EUROPE IN THE NINETEENTH AND TWENTIETH CENTURIES

VOLUME ONE

The second part in this two-volume
sequence is available as

EUROPE IN THE TWENTIETH CENTURY
1905–1970

by *Agatha Ramm*

GRANT AND TEMPERLEY'S
EUROPE IN THE NINETEENTH
AND TWENTIETH CENTURIES

Seventh Edition in two volumes

EUROPE IN THE NINETEENTH CENTURY 1789–1905

Agatha Ramm

LONGMAN
London and New York

LONGMAN GROUP LIMITED
Longman House, Burnt Mill, Harlow
Essex CM20 2JE, England
Associated companies throughout the world

*Published in the United States of America
by Longman Inc., New York*

First published (as Europe in the Nineteenth Century) 1927
*Fourth edition (Europe in the Nineteenth and
Twentieth Centuries)* 1932
Sixth edition 1952
First issued in paperback 1971
Seventh edition by Agatha Ramm (in two volumes) 1984

BRITISH LIBRARY CATALOGUING IN PUBLICATION DATA

Grant Arthur James
  Grant and Temperley's Europe in the nineteenth and
  twentieth centuries. — 7th ed. in 2 vols
  Vol. 1: Europe in the nineteenth century, 1789–1905
  1. Europe—Civilization—19th century
  2. Europe—Civilization—20th century
  I. Title II. Temperley, H. N. V. III. Ramm, Agatha
  940.2   CB415

  ISBN 0–582–49028–6

LIBRARY OF CONGRESS CATALOGING IN PUBLICATION DATA

Grant, A. J. (Arthur James), 1862–1948.
  Grant and Temperley's Europe in the nineteenth and
twentieth centuries.

  Rev. ed. of: Europe in the nineteenth and twentieth
centuries. 6th ed. 1971.
  Includes bibliographical references and index.
  Contents: v. 1. Europe in the nineteenth century,
1789–1905—v. 2. Europe in the twentieth century,
1905–1970.
  1. Europe—History—1789–1900. 2. Europe—
History—20th century. I. Temperley, Harold William
Vazelle, 1879–1939. II. Ramm, Agatha. III. Title. IV. Title:
Europe in the nineteenth and twentieth centuries.

D299.G7   1984   940.2′8   83–11986
ISBN 0–582–49028–6 (v. 1)

Set in 10/11 pt Linotron 202 Times

Printed in Singapore by Huntsmen Offset Printing (Pte) Ltd

CONTENTS

Contents

Contents

Contents

Contents

LIST OF MAPS

PREFACE

Dame Lillian Penson, who prepared the sixth edition of this work, died on April 17, 1963, and it seems fitting that this new edition should begin by acknowledging the value of her work. I should like also to acknowledge my own debt to her, who set the pattern of my own teaching and research. She records in her note to the sixth edition the death of Harold Temperley in July 1939 and of A. J. Grant 'who was his elder by several years' in May 1948. She writes that she, 'who was closely associated with both the original authors in historical work, was therefore able to discuss with Professor Grant the revision which has now taken place.' I have had no similar advantage. I must ask the indulgence of those who knew the earlier book both for the temerity with which I have cut, altered and perhaps injured the original work and for the absence of any personal participation, except as an observer, in the events which I narrate in the new chapters of Volume Two. The reader of the old work often had a vivid sense of personal contact with political events through the writing of the original authors, especially that of Harold Temperley. Dame Lillian in her note recorded the wish of the original authors 'that there should be successive editions which should maintain some at least of these characteristics' — 'and at the same time take into account the differing outlook of a new era.' This is my justification for what I have tried to do.

Taking account of a new outlook indicated that I should diminish the English reference of the old book. It is impossible nowadays to write of the continent of Europe as if it were seen by a more politically mature country with her revolution in the past and her parliamentary system the model for all to follow, or as if it were seen by the immensely powerful country that Britain still was in 1939. Indeed, it is difficult nowadays to write so often of 'England.' I have not changed 'England' to 'the United Kingdom' to conform with modern usage, but I have preferred a consistent use of 'Britain.'

More important, I have tried to bring out clearly a theme latent in the old book: that is, the importance in the nineteenth century of parliamentary constitutions and the whole liberal movement which aimed at obtaining them. I have also tried to show that this essential theme is not only the rise and operation of liberalism, but also its decline and the beginning of its supersession, as a cause of historical change, by socialism. This I have tried to do by adding a good deal of material on domestic politics, on economic history and on political ideas in Italy, Germany, France and especially Russia. I have incorporated the results of modern writing on, for example, the union of Belgium and Holland, or rather their reunion, and its break up in 1830; on the Italian Risorgimento, a word which is used nowadays for the movement of thought which preceded Italian unification and not of political unification itself; and on the German constitutions of 1867 and 1871. I have tried to leave untouched whatever was written on the Eastern Question and the Balkan countries which Harold Temperley knew so well. Volume Two, with two important exceptions, is much more my own composition than Volume One. Those who knew the old Grant and Temperley will even here, however, recognise the occasional untouched sentence, paragraph or page. The two exceptions in Volume Two are, first, the account of the Balkan Wars and, second, the account of the War of 1914–18 and of peace-making after it, in which Professor Temperley was a participant. He wrote the authoritative *History of the Peace Conference*. As for the rest of Volume Two, the introduction and chapters 1 and 7 to 10 are nearly all mine, chapters 11 to 16 and the conclusion wholly so. The reader will miss from these the slower pace and more reflective quality of the earlier writing.

In Volume One he will also miss two flight of fancy which are too characteristic of the old book to be altogether forgotten, though they no longer stand in the text. Polignac, the last Prime Minister of the Restored Monarchy in France, was described as 'this gingerbread conspirator.' The Confederation of German states, with scant justice either to states or animals, was likened to a hunting pack. 'It was like a number of animals formed into a hunting pack; the leader was Prussia, a huge grey wolf, at whose heels ran jackals, like Bavaria, Saxony, Württemberg and in whose train followed thirty-five smaller animals varying in size from large rats to small mice.' I hope I have preserved in both volumes the strongly personalised character of the narrative. I hope it is still history made by the decisions of known men and not by the action of anonymous forces. The earlier authors often thought it necessary to authenticate views or information which were new, when they wrote, with detailed references to their source in footnotes. When the views have become generally accepted or the information common knowledge, I have omitted the footnotes. When I thought authentication still useful, I have given references if possible to more recent books containing the same material.

I repeat, finally, two of the paragraphs which came towards the end of Dame Lillian's note. 'In the note to the fifth edition the authors referred to the personal experience of Professor Temperley in the British Imperial General Staff in the first World War and in the negotiations for peace. They acknowledged also the help given by a number of personal friends, some of whom are no longer available for consultation. In particular, acknowledgement was given for the criticisms made by Field Marshal Lord Birdwood on the chapter relating to the War of 1914–18, and to Mr J. M. (later Lord) Keynes for help in dealing with the Reparation and Economic Section of the Treaty of Versailles. Sir Arnold Wilson had given them advice in connection with all matters upon the then recent history of the East; Mr L. S. Amery had commented upon the section relating to the reconstruction of democracy after the first World War and Major-General A. C. Temperley (the brother of one of the authors) had given advice upon the history of Disarmament and the later developments of the League of Nations.

In the note to the fifth edition the debt of the authors was also acknowledged to Mr Raymond Postgate who had written part of the chapter which dealt with Marxism and with Russia.'

I think much of the debt to those named in this note may still stand; for, except that to which Raymond Postgate contributed, these chapters have been least altered in the whole work. Much, however, has been added on Marx, and the Russian section of that chapter rewritten as a separate chapter.

AGATHA RAMM

Introduction
MODERN EUROPE

Until late in the twentieth century 'Europe' implied not only a definite area of the earth's surface, but also a certain type of civilisation. The conceptions of the European states concerning social life and government, concerning religion and art and science, had, underneath all their differences, a certain resemblance which may have been difficult to define, but which appeared unquestionable when they were compared with the ideas of the old civilisations of Asia or the conditions in Africa or the New World. This basis of common ideas and practices was not the result of a common nationality, for the peoples of Europe are many, and some are widely removed from others; it was the result of the historical development of the European lands. All of them, though some to a greater extent than others, had inherited the science and art and philosophy of Greece. A large part of them had been incorporated into the Roman Empire, and even over those who were left outside that Empire the law and the language and the institutions of Rome had had a great influence. But it was during the Middle Ages that a real advance was made towards something that may be called European unity. The Christian Church, whether in its Eastern or its Western form, took up the task of Rome, though on a strangely different plane. Over all Europe the Christian ideas of faith, morals, and worship were accepted. There were wide differences between East and West, between nation and nation, but a common understanding was established which subsequent revolutions did not entirely destroy.

But though there was a certain common basis of culture in Europe this was very far from availing to keep peace among the different states and races. European history is a record of continual war from the second century A.D. onwards. The central doctrines of the Church recognised the unity of mankind and the blessings of peace; but there were no civil institutions that gave effective encouragement to these ideas and no organisation which could enforce them. Yet here, too, it is important to notice that most persistent efforts to

1

realise the unity of Europe as part of the greater unity of mankind were made during the Middle Ages. The Holy Roman Empire—so much misunderstood and so unfairly criticised—was an affirmation that Europe ought to have a single political organisation and an authority raised above the different states which could decide between them. It represented a system of rights and an ideal of justice, however ludicrously short of that ideal it fell. The organisation of the Church, too, was inevitably international in aim and character. Feudalism, chivalry, trade organisations, universities had an international character greater than anything that we find in the modern world until the nineteenth century.

The passing of the mediaeval world was accompanied, both as cause and effect, by the rise of national feeling and the assertion of the independence of each state. This is plainer among the nations that broke away from communion with Rome, but it is, in truth, a feature common to all. Spain and France were hardly less independent of papal control than England or Germany. The international ideas of the Middle Ages had been wearing very thin for some time; they now disappeared from the world even as an aspiration. From the end of the fifteenth to the end of the eighteenth century we have to look to solitary thinkers—to Sir Thomas More and Rabelais, to Sully and Leibnitz and Kant and Rousseau—to find even an echo of ideas that had once, in whatever strange form, been common—namely, that the Christian nations formed one whole and should have institutions to assert and to maintain their unity.

The nations of Europe, therefore, faced one another as armed and distrustful rivals, recognising no rule of conduct except their own advantage, and entering into transitory alliances on the promptings of fear or gain. These unstable and temporary relationships among the states of Europe have received the name of the Balance of Power. This has been idealised by some as a safeguard for European peace and the protection of the world against despotism; it has been denounced by others as the cause of the wars of Europe. It was, in truth, neither the one nor the other. It is simply a convenient name for the way in which states act towards one another when there is no influence to persuade them to concord, nor force to coerce them, nor any court whose authority they are all prepared to recognise. The working of the system—though indeed it was not a system—is seen at its clearest among the states of Greece in the fifth and fourth centuries B.C. It provides the explanation for the kaleidoscopic politics of Italy in the fourteenth and fifteenth centuries; and in the sixteenth century it passed from Italy to the larger state system of Europe, though during the Middle Ages the working of the same force had often been visible.

The most obvious feature of the state system of Europe under the influence of this idea is the recurring alliance of the weaker Powers against any state that seemed to exercise or claim a supremacy in Europe. Thus in the sixteenth century the Spanish power was resisted by a combination of states of which England and France were the chief. The seventeenth century saw the rise of France to the leading position in Europe; it saw, too, the union of her enemies against her, and the early years of the eighteenth century saw her overthrow. The union of forces which defeated the naval supremacy of Great Britain for a time in the eighteenth century and led to the independence of the United States has some features in common with these instances already given.

The end of the eighteenth century sees hardly a shadow of international action or aspiration. But with the French Revolution (it is important to note it) the era of international effort begins again, and in various forms, in spite of the wars with which the nineteenth and twentieth centuries are filled, has continued. We shall attempt in this book, while telling the story of the different countries of Europe, not to lose sight of the whole in the parts, and especially to examine the forces which from time to time made for war or peace.

It will be well to begin with a survey of the European Powers towards the end of the eighteenth century. Of Great Britain, it is enough to say that, despite the humiliation of the loss of the American colonies, she still ranked as one of the greatest of the Powers. Her navy had recovered from its momentary eclipse. The industrial revolution, which transformed her life, brought to her great wealth and the modern phenomenon of economic growth. Her Government was, in spite of names, a narrow oligarchy; but it worked in conjunction with a Parliament which had grown steadily more powerful since the end of the mediaeval period. It was in closer touch with large and important sections of the nation than any government on the Continent, and the large measure of support which it received accounts for its survival when nearly all the governments on the Continent perished in the revolutionary storm.

France had lost her military prestige when she was crushed by the alliance of Great Britain with Prussia in the Seven Years' War. King Louis XV, who died in 1774, was typical of the monarchical decadence. The French Monarchy owed its strength to the effective leadership which it had given to the nation in war, but he was without energy or military ardour; and under him the nation suffered great and irremediable defeats. His grandson, Louis XVI, succeeded in 1774, and in the War of American Independence fortune had returned to the standards of France. But the treasury was alarmingly empty, and the organisation of monarchical France was undermined by aristocratic opposition, by the growing strength and discontent of the middle classes, and by the new hopes and passions which were spreading throughout the country from the great writers of the time. The revolutionary storm first broke in France; and her constitution and social life have been often treated as if they were an altogether exceptional example of oppression, incompetence, and social distress. But there was very much in France that was representative of conditions that prevailed throughout Europe. Here was a monarchy which had done great things for the safety and the prosperity of France, which had overthrown all rivals for power—the feudal aristocracy, the legal profession, representative institutions, central, provincial and municipal—which ruled by 'divine right' without recognising any dependence on, or partnership with, the body of the nation, and which controlled France through its officials and its bureaucracy; the richest, the most splendid, and the most influential of the monarchies of Europe. The vigour and life had largely passed away from it. The mistakes and the defeats of Louis XIV and the neglect of Louis XV in part account for this. But the institution of autocratic monarchy no longer corresponded to the ideas or the needs of the time. The example of the Government of Great Britain was by reason of its success a great force throughout the century, and the time was soon coming when it would be necessary for all the governments in one way or another to take the people into partnership. On the eve of the Revolution the old system of government in France was almost without defenders. There was an almost universal aspiration after something new; all classes were touched in different ways by the new spirit, and the King himself was in sympathy with much of the humanitarian ideas of the time. What these new ideas were we will shortly examine. It is plain that the complete victory of the Monarchy over all rivals itself contributed to its overthrow and to the completeness of the triumph of the Revolution. When the central government was once overthrown there was no further resistance possible. The defenders of the old system—of what is usually called the old régime—were few, and they had no institutions through which they could work. France was, as it were, dominated by a single fort, and, when that fell, there was no further resistance.

The social system of France had many features common to many European states as well as some peculiar to herself. The population was divided—as most European populations were—into the privileged and the unprivileged classes. The Clergy, the Nobility, and office-holders were the privileged and belonged to an exclusive society from which the rest of the inhabitants of France were shut out. The Nobility did not, indeed, govern France; for the Monarchy had found its most dangerous rivals in the nobles, and had in its triumph excluded them from the most important administrative posts. But they and the Clergy and the courtiers enjoyed very considerable social privileges. They, like the office-holders, were exempt from many taxes paid by the unprivileged; the nobles alone were eligible for the higher ranks of the army, and formed the Court that shone with such great splendour at Versailles. The twentieth century has outlived most of these conditions; but they were then to be found, with modifications, in various parts of Europe, in Spain and Italy, in most of the German States, in Poland, and in Russia. Nor was the social condition of the people exceptional either in the character or in the extent of its grievances. The chief burden of the taxation fell upon the inhabitants of the villages and the peasantry. The peasants were owners of their farms, or, at least, either rent-paying tenants or sharecroppers, *métayers*; for the Revolution, though it increased the peasant proprietorships of France, did not, by any means, originate them. This class, which after the Revolution was the most contented and conservative in France, was before that event full of bitterness and protest. The peasants might own their lands, but they were burdened by a crushing load of taxes—crushing chiefly because the privileged classes had avoided their proper share of it—and they had also to pay many dues of feudal origin which had once represented their relation to their feudal superiors, but which had now lost all social meaning and were merely irritating burdens. They alone paid the *taille*—a tax on the houses and lands of the unprivileged—and in feudal dues they paid a proportion of their crops, dues for pressing their grapes or grinding their corn, and other burdens. The salt monopoly, which was known as the *gabelle*, obviously fell more heavily on those poor in cash than on the wealthy. Their position as free proprietors with their lands burdened by meaningless impositions was peculiarly irritating and easily accounts for the part they played in the early scenes of the Revolution. But again we must say of all this that there was nothing exceptional in their lot. Most European states showed something like it. In some, and particularly in Poland, the lot of the peasantry was far worse. The dwellers in the French towns had their own grievances: they found the decaying organisations of their trades guilds a restraint to their progress. They saw with natural jealousy the rapid advance in prosperity made by the commercial classes of Britain, and when the Revolution had begun they had far the chief share in directing and using it.

The great rival of France before 1789 was the House of Austria; or, to speak more accurately, the lands, various in character and origin, which were ruled, with many differences of method and power, by the great House of Hapsburg. Men spoke of France and Austria sometimes as the two ends of the Balance of Power. From 1500 their wars and rivalries fill a great part of the history of Europe, and France found in Austria her most constant opponent from the outbreak of the revolutionary wars down to the fall of Napoleon. The Austrian territories made a long and variegated list. Many nationalities, languages, and religions were found among the populations. They had been brought together by inheritance, by diplomatic marriages, by war, and even by purchase. The chief divisions or groups were the following: (1) The core of the Hapsburg power was to be found in the German lands in the neighbourhood and to the south-west of Vienna; there was no important difference either in language or race between these lands and those which are more usually classed as Germany. (2) To the north of the capital were Bohemia and Moravia, inhabited mainly by a Czech people, which had played a great part in European history, but which since the close of the Thirty Years' War in the seventeenth century had seemed content to be subordinate to the German Hapsburgs. (3) To the east stretched the great Magyar kingdom of Hungary, where the Magyars maintained their authority over many peoples—Rumanians, Croats, and Serbs. Divided in religion and feudal in the tone of their society, they yielded a grudging obedience to the Hapsburg sovereigns. (4) To the south of the Alps the Duchy of Milan, rich and populous, gave them rule over a mass of Italians alien in tradition and character. (5) Far to the west of Europe the accident of birth, in the first instance, and then the result of war had made Austria master of those Netherlands which we now call Belgium, the population of which, part Flemish and part French, presented a great contrast to the rest of the Hapsburg dominions.

The rule of these widely scattered and different lands was a difficult problem. The modern feeling that the nation and the state should be identical as far as possible was hardly known in the eighteenth century; but the difficulty of governing such varied elements was already apparent. The Emperor Joseph II (1765–90) had wished, in conformity with the general tendency of the age, to introduce a centralised and unified form of government into his dominions. He had tried to make German the official language everywhere; he had tried to bring all parts of his dominions under the direct rule of his officials, to introduce religious toleration, and to establish the equality of all his subjects under his personal rule. The effort was well meant, but it had broken down completely through the national pride and the religious prejudices of his various peoples. Nowhere were Joseph's projected reforms more revolutionary than in Belgium, where, moreover, he proposed to get rid of the restraints which the jealousy of Great Britain and Holland had for more than a century and a half placed on the navigation of the Scheldt, ruining thereby the prosperity of the great harbour of Antwerp. And nowhere more than in Belgium was there determined resistance to his schemes. The people, devoted for the most part to the Catholic Church, rose in violent protest against the proposals to suppress the monasteries and to secularise education; 'liberals' joined with them through dislike of the Emperor's autocratic schemes. It came to open war. Apparently suppressed in 1788, it flared out again in 1789 and was not suppressed. In 1790 when Joseph II died, the Belgians were demanding, through their delegates at Brussels, a federal republic. Joseph was succeeded by Leopold II, whose caution and love of the old routine was a great contrast to his predecessor's impulsive and imaginative temperament. He adopted the traditional Austrian policy of maintaining order by balancing the different interests against one another; and he gained much success. Yet when we come to speak in the next chapter of the great French Revolution it is well to remember that another revolution had already broken out in the neighbouring Belgian lands, very different indeed from what happened in France, but still a revolution which weakened the power of Austria and encouraged the French to believe that they would find allies on their northern frontier.

We have called Joseph II Emperor. He owed that title to the fact that he was head of the Holy Roman Empire, under which ancient and picturesque title were included little more than the states of Germany. It is of some importance to note that whereas Joseph had virtually no policy for the Empire, Leopold and Francis, who succeeded him in 1792, took their responsibility for what happened in Germany more seriously. Yet great difficulties hampered financial and military co-operation, even a common policy, among the German states. It is true that Voltaire's well-known gibe that the Empire was 'neither holy nor Roman nor an Empire' does injustice to its ideals, but that does not mean that it counted in international relations. It had no power.

Germany had been called in the seventeenth century 'a divinely ordained confusion,' and contained at that epoch over 300 'states.' The confusion was partly due to the mistakes of the German Powers themselves; but it had also been carefully and successfully fostered by a succession of French statesmen. The confusion was greatest to the west of Germany. No powerful state held the Rhine or watched the entry into Germany from France. Lorraine and Alsace had been in French hands since the end of the seventeenth century. On the western frontier were to be found the debris of states that had once seemed important: Württemberg and Baden especially; but the most characteristic feature was the ecclesiastical states on or near the Rhine, where bishops ruled, not cruelly nor oppressively, but very inefficiently and in a fashion which offered little likelihood of resistance to an invader. As we look farther east we find states stronger and better organised: Hanover at the mouths of the Weser and the Elbe, attached to Great Britain by the fact that its Elector was also King of Great Britain; Saxony on the upper course of the Elbe; and, farther south, Bavaria on the upper Danube, strongly Catholic and jealous of its northern neighbour, Prussia. Prussia passed through a fiery trial in the wars with Napoleon, and it seemed at one time as though she might succumb; but Germany for a century past and for more than a century afterwards found her destiny almost identified with that of Prussia. Prussia had no geographical advantages. 'Nature had not foreseen Prussia.' The core of the country lay on the middle waters of the Elbe and the Oder, with Berlin as its capital and Magdeburg and Frankfurt-on-Oder as its all-important outposts on the Elbe and the Oder. Without defensive frontiers the country had to rely on military force for self-preservation; and from the seventeenth century there was a tradition of military discipline and efficiency which helps to explain its continued progress. There were great Prussian rulers before Frederick the Great (1740–86), but it was he who raised the country from a second-rate to a first-rate Power. Using with great genius the fine army which he inherited from his father, he fought two long wars against a coalition of European Powers, in which Austria was his constant enemy and first France and then Great Britain his ally. He had won by the sword the rich upper valley of the Oder which is called Silesia. By diplomacy he gained in 1772 the northern part of Poland, which connected the central Mark of Brandenburg with East Prussia: this was the first step in the partitions of Poland which will occupy our attention later. Prussia had, after 1772, a large coherent mass of territory in East Europe; but this was separated from her lands on or near the Rhine (Mark and Cleves), and in the period covered by this book the Prussian sword would be called on to effect the junction with them. The latter part of Frederick's life had been devoted to peaceful and hard-working administration. The prosperity of the country increased greatly. Her prestige stood higher than that of any other country in Europe. Rulers like Joseph II, writers like Voltaire, looked to Prussia as the model of what a state shoud be. Her army seemed to possess an unrevealed secret of victory. Her triumphs had been won without taking the people into partnership or recognising the need of liberty. Only a few observers, such as Mirabeau—afterwards so famous in the story of the French Revolution—saw that the greatness of Prussia depended on the personal qualities of her king and prophesied trouble when his strong hand and subtle brain were removed.

Great Britain, France, Prussia, and Austria were the chief Great Powers in Europe, and they were mainly concerned in the outbreak of the war with France in 1792 to which our thoughts will shortly be directed. But Russia came little behind them in importance and, as the struggle went on, her influence—direct and indirect—became more and more important. Her vast and loosely organised population seemed hardly to lie within the circle of European culture. The gap between Russia and Western Europe in temperament and ideas has always been a wide one, and still is so. But in the Middle Ages she had accepted Christianity in its Eastern or Orthodox form, and its traditions and ideas had sunk deep into the national consciousness. Then in the seventeenth century Peter the Great, that strange and sometimes sinister genius, had carried her frontiers to the Baltic and for a time to the Black Sea, and had opened to her the civilising agency of maritime intercourse. He had, too, forced upon her aristocracy something of the external forms and something even of the language and science of Western Europe. It is impossible to think of Russia as lying outside the circle of Europe when she took so continuous and so important a part in its international relationships and in its artistic and philosophical progress. The work of Peter the Great in territorial aggrandisement and in the westernisation of the country had been carried on by the Tsarina Catherine II—a German by birth—who sat on the Russian throne from 1762 to 1796. For aggrandisement she looked both South and West. To the south lay the Ottoman Empire and, with Joseph II as her ally, she was engaged in one of Russia's periodic wars with Turkey (1787–92) when the French Revolution broke out. To her west lay Poland.

Poland had held a vast space on the map of Europe at the beginning of the sixteenth century. In language and people she was closely akin to Russia. Yet, while Russia moved forward to political unity and constantly widened her territories, Poland gives us a record of political and military decline hardly to be paralleled in the history of Europe. We can make no attempt here at any diagnosis of 'the Polish disease.' When we look at her towards the end of the eighteenth century we see a constitution that legalised anarchy by giving to any nobleman the power of veto in legislation, a social system that maintained the worst abuses of the feudal system without their excuses or the advantages of that system in the Middle Ages, and which especially condemned its peasant population to a condition of serfdom far worse than anything that was found in France; we see in the mass of the people great moral degradation, and few intellectual interests in the upper ranks of society. The frontiers of the country had no natural defences, and the government had not imitated that of Prussia in remedying this defect by the creation of a strong army. The result was that she was marked out as a prey to her neighbours. The first Partition of Poland had taken place in 1772. The incident was characteristic of the diplomacy of the time. A war threatened between Austria and Russia as ally and enemy respectively of Turkey. Frederick of Prussia intervened to suggest that the appetites of both Powers should be satisfied by the lands of the entirely inoffensive Polish state, and that he himself should take an equal share—as the idea of the Balance of Power would suggest—for Prussia. Even after that partition had taken place the territories of Poland were still wide and attractive. The appetite of her neighbours had not been satisfied by what they had taken, and they were thinking of a further and even of a final partition. Poland, at last really alarmed, was under her last King—Stanislas Poniatowski—seriously trying to set her house in order. When the French Revolution broke out in 1789, the Polish and Turkish questions were the most urgent matters for Prussia, Russia, and Austria. They were anxious for their booty, jealous of one another, and fearful of being outwitted. The interaction of the

Polish and Turkish problems with the French Revolution gives the clue to much of the diplomacy of the next years.

We must not speak in detail of the smaller Powers of Europe, though they had contributed much to build up the civilisation of Europe and were one and all drawn into the current of the French Revolution and the Napoleonic wars. Spain seemed to have almost stepped aside from the main movement of European progress in which she had once played so important a part, but her people would before long play again a great rôle in the story of Europe. Her monarchy was effete beyond anything that France knew. The royal house was a branch of the Bourbons who ruled in France, and the fate of the country had of late been intimately associated with that of France. Italy was divided into several nominally independent states— the republics of Venice and Genoa, the duchies of Milan, Parma, Modena, and Tuscany, the theocracy of the Papal States, the monarchy of Naples—but in fact the country lay under the influence of the Austrian House, which held Milan as a part of its territories and exercised great indirect influence over the rest of the peninsula. In Holland and the Scandinavian states there was a peaceful, vigorous and prosperous population whose annals had been uneventful of late. They, too, would be drawn gradually and unwillingly into the thick of the European conflict.

The states of Europe, then, towards the eve of the French Revolution, come before us independent and unrelated; pursuing their own advantage without any suspicion that there was any other possibility; arranging their temporary alliances as their immediate advantage and the idea of the Balance of Power seemed to dictate; repudiating in their public life any control of religion and any obligations to mankind. But there was in Europe at the same time a strong and strengthening current of thought and conviction of an entirely contrary kind. Perhaps the most revolutionary feature of the age is to be found in the antithetical contrast between the actions of statesmen and the best and most powerful thought of the age. We must try in a very short space to indicate the general character of this thought.

France held the foremost place in the world of thought, and the intellectual movement is usually treated as though it were solely French. But in reality the French were merely the leaders of general movement, long heralded by the work of such men as Locke and Leibnitz, Hume, Gibbon, Robertson, in England; Lessing and Kant, Herder, Goethe and Schiller in Germany; Benjamin Franklin in America; they are all part of the same movement with Voltaire and Montesquieu, with Diderot and Rousseau. Is it possible to determine the general characteristics of so widespread a movement? First of all it was universal in its outlook, and in this way was in marked contrast to the prevailing character of the politics of the time. In none of the countries mentioned was the tone of the literature patriotic or nationalist. France and England were at war during nearly the whole of the eighteenth century, but rarely has the intercourse of thought between the two countries been more constant or more useful to both sides. Frederick of Prussia had stirred the German temperament to patriotism, and there was in the literature of the time, in Herder and Schiller especially, some echoes of this, but the outlook of the great German authors mentioned was before all things wide and human. The second general characteristic of the thought of the time is its humanity. Never during the Christian era, or before it, was this note entirely absent, but in the eighteenth century it became dominant and essential. It is to the bar of humanity that religion, government, and social customs are brought, and they are for the most part condemned because they are found wanting in this respect. Thirdly and lastly, the thought of the time was critical and even hostile to the claims of the existing Churches and religions. Some of the writers possessed religious natures, but not one of them counted as a supporter of any ecclesiastical organisation or creed.

Voltaire, Montesquieu and Rousseau may be selected as the three most typical and influential men in all the group of writers. Voltaire was of all of them the best known and the widest read. His thought never went deep, and he has made no original contributions of importance to any side of European thought. But he was the most powerful influence in popularising ideas that Europe has ever known. His most sharply barbed shafts were directed against the ideas and practices of the Church; in politics he was neither liberal nor democrat, but regarded the honest and benevolent despotism of Frederick the Great as the form of government that should be imitated elsewhere. Above all he attacked in his writings and by his actions the religious intolerance of his time. The great days of the Inquisition were over, but still the Protestants of France suffered from cruel wrongs which sometimes led even to death. In protesting against all this and in many other ways Voltaire was the spokesman of the conscience of mankind. His wit and his satire, the clearness of his language and the humanity of his appeal, pervade the eighteenth century and the French Revolution.

Montesquieu was a profound student of constitutional problems, and by temperament conservative. His 'Spirit of the Laws' is a general discussion of forms of government and was the armoury from which those who were engaged in political reconstruction—a common task in the ensuing years—drew their ideas. The Constitution of the United States of America was largely influenced by it. Yet the book—as Montesquieu would himself admit with pleasure—was largely influenced by the English Constitution which he, like so many of the Frenchmen of his day, admired immensely. He praised a limited government, a machinery of checks and balances, and especially admired in the English practice what he called the 'separation of the powers'—the independence of the legislative, executive, and judicial branches of the state; though we see clearly now that he was wrong in thinking that in England the executive and the legislative were really separate.

Rousseau of all the writers of his age provoked the most opposite sentiments of love and hate, and he is still the most discussed. His emotional and meditative temperament hardly seems to belong to his age; and, though in many ways he is one of the most powerful forces in the main current of his time, in others he seems to throw himself across it and to try to swim against it. His moving style has none of the clarity of Voltaire. He was passionately religious in temperament, but neither Catholic nor Christian. He felt the evils of his age and the sufferings of the people, but none of the remedies proposed obtained his approval. The 'Social Contract,' published in 1762, summarises his ideas on the state but does it in such a way that men still argue as to his essential meaning. He opens with an indignant protest against the tyranny of his time. 'Man is born free and yet everywhere he is in chains.' The state owes its origin to the people; it belongs inalienably to them; the right always is theirs, in spite of all treaties or constitutions, to alter or abolish its government. Yet he does not think that democracy is possible, except in states of small size; he believes that it may be necessary to have recourse to a dictator, and he ends by insisting on the necessity of religion in a state, and proposes that a simple and civic form of religion should be imposed on all, even by the penalty of death. The influence of his ideas and phrases extended far beyond the students of his works. The French Revolution bears traces of his thought throughout.

No other French writers of the time have attracted so much attention from posterity as these three—Voltaire, Montesquieu, and Rousseau—but there was another group that had great contemporary influence and an important relation to the work of the Revolution. This group is known as the Economists or Physiocrats. They were much influenced by the writings of Adam Smith, the Scottish economist. Their chief representatives in France were Mirabeau, the father of the well-known statesman of the Revolution, Say, and above all Quesnay, the real thinker of the movement, whose obscure and difficult *Tableau Economique* was hailed by some of them as an infallible remedy for the troubles of France. They cared little for the abstract speculations of the time and failed to win the approval of Voltaire and Montesquieu. We may choose from their voluminous writings the following doctrines as central; that all wealth comes from the application of labour to land; that workmen are the most truly productive, perhaps the only productive, class; that the action of government should be reduced to a minimum; that complete free trade and the establishment of a universal system of education were the reforms most immediately requisite; and that all taxation should be reduced to a single land-tax. These principles, says Mirabeau, would suffice to 'set everything right and renew the age of Solomon.' Turgot was a discriminating disciple of this school, and both as an *intendant* and as a minister he made a great effort to put into practice the teaching of Quesnay. The Economists had a considerable influence on the course of the French Revolution, but never approached the importance of the followers of Rousseau and Voltaire.

When the great change had come the Revolution crystallised its aims in the triple watchword of 'Liberty, Equality and Fraternity.' All three words, but especially the first two, are difficult of definition, and they enlarged their meaning as the movement went on and have not yet ceased to enlarge it. At first by Liberty the French meant the security of the individual as against the action of the State; by Equality they meant equality of rights before the law and the abolition of privilege. The Fraternity that they thought of was chiefly among individuals and was exemplified in many an enthusiastic gathering on the eve of 1789, where nobles and peasants fraternised together. The thinkers of the time were not concerned much with international affairs nor with fraternity among nations. But two thinkers—Kant and Rousseau—saw the urgency of the problem and made some contribution to it. Rousseau wrote in 1756 a treatise on 'Perpetual Peace,' founded on the earlier work of Saint-Pierre, but embodying his own ideas and projects. He looked to a European confederation to establish that peace and security from the horrors of war of which he speaks with a noble emotion. He proposed that the sovereigns of Europe should found a perpetual and irrevocable alliance; that there should be a permanent Diet of their plenipotentiaries; that all should guarantee each against attack on their rights and territories; that any Power who did so attack should be put to the ban of Europe and crushed by the forces of Europe; that the Diet should work not merely for the preservation of peace, but for the general advantage of the human race. Kant reproduced these suggestions in 1795 with a clear acknowledgment that international peace depended ultimately not on contrivances but on men's resolution to have it and on greater public control of affairs within the several states.

Chapter 1

THE FRENCH REVOLUTION IN PEACE

Louis XVI, the last King of France to rule under the conditions of the ancient régime, came to the throne in 1774. He was guillotined rather less than twenty years later, and there is a danger of letting that tragedy and all that it symbolises influence unduly our judgment of the first fifteen years of the reign. We are apt to think that France engrossed the attention of Europe and that the atmosphere was heavy with the coming storm. But, in truth, the overmastering figure in the eyes of Europe was Frederick of Prussia. His wars were over and had left him and his state with a high reputation for discipline and success in war. The military and territorial ambitions of Prussia were, for the time, satisfied. The first partition of Poland, carried out in 1772 without the use of arms, had given more to Prussia than the long and tense struggle of the Seven Years' War. When in 1778 a difficult question arose as to the succession in Bavaria, in which the interests of Austria and Prussia were at variance, the conflict was settled by negotiation. Frederick's chief energies were now devoted to the promotion of commerce and industry, and to the building of the Prussian administrative system—autocratic, rigidly honest, and as efficient as any system can be that does not recognise the necessity of liberty. The new hopes of the age found a good deal of acceptance in Germany. Voltaire had been for some time a resident at the Court of King Frederick, and to Goethe and to Schiller and the thinkers of Germany the writers of France were a stimulus, sometimes to imitation and sometimes to opposition. But the Prussian king went on with his work, cynical and harsh in his manner and speech, but fundamentally in considerable sympathy with the new ideas.

In France the new reign of Louis XVI seemed to mark the coming of a better time. It was with real relief to nearly all classes in France that the reign of Louis XV came to an end. The frivolities of his Court had not been redeemed by success abroad, and, though France had enjoyed an immense prestige through her writers, the Court and Government had not profited by it, for the thought of France was as unfavourable to the system of Louis XV as it had been friendly to the régime of Louis XIV. The advent of the new king was welcomed because it was in any case a change, but there was also much to make Louis XVI popular. He was himself touched by the humanitarian hopes of the time and was ready for a change of system. He claimed for himself in the early years of his reign and in his last hours that 'he loved the people,' and history sees no reason to reject the claim. His wife, Marie Antoinette, was an Austrian princess, the daughter of Maria Theresa, a kind-hearted, brilliant, and really beautiful woman. Her Austrian origin was a disaster, both to herself and her husband. It made her unpopular in the country when France again came into antagonism with Austria (during the Revolution she was constantly denounced as 'the Austrian woman'), and it prevented her from understanding France or sympathising, as her husband did, with the new ideas; while her will, much clearer and stronger than his, made her a powerful and dangerous counsellor for him in his hours of crisis. But these considerations belong to a much later period. On the accession of Louis XVI France entered on a long and sincere effort under the presidency of the Monarchy to alter the character and aim of the Government, and at first found much enthusiastic support from the governing and the literary classes.

Humanitarianism counted for much in this effort; but the old system was in any case untenable, for the simple reason that it was not able to pay its way. Commerce and industry lagged far behind the great achievements of Britain. The land of France was rich and productive, but the system of privilege—which relieved the Nobility, the Clergy, office-holders and the Court from a large part, though not from all, of the taxation that they should have borne—made it impossible for the Government to use this wealth to meet their liabilities. The Revolution, or some revolution, would probably have come in France in any case; but it is through the channel of the financial needs of the state that it did actually arrive. The expedients employed to meet the expenses of the great wars of the eighteenth century had thrown the financial system of France into hopeless disorder. The first need was to balance income and expenditure, and that, as it turned out, could not be done without a complete change in French methods of government.

In Louis XVI's first Ministry Maurepas held the first position, but the name of Turgot, who was Controller-General of Finance, attracted most attention. He was a disciple of the Economists. His character and his writings had already made him well known, and he had valuable experience as *intendant* of the province of Limousin. He was only in office some twenty months, and what he did had little permanent effect; but men looked back to this short period as the time when there was a chance that reforms, wisely planned and vigorously carried out, might have averted the catastrophe of the Revolution. He wanted to introduce honesty and efficiency into the public services—a real revolution this; to check the dangerously great power of the Church; to introduce a juster method of taxation; to facilitate the circulation of goods, especially corn, within the bounds of the kingdom. He did not recognise the necessity of taking the people into partnership by the calling of any national assembly, though this was recommended to him by some of his colleagues. He worked at his schemes with a passionate zeal for justice and humanity. But his proposals aroused alarm in the classes whose interests seemed threatened. A Court cabal was formed against him, in which Marie Antoinette played a part, and Louis was not strong enough to uphold his Minister when he had become unpopular. Turgot was dismissed, and Necker became Controller General of Finance.

Necker was a Genevese banker and a Protestant. His appointment as Controller-General of Finance raised certain difficulties which were overcome by the exercise of the royal prerogative. He made the King's course easier, too, by renouncing the salary attached to the post. He was for a long period—down to 1790—the most popular of the public men of France; his unselfishness, his honesty, the belief that he represented the popular aspirations of the time and his connection with the literary world all contributed to this. He was a skilful financier, but not a great statesman. He accepted the administrative and financial system of France as it stood, and hoped, without introducing fundamental change, to carry on the government by means of economy and of loans, which his financial knowledge and reputation allowed him to contract at a cheaper rate than previously. All these efforts left little permanent trace on the history of France, and lie outside the limits of this book. For while he was in office there occurred a great event beyond the Atlantic, which exercised a powerful influence on European affairs. The tension between the British Government and the American colonies led to open rebellion in 1775. The Governments of France and of Great Britain had been constantly hostile during the eighteenth century, and in the wars between them France had lost to England nearly the whole of her colonial and Indian possessions. The memory of her defeats made France ready to seize the opportunity for retaliation that was thus clearly offered. The Government at first hesitated, fearful of the expense and afraid of the naval power of its rival. But private enterprise compensated to some extent for the inaction of the Government. Lafayette—courageous, romantic, and full of noble sympathy for the American cause—led across a band of volunteers. Americans have never forgotten this generous adventure. Public opinion soon forced the French Government to support Lafayette's effort by the action of the state. What followed is a matter of the utmost importance for world history and had an important bearing on the French Revolution. The help of France contributed decisively to the triumph of the American cause. Other European nations joined in a protest against the naval supremacy of Great Britain. The British fleet was defeated by the French off the coast of America, and so—as a direct consequence—came the surrender of Yorktown and the creation of a really New World. There was much in the struggle that left a deep impression on the minds of Frenchmen. An army of citizens had beaten the 'mercenary' soldiers of England. The Constitution of the United States was in process of construction. It was begun by the Declaration of Independence, through which the ideas of Rousseau rang unmistakably; the construction was carried on under the influence of Montesquieu's 'Spirit of the Laws' (the even deeper debt to the English Constitution was naturally kept in the background). The Liberty of which France wrote and talked and dreamed so much had arisen splendid and victorious beyond the Atlantic. The belief was strengthened that the soil of France might see movements and triumphs of the same kind.

But the most immediately serious result of the American War was on the finances of France. Necker's careful economies were insufficient to meet the expenses of the war. He issued a statement of the financial situation of France—his *compte rendu*. Both the accuracy and the motives of this publication have been questioned. But it was an appeal to public opinion, going quite beyond the ordinary administrative circles which had hitherto alone concerned themselves with finance. It was widely read and discussed. The royal circle regarded the step as dangerous, and Necker was dismissed from office (1781)—to return again when the storm was about to burst.

There were still eight years before the Revolution came, and there was nothing in the condition of France that made it impossible for the Government to set the finances in order. The wealth of the country was by no means exhausted. We have said already that there is no ground for thinking that France was distinguished from the other countries of Europe by the poverty and misery of her population. The Monarchy as an institution was still accepted by nearly all, and really popular with a large proportion of the people of France. Frederick the Great of Prussia had shown what might be done by a capable and resolute king in a situation far worse than that of Louis XVI. But Louis XVI was the very antithesis of Frederick the Great. His was a gentle, pious, kindly nature, without any of Frederick's demoniac energy; and the machine of French government was clogged by a long tradition of privilege and corruption. The iron will which alone could have made it work for national ends was altogether lacking in the occupant of the French throne. The charge, often brought against Louis XVI, that he resisted the Revolution too long and thus brought about his tragic end is almost the opposite of the truth. It was not inflexibility but weakness of will that was his bane. Out of weakness and out of genuine humanitarian sympathy he allowed the Revolution to come. When it had come, and in a shape very different from what he expected, he intrigued weakly and treasonably against it. So came for him deposition and prison and the guillotine.

Calonne was Finance Minister from 1783 to 1787. He was popular at the Court, with whose expensive pleasures he did not attempt to interfere; for he believed that an expensive Court made borrowing easier, and he lived by borrowing at an increasingly high rate of interest. Even to Calonne it became plain that the Monarchy could not solve the financial difficulty without taking some part of the people into its confidence. He went back to the traditions of the Monarchy of the sixteenth and seventeenth centuries and summoned a body of 'Notables,' who were men summoned by the King at his own choice to give him advice on any subject he might bring before them. They were not representative in any way, but consisted of members of the privileged classes. To this body, rather than to the Parlement of Paris, Calonne proposed a series of reforms including a land tax to be paid by privileged and unprivileged alike. The Notables demurred. To break the ensuing deadlock the King dismissed Calonne (April 1787). The Assembly of the Notables which remained in session had called forth a flood of discussion in which the States-General was increasingly mentioned.

The States-General—that is to say, a body representative of the Clergy, Nobility and Commons of the whole state, as distinguished from the States-Provincial which only contained representatives of a single province—had not been called since 1614. Their real character therefore was only known to the antiquarian and the historian. When the Monarchy had been weak they had often challenged its power: the triumph of the Monarchy under Richelieu had led to their disappearance. There was widespread enthusiasm for election and representation at the time, and the mind of France turned naturally to the one national institution in her past which had both these characteristics. And yet the States-General, in their traditional shape, were but ill-fitted for dealing with the national emergency. The three Estates—the Clergy, the Nobility, and the Commons—had each sat in separate rooms, and there had thus been two privileged Chambers, while the unprivileged Commons had only one. What was even more important, they possessed no powers: they could only put forward demands and make suggestions: the government of France had never conceded them any share in taxation or legislation. Each member brought from his constituency a statement of grievances: *cahier des doléances*. The business of each 'estate' was to draw up a general statement of their wishes and to present it separately to the Crown. When this had been done their work was over. It is a far cry from such a body to the contemporary British Parliament: a still further cry to the omnipotent Convention which was soon to direct the destinies of the French Revolution.

Meanwhile Cardinal de Brienne, who succeeded Calonne, had dismissed the Notables but not before they had advised the summoning of the States-General or still better the submission of the proposed reforms to the Parlement of Paris. The Parlement of Paris, a body of privileged persons, lawyers, had the duty of registering the King's edicts and until they were thus registered they were not valid. Strong in the assurance of the support of the privileged the Parlement refused to register the proposed new tax. The King used all the means that had been effective in the past; but in vain. This was the revolt of the nobles—*la révolte nobiliaire*—and it had begun in 1787. If there had been a strong King—Henry of Navarre, a Louis XI or a Louis XIV—the Monarchy might have emerged, changed but strengthened. Yet Louis XVI in face of the excitement and opposition took a wise step. He dismissed de Brienne, he recalled Necker, and he announced his intention of summoning the States-General. They were summoned first for 1788: but they actually met at Versailles, some twelve miles from Paris, in May 1789.

A King had been driven by national bankruptcy to call the representatives of his people into council. There was nothing necessarily catastrophic in such a situation; nothing that seemed necessarily to mark a new era in the world's history. But it became increasingly plain that under the hopeful appearance lay the reality of a breakdown of royal authority: indeed, of government itself.

There were no more critical days during the French Revolution than the first weeks of the States-General. There had been much discussion as to their constitution and procedure: and through the influence of Necker the Commons had got some 600 representatives, while the Clergy and the Nobles had about 300 each. But a difficult question of procedure still remained. How were the 1200 members to sit and debate and vote? Were they to sit in three Chambers and decide questions by a majority of Chambers, or were they to sit all together and decide by a majority of individual votes? The first method would give a majority of two Chambers to one for privilege: the second would secure a large majority for reform, for some of the Nobles and many of the Clergy were in sympathy with the Commons. And further, were they to be, as of old, a Council of advice or a real agency of government? And if they governed were they to be an instrument in the hands of the nobility or of the nation at large? The King's decision would probably have been accepted at first; but he had given no decision when the representatives met at Versailles.

Victory of the completest kind rested with the Commons. It was won by the beginning of July 1789, and in these seven weeks we may note the following decisive stages.

First the Commons refused to co-operate with the Government in any way, until the union of all three estates in one Chamber and 'vote by head' were conceded. They refused even to take the preliminary steps necessary to prove themselves legitimately elected until they were joined by the other orders. This system of passive resistance lasted until June 10. They were weeks of great anxiety to the King and his advisers. The country was falling into very grave disorder. Taxes were not paid. The States-General might be dismissed as stubborn and disloyal; but the financial difficulty would remain as great as ever. So nothing was done. The inaction of the Government gave the Commons or third estate confidence. They began to know their leaders and to understand their powers.

On June 10 the Abbé Sieyès—member of the third estate, celebrated for his study of constitutional forms—proposed that the Clergy and Nobility should be summoned for the last time to join the third estate in one Chamber; and that in case of the refusal of the Clergy and Nobility they should proceed to constitute themselves. and to take action without Clergy and Nobles. The third estate were determined not to yield to the other estates; they felt themselves strong enough to dominate them. Whatever the decision of the Clergy and Nobles, the Commons were determined to take a large part of the government of France into their own hands, and to assume some title which should announce to all the world the power that they claimed. On June 14 the debate began as to what the title should be. Sieyès proposed that they should call themselves 'The National Assembly'; claiming by this very title that they had the right, even though unsupported by the other orders, to speak and act for the nation. Some, and especially Mirabeau, wanted a less challenging title; but on June 17, by an overwhelming vote (491 to 90), they decided for 'The National Assembly.' It was the French Revolution in miniature. The Commons claimed to act for the nation in despite of the King and the privileged classes.

Would the third estate make good their claim? The King and his advisers were at last awake to the danger that threatened them. He was persuaded to use an almost forgotten method of procedure in order to force obedience on the third estate. In the old days if the King went down in person to the States-General and held a 'Royal Session' it was clear that his word must be obeyed. He would hold a Royal Session now: he would announce his will and France would accept it. But the plan failed. The third estate were in no mood for yielding. They were excluded from their Chamber by the preparations for the Royal Session, but they met in a neighbouring Tennis-Court and swore that they would go on with their meetings, in spite of opposition from whatever quarter, until they had 'made a constitution' (June 20). They were encouraged by the action of the Clergy, who were deeply divided in social origin and in their attitude to the claims of the third estate. The Church is often regarded as the implacable foe of the Revolution; but on June 19, by a majority of one, the Clergy had decided for union with the third estate, and on June 22—the eve of the Royal Session— nearly half of them joined the Commons. In the Royal Session, on June 23, the King announced many important reforms in finance and administration and accepted the States-General as a permanent part of the constitution, but he insisted on the 'three chamber' method of debating and voting. He thus surrendered into the hands of the privileged classes, not of the nation. It was a challenge to the Commons and was supported by a scarcely veiled threat that he would use force to crush opposition. Yet the sequel was amazing. When the third estate resisted by refusing to vacate their Chamber, the King declined to support his words by action. Instead he called upon the Clergy and the Nobles to disobey the orders he had given and to join the third estate. On July 2 all the members of the three estates who attended (there were many absentees) met in one Chamber in which the friends of reform were sure of a considerable majority. The courage and sagacity of the leaders of the Commons and the financial needs of the Crown had been the chief causes of this surprising result. But the divided counsels among the King's advisers had also had an important influence. Among them there were some who held that it was best to yield now in order to strike with more effect later.

There were now three main forces in France. First, there was the King and Court, which had surrendered to the Commons. There were elements in this group—we cannot be wrong in counting among them the Queen, Marie Antoinette and the King's youngest brother, the Comte d'Artois—who regretted the necessity of the recent surrender and watched for an opportunity of regaining lost ground. Then there was the Assembly which had at different times three different names. First it was the States-General; then, as we have seen, it became the National Assembly; soon it recognised the framing of a constitution as its all-important task and called itself in consequence the Constituent Assembly. A good many of the Clergy and Nobles continued to sit in it, but it was dominated by the Commons. The representatives of the third estate were drawn from the middle classes; many of them were prosperous and even rich members of the commercial bourgeoisie; the legal profession was strongly represented; there were no workmen nor special representatives of the working classes. They were determined to draw up a political constitution, and their ideas as to its general features were fairly clear. But in social questions they were much less interested and rarely advanced beyond vague and rather sentimental generalisations. Nor were their debates helped by the intrusion of non-members; the debates of the Assembly were open to the public from its early days. This public was sometimes, but not always, the spokesman of a third force, sometimes vaguely called the People, or the People of Paris, sometimes the Revolutionary Army. Taxes were not paid. In the country there were scores of attacks on the houses of the nobles and gentry. Trade was bad, unemployment was widespread. There were great numbers of half-starving workmen in Paris, whither they had come at the beginning of the Revolution. They were miserable and discontented, excited by the ideas of the times even if they did not understand them, demanding food first of all and generally better conditions of life. They provided the revolutionaries with a valuable and a dangerous weapon; difficult to control, but sometimes quickly responsive to suggestions. The Assembly, an essentially middle-class body, was carried to victory by its undeclared alliance with this revolutionary force. Leadership for it was provided first from a permanent headquarters in the Palais Royal where thousands congregated nightly round an original group of pamphleteers and journalists; second, from the Hôtel de Ville where the 407 'electors' of Paris—the large committee that had finally chosen the deputies for the capital in the States-General—sat in permanent session.

The King (we may use the word as a synonym for the Government: it is impossible to determine Louis XVI's personal share in what was done) determined to strike. Troops were ordered to concentrate on Paris, and their march continued in spite of the protest of the National Assembly. On July 11, 1789, all fears and suspicions seemed justified by the news which reached Paris from Versailles that Necker, the popular idol, was dismissed. A royalist *coup d'état* was clearly coming. Paris was in no mood to wait for it. The Hôtel de Ville reacted sharply. It began to organise a government, the municipality, and established what soon grew to be the all-important National Guard. It was a body of men midway between policemen and soldiers, citizens armed and drilled for the defence of the rights and the property of the people of Paris. The Hôtel des Invalides was broken into and a great store of weapons taken. So Paris had some means of defence. But of more real use than the National Guard were the French Guards, regular soldiers quartered in Paris who had become imbued with the spirit of the Revolution and who now openly joined the Parisians. On July 14 the tumultuous forces of Paris—led, if they could be said to be led by anyone, by Camille Desmoulins, a young lawyer, a brilliant writer and, despite his stammer, an effective speaker—attacked the Bastille. The great fortress had no longer any military importance. The garrison was small, the place unprovisioned. But the name of the Bastille had been the symbol of the old despotism, and it might have been made again a means of coercing Paris. A successful attack would be at once a warning to the Monarchy and a demonstration of the city's power.

The attack made no real impression on the fortress; but the Governor, de Launay, through failure of nerve or hopelessness of relief, surrendered in the afternoon. His life was promised him, but he was murdered in the confusion of the surrender. The Parisian army poured in to the great fortress, and almost at once began to demolish it. Its fall did not in any way alter the military situation, and the forces at the disposal of the King were large enough and loyal enough to crush the Paris rising. But again the King yielded, partly through timidity, but more through real feelings of humanity. He came to Paris to express his official sanction of what had been done, and attended a solemn Te Deum in Notre-Dame Cathedral.

The military importance of the fall of the Bastille, as we have said, was nothing, but its political consequences were enormous. The Commons were for the second time victorious over the King. He had been popular at first, but his popularity declined rapidly. Suspicion and distrust had taken its place. The National Assembly felt more secure in its constitution-building. Most important of all, Paris had come into self-conscious existence and had gained an effective government. A full Municipal Government was organised, and the first Mayor was M. Bailly, an astronomer of great distinction, who had been carried away from his scientific work by the enthusiasm of the hour. The National Guards, too, were fully developed, and the famous Marquis of Lafayette became their first commander. The control of the Revolution by Paris had begun.

The Constituent Assembly—for so we must call the National Assembly now—encouraged by these events went confidently on with its work. We will examine the results of that work in a moment. But first we must notice the strange events which three months later completed the work of the fall of the Bastille. First, under the influence of sudden and spontaneous peasant risings up and down France, the Assembly on August 4, amidst a scene of great excitement and enthusiasm, declared 'feudalism' abolished and the privileged classes themselves co-operated in destroying the legal basis of their position. It was a moment of really noble enthusiasm, but when the 'abolition' had been passed it was difficult exactly to define its import. In the end the important legislation enacted between August 4 and 11 meant little more than the suppression of most seigneurial rights. But the peasants, gripped by a great fear, had taken their part in the Revolution. They had joined the revolutionary force mentioned above.

Meanwhile the general features of the situation had not changed. There was a Court which had yielded reluctantly and watched for a chance of recovery; an Assembly confident and hopeful, but suspicious of the King and hostile to the Court; a crowd, hungry, excited, a ready instrument for the hands of conspirators. To what extent there was definite organisation of a royalist reaction on the one side, and definite conspiracy against the Monarchy on the other, it is impossible to say. Certainly the mood of Paris was more dangerous than ever. Newspapers had sprung up. The political newspaper was a new phenomenon in France and exercised a great influence. Clubs had been formed to discuss the questions before the Assembly and to mould public opinion. There were moderate and conservative clubs; but the most important were the revolutionary clubs, such as the Cordeliers and the Jacobins. This last came to be one of the great formative forces in the Revolution, rivalling the Assembly in influence, and sometimes coercing it. The presence of unemployment had led to the opening of public workshops—an expedient always attractive and disappointing. The unemployed of France came in great numbers to Paris, and became an intolerable burden on the straitened finances of the country. The workshops were in consequence closed at the beginning of October, and several thousands of men were thrown on the streets to beg or starve.

The doings at Versailles, where the King and Court still resided, provoked angry comment in Paris. A new regiment—the Flanders regiment, consisting mainly of non-French soldiers—had been brought to Versailles, and its arrival had been made the occasion of ultraroyalist talk at a banquet given to the officers. The opinion gained ground that the Court was preparing a blow against Paris. The desire that the King should live in Paris had been strongly expressed before the opening of the States-General, and it was supported now by the public press. The time had come to carry the wish into effect.

On October 5, 1789, a crowd, which had first demanded 'Bread' at the Hôtel de Ville, was persuaded to march to Versailles and lay its wishes before the Assembly and the King. It arrived there in the afternoon and was followed by Lafayette and the National Guards, which he commanded. The day passed over with petitions and demonstrations that did not seem of great importance. But soon after midnight the palace was penetrated by the crowd. The King and Queen were in some danger, but the arrival of Lafayette secured their personal safety. But Lafayette had himself presented a request that the King should come to Paris to live. And the King again, as usual, thought it wisest to yield. In the afternoon of October 6 he left Versailles, so closely identified with the glories of the French Monarchy, and came to the Tuileries, once the palace of the mediaeval kings of France, but now ill-provided for his accommodation. The Assembly soon followed. Paris henceforth enveloped and controlled the government of France. The Revolution more and more was concentrated in Paris, and in its character reflected the character of the great city.

That is the chief result of the fall of the Bastille and the march on Versailles. But there is another of great importance. What is known as the 'Emigration' had begun. To explain this we must understand that, though the King had yielded, there were large numbers of the nobles who regarded his concessions with contempt and hatred. Loss of tax exemption and seigneurial rights filled them with fear lest worse befall. They refused to live in a France dominated by principles which they detested, and in consequence they withdrew beyond the frontiers; a few to England, but most to the German states on the Rhine, to Mainz, and to Coblenz. Princes of the royal blood took the lead—the King's brother, the Comte d'Artois and the Prince de Condé—and they were followed by a crowd of nobles. In the German towns where they settled they aped the ceremonies of Versailles, talked of the imminent overthrow of the Revolution, and gathered troops in preparation for the day. They declared that the King's concessions to the Revolution were the result of his necessities, and therefore not binding. Their influence was evil in every way. The best hope for France was that the King and the Revolution should be really reconciled and should treat one another with confidence and respect. The 'Emigration' made this difficult, if not impossible.

Amidst all these alarms the building of the constitution had gone on unceasingly. There was an important preliminary. It was determined to draw up a Declaration of the 'Rights of Man' which should be the basis of the whole constitution. The Declaration was debated throughout August 1789. The following are some of its most prominent clauses:

> The representatives of the French people, constituted as a National Assembly, believing that ignorance, forgetfulness, or contempt of the rights of man are the only causes of public misfortunes and of the corruption of governments, have resolved to set forth in a solemn declaration the natural, inalienable and sacred rights of man; in order that this declaration being constantly before all members of the social body may always recall to them their rights and their duties; in order that the acts of the legislative and executive powers being constantly capable of comparison with the objects of all political institutions may on that account be the more respected; in order that the demands of citizens being founded henceforth on simple and incontestable principles may be always directed to the maintenance of the constitution and the happiness of all.
>
> Consequently the National Assembly recognises and declares in the presence and under the auspices of the Supreme Being the following rights of the man and the citizen.
>
> I. Men are born and remain free and equal in rights. Social distinctions can only be founded on public utility.
>
> II. The aim of every political association is the preservation of the natural and imprescriptible rights of man. These rights are liberty, property, security, and resistance to oppression.
>
> III. The principle of all sovereignty resides essentially in the nation. No body and no individual can exercise authority, if it does not take its origin from the nation.
>
> IV. Liberty consists in being allowed to do whatever does not injure other people. . . .
>
> VI. Law is the expression of the general will. All citizens have the

right to take a part personally or through their representatives in its formation. . . .

X. No one should be molested for his opinions, even for his religious opinions, provided that their manifestation does not disturb the public order established by law.

XI. The free communication of thoughts and opinions is one of the most precious rights of man. . . .

XVII. Property being an inviolable and sacred right, no one can be deprived of it except when public necessity, declared by form of law, makes it clearly necessary. . . .

It is easy to criticise this famous document. The practical needs of France were urgent and they were neglected during the interminable discussions on 'human rights.' It turned out, too, that some of the principles, so triumphantly enunciated, were decidedly inconvenient when the details of the constitution came to be arranged. Clause VI, for instance, clearly implied universal suffrage, and the Assembly in its later phase was in no mood to grant that. This disparity between principle and practice gave an opening for attack of which the later revolutionists were quick to avail themselves. But, after all, the Declaration of the Rights of Man is the most characteristic example of the nobler side of the Revolution—without which it would not have been the great event in European history that it is. The contrast with the English Revolution has often been pointed out. While the English Parliament in its Declaration of Right enunciated simply the historic and legal rights of Englishmen against the Crown, France based her action on universal principles, and in her Declaration made herself the spokesman of the human race. It is not strange therefore that, while the English Revolution has seemed to foreigners simply a businesslike and successful rearrangement of the constitution, the French Revolution gave a new starting-point for the hopes and efforts of all races and nations. For a quarter of a century the Declaration of the Rights of Man was the watchword and the charter of all the reformers and revolutionists of Europe.[1]

The constitutional debates are among the most interesting in the history of Europe. The political philosophy of Montesquieu and Rousseau had now to be translated into actual institutions and there was little in the past of France to help the legislators. They were to some extent influenced by the constitution of the United States; but their chief though undeclared model was the English Constitution. Not a single voice was raised to advocate republicanism; benevolent despotism, such as the Prussian, was no longer in fashion: and in

---

[1] It was, wrote Lord Acton, 'stronger than all the armies of Napoleon.' The text quoted above is taken from that prefaced to the Constitution of September 14, 1791, cp. J. M. Roberts, R. C. Cobb and J. Hardman, *French Revolution Documents* (1966), vol. I, pp. 171–4.

England men saw the one great example of the reconciliation of monarchy with popular institutions.

There were hot debates as to the position which should be accorded to the Monarchy. In the end Louis XVI was declared 'King of the French by the Grace of God and the will of the Nation.' In defining his power the Assembly was much influenced by Montesquieu's theory of the 'separation of the powers'—the view, that is, that the executive, legislative, and judicial elements in the state should be kept entirely separate. The King was the head of the executive: he was to appoint the chief officers of the army and the Ministers of State. But, in accordance with the above-named theory and through distrust of the royal power, the Assembly refused to follow the English plan whereby the Ministers have a seat in the Legislative Assembly and are dependent upon its support for their continuance in office. An unbridged gap was thus created between the representatives of the people and the Ministers of the King. If there was divergence of aim between them they could only be brought into harmony by impeachment or by revolution. This point had been passionately argued by Mirabeau, the most constructive and conservative among the popular leaders, but he had struggled in vain for the adoption of the English system. Nor did better luck attend his efforts to give the King of France the right possessed by the Crown of England to veto all legislation. The King received only a suspensive not an absolute veto: that is, he could delay the passing of a measure but only for the space of a session. The position thus accorded him was one of great dignity and influence, with more real power than belonged to the contemporary English Monarchy. But Louis XVI was the descendant of the most powerful of European kings, and what was offered him seemed a great humiliation. The revolutionary settlement in England had only been made possible by a change of dynasty. There were some who thought it might be well to follow the English example here also and to transfer the Crown to the House of Orleans, whose representative, Duke Philippe, had embraced the popular cause with apparent enthusiasm.

The legislative power was to be entrusted to a single Chamber of 745 members. There had been some question of a second Chamber, but it had been voted down by an overwhelming majority. A second Chamber, it was said, would be either the last refuge of the old aristocracy or the cradle of a new one: and France in her present mood wanted no aristocracy of any kind. The franchise was, in direct conflict with the Rights of Man, limited by a property qualification which excluded from the vote the great majority of the artisans of the towns.

The judicial system of France was remodelled. The judges were to be elected. Torture was abolished. The jury system was introduced. Elected officials and councils in departments, districts, cantons and communes—new divisions of the country—replaced the hierarchy of royal officials who had formerly administered the localities. Thus the position of elected municipalities, which had sprung up on the Paris model all over France, was regularised and a clean sweep made of the old system of local and provincial government. The old historic provinces of France—Brittany, Normandy, Champagne, Guienne, Burgundy, Provence—were abolished. In their place came eighty-three departments called after the natural features that belonged to them, without traditions and making no appeal to local sentiment. It was intentionally done. The fine local traditions were part of the past that the Revolution was determined to destroy. They stood, too, in the way of that national unity which the Revolution was determined to achieve and which, later, was emphasised by the motto: 'The Republic, One and Indivisible.'

Lastly, we will note the policy adopted by the Constituent Assembly with regard to religion. The question aroused violent passions. The intellectual movement of the century had been constantly directed against the power and claims of the Church of France. With the coming of the Revolution two sections of religious opinion, which had been driven out of sight by persecution, came again into the light of day. There were many Protestants in the Assembly and they had not forgotten all the injustice and cruelty that had been implied by the Revocation of the Edict of Nantes. The Jansenists too—the Methodists of the French Church, as they have been called—were well represented and were eager to settle old scores with the Church and the Monarchy that had so cruelly and so foolishly oppressed them. The intimate union, moreover, which had, since the beginning of the sixteenth century, existed between the Church and the Crown was now a source of danger to the Church. Now that the absolute Monarchy had gone, the Church, which had been its chief supporter, could not be left unchanged.

The first steps were concerned with the property of the Church. Tithes were regarded as a part of feudalism and had been abolished with the rest of it. Then the vast resources of the Church seemed to offer a means of escape from the bankruptcy which threatened the State. Upon the motion of Talleyrand, Bishop of Autun—who now begins his amazing political career—it was decided that the wealth of the Church should be surrendered to the state, and that the State should undertake to maintain the services of the Church and to pay the clergy. It was disendowment combined with a measure of strict establishment. Then the Assembly took the first step on a dangerous slope which was to lead France again to bankruptcy by issuing paper money (the notes were called *assignats*) on the security of the newly acquired property.

There was some protest against all this, but no danger of religious schism. Next, however, the Assembly turned to reorganise the government of the Church which had thus been taken into the pay of the state. The old dioceses were abolished and new ones were established to correspond with the new departments. The stipends of the clergy were rearranged. The bishops received much less than they were used to: the *curés* somewhat more. Then, worst of all, the method of election by all citizens, irrespective of their faith, was introduced into the appointment both of bishops and priests. It was defended as being a return to primitive custom, but when the question was referred to the Pope he denounced the new arrangements and threatened with excommunication all those who adhered to them. The Assembly did not recoil before the threatened conflict. They answered the denunciation of the Pope by enforcing on all clergy an oath of obedience 'to the King, the Law and the Nation.' The Law would, of course, include the new arrangements which were known as the 'Civil Constitution of the Clergy.' The Church was split into two sections: those who accepted and those who refused the new oath—the Dissidents and the Constitutionalists. At first the State generously accorded a pension to those priests who felt themselves unable to take the oath.

Among the evil consequences of this ecclesiastical legislation two are chiefly to be noted. First, it divided the people of France in their feelings towards the Revolution as they had not been divided before. The nobles who had 'emigrated' had, in effect, declared war upon it; but their opposition would rather strengthen the adhesion of the mass of the people. But now the seeds of division were sown throughout the country and they produced actual civil war before long. Next, the King, who had accepted the Revolution with hesitation, but still had accepted it, now found himself in decided opposition to it. The religious fibre in his nature was very strong. He gave his signature to the Church laws for fear of the storm of protest which his veto would have created; but the denunciation by the Pope made him profoundly uneasy. 'I ask God,' he wrote, 'to accept my profound repentance for having affixed my name, though against my will, to acts which are in conflict with the discipline and the belief of the Catholic Church.'

The ecclesiastical legislation was among the chief causes which impelled the King to his disastrous flight from Paris. At Easter 1791 he tried to go to his palace of St. Cloud (seven miles from Paris) to avoid receiving the Communion at the hands of a 'constitutional' priest. His way was barred by a suspicious crowd, which refused to give way even to the appeals of Lafayette. After this it was clear that the King was a prisoner in his palace at the Tuileries, and the tone of the press was growing even more hostile and suspicious. The boasting of the emigrant nobles that they would soon come and liberate him was a serious cause of annoyance and danger to the King. It had long been a fixed idea with him that he ought to get away from

Paris and revise and alter the constitution. Mirabeau, before his death in April 1791, had strongly urged that the King should boldly and openly go to Rouen, summon the Assembly to his side, and make certain changes in the constitution; but to do all this in such a way that his loyalty to the main principles of the Revolution should be beyond question. But neither the King nor the Queen really trusted Mirabeau. They inclined to think him a demagogue who had come over to the side of the Monarchy for selfish ends. His death destroyed the last chance of his plan being carried out. But more than ever the King was bent on escaping from the hateful restraint of Paris. His design was to get into touch with General Bouillé, who commanded the French armies on the north-eastern frontier, and with the backing of the armies to dictate the changes in the constitution that he desired; especially to annul the ecclesiastical legislation and to grant greater power to the nobility; and if necessary to appeal to the support of the Great Powers of Europe.

It was by no means a wild scheme and it came very near to success. Disguised as a servant of his children's governess, he escaped with the Queen and his children unnoticed from the Tuileries. He found a travelling carriage outside the city, and he reached Varennes, a small town on the Meuse. On the other side of the bridge he would have been in safety, but he had already been detected, and he was arrested by the mayor and an inn-keeper from a neighbouring village.

The greatest alarm prevailed in Paris when the King's flight was known. He had left a letter declaring his refusal to accept the constitution, and a foreign war was believed to be imminent. The news of his capture allayed these fears, but raised problems of the greatest difficulty. What was to be done with a runaway king? The example of James II of England and his fortunate escape suggested to some that it would have been well if Louis XVI, too, had managed to get away. There were some who advocated a change of dynasty and the recognition of the Duke of Orleans as king. But the majority of the Assembly determined to bring the King back to Paris, to suspend him from his royal functions until the constitution had received its last touches, and then to offer it to him for his acceptance. If he accepted he would be King once more; if he refused he would lose the throne, and the question of his successor would have to be faced. Such was the decision taken by the Assembly, but there was a small minority in the Assembly, supported strongly in Paris, which demanded the King's instant deposition and the declaration of a republic. Before this there had hardly been a sign of republican feeling. But now a petition was drawn up by the Cordeliers Club and placed on a table in the Champ de Mars for signature. There was nothing illegal in this; but disorder was feared, and Bailly, the Mayor of Paris, was instructed to disperse the crowd that gathered round the petition. The National Guard was called out and, as the crowd did not disperse at the first summons, a volley was fired and many lives were lost by the shots or in the stampede that followed (July 17, 1791). This became known as the Massacre of the Champ de Mars, and is the starting-point of the movement which in little more than a year made France a republic. Bailly, who had given the order to fire, became the object of the bitter execrations of the crowd. This was more dangerous than ever, for it was now the weapon of an organised working-class movement which had emerged in Paris in the spring of 1791. It had been prompted by a number of new clubs, often offshoots of the Cordeliers, recruiting their members among women and the unenfranchised generally. Thus the Paris *sans-culottes* challenged the power of the middle-class dominated Assembly and National Guard. The guilds having been abolished, they came forward with wage demands and threats of strikes.

In September 1791 the constitution was completed and was accepted by the King. The Revolution seemed at an end—unless, of course, the working-class challenge was to be taken seriously.

Chapter 2

THE REVOLUTION AT WAR

It is impossible to understand the French Revolution if its domestic aspects and developments are considered by themselves. The more its course is examined the clearer does it become that the whole of its later phase was conditioned by the great war which broke out and continued with no real period of peace for twenty-three years. We shall examine in a moment the causes of the war and the steps by which it came upon France. We must first consider the condition of the country at the time of its outbreak.

The new Legislative Assembly came into being in the autumn of 1791. It was decided that no member of the late Constituent Assembly could have a seat in the new one. The fortunes of France were therefore entrusted to a number of men without established reputations or definite party connections. The new Chamber was in consequence weak, and the real influence on the course of events was to be found rather in the newspapers and in the clubs than on its benches.

A great number of the members never definitely belonged to any political party, but we may notice the following groupings. The Conservative, or Right, party in the Chamber was known as the Feuillants, and represented in the Chamber the opinions of Lafayette outside. It was perhaps the largest party, but it was soon outstripped in influence by others. The Left, or Radical, side of the Chamber was later on divided into two groups. The first of these groups was known as the Girondists, because several of its leaders came from the Department of the Gironde. They were men, for the most part, young, enthusiastic, and eloquent. Though they accepted the Monarchy for the moment they regarded a republic as the ideal. Their main support was to be found outside of Paris in the provinces and country districts, and later on they came to be the special representatives of the middle class, but at first they were regarded with fear as dangerous and headstrong revolutionaries. Their chief leaders were Brissot, Buzot, Vergniaud, and Roland. The wife of the last named was always an important influence in the councils of the party, and because of her character and her tragic fate she has attracted more attention than any of them. The Jacobins were not distinguished at first from the Girondists. We have already seen the Club from which the party took its name. It was more influential in Paris than in the Chamber, and its leaders—Robespierre, Marat, and Danton—were the most powerful political influences in the city.

The King had the right of appointing a Ministry without regard to the wishes of the Assembly, and he chose his first Ministry from the Conservative, or Feuillant, party. Soon there came violent friction between himself and the Assembly. His flight had destroyed his former popularity, and his influence and his character were alike regarded with distrust by many. Whatever he did was interpreted in the worst sense. When he refused to accept a law condemning to death all emigrant nobles who did not return before January 1792 or when again he refused his consent to a very severe law against the priests who would not take the constitutional oath, this was regarded as a sign of sympathy with the enemies of the Revolution. So strong was the protest against his actions that he thought it best to allow his Conservative Ministry to resign, and he appointed a new one from the ranks of the Girondists. Roland was Minister of the Interior, but the most important name was Dumouriez, who, though not in any way closely connected with the Girondist party, had been appointed to the direction of foreign affairs. And as foreign affairs at this juncture became the all-important question, we must turn to consider them and the way in which France became involved in a foreign war.

The origin of the war has been a matter of dispute ever since it broke out. Some have ascribed it to the ambitions and passions of the Revolution; others to the jealousy and fear of the Great Powers. The situation in Europe had many elements of danger, and yet there was not, certainly at first, any inclination to go to war with France, while France on her side had in her constitution expressly repudiated war except for purposes of defence. Great Britain seemed at first disinclined to renew her age-long struggle with France. At the beginning of the Revolution the general feeling in England had been one of sympathy. It seemed that France was imitating the English example and was choosing a form of government closely resembling our own. A few warning voices were raised, and especially Burke's, maintaining that the spirit of the French Revolution was wholly different from that of the English movement in 1688, and that it threatened by its beliefs and examples the established order in every part of Europe; but such warnings were balanced by the enthusiasm of the poets and the acceptance of statesmen. Both Wordsworth and Coleridge wrote in glowing language of their high hopes when the Revolution broke out. Wordsworth has told us that it was 'bliss in that dawn to be alive' and that 'to be young was very heaven.' Coleridge was so convinced of the greatness of the movement in France that he 'hung his head and wept at Britain's name,' because Britain opposed herself to it. Among statesmen, Pitt was quite ready to co-operate with France, while Fox, on behalf of one section of the Whigs, hailed it with rapture. The English Government was concerned with a movement in Holland, where the governing Stadholder found his authority threatened by revolutionary parties. He entered into an alliance with Great Britain and with Prussia, and as Prussia easily suppressed the revolutionary movement in Holland people attached less importance to the danger from France.

It was in Central Europe that the events were to be found which were soon to lead to war, but even there there was a strong desire to avoid it. The organisation of the Empire was to the last degree inefficient. Its army and its funds depended upon contingents and contributions supplied by its members. Indeed, as we have seen in the introduction, the strength of Germany was to be found in the individual states, and especially in Austria and in Prussia. Austria and Prussia were old enemies and still jealous and hostile. The memory of the Seven Years' War and of the humiliation of Austria still rankled at Vienna, and the two Powers did not find it easy to co-operate. Moreover, Austria had many great tasks upon her hands. Leopold II was concerned to bring back calm where at present there was turmoil, and contentment where there was bitter opposition, in short, to mitigate in Belgium, Hungary and elsewhere in his dominions the disturbing effects of Joseph II's drastic changes.

Though he was always anxious for the safety of his sister, the French Queen, and offered her asylum if she would leave France, he was not prepared to be the single champion of the French monarchy against France—indeed, he did not wish to be champion at all. Yet whatever might happen in the future, he must at least make sure of his relationship with Prussia and this turned upon the Turkish and Polish questions. Frederick William II, a less intelligent and far-sighted man than Leopold, had succeeded his uncle in a mood of respect and had carried incomplete work of his to completion. But he soon fell into the hands of confidential advisers who needed better leadership than he could supply. His Prussian pride and his wish to serve his country led him in the end into a forward policy, as we shall see, which he was neither able nor strong-willed enough to sustain. But during 1790–91 he fell in with Leopold's policy of clearing away disputes as a preliminary to united action to protect their common interest in avoiding war with France. Leopold and Frederick William signed the Treaty of Reichenbach and the alliance of Vienna in July 1790 and then, meeting at the Castle of Pilnitz not far from Dresden, the Declaration of Pilnitz on August 27, 1791. At Reichenbach Leopold promised to make peace with Turkey without aggrandisement and a year later by the Treaty of Sistowa kept his promise renouncing

Joseph II's Turkish conquests. The alliance was concerned with Bavarian and other dynastic matters as well as a promise of mutual assistance if the internal peace of their dominions was disturbed. Its terms also contained a renunciation of the Polish crown and a pledge to protect Poland. To the Declaration of Pilnitz, which sought, too, to ensure the stability of Poland, we shall return presently.

The Polish question could not, however, be set aside by a stroke of the pen. Rather faced it must be because of the way in which the Russian Tsarina, Catherine II, was exploiting it. We have already seen how Poland's weakness had exposed her already in 1772 to the first partition at the hands of Prussia, Austria and Russia. Since then the prospects of Poland had much improved. Stanislas, who had been Catherine's favourite and her lover, was appointed to the Polish throne in 1764 through her influence. In his new role he displayed both energy and public spirit. He saw that the first thing necessary was to give Poland a constitution that should really be efficient, that should sweep away the anarchical privileges of the nobility, and be able to pass laws and to direct the foreign affairs of the country. Such a constitution he brought forward and he received a certain measure of support, but since it was possible for a very slight opposition to wreck a strongly supported plan, Stanislas in May 1791, by the use of the military forces of the State, forced through the amended constitution. Poland seemed then to enter upon a more hopeful era, but it was of the essence of the situation that her neighbours did not desire her to grow strong and prosperous. Among these neighbours Catherine was the most ruthless. She clearly and self-consciously interfered in Poland to check its growing solidarity, and with equal deliberation she set to work to embroil the other Powers in French affairs in order that, whilst they were occupied in the west, she herself might lay hands upon the Polish provinces that she coveted. When Leopold's death in March 1792 removed his restraining hand Catherine prepared to act. At the end of 1792 she occupied Poland with armed force and on January 23, 1793, signed with Frederick William the Treaty of St. Petersburg which effected a second partition of Poland. Until 1792 Catherine was at war with Turkey and it was Britain's as well as Austria's policy to resist her aggrandisement there. The suspicions between the Great Powers engendered by their Turkish and Polish policies is one clue to the amazing triumph of the French Revolution against the European alliance.

Meanwhile relations between France and the Empire had broken down. They had been difficult for some time past. Decisions which seemed at first sight to be purely domestic in character had affected the foreign relations of France. The abolition of feudalism, for instance, had led France to annex territory in Alsace and elsewhere on the left bank of the Rhine that was 'feudally held' by Leopold, by the Duke of Württemberg, the Margrave of Baden, Louis of

Hesse Darmstadt, the Duke of Zweibrücken or other Germans. The religious legislation of the Assembly had deprived the Bishops of Cologne and of Mainz of tithes which they had hitherto received from French subjects. The reorganisation of the bishoprics of France had taken from their obedience parishes and districts which had long been theirs. The Emperor Leopold, as in duty bound, had championed the claims of the Germans who alleged themselves to be injured and protested on their behalf, but he had not followed up his protest and instead had handed over their claims for settlement to the Reichstag of the Empire. Then, too, the French had their grievances against the Empire. We have seen how after the fall of the Bastille, and again after the days of October 1789, a considerable number of the princes and nobles of France had fled, in fear or in disgust, from the hated Revolution, and the majority of them had taken up their residence in the German states on the eastern frontier of France. There, at Trier and at Mainz, they kept the semblance of a Court, recruited and drilled soldiers, issued manifestos and talked of the coming restoration of the ancient régime. It was impossible for France to tolerate this challenge, contemptible though it might be. She had called upon the Emperor Leopold to disperse these *émigrés*, and he had expressed his willingness to do so. But they had not left German territory and France still nursed a grievance because of their residence there.

Finally the French totally, perhaps wilfully, misunderstood the Declaration of Pilnitz. It will be recalled that Leopold and Frederick William had adopted a policy of settling outstanding differences and the Declaration had begun with mutual assurances about Poland and a possible exchange of territories in Germany. It then asserted that the restoration of order in France was a matter that concerned all European States and that, *'provided other European States would co-operate'* with them, they would be willing to interfere to secure for Louis and Marie Antoinette a more tolerable position. Under the cautious language of diplomacy, this declaration seemed at first to carry a dangerous threat. It was really something different, for Leopold did not intend to follow it up by any action. He had left himself a loophole in the quoted phrase because he knew that Great Britain would not co-operate. He said in a letter to his Minister '*then* and *in that case* have been for me the law and the prophets; if England fails us the cause for interference does not occur.' But Frenchmen were unaware of the inner diplomatic meaning of the Declaration. It seemed to them that the Monarchies of Europe were threatening interference in the domestic affairs of France, and they were not more inclined to feel kindly to their King because the threat was made on his behalf.

It was at this juncture that the Girondist Ministry came into office, and the Girondists were generally in favour of a foreign war. Madame Roland regarded war as the force that was necessary to raise the feeling of France into republican enthusiasm and to overthrow the Monarchy. Dumouriez, the Minister of Foreign Affairs, dreamed of a diplomatic alliance that should give France an excellent chance of success. He hoped for the support of Great Britain and of Prussia; he even entertained the idea that the French armies might find in the Prussian Duke of Brunswick a commander who would lead them to victory according to the best traditions of the strategy of Frederick the Great. As the negotiations with Austria progressed the passion of France grew much inflamed. The possible revival of dynastic aggrandisement in Poland proved an irritant as well as an opportunity to show her own revolutionary virtue. There was a widespread readiness for war, and an outspoken opposition was only to be found among those who later came to be extreme Jacobins, men like Marat, Danton, and Robespierre. No wiser speech was made during the whole course of the Revolution than that in which Robespierre argued against the wisdom of the war, expressed his opinion that immediate success was improbable, and that it could hardly be fruitful either in France or in Europe of consequences favourable to the Revolution. But it fell on deaf ears, and even the Royalists in France welcomed the idea of a war. They believed that in war the need would be felt to strengthen the executive, and that this would make for the restoration of the royal power to something of its old strength. Under such circumstances the negotiations with Austria grew more and more strained and bitter. The Emperor Leopold II died on March 1, 1792. He was succeeded by Francis II, who had neither his experience nor his soberness of judgment. The demands of the French Foreign Office were refused, and on April 20, 1792, in accordance with the new constitution, Louis XVI went down to the Assembly and there, with tears in his eyes, declared war against Francis, not as Emperor, but as King of Hungary and Bohemia. Francis and Frederick William declared war on France in their turn on May 21 and a year later in May 1793 the Empire followed suit.

Thus Dumouriez's hopes of alliances were falsified. The French had planned an assault upon the neighbouring Austrian Netherlands, where they hoped to find sympathetic support for their invasion in consequence of the revolutionary movements already fermenting there. This, the first campaign of the revolutionary war, was a complete and humiliating failure. The troops of France were ill-disciplined; the officers to a large extent disloyal to the Revolution; the campaign ill-planned. The French armies penetrated Belgium some little distance, but retreated in disorder to the frontier, and the French had to confess the failure of a campaign on which they had placed high hopes. The failure produced an immediate consequence in Paris. The Ministers and the people entertained great suspicion of the honesty of the King's intentions. They saw in the failure, the consequence not merely of insufficient preparation, but of the trea-sonous designs of the King. On June 20, 1792, a crowd penetrated the badly guarded palace of the Tuileries, forced itself into the pres-ence of the King and Queen, insulted him by various cries and demands, and held the palace for some little time before it was driven out by the arrival of the National Guard. The incident is in itself without importance, yet it shows us in miniature the causes which led to the overthrow of the Monarchy, and even to the Reign of Terror. There was a dangerous foreign war; there was failure on the frontier; all men felt that the first necessary condition for success was energy and the will to victory in the head of the State. They believed the King lukewarm or treacherous. It seemed essential therefore to force on him a more energetic policy; or, failing that, to remove him from the government of France.

The Legislative Assembly, though not yet one year old, was utterly unable to control the situation. The real leaders of public opinion were not to be found there. It looked on at the development of events, anxious but helpless. In France generally it cannot be doubted that the prevailing feeling of the masses of the people, and especially of the peasantry of the country districts, was conservative, rather than radical. The Revolution had done much for them; it seemed to them to have gone far enough. They were by tradition attached to the Monarchy; they would be unwilling to take any violent action to overthrow the throne. If then action were to come, such action as seemed and probably was necessary for the saving of France, it must come, not from the Assembly, nor from the mass of the people of France, but from a resolute minority. That resolute minority was found among the Jacobins. They were men of various origins, but few, if any, of them were members of the working classes. They differed in opinion on many points and their differences led later to fierce struggles among themselves; but they were united in a fanatical and almost religious devotion to the principles of the Revolution, and in a love for France. It was the pressure of the for-eign war and the danger that it brought with it to the principles of the Revolution, which made them determine to overthrow the throne and to seize the government in the interest of the Revolution, and of France, which they regarded as identical. The middle class—the bourgeoisie—had dominated the Revolution so far. Power now passed rapidly into the hands of those who leaned on the support of the Parisian *sans-culottes*; and it was the war that caused this change with all its incalculable results.

The military outlook had grown worse since the failure of the Bel-gian campaign. The lead on the other side was taken by Frederick William, not surprisingly, since the Austrian military machine was cumbersome and the great reputation of the Prussian Commander-in-Chief, the Duke of Brunswick, was at stake. He now invaded

Champagne. The excitement of Paris under these circumstances can well be imagined. The troops that were raised in the provinces passed in many instances through the capital, and their passage was made the occasion for patriotic demonstrations. Especially was this the case with the troops from Marseilles, who arrived on July 30, and who sang for the first time the patriotic hymn, the 'Marseillaise.'

It is impossible to penetrate all the preparations for the blow that was soon to fall; but we know that a Committee of Insurrection was formed, consisting of some of the less-known Jacobins, and presided over by Danton, who now comes prominently into the story of the Revolution. We know that the assemblies of the forty-eight Sections, which roughly corresponded to the wards of a modern city, were declared 'permanent'—that is, were allowed to sit without any permission from the municipal authority—and that in them, the ultra-revolutionary party had won a predominant influence. We know, too, that the National Guard, once regarded as the mainstay of the middle class, was now thrown open to all citizens and became far more revolutionary in spirit. On July 11 the country was solemnly declared to be 'in danger.' On July 22 further excitement was caused by the hoisting of a black flag over the Hôtel de Ville. On August 3 there was published the manifesto of the Duke of Brunswick, the commander of the invading armies, threatening Paris with total destruction if any further insult were offered to the King. It naturally roused a more aggressive spirit in the people of Paris. The King and Royal family were living all this time in the palace of the Tuileries, and the defence of the palace was entrusted partly to National Guards, whose fidelity was now very doubtful, and partly to Swiss Guards, the traditional mercenary but loyal defenders of the Crown. The expected blow fell in the early hours of August 10, 1792. Then, first, new members elected by the Sectional Assemblies went at one o'clock in the morning and displaced the existing Municipal Council, though many of the old members were retained in the new one. This new Council then summoned Mandat, the commander of the Palace garrison, to report himself at the Hôtel de Ville. He was, on his arrival, ordered into arrest, and shortly afterwards murdered. The King early in the morning had reviewed the National Guards, but their cries had shown him how weak a support they would be in the hour of attack. At 8.30 in the morning, when the attack was already visibly threatening, he determined to leave the palace and to throw himself upon the protection of the Assembly. He was admitted into their Debating Hall, and given with his Queen and children a position in the reporters' box. During his absence the attack on the palace took place. The soldiers and the crowd penetrated into the gardens. When they approached the palace they were met by a heavy fire from the Swiss Guards, and would very probably have been driven out of the gardens. The King, however, from his retreat, heard the firing, and sent orders to the Swiss to surrender, as the struggle was now without meaning. They lowered their arms and began to march off, but a large number of them were killed by the invaders of the palace. After the capture of the palace, the excited mob came to the Assembly, where they demanded the deposition of the King and the declaration of a Republic. It was pointed out that this was impossible under the constitution of 1791; but the King was suspended from his functions, and a new Assembly, to be called the Convention, and to be elected by manhood suffrage, was to come into existence at an early date. It would decide what constitutional change was necessary, but the Republic already existed in all but name.

A little more than three weeks elapsed between the fall of the Monarchy and the September massacres. It is important to see the development of events. First, a new Ministry was appointed by the Assembly, drawn largely from the Girondist party. Roland was Minister of the Interior, Danton was Minister of Justice. We may note, too, that after the receipt of the news of the King's fall, Lafayette attempted to raise an armed protest among the troops. He found, however, that they were not inclined to support the Monarchy against the new revolutionary movement, and he soon felt himself in danger. He left the army, crossed the frontiers, and his part in the history of the Revolution was over. In Paris, meanwhile, the newly appointed Commune or Municipal Council was more important than the Legislative Assembly which was nearly deserted, and had only a few more days of existence. In the Commune Robespierre's was the chief influence. He demanded that the examination of crimes against the State should be attributed to the Commune, and the demand had to be granted. A Committee of Supervision, a kind of special Executive Committee, was also appointed, in which Marat was the guiding force.

The news from the frontier grew worse day by day. The fall of Longwy was known on August 26. It was reported, though prematurely, that the great fortress of Verdun had fallen too. The fever and the suspicion in Paris mounted daily higher. On August 28 Danton, as Minister of Justice, demanded that power should be given to him to search the houses of Paris for enemies of the Revolution, and by this means during the next three days some thousands of suspects were seized, and the city prisons were crowded to overflowing with men of various kinds; some innocent; many doubtless really guilty of conspiracy for the restoration of the Monarchy; all suspect of the crime of opposition to the Jacobin power. The position of the Jacobins was critical in the extreme. Danton in a well-known speech gives us the key of the situation. The Revolution, he said, was between two fires, the enemy at the frontier and the enemy at home. In order to survive, it was necessary 'to frighten the enemy.'

On September 2, Sunday, the business of frightening the enemy began. An extemporised tribunal was established by the Commune in the prisons of Paris. Prisoners were brought before it, more usually in batches than singly. They were roughly examined. Some effort was doubtless made to distinguish between the real enemies of the Revolution and others. If they were thought to be innocent, they were sent back to prison; if they were regarded as guilty, they were ordered to be removed to another prison. This was a sentence of death. They were thrust out into the street and murdered by those who were prepared for the work. In this way during September 2, and the two following days, many hundreds of people were killed in Paris; the exact number it is impossible to calculate. As to the origin, the responsibility and the aim of the September massacres there has been and there will long be discussion and controversy. It is clear, however, that whoever else was innocent, Marat was guilty, and that it is to the Committee of Supervision that much of the organisation and execution can be traced, though the passions of the revolutionary crowd, inflamed by the bad news from the frontier, doubtless made very little organisation or direction necessary. The massacres sprang rather from passion than from policy; they were a wild stroke at suspected enemies, at a moment when enemies were believed to surround the revolutionary leaders on all sides. Very soon even the most ardent of revolutionaries were anxious to free themselves from any share in the responsibility for the 'September Massacres.'

This same month of September 1792 saw also events of the greatest importance on the frontier. The victory of the Allies seemed assured, and the early occupation of Paris was confidently prophesied, but quite apart from the enthusiasm and courage of the French armies there were secret causes weakening and endangering the Allies. Austria and Prussia, though united against France, were at variance with regard to Poland, and it is certain that fears of what might happen in Poland had prevented the Allied armies from reaching anything like their projected strength. There was also difference of opinion between the Duke of Brunswick and Frederick William of Prussia, as to the conduct of the campaign, the King urging a rapid stroke, Brunswick advising care and caution. The armies that France opposed to the invaders consisted only to a very small degree of the new recruits. The chief command was in the hands of Dumouriez, and he had to rely chiefly upon the old army officered to a large extent by men out of sympathy with the Revolution, and irritated by many grievances, but the rank and file were largely moved by real enthusiasm for the Revolution. The fortress of Verdun fell on September 2; the road to Paris seemed open, but the lines of the Argonne Hills, which lay on the road to the capital, were occupied by Dumouriez, on instructions from Servan, the Minister of War, and here for some time the armies faced one another. When at last the invaders by means of a turning movement got into the rear of the

French, they found themselves opposed to a new French army on the hill of Valmy. Here, on September 20, 1792, there occurred an action, famous and important because of its results, but not worthy of the name of a great battle. The Prussians cannonaded the hill, and then tried to take it by direct assault. They were repulsed with some loss, but this small event was magnified by what followed into one of the decisive battles of the world. For there followed negotiations between Dumouriez and the Duke of Brunswick, full of subtlety and fraud on both sides. The Duke of Brunswick consented to retire and Dumouriez, believing that the Prussians might even now be induced to separate themselves from Austria, allowed him to reach the frontier in safety. But all this is of little importance compared with the fact that Paris which, on September 20, believed itself in imminent danger of attack and perhaps of blockade, found itself by this stroke liberated and triumphant.

The elections for the new Convention had begun about the time of the September massacres. It was believed at first that the result was a great victory for the moderates. Very many voters had abstained from the poll. Of the members returned only some fifty were declared Jacobins, one hundred and twenty were Girondists, and over six hundred were not definitely attached to either party. The new Convention appointed the Ministers and from the first gave executive power into the hands of committees.

The first thing to be decided was the fate of the King, and the decision came quickly. On September 21, 1792, by a unanimous vote the Monarchy was declared to be abolished and a republic established. Then came the question of the King's trial. There seemed no legal basis for his trial. The constitution had declared the loss of the throne the legal penalty for certain offences and especially for failure to resist a foreign invasion. He had perhaps committed the offence but he had certainly paid the penalty. What further charge could be brought against him?[1] It was clear, however, that the dominant party of the Assembly would not allow legality to bar them from their object, and the King's trial was decided upon. The indictment was presented on December 11, and the King was charged with plotting against the nation, with paying the troops raised by the *émigrés* abroad, and with attempting to overthrow the constitution. He was allowed counsel and was daringly and eloquently defended. The

---

[1] The two decisive clauses in the constitution are Chapter II, Section I, articles vi and viii: 'If the King puts himself at the head of an army and directs its forces against the nation, or if he does not formally resist such an enterprise when made in his name, he shall be judged to have abdicated the crown. . . . After such abdication, the King shall belong to the class of citizens and may like them be accused and judged *for acts posterior to his abdication.*' J. M. Thompson, *French Revolution Documents 1789–94*, (1948), p. 122; cp. J. M. Roberts, R. C. Cobb and J. Hardman, *French Revolution Documents* (1966), vol. I, p. 354 where the articles are summarised in one sentence.

votes of the Assembly were given individually and openly, and by a unanimous vote he was declared to be guilty. By a majority of one only, the capital penalty was decided, and, on January 21, 1793, he was guillotined in what had formerly been the Square of Louis XV, now re-named the Square of the Republic.

All the future of the Republic turned upon the war. This is really the decisive influence upon every detail even of the domestic history of France, and in spite of the victory of Valmy, the military outlook became rapidly worse. The most serious blow was that shortly after the execution of the King, Great Britain went to war with France. Many influences produced this result, for war rarely springs from a single cause. English opinion had been outraged by the attack upon the King, and still more by his execution: the French Ambassador was dismissed when news of it reached London. A powerful section of the people was lending a sympathetic ear to the splendid rhetoric with which Burke denounced the character and the aims of the Revolution: but there were more practical reasons as well. After the Battle of Valmy, the French had gained a series of important victories. They had crossed the Rhine at Mainz; more important still, they had invaded Belgium, and, on November 6, in the Battle of Jemappes (a much greater battle than Valmy), they had overthrown the Austrian army, and had by their victory made themselves masters of the whole country. A few days later Brussels fell into their hands. They then took two important and most questionable steps. On November 19 they solemnly declared that they would grant fraternity and help to all peoples who desired to recover their liberty; and this was a plain invitation to all people to rise against their governments and a plain menace to all governments who believed that their peoples were anxious to rise against them. Then a little later acting upon the supposed 'natural right' of a people to the possession of the mouth of a river that flowed through its territory, they declared that the river Scheldt, which as a result of many wars and treaties had been closed to the entrance of great vessels, should now be thrown open to all commerce. Great Britain, probably quite mistakenly, had for long regarded the closure of the Scheldt as a matter of the first importance for her commerce, and it has been asserted that she coveted some of the French West Indian islands. Pitt in Parliament presented war as the only way to impose peace on a troubled continent and peace as essential to preserve Britain's continental markets. On February 1, France anticipated Britain by declaring war against Britain and Holland. Spain joined the belligerents almost immediately.

France was thus at war with a great European coalition, which now numbered in its ranks Prussia, Austria, Great Britain, Holland, Sardinia, and Spain. The spring of 1793 saw dangers and disasters accumulating on almost every frontier. The first serious disaster came in Belgium, which had been the scene of the first decisive victory of the Revolution. There had been some readiness in the country to welcome the invaders, but the popularity of the French was soon effaced by the measures which they took for the government of Belgium. They oppressed the Church; they gave forced currency to their paper money. Worst of all, on the ground of a few petitions offered to them, they declared the country annexed to France. A probable ally was thus turned into a decided enemy. The policy had been dictated from Paris, and Dumouriez, the commander of the French armies, had protested in vain, Now there came to him from headquarters an order to advance into Holland, which he unwillingly obeyed, believing that Belgium was in too dangerous a condition to be left safely in his rear. The earliest stages of the war were successful, but on March 18, 1793, Dumouriez was forced to retreat in order to protect his Lieutenant, Miranda, who had been attacked by the Austrians. The great Battle of Neerwinden was fought, and, after a fierce and for a long time not unequal contest, it resulted in the victory of the Austrians. Defeat coming to the French where they had been accustomed to conquer was bad enough, but it was much worse that their commander began at once to treat with the enemy. We have seen that he was already on bad terms with the Paris Government. He had never been in real sympathy with the aims of the revolutionaries. He dreamed now of re-establishing the monarchy and giving the crown to the young Duke of Chartres, whose father, in spite of his royal blood, had thrown himself heartily into the revolution. Some suspicion of all this reached Paris and commissioners were sent to the army, but Dumouriez arrested them and went on with his plans. His army, however, refused to support him. He found himself in danger, and on April 5 fled over to the Austrians. The peril had been a very great one, and it left a very great fear behind. It is the second occasion (we have already seen the action of Lafayette) on which an army chief had attempted to raise the army against the Government. Fears of treason amongst the officers were henceforth one of the chief alarms of the revolutionists. In the action of Dumouriez, we may see the shadow of Napoleon beginning to pass menacingly across the Revolution.

The foreign situation was dangerous, and its danger was increased by serious disturbance at home. To the south of the Loire, in the district known as La Vendée, a movement broke out which culminated in civil war, and which for two years taxed all the energies that France could spare from the foreign struggle. La Vendée was different in character from the rest of France. The nobility and gentry were resident on their estates. The peasantry were devoted to the Church and not at enmity with the nobles. The country was, to a large extent, covered with forest, difficult to penetrate and easy to defend. At first the revolutionary movement, though not welcome in this backward part of France, had not been resisted, and some of its results had been popular with the peasantry. It was the demand for military service, and the attempt to enforce that demand, which led to rebellion in February 1793. The movement was stimulated by the priesthood, and found leaders in all ranks of society. The best-known names are Cathelineau, a peasant and a hawker, and La Rochejaquelein, a noble of high descent. A young naval officer called Charette had probably more military capacity than either of them. The Revolution, hard pressed by foreign war, could spare no troops for the west. The insurgents gained great advantages. In March 1793 Fontenay and Niort fell. The movement was clearly a dangerous one.

Against these accumulating dangers the Convention took resolute measures. They gave concentration to the Government; they gave to it a capacity for secrecy and rapidity of action, pushing aside all laws or institutions which were a check upon its effectiveness; and many Frenchmen accepted the action of the Central Government because it was fighting against the common enemy, even though they disliked what it was doing at home. On March 29, 1793, the Revolutionary Tribunal was appointed to deal, by a special procedure, with all those who were accused of hostility to the Government. On April 6 the Committee of Public Safety was appointed, the body which governed France for more than two years, and to which are to be traced most of those measures which gave the country salvation and victory. The Committee of Public Safety consisted of nine members: they had at their disposal a large amount of money to be used for secret services; they could override the action of the Ministers, who were reduced almost to their subordinate agents; they deliberated secretly, and they were only accountable to the Convention when they reported at stated intervals to that body. About the same time also the system of 'representatives on mission' was instituted. These were men appointed by the Convention, sent into all parts of France, nominally to enforce the general levy for the war, really to establish the supremacy of the Central Government in all parts of France. Thus the Revolution, which began by advocating a looser and decentralised form of government, was now, under the influence of the war, swinging back towards the old traditions of centralisation, characteristic of the French Monarchy during the seventeenth and eighteenth centuries.

It was the Girondist party that had suggested the Committee of Public Safety, but the members of the Committee were chiefly drawn from the Jacobins; and from the first the leading influence in it was Danton, already distinguished for the share that he had taken in the overthrow of the Monarchy. The figure of Danton is a somewhat strange one in the history of the Revolution. He was often regarded as one of the most blood-stained of the Jacobins. He had advocated, in the crisis of August 1792, 'Audacity, Audacity, and always Audacity.' Yet the more his career is scrutinised the more clearly do we see that, though he was capable of violent action when occasion seemed to call for it, his constant effort was to prevent the Revolution from falling into the abyss of anarchy and bloodshed which we know awaited it. He desired to return in many ways to ancient methods; he advocated, at a time when it was dangerous to do so, mercy, authority, and respect for government. Jacobin though he was, it was his aim at first to co-operate with the Girondist party, and he made overtures to them for that end. They rejected them decisively. They had come to regard the Jacobins as a party, not only of violence, but of brutality, and as the antagonists of all their idealistic and philosophic aims. Rejecting the overtures of Danton, they soon found themselves involved in a fierce contest with the whole Jacobin party. It is the first of those contests among the republicans themselves which continuously brought the government into the hands of smaller groups, until they led to the establishment of the personal despotism of Napoleon. In this struggle the Girondists had many elements of weakness. It was Paris that really dominated the Revolution now, and the Girondists represented the provinces and had little support in Paris. They were charged with 'federalism,' which was taken to mean that they wished at this moment, when France was faced by a European coalition, to break up the unity of the country and establish some looser form of government. Some wild threats that were used by one of their party, Isnard, against the city of Paris certainly tended still further to provoke the capital against them. They were weakened, too, by their connection with Dumouriez, who, since the Battle of Neerwinden, was always treated as the great traitor. The newspapers of Paris, edited by such men as Marat and Hébert, were opposed to them. In peaceable times the majority of Frenchmen would probably have voted in their favour, but at this particular moment they had no control over the actual forces that counted. On April 24 they brought the most detested of all the Jacobins, Marat, before the Revolutionary Tribunal, but he was acquitted, and the result of the affair was still further to exasperate the revolutionists of Paris against them. They were constant and loud in protest against the action of the Commune, which they declared was plotting against the liberty of the Convention. There was probably some truth in this, but their protest provoked a further attack. On May 31, 1793, a rising of the Paris crowd demanded the arrest of the Girondists as enemies of the Revolution. The first rising was dispersed, but a few days later, on June 2, came another. The Parisian crowd, fairly well armed and competently led, surrounded the hall of the Convention, and imprisoned the members until their demands were granted. It was necessary in the end to bow to popular violence, and a large body of Girondists were decreed under arrest and sent off to prison, there to pass through the Revolutionary Tribunal to the scaffold of the guillotine.

With the fall of the Girondists the Reign of Terror, which really began in August 1792, may be said to have reached its culmination. Its essential meaning is that a minority, and a small minority, of resolute men had seized upon the government in an hour of great crisis, and, dispensing with ordinary constitutional forms, pursued exclusively the defence of the country and the maintenance of power in their own hands. There have been many Reigns of Terror in history—many governments, that is to say, which have held power by violence and by frightening their opponents. What is peculiarly ironic about the position of the Jacobins is that their rule, though it rested upon the Revolutionary Tribunal and the guillotine, was exercised all the time in the name of liberty and the sovereignty of the people. In 1793 the Convention was dwindling in numbers, and its authority was passing over more and more to the Committees. Many of the members feared responsibility and did not attend. It was still, however, the nominal basis of the government of France, and all that was done by the Committees was submitted to its ratification.

The Committee of Public Safety was the all-important institution of France. It had been dominated by Danton up to July 10, and he had devoted himself to the raising of men and the equipment of the army, and to such diplomatic measures as the Convention and his colleagues allowed him. Even his opponents have admitted that the survival of France was largely due to his energy and devotion. Yet on July 10, when, according to the usual practice, the Committee of Public Safety came up for reappointment in the Convention, Danton's name was omitted. It is an obscure incident, partly to be explained by the rather careless temperament of Danton himself, partly by the eager ambition of his rivals. His place in the Committee was soon taken by Robespierre, who had hitherto been known as a follower of the doctrines of Rousseau, and as a persuasive speaker in the Assembly and in the Jacobin Club. He had taken no very prominent part in the overthrow of the Monarchy, nor ought his name to be closely connected with the September massacres. He had eagerly supported the declaration of the Republic and the execution of the King, and from now onwards, until his death in 1794, his was the most prominent name in the history of the Revolution. He remained to the end an idealist, dreaming of a social structure that should be erected in France when the present dangers were removed—a structure that should rest upon virtue and be supported by religion and should establish peace; but for the present he identified himself with those Jacobins who were for maintaining the Reign of Terror and throwing all the energy of the Government into the war against the foreign and domestic enemies of the Revolution. He was an admirable speaker—according to English taste the finest speaker that the Revolution produced—and some of his speeches are masterpieces both of style and of thought. It was as a speaker in the

Assembly and in the Jacobin Club that he had most power. He did not show much capacity for the details of administration, but he had devoted friends and colleagues who supplied what he lacked. The Committee of Public Safety now included twelve names. There is some truth, but not much, for factionalism split the Committee in every direction, in the classification given in Barère's memoirs. This distinguished the five men led by Carnot and exclusively concerned with the organisation of the army and navy; one man, a Dantonist nobleman executed for forgery when the Hébertists were liquidated; the so-called Triumvirate—Robespierre, Couthon and Saint-Just— chiefly responsible for the general policy of controlling the nation; and finally three men, Barère, Billaud-Varenne, and Collot d'Herbois—the true Revolutionaries according to Barère and usually in close connection with the Commune.

In 1793 the Jacobins brought forward a new and very democratic constitution. This was passed and presented to the people as an indication of the principles that the Jacobins still advocated, and which would guide their actions when peace allowed them to satisfy their true instincts, but the constitution was hardly brought forward before it was suspended.

During all this time the Revolutionary Tribunal was hard at work, and it was much helped by the Law of Suspected Persons, passed in September 1793, which allowed arrest and imprisonment without any proof of guilt. The prisons were crowded, and constantly men and women were brought before the Revolutionary Tribunal. Acquittals were rare, and the guillotine was the universal penalty. Among the most notable victims was, in October, Queen Marie Antoinette; Danton would have saved her life, for he believed that she might have been of use in bargaining with the enemy. But the passions of the hour were too strong; she was regarded as the chief enemy of the Revolution, and she followed her husband to the guillotine. On the last day of October a large batch of Girondists were executed. On November 6 Philippe, Duke of Orleans, who had championed the Revolution, had lent his palace to the agitators, and voted for the King's death, was nevertheless put to death. His connection with Dumouriez weighed heavily against him. On November 10 Madame Roland was executed, the charming and eloquent lady who had been a social centre for the Girondist party. On November 12 Bailly, astronomer and first president of the National Assembly, met his death for having given the order to fire upon the crowd that petitioned in 1791 for the declaration of the Republic. We may specially note that certain generals, such as Custine and Biron, were guillotined, charged either with treason or with slackness in pursuit of the enemy.

In August 1793 a *levée en masse* was ordered—all citizens were called upon, that is, to give their military services to the State. But by Danton's influence this was reduced to the more manageable shape of the conscription of all between the ages of eighteen and twenty-five. By this measure nearly half a million recruits were added to the army. In September 1793 was passed the Law of Forty Sous, whereby this sum was given to all those who attended the political meetings of the Parisian Sections or Wards. It proved a valuable incentive to the support of the Jacobin party. Thus in Paris was established a government, fierce, resolute and, except for the divisions in its own ranks, strong. Nowhere was its strength plainer than in the new economic régime which it introduced. It claimed for itself the right to buy before everyone else and to requisition goods and labour as needed for the war. It specified the price of bread, legislated against hoarding, and finally (September 1793) introduced an elaborate scheme fixing maximum levels in a scale of prices and wages. The controlled economy became isolated when the Committee banned the export of money and of goods needed at home and the English established a blockade. It entered the manufacturing field itself, at least for munitions; it took measures to stimulate agriculture and to increase industrial production and it enforced its economic policy by Terror. Not by intention but because of civil and foreign war, inflation and the collapse of private enterprise the Committee of Public Safety practised a kind of socialism.

A great civil war had broken out in addition to the Vendean war. This had been caused largely by the fall of the Girondist party and the fear that the new Government would be hostile to the provinces. It was believed at first that the greater number of the provinces of France had risen in rebellion against the capital and that an overwhelming majority of the people of the country were prepared to rise and crush the Jacobins. But this civil war was soon reduced to comparatively small dimensions. Lyons was in rebellion, and Toulon had not only declared against the Government but opened the harbour to Admiral Hood and the British fleet. Against both places the Jacobins sent considerable forces. Lyons was stormed in September 1793, and a cruel punishment was exacted from the inhabitants of the city. The army that advanced on Toulon had a harder task to face, for the inhabitants were assisted by the crews of the British and Spanish ships. The French Commander was Dugommier, but the chief attention of posterity has been given to the action of his subordinate Napoleon Bonaparte. The siege lasted some time, but on December 19, 1793, the city was taken and the British fleet forthwith evacuated the harbour, burning the shipping and many of the warehouses before they left.

The Vendean war remained, and was a harder task. In their own country and against the hasty levies that the Republic could send against them, the insurgents proved invincible, and the Republicans were again and again driven back. When, however, victory encouraged them to extend their operations the limits of their powers were soon made apparent. It is true that in June 1793 they managed to take the important town of Saumur on the Loire, and from there they advanced to the attack of Nantes, but the attack on that town was a failure and their leader, Cathelineau, was killed. In July 1793 a much more efficient French army was free to operate against the insurgents, for in that month the city of Mainz capitulated to the Prussians. The garrison was allowed to march out on giving its promise not to fight again against the Allies. This was interpreted as making them free to fight against the Vendeans. When they arrived on the western theatre of war a change was quickly seen. In October 1793 was fought the Battle of Cholet. The Vendeans were thoroughly defeated and their leader slain. Henceforth they struggled against an enemy manifestly superior. They made one more effort to cross the Loire, hoping to penetrate as far as Normandy and secure the help of sympathisers there, but this effort also met with disaster at Angers. The movement would probably have given no further serious trouble if it had not been met with brutal and cruel repression from Carrier, the Jacobin representative. His executions and brutalities stimulated further resistance and the country blazed up more than once into renewed rebellion. When Hoche, one of the new generals who had risen from the ranks, was sent to take charge of the war, he adopted more humane methods. In December of 1794 he granted the Vendeans an amnesty, and in February 1795 the war in the west was brought to an end by the Treaty of La Jaunaie.

The foreign war showed alternations of failure and success; failure in the spring and summer of 1793, and then recovery and victory in the autumn of 1793 and in the years 1794 and 1795. Things were at their worst about midsummer 1793. In July of that year the city of Mainz had been recaptured by the Prussians, whose troops proceeded to invade Alsace. Then, in the same month, the important northern fortress of Condé was taken by the Austrians, Dutch, and British. In August of the same year, as we have seen, the harbour of Toulon was surrendered into the hands of the English Admiral, Hood. Thus the French frontiers were pierced at three important points, and with rebellion active in several districts foreign opinion assumed that the collapse of the revolutionary Government was not far off.

And yet it was not collapse but complete victory that awaited France. Before we glance at the events which show this victory we will briefly consider the question of its causes.

In the first place, France had now an efficient and energetic Government, wholly determined to control the country, economically as well as politically. Secondly, Carnot had not only infused into the army a new energy, he had also introduced improved weapons, a better discipline, and new ideas in tactics and in strategy. The chief quality of this was the abandonment of a passive defence in favour of a resolute and continued offensive. The secret of all defence, he said, lay in the counter stroke. New officers, too, were rising from the ranks—men usually drawn from the middle class of society who had been trained indeed in the old army, but who found an opportunity for their talents or their genius in the new conditions. Chief among these were Hoche, Jourdan, Pichegru, and Murat. They were ardent supporters of the Revolution, which alone had allowed them to rise to the highest commands, and they fought against the enemy without any consideration for the Monarchy or the ancient régime. Something of their enthusiasm pervaded all ranks of the army, and enthusiasm counted for much. Yet French military writers are at one in telling us that too much stress must not be laid upon this quality of enthusiasm, that enthusiasm alone will win neither battles nor campaigns, and that the tradition that the French revolutionary wars were won by enthusiasm has on some subsequent occasions materially injured the military plans of France.

To France herself belongs the chief credit for the reversal of the fortune of the war and the winning of complete victory over the Allies. Yet all the causes of this change were not to be found in France. It is most important to recognise that the Allies were by no means a united body; that there was divergence of interest and of aim among them, and that on one question—the future of Poland—the tension between Prussia and Austria was so great as almost in itself to ruin the chances of the campaign. It will be recalled that in January 1793 the second partition was agreed upon. Prussia and Russia were to take Polish lands, while Austria was to receive the compensation, which was her due according to the idea of Balance of Power, in Alsace and in Lorraine, when these provinces were won from France. As time went on there was less and less prospect of these provinces being conquered. The second partition was enforced upon the Polish Diet at Grodno in September 1793. The attitude of Austria to Prussia became therefore one of almost unconcealed hostility. Just when a decisive blow was possible against France, Polish affairs rather than French claimed the attention of the Eastern Powers.

It is under these circumstances that the tide of battle turned in favour of France. It is not the object of this book to give any detailed military narrative, but we must notice the outstanding facts. In September 1793 the French army marched to the relief of Dunkirk which was being besieged by an British army under the Duke of York. In the battle fought at Hondschoote the French were completely victorious, and Dunkirk was relieved. It was believed later that if the French Commander, Houchard, had shown greater energy the defeat might have been an overwhelming one, and he was guillotined for his supposed failure. In October 1793 Jourdan gained a victory at

Wattignies, and the French troops once more crossed the Rhine. Then in 1794, in June, Jourdan defeated the Allies under the Duke of Coburg at Fleurus. No further effort was made to regain Belgium from the French, and the Prussians, disappointed with their failures and suspicious of the designs of their allies in Poland, were now admittedly anxious to retire from the war. At the end of 1794 the French army was sent again to the conquest of the United Provinces (Holland), which had been attempted in vain by Dumouriez in 1793. This time there was no mistake. The French commander, Pichegru, entered Amsterdam in January; the Dutch navy was ice-bound off the coast and was actually, to the amazement of all Europe, captured by a detachment of French cavalry. The war was not over; but with the spring of 1795 it was fairly clear that France would be able to make terms with, at any rate, some of her enemies.

We must turn from these military triumphs of the French Revolution to its domestic history. The Jacobin party, which had acquired complete victory over its rivals, whether Girondists or Constitutionalists, was now deeply and bitterly divided. We have already seen how, on July 10, 1793, Danton had been left out of the Committee of Public Safety in favour of Robespierre. Danton's aims changed with the changed situation, and he who had been reckoned the most vehement and violent of revolutionists became now an advocate of milder measures and of the restoration of order. He was now closely associated with Camille Desmoulins. He and Danton, on the benches of the Convention and in the pages of a new journal which they founded—the *Old Cordelier*—recommended, often under the veil of allusion and irony, the abandonment of terror and the return to a system of humanity and of law. These men had a considerable following in the Convention, though they had never again controlled any of the great events of the Revolution.

Robespierre and his allies controlled events from the autumn of 1793 to the summer of 1794. This was the period when the Committee of Public Safety exercised a control over the nation unknown till then. Robespierre was without question an extremely popular figure in Paris, supported by a large number of admiring and devoted friends. It was the tragedy of his life and the cause of his failure that the attempts which he made for the reconstitution and regeneration of French society had to be accompanied by violence. Their failure was probably in any case certain; it was under the circumstances rapid and fatal to himself. He was aloof and a puritan, wedded to duty and to service, masterful and ready to take cruel measures. He was also vain, and his vanity was increased by the admiration of his friends. Thus it comes to pass that the period during which this prophet of humanity and disciple of Rousseau dominated France is also the period when the Reign of Terror was seen at its worst and most destructive.

Hébert and Chaumette were powerful in the Commune or Municipal Council of Paris. From this source emanated many important measures subsequently accepted by the Convention. It was from them that reforms were introduced into the hospitals and cemeteries of Paris; it was from them that the first idea came of that admirable decimal system of weights and measures which has been adopted by the greater part of the world. This last measure is eminently characteristic of their ideas; they discarded what was traditional; they adopted standards which seemed logical and 'natural': as the unit of measurement, a certain portion of the circumference of the globe; as the unit of weight, a certain portion of its volume. From this party also came the proposal to adopt a new calendar. The first day of the first year was to be that of the declaration of the Republic in September 1792. The months were re-arranged, and an effort was made, by no means the first in history, to substitute for the traditional names of the months titles derived from the physical phenomena associated with them. After the year and the month came the turn of the week; the week of seven days with its Oriental origin and its religious association was to be thrown aside. The year was to be divided into decads, divisions of ten days, of which one day should be a holiday. This new calendar with its many interesting features was maintained in France until the establishment of Napoleon's Empire in 1804. Then there came the idea of the adoption of a new religion. The Christian religion, especially in its Roman Catholic form, was still without doubt the religion of the vast majority of the French people, and the future was to show that hardly anything would be more popular than its restoration to honour and official recognition. But the Revolution in its Jacobin form was decidedly opposed both to Christianity and to Catholicism. There was too a very general feeling that the revolutionary settlement could not be completed unless it were accompanied by a positive religious change, as had been clearly declared by Rousseau in his Social Contract. Before the movement was adopted in Paris it had begun in provincial centres. There was indeed a spontaneous effort among the revolutionaries in various parts of the country to find something which might be substituted for the Catholic Christianity which they were prepared to abandon. The movement, it is important to notice, never became thoroughly national; it is untrue to say that Christianity was abolished in France by the Revolution; it was Paris that was mainly concerned with the new movement. In Paris, during the autumn of 1793, various inducements were offered to priests to abandon their orders and abjure their faith. Early in November the Archbishop of Paris, Gobel, a Constitutional Archbishop, not therefore in communion with Rome, abjured his faith, before the Convention. On November 10 the worship of Reason was celebrated in an absurd ceremony which was held in the desecrated cathedral of Notre-Dame. The new worship was not atheism. It approached more nearly to a very vague form of theism. On November 24 all churches were closed in Paris. The movement spread into the provinces and it is estimated that something like 2400 churches in France were turned into Temples of Reason. The movement was more than questionable as a matter of policy; it offended still further the Catholic sentiments of France, and it by no means satisfied all the revolutionaries themselves. Robespierre and his important following would have nothing to do with the worship of Reason. They rejected the traditional faith of France, but they were anxious to introduce a more definite declaration of theism, and this new ceremony made a wide gulf between Robespierre's group and the party of the Commune, which had important results.

By the spring of 1794 factionalism had reached a new level of bitterness; but it is the way of revolutions to turn all divisions into fanatical hatreds and to make men believe that their ideas must triumph by the death of their opponents. It was not only enthusiasm or fanaticism that produced these results: it was above all fear. The Revolution had spilt so much blood that all men's nerves were shaken and all were inclined to see in a political rival a potential assassin. The Hébertists were the first to be liquidated. For a time they had seemed likely to triumph and Robespierre had drawn nearer to Danton in resistance to them. The measure which gave to Robespierre and his friends their victory was probably a law suggested by Saint-Just, whereby all the property of those who were arrested on suspicion was to be devoted to the relief of the poor. It was a great bribe to Paris, and the pendulum swung decisively in the direction of Robespierre. On March 17 the Hébertists were arrested, and on March 24 they were executed. The turn of the Dantonists came next. Danton and Robespierre were old friends and the reason for the tragic struggle is not clear. The charge against Danton was that he leaned too much towards mercy and conciliation. He was not a danger to the life and power of Robespierre and his friends, yet it was always possible that in the Convention he might have organised some movement against the Terrorists, as he had organised the great movement against the Monarchy. Robespierre felt himself threatened whilst Danton and his associates lived. On March 31, 1794, Danton, Camille Desmoulins and others were arrested. On April 2 they were tried before the Revolutionary Tribunal. Their trial was one of the most famous of the many that have attracted the attention of posterity. It seemed at one moment as though the sight of these famous champions of the Revolution in the dock might make an appeal to public opinion that would result in some serious rising. Orders were therefore sent down from the Committee of Public Safety that the trial should be brought to a speedy end. A verdict of guilty was of course found, and on April 5 Danton and Desmoulins were executed.

The fall of Robespierre, Couthon and Saint-Just came last. The worship of Reason, as we have already seen, conflicted with the ideas of Robespierre. He followed Rousseau in desiring a form of religion that should be avowedly though simply theistic. He was now so much master of the situation in all that concerned the domestic policy of France that the Convention which a short time before had decreed the worship of Reason now decreed that that worship should be changed into the recognition of the Supreme Being. On June 8 the festival inaugurating this new and pure and, as Robespierre hoped, permanent religion, was carried out. Robespierre himself was made President of the Convention for the occasion. There was a procession of its members and others to the garden of the Tuileries where there was much allegorical burning of images, and the festival ended with a great deal of speech-making in which Robespierre's vanity was extraordinarily illustrated. From this date he was vulnerable. It is doubtful whether the movement was really in harmony with the wishes of many Frenchmen, yet it was accepted with some favour because it was hoped that it might bring the cessation of the Reign of Terror.

The Reign of Terror, however, could not cease; it rested primarily as we have seen on fear, and although one fear, the fear of the foreign enemy, was rapidly passing away, another fear still remained, the fear that each political leader had of his rivals and of the fatal consequence to himself of failure or overthrow. Instead then of the terror ceasing it became very much hotter than before. On June 10, 1794, a law was passed, known as the Law of Prairial from the revolutionary month in which it was carried, by which the procedure of the Revolutionary Tribunal was changed and quickened. All the citizens were now called upon to denounce traitors; members of the Convention were no longer immune from arrest; the kind of evidence that was permissible was rendered even more vague and dangerous than it had previously been. So the number of victims rose rapidly. From June 10 to July 27, the date of Robespierre's fall, there were at Paris 1376 victims, a half of the total number (2750), and in this number members of the old privileged classes and even of the middle class counted only 650. Thus Robespierre's challenge to his rivals, in the Convention, and to what remained of human sentiment among the revolutionaries, was direct and provocative. It was not long in producing the natural result. Saint-Just had some time back proposed, in accordance with the suggestion of Rousseau's Social Contract, the establishment of a Dictatorship, and although that had not been accepted, it is certain that Robespierre and his friends in council together had determined to establish some more concentrated form of government which should give them more security and allow them to go on with the work of social regeneration, which we cannot doubt was really dear to them. On July 26, 1794, Robespierre opened the campaign by a speech in the Convention—a strange speech, well written and eloquent, as all his speeches are—defending and even eulogising his own career, speaking of the unfairness of the opposition to him and of the number of enemies by whom he was resisted, but actually mentioning no one. It was probably the vagueness of the attack which led to his failure. Had a list of victims been mentioned the Convention might have accepted their arrest, but these vague phrases might threaten almost any one in the Convention. When Robespierre had finished, the Convention plucked up courage to indicate its disapproval by refusing to have the speech circulated as an official utterance of the Revolution. It was a rebuff such as Robespierre had not known of late. Deeply indignant he went to the Jacobin Club where he repeated the speech amidst universal applause. He determined to strike again; and next day, July 27 (or in the Revolutionary Calendar the 9th Thermidor), he presented himself at ten in the morning at the meeting of the Convention. He no doubt intended to remove the vagueness of his previous utterance and to define his aims; but his enemies, or those who feared him, had already made their preparations and had agreed to refuse him a hearing. When he mounted the tribune from which all speeches were made, his first words were interrupted by a violent uproar which was renewed whenever he attempted to speak. Nor were the attempts of his followers to get a hearing more successful. The scene was one of the greatest possible confusion, passion and violence, for most actors in it must have felt that their lives might be at stake. At last it was moved and carried that Robespierre, Saint-Just and his immediate followers should be declared under arrest. They were handed over to the officers of the Convention to be taken to prison and the struggle seemed to be at an end.

It was, however, by no means at an end. Since the fall of Hébert and Chaumette the organisation of the Commune, or Municipality of Paris, had passed under the influence of Robespierre and his friends, who thus controlled the prisons of Paris. When it was found at the Hôtel de Ville that Robespierre had been imprisoned an order was sent for his liberation, and he was brought back in triumph to the Hôtel de Ville. The Convention therefore, when it met again in the afternoon, found that its great enemy was at large, and that the decision would not now rest with decrees or majority votes, but with force and arms. They passed a decree declaring Robespierre an outlaw, and turned to the organisation of the fight.

Late that evening the defences of the Hôtel de Ville were broken through. The assailants from the Convention rushed up the staircase to the room where Robespierre, Couthon and others were. Robespierre was found with a shattered jaw, whether self-inflicted or not is uncertain, lying upon the table. As Robespierre had already been declared an outlaw there was no need for any trial; a form of identification was sufficient, and he went, a strange and tragic figure, to the fate to which he had sent so many hundreds. Robespierre fell when arrested by the Convention, although he had the Jacobins and the Commune on his side, because he made an error of judgment, not because he scrupled to trust to a rising of the Jacobins and Commune on his behalf. He misjudged in that he simply could not believe that he could not win back the mass of the Convention if only he could address it.

The fall of Robespierre might perhaps have been simply one incident among many in the Reign of Terror; it might have led up to the rule of some fiercer and less scrupulous terrorist; but, as a matter of historic fact, from the moment of the fall of Robespierre the Reign of Terror began rapidly to pass away. The reasons for this are many. The situation was essentially unstable. The rule of the guillotine could not have been made permanent in eighteenth-century France, and public opinion in Paris was turning clearly and violently against it; but there are two reasons more important than any others which rendered the disappearance of the Reign of Terror at this moment inevitable. The first is that the foreign danger was now rapidly disappearing. We shall return to this at the end of the chapter. It is enough to say that, after the Battle of Fleurus, France was herself an aggressive Power, and that the assault upon her frontiers, north and east and south, had proved an entire failure. There was rising up in the country a feeling of military confidence and pride that made the Revolutionary Tribunal and the constant batches of victims for the guillotine seem both criminal and absurd. The Reign of Terror was primarily a military measure, and as the military danger passed away the Reign of Terror passed away with it. And then, though less important, whatever else the fall of Robespierre meant, it meant the victory of the Convention. There had been a direct conflict between the forces of the Convention and the forces of the Commune, between the body that represented France and the body that represented Paris. It was the Convention, it was France, that had won. For the first time in the history of the Revolution an attempt to crush by popular force the elected representatives of France had ended in failure and defeat.

This was the meaning of the so-called Thermidorian reaction which followed immediately after the fall of Robespierre—that is, that France should have parliamentary government, civil liberties and legal equality but not social regeneration nor as yet religious peace or economic stability. The Commune was closed and broken up, and its work was delegated to Committees and Commissioners. On August 10 the Revolutionary Tribunal was reorganised so as to bring it more into harmony with the ordinary procedure of French law, and the Law of Prairial was repealed. On September 1 the Executive Committees were reconstituted and brought under the direct control of the Convention. The Committee of Public Safety, although it continued to exist, was no longer the independent body it had been. On November 12 the Jacobin Club, that constant source of revolution, was finally closed. Meanwhile the executions had very much diminished, and with the winter of 1794 the Reign of Terror may be said to have passed away. It was a striking and a symbolic fact that seventy-five of the Girondist party who were in prison were allowed to return to the benches of the Convention, where they strongly reinforced the movement of reaction against the Terror. The storm, however, did not settle into a calm without occasional returns of the old troubles. These were stimulated by the fact that the winter of 1794–95 was a terribly severe one. The suffering would have been great in any case, but with poverty and dislocation of trade and commerce it was trebly felt. In April of the year 1795 there was a rising of the old kind that Paris had grown to know so well, which, from the revolutionary month in which it took place, is known as the rising of Germinal. The demand of the insurgents was for 'bread and the Constitution of 1793.' It was probably never really dangerous, and it was easily crushed by Pichegru, in command of the armed forces of Paris. Again the Convention had triumphed. Its triumph was marked by further reaction against the Jacobins and the Reign of Terror. Prominent Terrorists were exiled. The National Guards were reconstituted so as to be a defence for the middle class. The property of those who had been guillotined was restored to the relations of the victims.

Another rising took place in May 1795 (the rising of Prairial). This was more definitely political in its aims, and was organised by the members of the old Jacobin party. It was for a time dangerous. The hall of the Convention was occupied by the insurgents; an attempt was made to pass legislation that would have taken France back to the principles of 1793 and 1794; but then there came to the assistance of the Convention, not the National Guards, but the regular troops under the command of Menou and Murat. The insurgents were driven out without difficulty, and further steps were at once taken for the defence of the Convention against such a danger in the future.

Then on June 10, 1795, there came an event which had serious consequences. The little son of Louis XVI, recognised by all Royalists as Louis XVII, died in prison. The details of his piteous and tragic existence need not concern us, but it was of much importance that henceforward the unquestioned heir to the French throne was the late King's brother, the Comte de Provence, who was destined to reign in 1815 as Louis XVIII, but who was at present serving in the armies of the foreign enemy against France. There were many Frenchmen, nominally Royalist, who would be unwilling to support the claims of a national enemy. It was thought wise, therefore, to bring forward a new constitution at once in order to clear up ambiguities as to the nature of the Government and to conciliate those who were capable of being brought over. This is known as the Constitution of the Year Three, which lasted, with very slight change, until it was overthrown by Napoleon in 1799. It opened with the declaration of the duties of the citizen as well as of the rights of man. It established a limited franchise which was dependent upon a term of residence and the payment of certain taxes. It reversed the decision of 1790, whereby the idea of a Second Chamber had been pushed aside, and it established not only a 'Council of Five Hundred,' consisting of representatives over the age of thirty, but also a 'Council of Ancients,' consisting of men over forty, and this Council of Ancients was to have the right of vetoing legislation by the other Council for the space of one year. Both Councils could hold their meetings elsewhere than in Paris. This provision was introduced to avoid the dangerous influence of the Paris crowd which had been so frequently felt during the Revolution, and it assisted, as we shall see, the rise of Napoleon to power. At the head of the State there was to be, of course, no King; neither was there to be a President nor a Consul. Instead there was to be a Committee, or as it was called a Directorate, which was to take the place of the Committee of Public Safety, of five persons of whom one was to retire every year. A last regulation was the immediate cause of the next outbreak of violence. It was laid down that one-third of both Councils was to retire every year, but that two-thirds of the first Legislative Councils were to consist of members of the existing Convention. It was against this 'regulation of the two-thirds' that the rising took place; for it meant that the elections could produce no immediate change in the character of the Government, and that the Convention would prolong its rule, at any rate for a time; and so Jacobins and Girondists and even Royalists were ready to join against this detested regulation. On October 3 there came the last rising that we need note—the rising of Vendémiaire. Paris rose, as so often before, but with rather more organisation than she had usually shown. On the side of the Convention, however, there was great determination and a perfect readiness to meet the popular display of force by appeal to the army. The defence of the Tuileries and of the Convention Hall was put into the hands of Paul de Barras, and he had as his subordinate Napoleon Bonaparte, already distinguished at the siege of Toulon. When, on October 5, the attack upon the Convention took place it was met by artillery fire and was easily beaten off. The extent of the fighting has indeed been very often exaggerated: the total loss of the insurgents seems not to have exceeded 100. The significance is that the Central Government once again, and much more decidedly than ever before, had repressed a popular rising. The name of the people no longer exercised its old paralysing charm. The Government maintained its rights even against the claims of the people. It is a significant event, also, because Napoleon, in recognition of the part that he had played in the repression of the movement, was given the command of the home army, and thus got his foot upon the ladder that was to lead him so far and so high. Soon after this, on October 26, 1795, the Convention came to an end. History knows of no representative body more important than this. Its only rival to an equality of importance is to be found in the English Long Parliament of the seventeenth century.

We must end this chapter by noticing very briefly the military situation. On June 1, 1794, there had come the first important naval action of the war. French ships with supplies were being brought into Brest. The French fleet went out to convoy them and was met by the British fleet under Lord Howe. The battle was not an overwhelming defeat for the French, but it was decisive. For long after this the British naval supremacy in the Channel was not challenged. In June of the next year (1795) the British co-operated with the emigrant nobles in organising an attack upon Brittany. It was hoped that the French force, which was to be landed in Quiberon Bay, would receive the assistance of the scattered remnants of the Vendean war. The French force was landed, but it found itself cooped up in the Quiberon Peninsula by a French army under General Hoche. In the end the Royalists were forced to surrender, and a large number of them were executed. Thus ended all hopes of a successful insurrection in the west against the Revolutionary Government. On land, too, the French arms were almost everywhere successful. There was little fighting of note. The most important fact was that Prussia and Austria, still allies in name, were almost avowed enemies. One cause of this contention between them was to be found, as before, in Polish affairs. The second partition had left the unhappy country totally incapable of managing its own affairs or of sustaining its position as a European State. Those who had robbed already twice, determined now to rob a third and a last time. The negotiations for the third partition took place between Austria and Russia. Prussia was not admitted to the secret of the negotiations, and although she was given some share of the spoil, that did not in the least appease her hostile and suspicious humour. The Prussians for some time past had only been kept in the field by financial subsidies from the British Government. Their historians recognise and deplore the humiliation of their position. Now, in 1795, peace was at last made between Prussia and France—the Peace of Basel. Its terms, which are important, may be summarised as follows. Certain terms were publicly announced. France was to occupy the left bank of the Rhine until the conclusion of the general peace. Further, France promised to undertake no military operations in Northern Germany, and to recognise the right of Prussia to act as intermediary for any German state which required peace. This article, a challenge to the authority of the Emperor, was not in the event used. The states of the Empire nevertheless followed Prussia out of the war. The delimitation of the territory in North Germany, where France agreed to carry on no military operations, was to be secretly agreed upon between France and Prussia. That north Germany was at peace from 1795 to 1805 was of great importance culturally and economically.

The peace was an immense triumph for France. It was victory, though not entirely one of arms, still victory over the greatest military Power of the Continent. It seemed to portend a general break-up of all resistance to the Republic. In May 1795 Holland made terms with France, promised to join her in war against Britain, and was annexed to the French Republic in all but name; and in July 1795 Spain withdrew from the contest, surrendering the island of San Domingo to the Republic and promising certain further concessions. Austria and Britain remained alone in the field. It would take several years of war yet to reduce both of them to peace, but the triumph already acquired was an amazing one. When men thought of the confidence with which the speedy overthrow of the Republic had been anticipated in 1792, and again in 1793, and then looked at the aggressive action, the novel tactics, the daring strategy, and the ultimate victory of the French Republican armies, it was clear that a new Power of an incalculable and dangerous kind had come into the history of Europe.

Chapter 3

THE RISE OF NAPOLEON TO POWER

From this time the interest of the domestic development of France is rivalled by the story of the victories of the French armies until we are in danger of forgetting what is happening in France altogether, and of fixing our eyes only upon the personal triumphs of Napoleon. Napoleon was without question a man of extraordinary force of brain and character, who under all circumstances and in all countries would have won for himself a high position. He had great powers of work and of organisation, exactitude, rapid insight, courage, willingness to accept responsibility, resolution in following a plan once under-taken—all the qualities of the soldier in their highest development; and with all he had the gift of genius which defies analysis. But his rise is much more than the story of a capable man winning for himself a high place in the world. It reflects also one of the most general laws that may be observed on the surface of history. We can see constantly how a period of confusion and of revolution ends in the establishment of some strong and often of a personal power. The instances that are usually quoted in comparison with Napoleon's life history are the establishment of the Roman Empire by Julius Caesar after a century of confusion and revolution in Rome, and the personal rule of Oliver Cromwell which followed the Puritan revolution. But these are only the most obvious instances. We may see something of the same sort when the Tudor Monarchy follows the Wars of the Roses; when the strong concentration of the French kings under Charles VII and Louis XI brought to an end the long agony and turmoil of the Hundred Years' War in France; or, again, when the Thirty Years' War in Germany is followed very generally by the establishment of personal rule. So general a development must have common causes, and they are not difficult to determine. In the first place societies that have undergone great confusion from whatever cause feel the need of some established order as the first necessity of their social life. If they cannot obtain it by constitutional means, by mutual agreement, and through the employment of liberty, they are willing that it should be secured by the strong hand of a soldier. And again, in a revolution such as that which we have been examining, and in periods of confusion such as the others that we have referred to, we may see the decision slipping into the hands of those who control the largest amount of physical force. In France especially the will of the people and the votes of citizens, though often praised and idealised, had hardly decided any important issue since 1793. The Monarchy had been overthrown by violence, the Republic had been established and had been saved by violence, it was by violence that Robespierre had risen and by violence that he had been overthrown. It was natural therefore that France should be at last ruled by violence in its highest development; not by the unruly mobs of the Paris streets, but by the trained and victorious legions of France herself. Lastly, we may note that France was growing weary of political and social controversy. The ardent hopes of 1789 had in part been realised, but more generally they had been proved incapable of realisation, and whilst men were growing cynical or hostile to the squabbles of party politicians whose great words and aspirations were never translated into action, they were more and more dazzled by the victories that had been won in the past by the Generals of the Republic, and which were now to be won in an even more dazzling form by Napoleon Bonaparte. What Rousseau almost recommended in his *Social Contract* and Burke had prophesied in a splendid passage of the *Reflections* was now to come to pass. A movement that had begun in a passionate and even extravagant desire for liberty was to end in the rule of a soldier-dictator.[1]

Napoleon was born in 1769 at Ajaccio in Corsica, of Italian stock. Just a year before, the long connection between Corsica and Italy had been broken and the island had been incorporated with France, in spite of Paoli's effort to maintain independence and the sympathy and occasional support of Great Britain. Thus, Napoleon was from his birth a French citizen. One of a large family, he was destined from an early date for a military career, and in 1779 was sent to a

---

[1] Near the end of the *Social Contract* Rousseau had contemplated the necessity of a special act entrusting the care of the State to its most worthy citizen, when the safety of the country is at stake. Earlier in the book he says, 'I have some presentiment that this small island (Corsica) will one day astonish Europe.' This is nothing more than a lucky hit. Burke's words, written at the beginning of the Revolution, to 'a very young gentleman at Paris' are genuine historical prophecy, for they spring from a real understanding of the situation. 'In the weakness of one kind of authority, and in the fluctuation of all, the officers of an army will remain for some time mutinous and full of faction, until some popular general, who understands the art of conciliating the soldiery . . . shall draw the eyes of all men upon himself. Armies will obey him on his personal account . . . But the moment in which that event shall happen, the person who really commands the army is your master, the master (that is little) of your king, the master of your assembly, the master of your whole republic.' *Reflections on the Revolution in France* (October 1790); see Burke, *Select Works* (1898), vol. II, p. 260.

military academy at Brienne. In 1785 he had become sub-lieutenant in an artillery regiment, and was at this time full of enthusiasm for Rousseau and a Republic after the classical model, and for the independence of Corsica. When the Revolution broke out he welcomed it. His enthusiastic admiration was given to the Republicans, and he had a somewhat close friendship with Robespierre's brother. He was out of employment when, on August 10, 1792, the Monarchy was overthrown by the attack of the Paris mob. He saw something of the events of that day, and has left on record his belief that the victorious crowds could have been easily dispersed by trained soldiers. He served a little later in the suppression of a rising in Corsica, and henceforth his local patriotism gave way before his ardent devotion to France. In December 1793 he had played an important part, though not so important as has sometimes been represented, in the capture of Toulon from the British, and in September 1795 he had, as we have just seen, saved the Convention from the attack of the Revolutionaries. In 1796, when twenty-seven years of age, he had married a widow, Joséphine de Beauharnais, who was then aged thirty-four. She seems to have had no idea at all of the nature of the man whom she had married, and of the career to which he was destined, and refused to accompany him or share in the hardships and the glories of his first great campaign.

The Republic, as we have seen, though it had driven from the field the greater number of its enemies, was still left at war with Great Britain and Austria. Of Great Britain we need hardly speak. It had abandoned, after a series of failures, any attempt to defeat the French on the mainland; but the British control of the sea was a permanent threat to the colonies and the possessions of France, and indirectly of great help to Austria. The Directorate, as the new French Government was called, was now aiming a blow at the very heart of the Austrian power which they hoped would give them victory and peace. The main armies of France were to advance on Vienna, under Generals Moreau and Jourdan, by the well-known route of the Black Forest and the Danube. Another army was to attack the Austrian power and possessions in Italy. It was this subordinate attack which was entrusted to Napoleon Bonaparte, and which his genius converted into the most important stroke.

Italy had shared the intellectual movement of the eighteenth century. It showed itself there in economic and legal thought. Pietro Verri and Antonio Genovesi were political economists and Cesare Beccaria and Gaetano Filangieri were great jurists, the originators of some of the ideas which Jeremy Bentham afterwards made famous. At the end of the eighteenth and beginning of the nineteenth century the dramatist Vittorio Alfieri and the poet Ugo Foscolo touched men's imagination with the idea of an Italian nation. Nor were there wanting in Italy adherents of those universal ideas of liberty and justice which make men wish to govern themselves. But Italy consisted of several states. There was first, sitting astride of the western Alps, the kingdom of Sardinia, a name, originating in events after the Peace of Utrecht, for a state whose real nucleus lay in the upper valleys of the Po, which are known as Piedmont, and in the vigorous military and well-disciplined population of the mountains of Savoy. A little farther east there came the Duchy of Milan, an important appanage of Austria—important by reason of its very great wealth and commercial possibilities; important also because it commanded the road by which Austrian troops would pass through the Tyrol into Italy. The famous quadrilateral—the four fortresses of Mantua, Legnago, Verona, and Peschiera—maintained the connection between Austria and Italy. Further east we see the Republic of Venice, the oldest of European states, and in some respects the most notable, now sunk far into decline. A little further south there were the Duchies of Modena, Parma, and Tuscany, all of them by dynastic or political arrangement closely attached to the House of Austria. In the west was the Republic of Genoa, a less interesting counterpart of her Venetian sister, and like Venice sunk in decay. Across the centre of Italy stretched the Papal States, fulfilling few of the requirements of the modern state, but regarded with special veneration by a large part of Europe on account of its connection with the head of the Roman Catholic Church. The south of Italy was occupied by far the largest state of all, covering as it did not far from one-half of the whole peninsula: the kingdom of Naples. The King of Naples was a member of the Bourbon family, and was connected by marriage with the House of Austria. It was thus at once exposed to the special hostility of France, and had a special claim upon the support and friendship of Austria.

The campaign which now opens has the special interest that it first gave the measure of Napoleon's genius. It exhibited his daring, his rapidity of decision and of action, and at the same time (what did not fail him until late in his career) the sureness with which he could distinguish between what was possible and what was not. From the merely military point of view we may note the great importance that he attached to the use of artillery, his insistence upon never standing on the defensive, but, even with fewer troops than those of the enemy, conducting the campaign always on aggressives lines. We may note too, as soldiers of the time noted, how the character of his army allowed him to do what other armies could not. It was composed of many elements, but it consisted largely of men who were themselves interested in the cause for which they were fighting, and who did not think of their commander merely as a hard ruler and a grudging paymaster. He could send his men out as scouts singly, or in small parties, with little fear of their desertion, whilst such action was impossible to the troops against which he was fighting. We shall devote the least possible attention to the details of these remarkable campaigns, but this neglect of the details must not be taken to imply that the campaigns were not themselves of the utmost importance. To trace the fortunes of the Continent without considering the wars which have so frequently passed across its surface, would be in the highest degree absurd. Neither the economic nor the intellectual nor the political life of Europe is intelligible without reference to its military history.

When Napoleon took up the command of the French army, it was at Savona to the west of the Italian Alps. There it had been for some time trying in vain to find or force a road across the mountains. Soon after Napoleon took charge of it the road was found. A joint army of Sardinians and Austrians was opposed to Napoleon. He managed, however, to separate them, and in the Battle of Mondovi defeated the Sardinians and drove them to accept the Armistice of Cherasco (April 28, 1796), whereby they retired from the war and ceded Savoy and Nice to France.

Austria remained, and Napoleon lost no time in coming to blows with her. He marched on to Milan, desiring not only to capture the Milanese but to isolate the Austrians from Piedmont. His first big battle was fought at Lodi on May 10, 1796. It was a great victory, and the Austrians at once retired, abandoning Milan to the conqueror. He entered amidst immense popular enthusiasm. He seemed at first no conqueror but a liberator, and was accepted not only by the liberals but by the clericals of the city. When the Italians found that Napoleon intended them to pay for the war, when they found that he imposed heavy taxes and sacked their cities if they refused to pay them, their mood soon changed. If Napoleon, at this time, was a stimulant to Italy's national feeling it was because he was yet one more foreign invader in Italy's long history of foreign invasion, against whom it behoved Italians to unite. Napoleon next laid siege to the great fortress of Mantua, the central Austrian fortress in Italy, strongly defended with artillery and surrounded for the greater part of it by impassable lakes and morasses. It was understood that the fall of Mantua would mean the fall of the Austrian power in Italy, and the Austrians were as determined to relieve it as Napoleon was tenacious in maintaining his hold upon it. On four different occasions Napoleon had to relax his hold upon the place in order to march to the encounter of Austrian armies. They were defeated over and over again; the last and the decisive blow was delivered on January 14, 1797, when an Austrian army of seventy thousand men under Alvinzi was scattered at the Battle of Rivoli. After that there was no more hope for Mantua, which shortly afterwards surrendered. Peace did not come immediately, and in order to force it Napoleon pressed forward through the north-east of Italy into the eastern Alps and reached the town of Laibach (Ljubljana). Napoleon's own position was not without its difficulties. The French advances in Germany had shown nothing in any way corresponding to his own meteoric movements in Italy. It was therefore out of consideration for his own position, as well as for the needs of France, that he appealed to the Austrian Archduke Charles to stop the war. An armistice was arranged at Leoben in April 1797. But though preliminaries were signed they were not developed into a peace for some little time. The Austrians were unwilling to admit defeat; they were watching events in Paris, hoping for a Royalist revolution there, but they were disappointed in their hopes. The French armies were now pressing not only east of the Adriatic, but also on the Danube, and so, on October 17, 1797, the definite Peace of Campo Formio was signed. There were in the Peace open and secret articles. By the open articles, the Belgian lands were abandoned to France; a republic was set up in Northern Italy, to be called the Cisalpine Republic; France was to take the Ionian Islands; Austria was to be allowed to hold Venice and all her territory in Italy and the Adriatic. (This policy will be more carefully examined.) Lastly, a congress was to be called at Rastatt, wherein the affairs of Germany were to be settled at conferences of representatives from France and the states of the Empire. Besides these open articles there were secret ones, wherein the Emperor repeated the promise already given by Prussia at Basel in 1795 of the cession to France of the German territory on the left bank of the Rhine. France, too, promised that Austria should receive the important ecclesiastical state of Salzburg and a part of Bavaria. Such was the Peace of Campo Formio, characteristic of the diplomacy of Napoleon, in which he showed himself almost as much a master as in the art of war; characteristic, too, of the way in which the Hapsburg Emperor all through this period was forced to abandon the defence of Germany; characteristic, lastly, of the method pursued by Napoleon frequently during his career of appeasing the hostility of his greater opponents by allowing them to absorb the territory of smaller states. It should be noted in passing that Talleyrand had been appointed Foreign Minister in France in September 1797 and that his partnership with Napoleon in diplomacy had begun with the negotiation of Campo Formio.

We must look now a little more carefully at the settlement of Italy by Napoleon on which so much of its future destiny depended. We have seen how Sardinia was treated by the Armistice of Cherasco. We have seen, too, how by the Peace of Campo Formio the Cisalpine Republic was recognised. This strange title was adopted from the history of Ancient Rome, which made during all this period so strong an appeal to the imaginations of Frenchmen. It consisted at first mainly of the territory of Milan, but then there came risings in the districts further south—in Bologna, Ferrara, Ravenna, and Reggio— all districts loosely attached to the Papal States, and these were by their own wish incorporated into the new Republic. Thus there arose on Italian soil a republican state of the modern pattern influenced by all the political and social ideals of the French Revolution. Its form would soon be changed into monarchy, its character would alter, and it was not destined to survive the battle of Waterloo. Napoleon had now given stimulus to Italian national feeling in another way: he had begun the work of furthering political cohesion. Next the corrupt and antiquated Republic of Genoa was overthrown, democratic principles were introduced, and it was rechristened the Ligurian Republic, the name being again borrowed from classical history. More important than what happened to Genoa is the fate of Venice. This famous Republic had done its utmost to maintain neutrality during the collision between Napoleon and Austria, and to stand quite apart from the war that raged at her frontiers. When Napoleon made peace with Austria and desired to establish good relations with the vanquished enemy he could find no better means of doing so than by throwing to Austria the possessions, the liberties, and the existence of the glorious and inoffensive Republic.

The Papal States had also to pay the price of defeat, but Napoleon was anxious to leave the way open to the renewal of friendly relations with the Pope. By the Peace of Tolentino (February 1797) the Pope ceded Avignon to France, and Bologna, Ferrara, and the Romagna to the Cisalpine Republic. He handed over to Napoleon money, manuscripts, and pictures; but the Directory would have liked still harsher terms, and the Pope was grateful to Napoleon for his escape from a deeper humiliation or even from destruction!

As the future destiny of Italy was influenced by Napoleon, so too was that of Germany. We have seen that it had been arranged that a congress should meet at Rastatt to settle her affairs. This meant in real terms settling the compensation to be received by states which would lose territory when the left bank of the Rhine was incorporated in France. The congress sat from November 1797 to April 1799 and was a strange encounter between old and new ways of doing business. Two French plenipotentiaries—Napoleon did not think it worth more than a brief visit—engaged in negotiations with a deputation from the states of the Empire of seventy-six members who communicated with them in long written memoranda. Though, as will be seen, the Congress dispersed before it made any formal decisions, its discussions implied that two principles would be adopted in reorganising Germany: secularisation of former ecclesiastical territory, since the most powerful states to be compensated were lay; and mediatisation, the name of a process whereby independent imperial cities, bishoprics or other small states were absorbed by larger ones. When these principles were applied they would lead to the end of the Holy Roman Empire. The Congress of Rastatt, it should be noted in passing, coincided with the last popular movement in Germany in imitation of the French Revolution. It was an abortive effort to introduce parliamentary methods into Württemberg. Later popular movements were to be anti-French.

We must return from the campaigns of Napoleon to the domestic difficulties of France. From 1795 to 1799 her internal history loses the interest and importance which attached to it up to the day of Vendémiare. The struggles among the leaders were for the most part personal and egoistic. The interference of the army occurred from time to time. Military rule drew visibly nearer.

We have seen the nature of the Constitution. A recurrent difficulty was the absence of harmony between the Directors, who formed the executive, and the two legislative Chambers. 'The Separation of Powers' was still dear to the minds of French theorists. One-third of the Assemblies retired every year; but only one of the five Directors. The Directory, therefore, was not necessarily in sympathy either with the Assemblies or with the constituencies. The first Directors were Carnot, 'the organiser of victory'; Letourneur, an engineer; Barras, who had shared with Napoleon in the defence of the Convention against the rising of Vendémiarie; Larevellière-Lépeaux, a Girondist; and, most important of all, Rewbell, an Alsatian and a Jacobin, in whose hands lay the chief authority.

The problems that these men had to face were many and difficult. The financial situation seemed hopeless. Inflation had caused the *assignats*—the paper money of the Revolution—to fall to one per cent of their face value. The religious situation was full of menace. The 'Constitutional Church' set up by the Revolution had no vitality and had almost disappeared. A new religious movement called 'Theophilanthropy' patronised by the Directors, had no real following. Events were soon to show how popular the Roman Catholicism of the old and proscribed type was, and how ready the mass of the people would be to welcome it again. Then there was the question of the *émigrés*, of whom there were perhaps 300,000. The property of all was confiscated, and in many instances men had been declared to be *émigrés* in order that their property might be seized. Their relatives raised bitter protests against the injustice of the act. Conspiracy and *coups d'état* are the outstanding features of this period. Baboeuf conspired to replace the Directory by a communistic régime—unavailingly but he bequeathed a legend. The first *coup d'état* occurred in 1797.

In March 1797 the elections took place to fill the places of one-third of the Assemblies. The results showed great gains for the Moderate and anti-Jacobin party, while three out of the five Directors were decidedly Jacobin. Here was a difficult situation. A general election (on a small scale) had decided against the Government, but the Government was not in the least inclined to yield. Many believed that a wave of reaction was about to sweep the country; and the

Austrian Government delayed to convert the Truce of Leoben into a Peace until the issue was decided in Paris. It would not be decided now by the crowd of Paris but by the army. The Directors first appealed to Hoche, but he declined the part suggested to him. Then they were forced to apply to Napoleon, whose character, genius, and success were already beginning to alarm them. He sent his officer, Augereau, to carry out his instructions. It was not necessary to use force. The appearance of this showy and empty-headed soldier was enough. His orders were obeyed. Carnot, who had made himself the spokesman of the Moderates, was deposed from the Directory. A number of deputies were arrested, and among them Pichegru, a soldier of repute. Then at the order of the Directors the results of 154 elections were annulled. The effort to introduce more tolerant measures was dropped. The religious dissidents and the *émigrés* were treated with all the old rigour. The assumed connection of the reactionaries with the designs of the Austrian Government had been fatal to them. The army had re-established the Jacobins in order to dictate terms to the enemy. This is known as the *coup d'état* of Fructidor. The future was to show that the alliance between the Jacobins and the military chiefs was not natural or permanent. In the next year something of the same sort happened again, when the elections in thirty departments were annulled because the results were not acceptable to the Directors.

Events in Paris were now directly dependent on the war, and we must turn to that to understand the next great domestic movement in which the army, through its great chief, interfered and swept the Republic and the Jacobins out of France.

Austria had accepted a dictated peace, but Great Britain still remained, victorious and impregnable on the water. The Directory sought to find some vulnerable spot. It seemed at times that they had found it. In 1797 there had broken out the great mutinies in the British fleet at The Nore and at Spithead. It seemed for a moment as if the trident were broken in the hands of Britain, but the mutinies were settled and the sea power of Great Britain not diminished. In 1798 there came the great Irish Rebellion. A French army managed to reach Ireland to support it; but, as so often before, an Irish rebellion proved a great disappointment to the enemies of Britain. The movement collapsed, and the bitter memories that it left behind were of no use to France. How was the land power to inflict a dangerous blow on the sea power? How was the lion to destroy the shark? It seemed to the Directors that they might find in Egypt 'the Achilles' heel of invulnerable England.' France had no cause of war, nor even any grievance which could be seriously alleged against Egypt, which was governed by the military caste of the Mamelukes, nor against the Sultan of Turkey, with whom lay the nominal suzerainty. It was really Britain that was attacked when the French expedition sailed for

Egypt. The rapid growth of British influence in India had increased the zeal of Frenchmen for the recovery of their former pre-eminence. A French force in the Isthmus of Suez would threaten the British in India, for France would then be far nearer India than Britain was. The instructions of Napoleon when he was depatched to Eygpt contained as their first point 'to drive the English from all their possessions in the East which he can reach.' There followed other instructions: the Isthmus of Suez was to be cut; the condition of the natives was to be ameliorated; and peace was to be maintained with the Sultan. Napoleon took with him, also, learned Egyptologists to throw light on the monuments and antiquities of the then little-known country. The deciphering of the hieroglyphics was one result of the expedition.

At first all went well with it. The island of Malta surrendered to Napoleon on June 11, 1798; on July 1 he reached the coast of Egypt, and six days later began his march to Cairo. He tried to conciliate the native population, but the Mamelukes fought for their power. On July 21, in a battle fought within sight of the Pyramids, they were entirely defeated, and Napoleon was master of Egypt. A few days later bad news came from the coast. Nelson had found the French fleet at Aboukir Bay and had destroyed it in the Battle of the Nile. Napoleon realised at once the importance of the blow. It meant that there would be no more reinforcements from France, while Britain could send what troops she liked into Egypt. He made light of the situation: 'We must remain in these lands and then come forth great like the ancients'; but the fate of the expedition was sealed by the maritime supremacy of Great Britain which was to decide so many issues in Napoleon's career. Turkey now joined herself definitely to Britain, and Napoleon determined to anticipate an attack from the north by a march into Syria. He spoke later of his design of marching on Constantinople or on India, but those were second thoughts; at the time he thought only of the immediate danger. His Syrian campaign opened well. El Arish fell into his hands; Jaffa was occupied. At Jaffa the slaughter of prisoners, 'after much deliberation,' in order to avenge the murder of a French envoy did much damage to his reputation, and the outbreak of plague in his army seriously weakened his strength. He pushed on, nevertheless, to St Jean d'Acre and laid siege to it. The town was assisted by Sir Sidney Smith with British ships, and in the end, after the prize had often seemed within his grasp, Napoleon was beaten off. He retreated to Egypt after suffering heavy losses (May 1799). He was still strong enough to destroy a Turkish army which was sent into Egypt, but the outlook for the campaign was not really improved, nor could it be while the British had control of the sea. The news from Europe was disquieting. A new coalition had been formed against France and she had suffered severe defeats. For his own sake and for the sake of France it was best that he should leave Egypt. He sailed from Alexandria on August 23 and, after running great danger of capture, reached France at Fréjus on October 9.

The end of the Egyptian expedition may be quickly summarised. The French army had been left under Kléber and Menou. Kléber at once began to negotiate for terms, but Nelson would grant nothing but surrender at discretion. In June 1800 Kléber was assassinated; and the Turks and British planned a threefold attack on the French in Egypt. It was impossible to resist longer and, in August 1801, 20,000 French troops surrendered at Cairo and Alexandria.

The outlook in Europe had changed very much since Napoleon left for Egypt. The Treaty of Campo Formio had given Europe little more than a year of peace. The cause of the new war—which is just a continuation of the old one—is plain. France was immensely powerful. The force of her arms and the attractiveness of the new political and social principles which she championed won for her great gains even during the period of nominal peace. Before Europe could begin to enjoy the hard-won peace she was stirred to panic again, and once more most of the nations of the Continent united with Great Britain—who was still in arms against France—in another league against a pressing danger.

First there had come a revolution in Rome. The papal power was opposed there by strong elements in the population. These were incited by the agents or the example of France to demand democratic reforms. They were supported by the French general, Berthier, who established a republic with a government vested in seven magistrates who bore the venerable name of consuls. The Pope—Pius VI—was expelled by the French and was deported first to Siena and then to Valence, where he died. But it soon proved that the republic was little more than an agency of France. A French garrison remained, and Rome was treated almost as a conquered country. What happened in Holland was not very different. The Batavian Republic had been declared there, but its form had not yet been determined. The country was much divided in feeling: some desiring the return of the House of Orange; some a federal republic in accordance with the old tradition of the land; others, backed by France, supporting a centralised state after the fashion of France herself. The question was put to the vote, and a large majority of those voting declared for the French model. The majority, however, of the citizens did not vote at all. The influence of France had been apparent throughout, and Holland under the new form was only 'a thinly disguised annexe of the French Republic.' By similar methods France came to control the north of Italy. The Cisalpine Republic showed itself inclined to take an independent course. General Berthier had thereupon 'purged the Council of the Republic' and reduced the Government to complete dependence on France. A little further west a more naked extension of the power of France took place. Piedmont had remained attached to the kingdom of Sardinia after the Armistice of Cherasco. An excuse was now found to expel the King from his Italian territories, and Piedmont was annexed to France. At the same time the Grand Duke of Tuscany was expelled, and France seemed to threaten the independence of the whole of Italy.

Even more important were the steps by which the French Republic became practically mistress of Switzerland. The Helvetic Confederation—to give the country its correct political title—was ruled by a narrow oligarchy, though there were wide differences in the conditions of the different cantons. The oligarchy of Berne was specially powerful and notorious for its narrow exclusiveness. The Canton de Vaud petitioned France for help against its oppressors. Ever since 1792 the Republic had declared that it was ready to help oppressed peoples against their rulers. In accordance, therefore, with the traditions of the Republic a French army of 15,000 under General Brune entered Switzerland and overthrew with unexpected ease the Confederacy, whose proud boast it was to have maintained its liberties against so many tyrants and aggressors. The Helvetic Republic 'one and indivisible' was set up, centralised and unitary after the pattern generally approved of by France; and, like the other republics set up under French influence, strictly subordinated to France. Swiss independence was at an end and her valleys were again, after a long interval, to be full of the noise of war on a great scale. These events did not pass without protest even in France. Carnot, who held by many of the ideals of the early Revolution, refused to acquiesce in the overthrow of the independence of Switzerland. Wordsworth was prompted by the depressing news to write his great sonnet in which he deplored the extinction of the 'two great voices of liberty'—Venice and Switzerland.

Then came a blow against the kingdom of Naples. King Ferdinand IV—a Bourbon—ruled there and his queen was Marie Caroline, sister of Marie Antoinette. The miserable inefficiency of the Government was notorious, but the population was very backward, and an attempt by Italian Jacobins in 1794 to raise it against the King had failed. When the Battle of the Nile had seemed to show that the cause of France was weakening and had brought the British fleet and Nelson into the harbour of Naples, the King despatched his general, Mack (an Austrian), to attack Rome and drive out the hated republicans. The French garrison found itself taken by surprise. Championnet, the French general, had to evacuate Rome, and Ferdinand entered to enjoy a short-lived triumph. Soon French reinforcements restored the balance in their favour. Naples was attacked and occupied; the Neapolitan royal family took refuge on the English fleet; and another republic—the Parthenopean—was set up. One incident may be noted as casting light on forces at work below the surface of

Europe, which would ultimately prove too strong even for Napoleon. The armies of Naples had shown their proverbial incompetence and had fled before the French attack. But, when Championnet believed that all resistance was at an end, the despised *lazzaroni* of Naples— the lower classes of the town and country—carried on an irregular warfare that proved more serious than the resistance of the regular troops. It was beaten down in the end, but it is the first hint of popular national resistance to the French, even when they came offering liberty and equality; it is the first appearance of that passionate popular resistance which later in Spain and in the Tyrol, in Russia and Prussia and Germany, wore down the might of Napoleon.

France brought to these sister republics, which she set up, better government, higher ideals of social life, and relief from many burdens. But it is not to be wondered at that the states of Europe saw with alarm the advance of the French flood and looked round for means to resist it. Great Britain, under the guidance of Pitt, was ready with advice, money, and co-operation. But the most eager advocate of war against France was found in an unexpected quarter. In 1796 the Tsar Paul had succeeded the Tsarina Catherine on the Russian throne. He was probably 'a dangerous madman,' but he took his position in Russia and in Europe very seriously. He had been made Protector of the Order of St. John, from which Napoleon had taken the island of Malta on his road to Egypt, and he dreamed of making Russia an important Mediterranean Power. French schemes in Poland gave him a more justifiable cause for action. In December 1798 he joined hands with Pitt and Britain. She was to pay a large subsidy to the Russian armies, and together Britain and Russia were 'to bring back France to her pre-revolutionary frontiers.' Austria at first hung back, but the French interference in Naples had great influence in making her accept the idea of a new war. Nor was she uninfluenced by the difficulties encountered with the French at the Congress of Rastatt. That Congress ended under the shadow of the murder of the French representatives. The affair still remains obscure. In March 1799 Austria declared war.

France had a very serious task to face. Her armies were vastly outnumbered; it is reckoned that at first she had only 170,000 men to oppose to 350,000. Her greatest general was in Egypt; and on the other side there were in command men of real energy and talent. Suvorov, the Russian general—Byron describes him as 'hero, buffoon, half demon and half dirt'—had a fiery energy that sometimes touched genius; and the Archduke Charles of Austria gained important victories. Yet in September 1798 France had laid the basis of her future success when she rationalised and tightened up the rules governing universal military service between the ages of twenty and twenty-five, already introduced by the *levée en masse* of 1793.

The war was on a vast scale. Italy and Switzerland were the chief theatres of the war, and at first fortune seemed decisively to favour the enemies of France. The French power was driven from Naples. The French armies were defeated in Switzerland. The most complete victory of all was won by Suvorov in Italy. He utterly defeated the French under Moreau at Novi (August 1799) and the Cisalpine and Roman Republics collapsed at once. The omens were very favourable for the allies. With close union and agreement as to the plan of campaign victory seemed assured.

But union and agreement were lacking. Though the Polish question was no longer there to paralyse the action of the allies, there was wide divergence of aim among them. Austria aimed at annexations in Bavaria and North Italy. The Tsar was anxious, above all things, to restore the King of Sardinia to Piedmont and the Bourbons to France. Suvorov was a most difficult man to work with, and he was at cross purposes with the Austrian war council. This led to disaster in October 1799. Suvorov was ordered to enter Switzerland in order to join another Russian general before Zürich. He was most unwilling to leave Italy, but moved at last. The Austrians did not cooperate, and Suvorov believed himself betrayed. His march across the mountains was a great achievement, but he found the army that he was to join already dispersed and with great difficulty escaped from the surrounding French armies. There followed bitter recriminations between the generals and the Governments. The alliance was clearly falling to pieces. All this, it must be noted—both the failures of the French and their recovery from them—had happened while Napoleon was away from France.

We must return to Paris, where the Directory was in great difficulties. Its own character was in part responsible for these, for the Government was full of corruption and scandal. But before it passes out of view we should do justice to what it had achieved. It had in fact succeeded in stabilising French finances. It had coped with continued inflation and a continued fall in the value of the paper money by returning to a metal currency and promoting deflation as far as it could. The fall in prices was hard on the peasants with agricultural products to sell and the Directors were helped by Napoleon's exactions from foreign countries. Yet financial stability was a permanent gain, for it restored business confidence and promoted prosperity. The Directors took drastic measures to cut the National Debt and added a new tax on windows and houses to the three direct taxes established in 1790. Direct taxation in France remained until the eve of the War of 1914–18 as the Directors had left it. It was not the failure of the Government but the failure of the war that overthrew the Directory. Twice the Directors had used the force or prestige of the army in order to exclude from the Councils representatives elected by the country but hostile to their power. But now in June 1799, in presence of defeat, actual and threatening, the support of the army failed them. The Councils took action: deposed one Director and forced the resignation of two others. The new Directors— the last to hold office—were Sieyès, Barras, Ducos, Moulin, and Gohier. Democratic Jacobinism raised its head again. The country was restless and ready to acclaim anyone who would give them honour and security.

Napoleon reached France in October 1799. He was hailed with immense enthusiasm. The failure of his Egyptian adventure was not reckoned against him. That failure had happened in a distant theatre and under obscure circumstances. Men remembered only the way in which in his Italian campaigns he had forced the Austrians to accept peace. His behaviour increased his reputation. He was modest and reserved. He boasted little of his victories, and associated more with men of science than with soldiers. Yet there can be no doubt that his eyes were always set on his great political enterprise, and that he considered carefully the problem and its solution from his arrival in France.

Some change in the Government was certain. What should be its character? Napoleon entered into close relations with Barras, his old ally; with Sieyès, the political theorist; with Talleyrand, ex-bishop and Jacobin and the subtlest and coolest of intriguers. He listened to them all, but he took chief counsel with himself. His hope was that his popularity with nearly all classes would be so great that he would be spontaneously acclaimed as head of the State. He would thus rule by something as near to constitutional right as could be obtained in revolutionary France, and would not have to draw the sword or shed blood. It makes clearer the great intrigue on which he entered if we realise that it did not work out according to programme; that the show of force was not what he wished; and that the need to display, if not to use, force considerably influenced his future career.

The scheme was helped by the fact that his brother Lucien was President of the Council of Five Hundred. Napoleon hoped that the Councils would use their constitutional right to move their sessions to St. Cluod—for Paris was not a suitable environment, even now, for a counter-revolution; that they would invest him with the command of the Paris troops; and then, meeting in the midst of the troops, would vote for constitutional revision and give him the duty of presiding over and directing the work. He did not doubt that if this were done it would result in something like personal power for himself. The Directors would have to be got rid of, but it was hoped that they could be induced to resign.

The programme was followed up to a certain point. Sieyès and Ducos, who were in the plot (though not as completely as they thought), resigned and hoped that the others would do the same. Barras had hoped for a share in the work and the power, and was deeply chagrined to find that his part was to be a negative one; in the end he, too, resigned. The other two Directors, who refused, were placed under arrest. Early on November 9, 1799, the Council of Ancients voted for the transference of the sessions to St. Cloud and conferred the desired command on Napoleon. November 10 (the 19th of Brumaire in the revolutionary calendar) was the real crisis. Napoleon knew that all his future lay on the event of the day; he said to Sieyès, as they drove to St. Cloud, pointing to the place where the guillotine had stood, 'We end there, or in the Palace of the Luxembourg.' At St. Cloud he addressed the two Councils in turn. But now the programme no longer worked; for the Councils were not so influenced by Napoleon's popularity as to be willing to vote away the Constitution and their own existence. The Ancients listened to Napoleon's address coldly and declared their devotion to the Constitution and cried 'No Cromwell!' The Council of Five Hundred, when he appeared before them drove him, with some show of violence, from their hall. Popularity and fine phrases would not solve the problem; unwillingly Napoleon had to appeal to the sword. When his brother brought him word that the Council was getting out of hand he called upon the troops to enter the hall and drive the councillors out. It was for him a moment of tense anxiety. Would the soldiers of the Republic turn their bayonets against the free Government of France? They obeyed with little hesitation. The majority of the legislators fled. The rump of those who remained, acting in collusion with the chief conspirator, voted for constitutional revision, and appointed three consuls to carry it out. The names of the three were Napoleon, Sieyès, and Ducos. Early on November 11 Napoleon was back in Paris and the *coup d'état* was over. Paris and France accepted it with surprising calm. There was no sympathy with the Councils or with the Directors. The country was ready for a new experiment.

The Revolution of Brumaire had decided that the Constitution was to be revised. But what was to be the nature of the revision? On that there were widely differing ideas among the chief actors in the drama. Napoleon Bonaparte and the Abbé Sieyès had been the chief agents of the *coup d'état*: the one was a soldier, the other a man who had devoted much thought to questions of political theory and had exercised a decisive influence in the early stages of the Revolution. He expected that at this crisis the Government would be remodelled according to his ideas and that the soldier would recognise the thinker's superiority. He had a clear if rather elaborate system of government in his mind. He still held by Montesquieu's doctrine of the 'Separation of Powers.' The executive was to be independent of the legislative; the Government was not to rest directly upon the support of the elected representatives of the people. Yet he knew the danger of collision between Ministers and Parliament; the history of the Revolution had made that plain. There was the problem! How to fashion a government that should not depend for its existence on the people and yet should have the confidence of the people? The formula that he adopted—he was fond of formulas—was 'Confidence from below; power from above.' The practical application of it was curious. The people were to draw up lists of men who, in their opinion, were worthy of holding office and who would enjoy their confidence as administrators. These lists were to be drawn up by an elaborate method which we need not follow. Then power was to come from above. A Great Elector was to be appointed at once. He was to be well paid and was to fulfil almost exactly the functions of a constitutional sovereign. His business was to appoint, from the lists sent up to him, all the agents of government and the members of the councils. There were to be two consuls—one for home and the other for foreign affairs. There was to be a council of state to initiate legislation; a tribunate to discuss legislative proposals; a legislative assembly that was to hear the arguments for and against the proposed measure, and was then to vote without discussion. There was to be a senate with the right of veto.

Napoleon was in agreement with many superficial features of this scheme. He distrusted popular control; he preferred nominated assemblies to elective; he disliked and feared parliamentary discussion. But he was utterly opposed to what was fundamental in Sieyès's proposals. It was a system of checks and balances; the nominal head of the State was to have no real control; the head of the army was to be strictly subordinate. Napoleon desired a strong government, centralised in the hands of the head of the army, moving at once in obedience to a command; a government personal, efficient, and bureaucratic; and he desired that the head of the government should be himself. Here was an antagonism that could not be settled by vague phrases. Sieyès and Napoleon were in conflict, and the issue was not in doubt. It was the soldier's prestige and the soldier's sword that had triumphed at Brumaire, and Sieyès must necessarily yield. Fifty members were chosen from the two Councils to decide between the rival schemes, and Napoleon, of course, triumphed.

There was a good deal of make-believe in the scheme that was adopted. Sieyès's scheme of elective machinery, whereby confidence was to be elicited from below, was maintained in theory though it was never actually applied. The wheels in the machine bore the same names as in Sieyès's plan, but the driving force was utterly different. The executive government was to be vested in one First Consul, who could be none other than Napoleon himself. There were to be—in partial agreement with Sieyès's suggestion—two other consuls, but these were rather vice-consuls than colleagues. Cambacérès and Lebrun were appointed to these posts. They would not rival the importance of Napoleon. A nominated State Council was to initiate all legislation. The State Council (Conseil d'État) deserves a pause: for it was the most characteristic of Napoleonic institutions. It com-

prised the men of talent and expertise whom Napoleon particularly
valued. Its two functions of drafting laws and settling administrative
disputes enabled it, especially when presided over by Napoleon, to
be the dynamo by which Napoleonic power was generated. Then
there was to be a 'Conservative Senate' of sixty members chosen by
the consuls. They were to make appointments; fill the consular
vacancies; appoint a tribunate of 100 members which was to debate
legislative proposals; appoint a legislative assembly of 300 who were
to listen to speeches on both sides, and then vote on proposals that
had come down from the tribunate. The scheme was submitted to a
plebiscite—another characteristic Napoleonic institution. It was
announced that 3,012,000 votes had been cast for it and only 1562
against it. The meaning of these details is more interesting than the
details themselves. They meant that the victorious leader of her
armies ruled France with institutions which would be the means of
strengthening that rule—perhaps by giving it access to public
opinion—not of enabling France to rule herself.

Chapter 4

NAPOLEON, EMPEROR AND STATESMAN

Napoleon had won his power in the Revolution of Brumaire as a victorious leader of the French armies, and he well knew that victory alone could maintain the position that he had won. It was a good deal later that he said to a friend, 'I act only on the imagination of the nation. When this means fails me I shall be reduced to nothing, and another will succeed me.' It is a sentence which gives us a clue to much of his history. He could not lay down the power that he had won; he was master, but he was also slave. If the French were not continuously dazzled by victories and glory the old ideals of the Revolution—liberty, equality, and fraternity—would come back to their minds, or they would think again of the high place held in an admiring Europe by the old Bourbon Monarchy.

Austria and Great Britain alone remained under arms against France. The position of Great Britain was at present unassailable. Napoleon made overtures to King George III to find some road to peace. George III only answered that it was necessary to restore to the throne of France her legitimate kings, and laid himself open to the retort that, if legitimate kings were never to be expelled, he himself, owing, as he did, his position to the revolution of 1688, had no right to the English throne. It seemed that peace was only to be won by victory.

A twofold attack was planned against Austria, very much after the fashion of those operations of 1796 which had first made Napoleon's name known in Europe. First, Moreau was to lead an army across the Rhine and into the Danube valley in order to attack Vienna by that well-known route. At the same time Napoleon was to take an army into Italy by the passes of Switzerland, which, since recent changes there, were open to him. This Italian expedition was now, however, no subordinate one; it would be upon it that the failure or success of the French Government would depend.

The French power had nearly gone from Italy. The Cisalpine Republic had collapsed, and with it all the other spheres of influence in Italy which France had established. A French army under Masséna was at this time being besieged in Genoa by the Austrian, Melas, and nothing besides this was left of French power in Northern Italy. Napoleon determined to enter Italy, not by his old route of the Mediterranean shore, but across the pass of the Great St. Bernard. He made much of this march of his across the mountains, and it was compared by his flatterers with the exploits of Hannibal and of Francis I, for Napoleon was not only a great general but also an incomparable journalist. In truth, however, there was no great difficulty in the exploit. There were only five leagues which were impracticable to carriages, and that space was quickly made available by his engineers. He descended into the Val d'Aosta, and came down into Piedmont. He hesitated for a moment as to whether he should march on Milan or Genoa. Had he marched on Genoa the French army under Masséna might perhaps have been saved. Napoleon determined, however, to make for Milan, which he entered without opposition. Masséna was in consequence forced to surrender with his army of twenty thousand men, but by a curious oversight these men were allowed to march out in the direction of Napoleon still bearing their arms. Napoleon advanced towards Alessandria, which was the headquarters of the Austrian force, and on June 14, 1800, the Battle of Marengo was fought in the neighbourhood of Alessandria. This was the first battle fought by Napoleon since his assumption of the new title of Consul, and counts as one of his great victories. In truth, it was very nearly a defeat. The French army was attacked unexpectedly whilst it was divided into three parts. It was driven back with considerable loss, and the Austrian general, wearied with heat and age, retired into Marengo, confident that he had won a victory which he might leave a subordinate to complete. It was at this moment that, with dramatic suddenness, a French force, recently detailed to watch the Austrians at Genoa, arrived under Desaix. He had no instructions from Napoleon, but he heard the noise of the guns and marched straight to them. He arrived to find Napoleon defeated, but in time to win a second battle, and this second battle was a complete French victory. The Austrians withdrew behind the river Mincio; and all the results of the victories of the Austrians and the Russians since 1798 were undone at a blow. Before the end of the year there came another heavy disaster upon them north of the Alps. There Moreau came into conflict with the Austrian army under the Archduke John, at Hohenlinden. A severely contested battle ended in a complete French victory, and Vienna itself was in danger. It would have been necessary in any case for Austria to accept peace after these two staggering blows, but a strange change which passed over Russia at the same time made it still more obviously necessary. The half-mad Tsar Paul, who had for some time been a champion of legitimate monarchy and a bitter enemy of the French, had now become an eager partisan of the French and was ready to co-operate with Napoleon. So on February 9, 1801, the Austrians accepted the Peace of Lunéville, which was in many respects a repetition and reinforcement of the Peace of Campo Formio. The chief clauses affected the future of Germany and Italy. The cession of all the territory on the left bank of the Rhine to France, already promised by Prussia at Basel and by Austria at Campo Formio, now became effective. The process of ending the Holy Roman Empire which we have seen beginning at the Congress of Rastatt was now continued at the Congress of Regensburg, which lasted from 1801 to 1803. The Main Decision of the Imperial Deputation, as it was called, sanctioned by the Reichstag in April 1803, was the legal document which enacted the secularisation and mediatisation first discussed at Rastatt. It it more vividly called the Princes' Revolution, for it meant a revolutionary consolidation and increase of the territories of Baden, Württemberg, Bavaria and the two Hessen states. The content of the document in the event was determined beforehand by separate agreements of the rulers of these states with Napoleon and by mediation of Alexander of Russia who by 1803 had succeeded Paul. The Italian stipulations of the Peace of Campo Formio were also reaffirmed. The process of enlargement and consolidation was, however, also applied when the Duchy of Tuscany and the island of Elba were ceded to the Cisalpine Republic. It was agreed that the Duke of Tuscany should receive in Germany compensation for what he lost in Italy. The independence, it may be noted, of the sister republics which had been set up by France in various parts of Europe was guaranteed.[1]

Great Britain alone now remained, and Napoleon despaired as yet of striking any blow against her through direct action at sea, but cherished for a time the hope that what he could not do directly he might do indirectly. It was well known, and had become quite apparent during the war with the American colonies, that every nation that possessed any maritime power resented the claim of Great Britain to be allowed, in time of war, to search all vessels of whatever kind, even those belonging to neutral Powers, in order to see whether they were carrying goods belonging to the enemies of Britain and to destroy such goods if found. There had been a league of neutrals against this practice at the end of the American War, but the practice still continued. Now, under the direction of Russia, Denmark and Sweden joined with Prussia in a league of protest against this right of search. It seemed possible that a formidable naval Power might be created in the Baltic hostile to Great Britain and capable of serious action against her. Great Britain, however, struck too swiftly. On April 2, 1801, Copenhagen was attacked, the Danish fleet destroyed,

---

[1] These sister republics, it will be convenient to note, were the Batavian (Dutch), the Helvetic (Swiss), the Cisalpine and the Ligurian (Italian).

and the league broken up. At the same time events in Egypt were obviously leading up to the surrender of the French armies into British hands, which occurred during the summer.

The war seemed as though it might go on for ever. Yet peace was desirable for both parties to it; and in Britain, where Pitt had resigned owing to his sharp difference with George III about the conditions of the union with Ireland, the new Prime Minister, Addington, was less determined in his prosecution of the war. Negotiations were opened, and the Peace of Amiens was signed (March 27, 1802). It is a peace of many clauses, but they may be shortly summarised. All British conquests from France were to be restored, but Ceylon and Trinidad, which had been ceded, the one by Holland and the other by Spain, were to be retained by the British. Malta, which had recently been retaken by the British from Napoleon, was to be restored, not to France but to the Knights of St. John. It is a long clause that lays down the method of this restoration. The independence of the island was to be guaranteed by Great Britain, Austria, Spain, Russia, and Prussia. The King of the Two Sicilies was to garrison the island with two thousand troops. There are other details also. We shall see that they were never carried out; and that Great Britain, on that ground, refused to hand over the island. Such was the Peace of Amiens. It was greeted with immense jubilation in France and in Great Britain. It opened Europe again to the visits of British tourists. Many regarded it as the end of the period of war and the establishment of a durable peace, and some were ready to see in Napoleon a great benefactor of mankind. It proved, however, to be only a precarious and deceitful truce. In England the early enthusiasm for it soon passed away. Public opinion, especially among the commercial classes, was irritated because France still held Belgium and Holland—still, therefore, controlled those lands which in the hands of a rival Power seemed to us 'a pistol pointed at the heart of London.' The hopes of trade with France, too, proved illusory; nowhere was trade readily admitted, and in some places it was absolutely prohibited. Such as it was, however, the Peace gave to France a much needed breathing space during which great changes were introduced into her political, social, and religious life.

Napoleon ruled France as First Consul. He disregarded the machinery which had been set up after the Revolution of Brumaire. Those institutions had perhaps been useful in the first instance as screens to his personal power, but as he grew more confident and more assured of public support he swept them away and ruled without even pretending to take the people into partnership. Not only did his power tend more and more to become an avowed autocracy; it also, little by little, dropped all trace of its revolutionary origin, and became more conservative and more dependent upon the conservative support of the Church and the peasantry. Napoleon disliked later to be reminded in any way of his early revolutionary connections and beliefs. In December 1800 a bomb was thrown at him as he was going to the opera. It was declared to be the work of the *septem-briseurs*, the contemptuous phrase that was now applied to the violent Jacobins. After an inquiry 130 Jacobins were banished, not for the bomb throwing but, as the edict said, 'for the massacres of September 2, May 31, and every subsequent attempt.' The Government made war even upon women, and the widows of Marat and Chaumette were imprisoned. It is noteworthy, as showing Napoleon's old connections, that the sister of Robespierre was awarded a pension.

These attacks on the First Consul were the cause or excuse of a further hardening of the constitution. Then, in March 1802, came the Peace of Amiens, and France saw herself victorious over all her enemies and in the enjoyment of a military prestige that even Louis XIV at the height of his power had never possessed. She seemed to owe all to the marvellous man who had led her from victory to victory. Liberty had few enthusiasts now; personal rule seemed to bring success and might bring prosperity. Doubtless Napoleon desired to secure his personal power on a more durable and unchallenged basis; but the desire of his people seconded and even outstripped his ambition. In gratitude for the Peace it was proposed to extend his consulate to a second period of ten years. It was due to Napoleon himself that this proposal was enlarged and changed into the consulship for life. The office was not to be hereditary, but—in imitation of Roman models—the Consul was to be allowed to choose his own successor. Changes in the constitutional machinery were made at the same time. The State Council became the Privy Council; its members were nominated by the First Consul and it was given the initiative in all proposals. It was only in the Tribunate that any discussion was allowed. There was nothing that Napoleon so much disliked and feared as discussion, whether in an Assembly or in the press. Already, after the attack on his person, the Tribunate had been remodelled; those who were to retire each year were chosen by the First Consul, who could thus get rid of opponents; and strict limitations were placed on their debates. Now the Tribunate was divided into five sections and the deliberations of each were held in secret. The electoral machinery was still kept in name, and even revised; but the electors were not allowed really to influence the Government in any way. France had now a personal government, with fewer checks upon it than had existed in the time of the old Monarchy. All citizens were asked to give their opinion on the new proposals. They supported Napoleon's extended power by three-and-a-half millions of votes to less than ten thousand. The imperial plebiscites are not above suspicion; but it is clear that the people desired that Napoleon should rule.

He was Emperor in all but name. The name came soon, and it will be well to trace the way by which it came without casting more than a rapid glance upon foreign affairs, which had a profound influence on the assumption of the new title. For in May 1803 the Peace of Amiens broke down and the new war, first with Great Britain and then with a wide European alliance, seemed a personal challenge to the power and character of Napoleon. In face of such an attack it was inevitable that France should rally with enthusiasm round the man of her choice. A similar effect was produced by the Cadoudal plot which came to light in February 1804. This was a really serious affair. Georges Cadoudal was a Vendean Royalist and he had sworn to kill Napoleon. Greater names than his were associated with him; Pichegru, the revolutionary general, and Moreau, the victor of Hohenlinden. The British Government, too, was not ignorant that something was in the wind. But a fellow-conspirator revealed the plot. Cadoudal was executed; Moreau was banished; Pichegru died in prison, not without some suspicions of foul play. The plot, too, caused the death of one who was in no way connected with it. The Duc d'Enghien was a prince of the House of Condé and one of the emigrant nobles. He was resident at Ettenheim in Baden, not far beyond the frontier of France. The reason for the outrage that followed is difficult to make out. Napoleon felt himself surrounded by plots. He was exasperated against the confederacy that was growing up against him. He seems to have believed that some invasion of France was preparing in which Enghien was to be assisted by Dumouriez. A body of cavalry rode to Ettenheim, seized the Duke, and brought him first to Strassburg, and then by rapid marches to Vincennes, near Paris. A court-martial was held upon him, and after the mockery of a trial he was shot at once. Nothing has weighed more heavily on the reputation of Napoleon than this crime. Rumbold, the British representative, was about the same time abducted from Hamburg and his life was with difficulty saved from the anger of Napoleon. Several of the German states were forced to dismiss their British representatives.

Plots real and supposed; the frantic hatred of Europe, and especially of Great Britain—these only increased the readiness of France to testify her confidence in Napoleon. A proposal was made in the Tribunate to make the power of Napoleon hereditary. It passed as a matter of course, Carnot alone maintaining a republican attitude of opposition. Then a little later—on May 18, 1804—a decree of the Senate gave him the title of 'Emperor of the French.' The Pope was in official relations with the new Government of France in consequence of the legislation shortly to be examined. He came to Paris and crowned Napoleon and Josephine in the cathedral of Notre-Dame. All the details of the ceremony were carefully considered. Napoleon avoided the recognition of any superiority in the Pope. He took the crown from the Pope's hands and placed it on his own head.

Napoleon's claim to statesmanship, which gives him a unique place among soldiers of genius, rests primarily on the measures of domestic policy of this period. They are numerous and of vital importance in the history not only of France but of Europe as a whole. In their formulation many people besides Napoleon took a significant part, but Napoleon's direct responsibility is great, for his inspiration and influence affected them all.

First, he found a settlement of the religious question which had for so long been a festering sore in France. The challenge of the Revolution to the Catholic sentiment of France and to the organisation of the Catholic Church had been the source of many of the gravest difficulties which had beset her. The attempt to set up a constitutional Catholic Church independent of Rome and the Pope had proved a dismal failure. The constitutional priests had no following. In many cases they had married and adopted a secular life. Theophilanthropy, in spite of the support given to it in Government circles, had been an entire fiasco. Religious France was at heart Catholic, and a greater part of France was religious than is usually assumed.

Napoleon approached the matter from the point of view of statesmanship. His own religious views do not seem to have gone beyond a vague deism. But he had a just instinct of the strength of the Catholic Church and of the danger of collision with a body that commanded the loyalty of so many Frenchmen. He wanted an established church as a support for his throne. 'A state without a religion is like a vessel without a compass,' he said. Even in his first Italian campaigns he had shown himself more friendly to the Papacy than the French Government quite liked. After the Battle of Marengo, the *rapprochement* between him and the Papacy was hurried on. The Battle of Marengo was celebrated by a religious thanksgiving. Pope Pius VII was restored to the Papal States. The attitude of the First Consul clearly invited friendly overtures. At the same time hints of threats were not wanting. A French garrison was maintained in Rome and might at any moment make its presence unpleasant. There was some talk, too, of carrying farther the traditional idea of Gallican liberties and erecting in France a Church, Catholic and orthodox, but independent of Rome. So the Concordat was passed and at Easter 1802 France went back in the main to the ecclesiastical constitution which had existed before the Revolution, except that the Church was without property and all clerical stipends were paid by the State—a system which lasted until 1905. The Church entered again into communion with Rome. Catholicism was once more the religion of the State. Its services and organisation were to be supported by State funds. On the other hand, all the higher Church dignitaries were to be nominated by the First Consul; the Pope could only reject his nominees on the ground of heresy or immorality, and, if there was no fault to be found with them on these points, was bound to grant canonical investiture. The First Consul would thus be able to maintain authority over the Church by appointing to the important posts men of whose support he could feel sure. This, however, was not the end nor, in the Pope's view, the worst. In the Concordat there occurred the clause that 'worship should be public so long as it conformed to the police regulations, which the Government should judge necessary in the interest of public tranquillity.' These regulations were soon produced. It was declared that no papal bulls were applicable to France; that no synod of the clergy of France could be held without the permission of the First Consul; that no bishop might leave his diocese even if summoned by the Pope. Worst of all, it was laid down that the declaration of Gallican liberties—that is, the special rights and liberties of the Catholic Church in France—were to be taught to all those who were preparing for the priesthood. This declaration, formulated in 1682, had been a matter of long controversy between the old Monarchy of France and the Papacy. In sum it curtailed the authority of the Pope within the Church of France, and declared that that authority was not final until it had been corroborated by the assent of the Church. So bitter was the draught that the Pope hesitated about accepting the Concordat as a whole, now that this declaration had been attached to it; but he accepted it in the end.

Napoleon's central idea in all this was to control a great force that influenced the actions of men through their feelings and beliefs. Other Churches were not left out of account. The Lutheran and the Calvinist Churches were brought under State control and into State pay. Government support was also given to the Jews. The religious life of France was thus to be established and endowed. The throne, though much changed in style, was once again to lean on the altar or altars of France. There have been widely differing judgements on all this in respect of both religion and policy. The question certainly was settled. Yet the Churches, more especially the Catholic Church, may not have benefited from being thus identified with the interests of Napoleon. Napoleon may well not have profited particularly from alienating a section of France which still thought the essence of the Revolution was that it had freed France from clerical ascendancy. 'A million men have died,' said one adviser, 'to destroy what you are re-establishing.'

The same period sees also the elaboration and completion of the Napoleonic codes. They are one of Napoleon's greatest claims to be considered a benefactor of mankind. In his exile in St. Helena he claimed that the Civil Code, and not his victories in war, was his most real claim to fame. The French codes, too, were the most effective instrument in carrying over a large part of Europe the ideas of the

French Revolution so far as they were accepted and promoted by Napoleon. The idea and the work of codification were not new in France. There was indeed something characteristically French in this effort to carry forward the work of the Roman Empire and to present the laws of France within the smallest possible compass and in a form clear, logical, and complete. Louis XIV had done something towards this end. The Revolution had expressed a desire to see that work carried farther. Such work has always required for its accomplishment the force of a strong government and usually of a powerful single will; and this was supplied in full measure by Napoleon.

Napoleon was the child of the Revolution, but in many ways he reversed the aims and principles of the movement from which he sprang. And this was particularly true of the codes. The Revolution had not only swept away what remained of feudalism and ecclesiastical control of the State, but it had attacked the cherished traditions of the lawyers of France. It had striven, above all things, for equality. It had insisted that the inheritance should be divided in equal shares among the children; it had limited very strictly the power of testamentary bequest; it had offended Catholic sentiment by introducing divorce; it had removed all control over questions arising out of births, deaths, and marriages from the Church. There was much in all this of which Napoleon in his new mood did not approve. He had made friends with the Church. He valued authority. He had little love for equality. The codes, then, proved to be a work of reconciliation in which he returned in some respects to pre-Revolutionary ideas but also summarised the legislation of the Revolution in a short and logical form.

Napoleon was not a lawyer, and he approached the questions with the open mind and also with the ignorance of a layman. But his influence was very great. He not only gave the impulse and insisted on the work being carried out: he also presided at many of the sittings, especially of those devoted to the Civil Code, and interfered often with decisive effect. Some utterances of his with regard to the work of lawyers are of sufficient interest to be quoted: 'I first thought that it would be possible to reduce laws to simple geometrical demonstrations, so that whoever could read and tie two ideas together would be capable of pronouncing on them; but I almost immediately convinced myself that this was an absurd idea . . . I often perceived that over-simplicity in legislation was the enemy of precision. It is impossible to make laws extremely simple without cutting the knot oftener than you untie it.'

There were five codes in all: the Civil Code, the code of civil procedure, the code of criminal procedure and penal law, the penal code, and the commercial code. Before they became binding on France they passed through many stages, but the really decisive agencies were a preliminary committee, in which the project of the Civil

Code was drawn up, and the Council of State before which the suggestions were brought, and which was often presided over by Napoleon himself. He was present at thirty-five out of the eighty-seven sittings devoted to the Civil Code. The Civil Code, called the *Code Napoléon*, promulgated on March 21, 1804, was the most important. It protected the great achievements of the Revolution: individual freedom, freedom of work, freedom of conscience, the secular character of the State and equality before the law. On the other hand, it cast back to the old régime in the space it gave to defining, preserving and protecting property, especially landed property and acquired wealth. It cast back, too, in the protection it gave to authority: the authority of the father over his children and over his wife was absolute. Divorce was allowed but hedged about with restrictions. Freedom to will one's property as one chose was restricted to a small part of it and equal division among the children preserved from the revolutionary legislation for the rest. It gave complete freedom to employers whose testimony alone was acceptable in wage disputes. It was only reflecting the economic organisation of the country in paying little attention to work for wages. The Code of Criminal Procedure followed in many respects the example of British practice. Yet the institution of the jury was hotly attacked. Many held that it was too favourable to the accused and limited dangerously the power of the Government. In the end, and largely through the influence of Napoleon, it was maintained. Its decisions were given by a majority; trials were to be held in public; counsel was to be allowed in all cases. The characteristic French procedure of a preliminary and largely secret indictment of the accused by the *juge d'instruction* was maintained, in spite of the protest of the revolutionary statesmen against it. In the penal code branding and confiscation of property were allowed as penalties, and the right of association was only allowed under strict limitations. The codes were influential with the rulers of Germany and Italy where they were considered to present in clear and compact shape rules which they could follow in modernising their states.

Napoleon also reconstituted the general administration of France, and all he did was inspired by the same spirit; both reconciling and authoritarian. In local administration he preserved the departments. but their subdivisions were altered. The great innovation was the appointment of officials nominated by the Government and subject to dismissal by it, at the head of departments and *arrondissements*. The Prefects, sub-Prefects and Mayors had councils attached to them but with restricted powers. The Prefects were a characteristic Napoleonic institution both in reviving the traditions of the old-régime *Intendants* and enabling Napoleon to win over many sections of the political world. The first batch of Prefects included men from all the elective Assemblies and the Directors' Councils of the revolutionary period. In many respects his reign saw a continual reaction towards the ideas and forms and practices of the old Monarchy. Thus he revived by successive enactments the hierarchy of rank which the Revolution had so resolutely abolished. The beginnings of this may be found in the establishment of the Legion of Honour in 1802. France was then still a republic, and Napoleon spoke the language of the Revolution; but the men of the Convention would have regarded with horror the new distinction which he distributed primarily to soldiers but also to civilians of high achievement in all walks of life. From 1804 onwards a vast and stately hierarchy of rank grew up. Under the princes of the imperial family there were established the six 'grand imperial dignitaries'—the Grand Elector, the Arch-Chancellors of the Empire and of the State, the Arch-Treasurer, the Constable, and the Grand Admiral. Then came the Grand Officers of the Empire, ranging from the Marshals of the Empire to the 'Grand Almoner' and the 'Grand Chamberlain' and the 'Grand Huntsman.' In 1808 the full system was completed, and the imperial throne was surrounded by as thick a crowd of 'Princes and Dukes and Counts and Barons and Knights' as had ever supported the throne of Louis XIV. Many of these dignitaries were 'new men' who had been raised from the ranks of the middle or lower classes by the revolutionary storm; but the tendency was for Napoleon to look to the members of the old families for his servants and his titles. The revolutionists could no longer see in him an ally, but the members of the ancient régime felt no loyalty to him and showed him little fidelity.

The Revolution had had aspirations towards the organisation of an educational system in France. Here, too, Napoleon in characteristic fashion, by his powers of energy and will, translated ideas into facts, but altered all according to his own bias towards rigid centralisation and authority. There were to be schools of four grades; primary, secondary, the characteristic semi-military boarding schools, which were called *lycées*, and special schools for technical training. At the head of all and controlling all came the Imperial University, which was definitely constituted in 1808. There was to be one single organisation for all France, with seventeen subordinate provincial institutions controlled from the centre. It was intended to bring the whole educational system of France under the control of the University, an administrative body, not a society of scholars and students. No one was to be allowed to teach who was not a graduate in one of the faculties of the University, but the vast military and political tasks which claimed Napoleon's attention prevented him from reaching his aim, and, when the Empire fell, the majority of the pupils in French schools were under private and voluntary instruction.

The famous *Institut de France* had been established in 1795 for higher study and research. Napoleon's relation to it is curiously significant. He supported it in the main, and was pleased with the work it did in physical science and the fine arts, in mathematics and literature; but he reorganised it. He disliked the study of moral and political sciences, and, by his decree of January 23, 1803, suppressed the department that was devoted to these studies. There is nothing more characteristic of despotism than suspicion of the studies and speculations that touch human life and conduct, and nothing reveals the essential despotism of Napoleon's outlook more than this hostility towards the moralist and the politician.

He was equally opposed to liberty of expression in the press and in literature. Newspapers were strictly censored, and at last almost suppressed. All books had to be submitted to examination before they were published. The theatre, too, was submitted to a peculiarly rigid control.

Napoleon imitated too the better features of the age of Louis XIV with curious closeness. He inaugurated a vast series of public works. Roads were projected and many constructed; canals were cut; French manufacturers were fostered by a protective system which had its origins partly in the political and military relations of France with Europe, but also corresponded to Napoleon's own ideas. Colbert— the great Minister of Louis XIV—would have been delighted by the tariffs by which foreign manufactures were excluded, by the regimentation of French industries in guilds once more, and by the steps which were taken to introduce into France some of the methods of the industrial revolution which had made so profound a change in the life of Great Britain. Agriculture was improved by the introduction of new methods from Belgium and England. The Lyons silk industry was revived, partly through the adoption of the new Jacquard loom. Cotton was introduced from the East, and was manufactured by means of the spinning-jenny, which came from England. Gas was adopted as an illuminant. The general condition of France, until the Empire touched its period of ruin, showed an air of prosperity in all classes. The economic situation was indeed thoroughly artificial, and depended in every part on war. Yet work was plentiful and wages good. Those who looked beneath the surface saw that there would be a Nemesis at last.

Napoleon's ministers and agents depended on him alone. Neither popular approval nor popular censure affected their tenure of office. He was at first served by men of great ability, both in the army and in the domestic administration. In the last category two names stand out pre-eminent: Talleyrand for the management of foreign affairs, and Fouché for the maintenance of order at home. They were both men of something like genius in their widely different ways; the one subtle, ironic, a master of finesse, and a skilful reader of the barometer of Europe; the other brutal and corrupt, the head of a network of spies and secret agents, quick to detect and to suppress conspiracies against his imperial master, and not above the suspicion that he sometimes fomented the conspiracies that he discovered. Both men rendered Napoleon most valuable services, but both fell under his suspicion. They probably saw clearly the dangers that threatened his power in spite of his immense victories, and both prepared the way for a favourable reception in the camp of his enemies. Talleyrand is strongly suspected of having communicated with the British Government at the time of the Treaty of Tilsit in 1807. He quarrelled with Napoleon in 1808, and was not employed again as his chief agent in foreign affairs. Fouché's power lasted longer, and he was for a time the chief man in France next to the Emperor. But he was more guilty than Talleyrand of facing both ways and of thinking of a possible refuge when Napoleon's power was gone. He was dismissed in 1810. Henceforward the Emperor ruled by weaker and more submissive instruments. Like Louis XIV and many other representatives of sovereign power, he became suspicious of great ability in his subordinates, and tried to manage the whole of his vast Empire himself.

In one respect he was less fortunate than the great French king with whom we have compared him. The throne of Louis XIV was glorified and strengthened by the array of men, great in every department of art and thought, who surrounded it and paid willing homage to it. Napoleon was quite awake to the importance of such support, but his Court was always something artificial and exotic, and it was not connected with any high standard of manners or with any great names in the domains of art or thought. The mind and heart of France were active, but they owed little to Napoleon, and expressed no gratitude to him. The greatest names in literature were in decided opposition to his power. One of them was that of Chateaubriand, who had at one time been in the service of the Empire. He exercised a great influence over the mind of his contemporaries, and his book called 'The Genius of Christianity,' published in 1802, had made him famous. He was not persecuted by Napoleon, but all his influence was thrown against the Emperor. The conflict between the Emperor and Madame de Staël was more direct. She was the daughter of Necker, famous at the beginning of the French Revolution, and was the author of novels and treatises. Though thoroughly French in her character and in the style of her writings, she had written a book 'On Germany,' in which she analysed and praised the characteristics of the people, and in so doing managed to strike more than one shrewd blow against the methods of Napoleon. She was subjected to supervision and almost to imprisonment at Napoleon's hands, but she escaped and published her book in England. Europe looked on and applauded the daring woman's resistance to the tyrant, and exaggerated her value both as thinker and artist. France had famous names in science and important names in art at this period, but the fifteen years during which Napoleon was the supreme figure in France are not a great period in French literature, art, or thought. The chief strength of the Emperor's Court lay, probably, in the Empress Joséphine. She was prodigal of money, and is estimated by Masson, the biographer of Napoleon, to have spent over a million francs a year on dress alone. But she was beautiful, charming, and, to a large extent, popular. Her divorce was prompted by political and international considerations, but it was probably a mistake. France never took her successor into favour, as we shall see on a later page.

It has been claimed that Napoleon was equally great as statesman and as soldier. Can that claim be justified? Doubtless he had no chance of developing all his ideas amid the hardly interrupted storms of war; his domestic policy was throughout subordinated to military necessities. But we must remember that the European situation was largely his own creation, and that his power in France itself was always intimately bound up with his military prestige and victories. In his social and political schemes there is very little that is original. For a part of it the way had been prepared by the Revolution; for another part, by the old Monarchy. The great feature about his statesmanship is not its originality, but the immense energy and strength of will and attention to detail with which he carried it out. It was not so novel, nor perhaps so well adapted to the needs of the time, as the work of Colbert, which it so closely resembles. Finally, it is obvious that in all his work he showed no appreciation of the value of political liberty. That first great watchword of the Revolution had perhaps at one time appealed to him, but his early enthusiasm was quite dead. He thought of liberty as a disturbing factor that prevented the efficiency of a state. There is no hint in anything that he said or wrote that he thought of it as the great force making for stability, order, and efficiency.

Chapter 5

THE DEFEAT OF THE GOVERNMENTS OF EUROPE

The Peace of Amiens had been welcomed with profound relief by all the nations of Europe, and nowhere more than in Great Britain. Many hoped that the storms of the revolutionary period were over, and that Europe might enjoy at any rate a space of tranquillity and peaceful development; and yet the Peace of Amiens lasted less than two years, and quickly gave place to a war of greater intensity and longer duration, which did not really cease until the Battle of Waterloo. What were the causes of the new war? Though the rupture of the Peace of Amiens has had many books written about it there are certain points about which there is still real difference of opinion among the best informed historians.

Generally, that rupture illustrates the working of the idea of Balance of Power. The various nations of Europe regarded one another as potential enemies; the power of one seemed to be the danger of the rest. With these ideas it was inevitable that the great position which France had attained before the Peace should seem a real menace to the safety of the other European States, and the gains which France made after the Peace were still further unsettling and alarming to the minds of traditional European statesmen. We must turn, therefore, to notice what these fresh developments were which were the excuse, and to a large extent the real cause, for the outbreak of hostilities.

We have already seen the encroachments of the French power upon her neighbours during the Peace of Lunéville. The same process may be observed after the Peace of Amiens. France had established six sister republics in Europe. These were expressly recognised as independent by the Treaty of Lunéville, but France treated them in such a way as to imply that they were, in effect, at her disposal. French garrisons were maintained in all of them. The Cisalpine Republic was already in its foreign policy dependent upon the decision of Napoleon. It was now all but openly annexed. Four hundred and fifty representatives from the Republic came to Lyons. There they debated the form of their constitution. It was agreed to adopt one precisely parallel to that of France. The title of the Cisalpine Republic was changed to that of the Italian Republic, and Napoleon was chosen as its President (this was before his own assumption of the imperial title), 'not as being First Consul of France, but as an individual.' The distinction really made no difference: the Italian Republic was closely bound to the fortunes of France. Piedmont, as we have seen, was definitely annexed in September 1802, and no compensation was paid to Sardinia. France had not ceased, moreover, her interference in the affairs of Switzerland. The French troops were not withdrawn, and this gave her the opportunity of deciding on the issue of the internal political strife which now broke out. There was a democratic party at daggers drawn with an oligarchical party. There was one party which desired a centralised government, while another was in favour of a form of federalism. Napoleon declared that Switzerland must be saved from herself, and he imposed upon her a federal constitution in which nineteen cantons took part. Again the independence of Switzerland was declared, but she was bound to contribute troops to France, and her independence, therefore, was a mere form and shadow.

All these things concerned Great Britain and the Powers of Europe equally, but there were certain incidents which touched Great Britain particularly, and which even alarmed her as implying that France and the ruler of France had not yet given up the idea of challenging the colonial and maritime power of Great Britain.

There were strange events in San Domingo. This island, better known to us as Haiti, was inhabited almost entirely by a population of negro origin. The French Revolution had declared slavery abolished throughout French dominions, but the result had not been to procure peace in San Domingo. On the contrary, a violent servile war had broken out, and in this war there appeared Toussaint l'Ouverture, the greatest military general who has ever come of negro stock. He made himself the leader of the insurgent blacks, occupied practically the whole island, and treated it as belonging to him personally. The offers of the British to help were rejected, and their efforts to occupy the island were defeated. Toussaint began, with victory, to ape something of the manners and ceremony of European military command. In 1801 he took to himself the title of consul for life, and gave to the island a constitution on the model of what had been adopted in France. The constitution, of course, never existed except on paper. When, therefore, the Peace of Amiens gave to France once more the power of despatching ships across the Atlantic the island was practically independent of France and in the occupation of this remarkable negro chief. It was inevitable that the French should try to recover it. Nor does there seem to be any good reason for the objection felt by the British Government to the method in

which it was done. General Leclerc, the husband of Pauline Bonaparte, was sent out with an army of twenty thousand men. Against
this force Toussaint could make no effective resistance. He showed
great energy and some tactical skill; in the end, however, his surrender was obtained, and he was deported to France and imprisoned
there. The French army that was left behind was attacked by disease
and reduced to a very small force. San Domingo ultimately became
again independent of the French Government. Great Britain saw
with alarm, however, that France was capable of sending a large
expedition across the seas, and believed that General Leclerc's force
implied a readiness once more to dispute with the British the control
of the West Indies, then so valued a part of the colonial empire of
Great Britain.

There were reports also from India which gave ground for anxiety.
The French general, De Caen, had been sent out to India to visit the
French possessions that still remained there, to revive French influence, and to report upon the general situation. The instructions that
were given to him seemed to show that Napoleon did not really contemplate any permanent peace with Britain. Another French agent,
Sébastiani, was sent to the Levant and Syria in order also to report
on the prospects of France there; and by some strange oversight—
if it was an oversight—his report was published in the offical newspaper, the *Moniteur*, and in it occurred the phrase that an army of
6000 Frenchmen would be enough to conquer Egypt. It seemed,
then, that through the mind of the First Consul was at any rate passing the idea of taking up again his Egyptian projects. Besides those
matters which concerned British interests overseas, there were others
that worked also to produce a feeling of exasperation and unrest.
The hopes entertained by Great Britain that the peace would open
commerce in France proved to be illusory. On the contrary, British
commerce was almost totally excluded from the French possessions,
and the indignation of the commercial classes in London was very
great. Napoleon, on his side, complained bitterly of attacks made
upon him in newspapers that were published in Britain. Certain
French *émigrés* were using those for continued and violent attacks
upon the First Consul. Napoleon demanded that these papers should
be suppressed, and he would not accept as a sufficient excuse the
British freedom of the press. He complained at the same time that
the British were harbouring on their soil the Bourbon princes, still
the claimants to the throne of France, and he called upon the British
to expel them; but he called in vain.

There was, then, during the period of the Peace a gradual increase
in the tension between the two Powers, and this tension became in
the end concentrated on the question of Malta. That island, important by its natural strength and its geographical position, had, as we
have seen, first fallen into the hands of Napoleon. It had then been

taken from him by the British, and at the Peace of Amiens the promise had been given that it should be restored to the Knights of St. John under certain conditions. These conditions were not fulfilled. Great Britain had, as a result, a reasonable excuse for her refusal to evacuate the island. It must be noted at the same time that no effort was made to procure the fulfilment of these conditions, and that there is strong evidence that Great Britain was determined to maintain her possession of the island on whatever grounds.[1] With the signing of the Peace diplomatic relations were resumed with France, and Lord Whitworth was sent to Paris as British representative. From the instructions which were given to him when he went, it is clear that the British Government had made up its mind to maintain its hold upon Malta. Between Lord Whitworth and the First Consul there ensued a controversy of the most interesting and often of the most dramatic kind, which is presented to us in his despatches. He was a characteristic Englishman of the period, with an Englishman's contempt for France and its ruler, blind to many of the strong points in the French case, but at the same time stiff and determined to do his utmost for the country that had sent him to Paris. Napoleon, on his side, demanded the execution of the Treaty of Amiens. 'The Treaty of Amiens,' he said, 'and nothing but the Treaty of Amiens.' And Lord Whitworth, on his side, took as his ground that the execution of the treaty was dependent upon the condition of Europe when that treaty was signed, and that the execution of the treaty, therefore, could not be claimed in face of the great strides which had been made by the French power since the signature of the treaty. There were efforts, perhaps genuinely meant, on both sides to find some compromise. Napoleon's brother Joseph took a leading part in these overtures. No good result, however, was obtained, and in March 1803, after a scene of great violence at the Tuileries Palace, relations were broken off between Great Britain and France. Napoleon laid hands upon all those Englishmen who in great numbers had availed themselves of the Peace to resume the habit of continental travel, and many of these unfortunate men remained prisoners for ten years.

War had come, but the extent of the war was yet uncertain. It might possibly be confined to the two great Powers whose quarrel had been the cause of it. On both sides there was keen competition

---

[1] Lord Hawkesbury in a secret letter of instructions to Lord Whitworth wrote: 'If the French Government should enter into any conversation with you on the subject of the Island of Malta, it is of great importance that you should avoid committing his Majesty as to what may be eventually his intentions with respect to that island . . . I recommend you, however, to avoid saying anything which may engage his Majesty to restore the island *even if these arrangements could be completed according to the true intent and spirit of the 10th article of the Treaty of Amiens*' (November 14, 1802). *England and Napoleon in 1803*, being the Despatches of Lord Whitworth, ed. O. Browning (1887), pp. 9–10.

for alliances, and in the end practically the whole continent of Europe was involved in the struggle.

Napoleon, on his side, maintained at once that the obligations of the Peace of Amiens were at an end. He reoccupied Naples; he sent an army of 30,000 men into Holland; he saw too that he could secure in Germany a valuable pledge against England by seizing Hanover, which was under the English King, though not of course incorporated in the English State. Hanover was overrun with 40,000 men, and Napoleon declared that he would keep Hanover as long as Britain kept Malta. He made overtures to Russia and to Prussia for alliance; but in Russia the mad Tsar Paul, with his passionate admiration for France, had been succeeded by Alexander, a man of different temperament and aims, and the French overtures were decidedly refused. There was a tradition of friendship between France and Prussia which had been maintained with some care since the Peace of Basel, but this was too weak to bring Prussia in on the side of France. It was only with Spain that Napoleon had any real success. The existing Government of Spain was one of the most corrupt and inefficient to be found in all Europe. The chief figures were King Charles IV; his Queen, Louisa; and the Minister Godoy, the lover of the Queen, and unquestionably corrupt in his management of the affairs of the kingdom. In March 1801, negotiations between Napoleon and the Spanish Government resulted in the Treaty of Madrid. By this treaty Spain handed over to France Louisiana in America, and promised to make war against Portugal, the age-long ally of Great Britain. Napoleon, on his side, promised to set up a kingdom of Etruria in Italy, and to give it to the Duke of Parma, the son-in-law of Charles IV. In accordance with this treaty Portugal was invaded by Spain, but was not occupied with the thoroughness that Napoleon had desired. After the rupture of the Peace of Amiens, Spain was induced, or in truth forced, to contribute a sum of four million francs a month to the French treasury. Napoleon knew so much about Godoy that he could threaten revelations with regard to his character and practices if he refused to comply with his demands. Spain was, in effect, dragged helplessly at the chariot wheels of France.

On the other side a great coalition soon sprang into being. Pitt emerged from the retirement into which he had gone as the result of his difference with King George III over the Irish union, and, in 1804, he resumed power, eager to strike a blow against France and Napoleon. His knowledge of the diplomacy of Europe was unrivalled, as was also the tenacity with which he struggled against his great enemy. He soon built up a new and powerful coalition against France. First he won over the power of Sweden, which hitherto had not taken an active part in the European wars against France. The King of Sweden was Gustavus IV, who began to rule in 1792. He was a narrow Lutheran in religion and fiercely hated the principles of the French Revolution and Napoleon. Without hesitation he joined the Third Coalition. Russia, too, joined eagerly. The pro-French policy of the Tsar Paul had merely been an accidental interlude, and the general bias of Russia was hostile to French ideas, character, and aims. Nor could Austria remain neutral. France had crossed the path of Austria at many points and had already inflicted upon Austria two humiliating peaces. French influence in Germany was already stronger than her own and Francis marked his sense of the decline of his German position by assuming in 1804 the title of hereditary 'Emperor of Austria'. The creation first of the Republic and then of the Kingdom of Italy was exasperating to the traditions of Austrian statesmanship. It was believed that her finances had been re-established and that the weakness of her army had been remedied. She entered the war once more and brought in with her the Kingdom of Naples, which was always a dependency of Austria.

An important question was the future action of Prussia. She had remained obstinately neutral since the Peace of Basel in 1795. She saw the advances of French power with real alarm, but was bitterly jealous of Austria and refused the overtures that were made to her by the Alliance. She declined also the proposal of Napoleon that she join with him, even though he offered the Kingdom of Hanover to her as the price of that alliance.

So, then, the great Alliance faced France and Spain. The declared objects of the Coalition were to reduce France within her ancient limits, to call a congress to settle the various international questions that had arisen during the war, and to draw up a federal system for the maintenance of the peace in Europe. This last clause may be particularly noticed. It shows us how, even so early during the struggle with Napoleon, the notion of finding some settled basis for European order had come to men's minds. We shall see how it was this idea that produced the Quadruple Alliance and Congress system after the overthrow of Napoleon.

The enemy that Napoleon had to face consisted of, firstly, the overwhelming naval power of Great Britain and, secondly, the apparently vast military strength of Austria and Russia. How was he to attack them? He had beaten his enemies on land before, and he had found that that did not lead to the surrender of Great Britain. She was impregnable behind her seas. But if Great Britain could be beaten down he had every reason to think that such a defeat would have a great and probably a decisive effect upon her military allies. His first idea, then, was to settle the war by a direct blow against Great Britain, and by her invasion and conquest. Napoleon knew little himself of naval matters, and he may on this account have felt some jealousy of the French navy and its commanders. At this juncture, however, he devoted most seriously his genius and capacity for detail to the organisation of a descent upon the coasts of England. A large fleet of flat-bottomed boats was collected at Boulogne. The manœuvre of embarkation was constantly practised, so that when conditions were favourable the armies might be got on board and taken across the Channel in the shortest possible time. It was at first his hope that the crossing might be effected under some favourable conditions of the weather without a previous battle against the British Navy; but the more he studied the problem the clearer it became that success could not possibly attend such a scheme, and that the Channel must be held by a French naval force before the fleet of transports could with any prospect of success be launched upon the waters. There were three French squadrons: one at Toulon, the second at Rochefort, and the third at Brest. Napoleon projected a scheme for decoying away the British fleet from its watch over the Channel by an attack upon the West Indian Islands. His aim here was a double one: if the British West Indian possessions really fell into his hands, that would be a great and most valuable prize; if the British fleet left the Channel in order to protect them, that might give to Napoleon the period of safety which he required for the crossing of the Channel.

The incidents that follow, culminating in the Battle of Trafalgar, form the most famous chapter in the naval history of Great Britain. The genius of Nelson, the efficient organisation of the British fleet, resting on a long tradition and improved under Rodney's influence after the failure in the war against the United States, and the conspicuous absence of these very qualities in the French navy, are sufficient to account for the victory which established the naval supremacy of Great Britain for the rest of the war. Opinions have differed as to the influence of the battle on the course of the struggle of Europe against Napoleon. It did but reaffirm the strength of British naval power which was clear before; it did not materially increase that supremacy. Napoleon had known before that the British fleet was his greatest enemy, and that conviction was deepened. Had the battle not been fought at all the issue of the struggle would probably not have been seriously altered. And if Napoleon had won? He is reported to have said: 'If I can only be master of the sea for six hours England will cease to exist.' But if he really believed this he was certainly in error. The nation was identified with the Government in Britain as it was not elsewhere among the enemies of Napoleon, and there can be no doubt that a fierce national resistance would have followed under conditions favourable to the defence. If the Grand Army had disembarked on the shores of England it would almost certainly have won victories, but Napoleon would have found himself committed to a struggle that would have anticipated the exhausting war in Spain and might have been as fatal as his march on Moscow.

Before the Battle of Trafalgar had been fought Napoleon had

abandoned the enterprise against Britain and was in full march for Germany. The unprecedented victories that awaited him there soon made Trafalgar appear to contemporaries of little importance. Austria and Russia stood determinedly against him. Prussia watched the course of affairs in alternations of hope and fear. If she would have to fight France some time there was no time so favourable as the present, when she would have the alliance of the Tsar and the Emperor. Were the forces of Prussia joined to theirs Napoleon would not dare to undertake his daring march into the heart of Germany. On the other hand, Napoleon would pay highly for Prussian neutrality. Much might be won by dexterous diplomacy. Hanover might be taken from the King of England and attached to Prussia, whose territories it would so valuably increase. Prussia might become the head of North Germany and might even assume the imperial title with the approval of Napoleon himself. The King and Government of Prussia were incapable of clear thought and direct action. The King—so it was said—'hoped to deceive all the world and yet remain an honest man.' So nothing was done when to do nothing was fatal. But though Napoleon failed to win over Prussia he secured the alliance of Württemberg and Bavaria. Frederick II, the Elector of Württemberg, could not in any case resist Napoleon, and might get from him an increase of territory that he desired. An alliance was made, and Napoleon was received with all honour on his arrival. Bavaria had already been cajoled or forced into the same alliance. The Elector Maximilian Joseph had a real admiration for French ideas and for the great ruler of France. His state was already, to some extent, reorganised on a French model. He could not resist France, and Napoleon would not listen to his plea that he should be allowed to remain neutral. The Elector of Baden was drawn over to the same side. So Napoleon entered upon his campaign in Germany with considerable German support.

The victories that he won in 1805 and 1806 are the most amazing of his career. Three great military states were overthrown one after the other— Austria, Russia, Prussia. A new Charlemagne, or even a new Julius Cæsar, seemed to have arisen, and some thought that the future had in store for Europe some new and enduring organisation. Only a few thinkers and patriots could believe that the storm would pass as quickly as it had come, and that for better or worse the old features of European life would reappear. But at the distance of nearly two centuries we can see that what happened was not miraculous. A general of genius with the best equipped army in the world attacked troops that still followed an old routine. A government, that had sprung from a popular rising and which still identified itself to a very large extent with the interests and aspirations of the people, came into conflict with governments of the old type: governments that were machines rather than organisms, which were in no vital connection with the people, which in consequence inspired little enthusiasm or self-sacrifice.

So the armies of Napoleon marched from victory to victory. The Austrian general, Mack, was in Ulm with a considerable Austrian force. He had spoken confidently of the victories that he was going to win, but he was alarmed by the size of the armies which marched with unexampled rapidity from Boulogne to the Danube. He tried to withdraw when it was too late, but found himself surrounded, and surrendered with a force of about 33,000 men. There was much worse to follow. Vienna was abandoned without a struggle. The Tsar Alexander and the Emperor Francis joined their forces near Austerlitz, to the north of Vienna. There, on December 2, 1805, was fought the Battle of Austerlitz—'the battle of the three Emperors,' as it is sometimes called. The armies of Austria and Russia were hopelessly broken. The Austrian armies could not be re-formed again; the Russian army withdrew to the north-east and had still some heavy fighting before it. For the moment Napoleon the soldier had done his task; but there was much for the diplomatist to accomplish.

Germany lay in his hands, though there were strange and ominous movements reported from Berlin, to which we shall come in a moment. What did Napoleon intend to do with Germany and Central Europe? He had already given hints of great changes that he intended to introduce. In a proclamation, when he crossed the Rhine, he had said: 'We will not stop until we have secured the independence of the German Empire.' And to the Elector of Württemberg he had said: 'The House of Austria does not disguise its intention of getting hold of the Germanic body and destroying all the sovereign houses.' He would endeavour, therefore, to give to his action in Germany the appearance of a war of liberation and pose as the protector of Germany against Austria. Some hoped even that he would give new vigour to the old machinery of the Holy Roman Empire. But Napoleon was still at heart a revolutionary. He determined to do away with it: to rationalise and to modernise.

It is important to understand the process whereby the destruction of the Holy Roman Empire was completed and Germany lost her mediaeval character; for it is the beginning of the movement which was to lead her to unity and to power in the second half of the nineteenth century. We have seen in the introduction how the Empire stood for an ideal of justice. Whatever government was like in practice, it had afforded protection on an equal footing to the rights of free cities, even of free villages, of the imperial knights and counts, of rulers of large states like Prussia, Saxony or Bavaria. We have seen how the Treaties of Basel, Campo Formio and Lunéville resulted in Germany's spoliation. She lost one-seventh of her population and important cities such as Aachen, Cologne, Trier and Mainz, when the left bank of the Rhine was annexed to France. The process of secularisation and mediatisation, heralded by the Congress of Rastatt and implemented after the Congress of Regensburg, produced a smaller number of large, consolidated lay states instead of the old mosaic of principalittes, bishoprics, cities and knights' domains on the right bank of the Rhine. The old number of some three hundred states had been more than halved. In the war of 1804–06 all the German states were either neutral or on the side of France. The peace of north Germany was assured when Prussia obtained from both Russia and Napoleon promises to enforce or to respect its neutrality. In the south the newly consolidated states, Baden, Württemberg and Bavaria, but not at first Hesse Darmstadt, put armies in the field on the side of France.Thus when on December 26, 1805, Napoleon signed the Peace of Pressburg with Austria he inserted provisions for their further aggrandisement, mostly at the expense of Austria, and in addition declared that the title of King had been assumed by the rulers of Württemberg and Bavaria. These rulers were recognised as independent sovereigns. They passed, that is to say, out of the Emperor's allegiance. The dismantling of the Holy Roman Empire continued between 1805 and 1806. The imperial knights and counts lost their status. They were recognised as noblemen and landowners, but they became now also citizens and subjects of the small states where their lands lay. This is the so-called Knights' Revolution, initiated by Article xiv of the Treaty of Pressburg and not completed until 1810. Next Napoleon signed the Treaty of the Confederation of the Rhine on July 17, 1806, with the rulers of Baden, Württemberg, Bavaria, Hesse Darmstadt, Nassau, the former ruler of Mainz (the so-called Arch-chancellor of the Empire) and ten other princes on the right bank of the Rhine or in south Germany; the King of Saxony acceded; the Arch-chancellor's lands were reorganised as the Duchy of Frankfurt: a second new state, the Duchy of Berg, was created and it too acceded; the number of free cities dropped to three. To the three Kings were now added two Grand Dukes, the titles adopted by the rulers of Baden and Hesse Darmstadt. The old constitutional machinery of the Holy Roman Empire was swept away and in its stead was the Confederation of the Rhine, consisting first of sixteen states and then as Saxony, Berg and others were admitted, enlarged. It was headed by the Duke of Frankfurt with a title of Prince Primate and it was supposed to have a Diet. In reality it was a mere military alliance between its members and Napoleon. By Article xii he took the title of Protector of the Confederation. Its members were bound to supply large contingents and large subsidies to him. On August 6, 1806. Francis dissolved the Holy Roman Empire by proclamation.

The rulers of the states of the Confederation of the Rhine were under pressure from Napoleon so that they could supply the soldiers and subsidies due from them; under pressure from the landowners and nobility to reform their constitutions; under pressure from progressive officials and the articulate classes to summon elective parliaments, to make taxation universal, to abolish serfdom and to grant civil liberties. It was thus that Max Joseph of Bavaria, King since 1805, aided by an able Minister, Maximilian von Montgelas, published a constitution for Bavaria in 1808, establishing a single-Chamber legislature. He also introduced universal liability to taxation and military service, reformed and centralised administration and established a variety of civil liberties, abolished serfdom and a number of antiquated restrictions on trade and industry. The rulers of Baden, Württemberg and Hesse Darmstadt similarly consolidated their states into modern territorial units, though not yet with representative institutions, got rid of exemptions and immunities, streamlined administration and made other reforms which contributed to social cohesion.

Western Germany had accepted the French supremacy; Austria had submitted and by the Treaty of Pressburg lost not only German territory but the recently acquired Venetian lands which now went to the kingdom of Italy. She could not for the present make any resistance. There remained Prussia—Prussia, which under Frederick the Great had so humiliated France; Prussia, which despite the alien elements in its population had come to be regarded by many—even by Goethe—as the special representative of German nationalism. What would Prussia say to this new organisation of Germany?

Prussia was too much divided to speak with a decisive voice. The young King was pulled hither and thither by the parties at his Court. On the one side were the 'patriots,' who saw in France the great enemy of Germany and desired to draw the sword to save Prussia and Germany; to this party belonged the Queen, Louise, 'the good angel of the good cause,' Hardenberg the Foreign Minister, and Blücher the soldier. But the King himself inclined to seek safety in the friendship of France, and found support from many of his Ministers. It must be remembered that Berlin and Paris were by no means then in that decided antagonism that grew up in the nineteenth century. There was between them a tradition of mutual help and admiration. But the march of Napoleon into Germany and violation of the Prussian territories of Anspach and Bayreuth during that march gave the victory to the war party. The Tsar Alexander visited Berlin. He had a solemn interview with the young Prussian King, Frederick William III, at the grave of Frederick the Great. War against Napoleon was determined on; Haugwitz was sent to the French camp with an ultimatum. But the Battle of Austerlitz was fought before the ultimatum was presented; and Prussia in a sudden panic—justified by the situation—sought not war but peace, even at the price of humiliation. Napoleon quite understood the position at Berlin; but he was ready to make concessions to Prussia which were indeed the deepest of humiliations. Hanover was the key of Prussian diplomacy. The Prussian King had promised Britain to respect the independence and the British connection of Hanover. But now Napoleon offered the bait: Prussia might have not only peace but Hanover as well; and Prussia swallowed the bait. Fox denounced the policy of Prussia as combining 'everything that is comtemptible in servility with everthing that is odious in rapacity.' She had betrayed Germany, but she hoped she had enlarged her boundaries.

Prussia, however, did not receive the price of her shame. The possession of Hanover was by no means assured. It was known that Napoleon was making a tentative offer to restore the country to Britain. Then, too, the King of Prussia had formerly received from France the suggestion that he should form a Confederation of North Germany and rule over it with the title of Emperor; but now Napoleon showed no inclination to allow that splendid vision to materialise. And while the gains of Prussia were doubtful, the losses were painful and certain. Napoleon's general, Murat, had been made Duke of Berg and given a place in the Confederation of the Rhine; he was claiming, as part of his dominions, Essen and Werden and Elten, which were undoubtedly Prussian territory. And meanwhile the patriotic war fever was growing in the army and the country. The army chiefs were confident of victory. Prussia looked round for allies and got promises of help from Russia, which had not been crushed to extinction by Austerlitz, and from her neighbour Saxony. Then an ultimatum demanded that the French troops should be withdrawn west of the Rhine. That could only mean war.

The decision came with amazing suddenness and completeness. On October 14, 1806, the prestige of the Prussian armies was destroyed on the heights of Jena and at Auerstädt, a few miles to the north. No Austrian army had collapsed before Napoleon so completely as these once invincible Prussians. And the battle was clearly no accident; for blow followed upon blow, and Prussia made no further effective resistance. The French entered Berlin, captured fortresses and towns with amazing ease, and at last forced even Blücher to surrender near Lübeck. The King of Prussia had joined the Russian army in the north-east, and the Russians showed something of their old stubborn powers of resistance. At Eylau, in February 1807, they fought against Napoleon a battle that was no real French victory, but, in June 1807, Napoleon struck again at Friedland, and this time he made no mistake. The Russian army could struggle no more after this battle. The Emperor of the French stood at the very height of his power.

We shall examine in the next chapter the new Europe that was rising up under the ruins of the old, and the new economic form which was taken by the Emperor's struggle against Great Britain. That struggle had already begun, and Napoleon was anxious for the support of all Europe in his effort to overthrow by indirect means the Power whose navy he had failed to cope with. He found the Tsar of Russia unexpectedly ready to co-operate with him. The Tsar had already much of the instability which was to characterise him in later years, and he had his own grievances against the Government of Great Britain. Since the Battle of Jena he had had to bear the chief brunt of the war; he had asked for the guarantee of a loan of six millions from Great Britain, but this had been refused in language that was likely to hurt Russian susceptibilities. He had urged the British Government to make diversions in his favour so as to draw off some part of the French forces; but nothing of importance had been done. The irritation against Great Britain in Alexander's mind boiled up into fierce hatred. He made an armistice with France, held his famous interview with Napoleon in a pavilion built on a raft in the middle of the river Niemen, and established the bases of a peace. Its terms, which concerned Prussia as well as Russia, were subsequently agreed on in a series of meetings held between the Russian, French, and Prussian representatives in the town of Tilsit; but the part played by the Prussians was humiliating in the extreme. Napoleon seemed to delight in insulting the King and Queen of Prussia. The fate of the country was settled by the Russian and French Emperors.

The terms that concerned Prussia were declared in the treaty to be due to the desire of the French Emperor to establish friendship with Russia on unshakeable foundations. He implies, therefore, that but for the Tsar's mediation the terms would have been even harder. Confiscated Prussian provinces with Hesse Cassel were to form a new kingdom, to be called the Kingdom of Westphalia, which was to be given to Napoleon's brother Jerome. The greater part of the Prussian territories of Poland was to form a duchy of Warsaw and to be given to the King of Saxony; there were many who hoped that this might be the beginning of the restoration of an independent Poland. Prussia lost nearly half her territory, and her population was reduced from ten to five millions.

Russia had no such humiliations to suffer. On the contrary, her territories were increased by Finland and a part of the Polish possessions of Prussia. She was, of course, forced to recognise all the regulations which Napoleon had made for Central Europe. There were secret articles as well as the published ones.[1] It was agreed that Great Britain should be summoned to make peace and to renounce her claims to maritime supremacy; and that, if she refused, Russia and France should make common war against her, and should force Denmark and Sweden and Portugal to close their ports against Brit-

---

[1] The full text of the secret articles was not published until 1890. It is to be found in A. Vandal *Napoléon et Alexandre I*. Vol. I. *De Tilsit à Erfurt* (1891), pp. 499–507.

ish merchandise and join in the war against her. Something of the nature of these secret articles was known with extraordinary rapidity in London, and the channel of their revelation is still an unsolved problem. Were there British spies who learned something from high-placed Russians? Or was it Talleyrand who, anxious to make friends with the enemy in case of Napoleon's fall, revealed them to the British Minister, Canning? The British Government acted on the information, however it came. Demark was summoned to surrender her navy and on her refusal was forced to do so by a naval and military attack on Copenhagen.

The territories of Napoleon received considerable additions after this date. They reached their maximum in the year 1811. But 1807 marks the zenith of his power. Had he died in that year his career would have seemed the most miraculous in the military annals of Europe and perhaps of the world. He had succeeded in every task, overthrown every enemy. He had rearranged Europe according to his liking. He had no military rival, and he was in apparent close and friendly alliance with the Tsar of Russia. The French Revolution was left far behind now. It was not France but Napoleon who commanded in Europe. And he had carried with him his family to wealth and fame and power. His mother, once the simple housewife of Ajaccio, was installed as the Empress-Mother in Paris. His eldest brother, Joseph, had just been made King of Naples—from which Ferdinand had been driven in 1806—and then later he ascended the great historic throne of Spain. His third brother, Louis, was made King of Holland, which had hitherto been treated as an independent republic. Another brother, Jerome, as we have seen, was King of Westphalia. His sister Caroline had married Murat, who was now Duke of Berg, and who would by and by, when Joseph moved to Spain, become King of Naples. Pitt, Napoleon's most determined and most capable enemy, was dead. He seemed a god to kill and to make alive.

Chapter 6

THE RISE OF THE NEW EUROPE

For ten years the personality of Napoleon dominated the life and thoughts of Europe as they had never before been dominated by one man. For any parallel we should have to go back to the careers of Julius Caesar or of Charlemagne, and they can not, for obvious reasons, have exercised the same universal influence that Napoleon did. From 1795 to 1807 it is difficult to take sufficient notice of the internal affairs of other countries. But after 1807 the condition of Europe changes. Napoleon is still the central figure in the drama, and will remain so until his public life is done; but his armies and his policy no longer monopolise attention. A little below the surface we can see other forces rising up which make even his greatest victories fruitless. The ultimate catastrophe seems already in sight.

Could he have closed his military career at Tilsit? Could he have given to the Europe, that he had made, a permanent settlement and a peaceful development? Napoleon might have been glad to accept a condition of peace if it gave him a secure position of power at home and in Europe; but, as we have seen, and as he knew, peace was dangerous to his position in France. The Governments of Europe whom he had beaten had by no means given up any idea of another round in which they would win; for they had acquired from France new standards of streamlined administration, military recruitment and effective and universal taxation which they could apply. They were also learning from the French example what individual initiative and individual patriotism could do. They would turn all these lessons against her. There was one Power, moreover, that had not been beaten: Great Britain. Fox, a strong critic of war with revolutionary France and Napoleon, had succeeded Pitt, but his effort to establish peace had failed. He too continued the war as did his Tory successors after his death, with the support of the vast majority of the nation.

The struggle with Great Britain had taken a new character which profoundly modified the course of European affairs until Napoleon fell. The Committee of Public Safety had already, in 1793, had recourse to economic warfare. Napoleon now adopted it with some drama; for he declared it from Berlin in November 1806. No rhetoric could give such emphasis to the position of Napoleon as the fact that he sent out his decrees from the conquered capital of Federick the Great. The British Isles were declared to be in a state of blockade, and all commerce was prohibited between them and the lands over which Napoleon had power or influence. The result, however, since Napoleon without naval predominance could not enforce the blockade, was to check British exports but to leave her imports much as they were. It has been called 'a boycott not a blockade.' The British Government answered by the Orders in Council of January and November 1807 requiring neutral ships to be furnished with a licence in a British port. If Great Britain could not trade with Europe neither should the neutral States. The French lands were placed under blockade and Britain with her navy could cut off trade more effectively than France. Napoleon held to his new policy as a certain means of ruining Britain. All nations which came under his influence were forced to adopt it. The desire to extend it was the cause of other wars. In November and December 1807, after Tilsit, by the Decrees of Milan he reaffirmed and strengthened his declarations against all commerce between Europe and Great Britain.

Unquestionably Great Britain suffered from the so-called Continental System. There was much unemployment, many bankruptcies and economic setbacks to individuals from the commercial dislocation. But British goods did not altogether cease to reach European markets. Moreover, in the years 1803–05 only 33 per cent of British exports had been sent to Europe. The rest of the world, which took the remaining 67 per cent, was still open to her. And in production the new machines and new industrial methods gave her great advantages. Britain suffered, but only to the point where suffering hardened her determination to struggle on.

The inhabitants of France itself were in many ways prosperous during these years. The conquests of Napoleon opened up to their trade new and wide districts. The results of the social legislation of the Revolution were seen and felt in the flourishing condition of agriculture. When France began to suffer from the failure of the colonial products, which had been stopped by the policy of Britain, French science, supported and directed by the State, was able partly to provide a remedy. The price of sugar reached a prohibitive figure, but then the manufacture of beet sugar was developed and improved and became a lasting source of French wealth. Indigo was made, or a substitute for it. There were indeed some trades that found no such relief; but the worst results of Napoleon's Continental System were not to be found in France but Holland and the German states which had fallen under French control. This was all the more apparent when Napoleon placed on all colonial products a high tariff, amounting usually to about half their value.

Holland, which was ruled by Napoleon's brother Louis as king, found her whole commercial life overthrown by the new arrangements. She complained and protested, but in vain. King Louis sympathised with his people and was doubtful of his brother's success, and in the end he abdicated his uneasy throne. His abdication won no relief for the country. Holland was formally annexed to the French Empire in July 1810. Similar motives produced the annexation of the north-west coast of Germany in December of the same year. This violent act was officially justified, on the ground that British commerce would 'continue to flow into the Continent—if the mouths of the Weser and Elbe were not closed against it for ever.' If there had ever been any chance that Central Europe would be reconciled to the dominion of Napoleon, it was destroyed by the Continental System. The rule of France had brought welcome social freedom and the humane provisions of the Civil Code, but for most of the population these advantages were quite outweighed by the high prices and semi-starvation which were produced by the economic war against Britain.

Let us turn to Germany and to Prussia and see what shape was taken by the forces that fermented there. The overthrow of Prussia was amazing, but not so remarkable as her recovery, which is among the heroic things of history, to be classed with the triumph of the Romans after Cannae, and of the French after Agincourt. The catastrophe of Jena did not at all mark a crumbling and decadent State. The causes of the catastrophe are plain. Prussia's initial mistake was to adopt a policy of neutrality without strengthening her army. During the campaign her generalship was at fault and there were many tactical errors in the battles themselves. But the whole army was rotten: with its regiments recruited abroad; with its brutal code of discipline, its universal obligation to serve riddled with exemptions, so that it fell on those who did serve, serf-peasants and craftsmen, as an intolerable burden; with its noblemen officers, young and inexperienced, or peacetime soldiers arrogant and prejudiced, or elderly with experience dating from the Seven Years' War. The deepest cause of Prussia's fall was the disorganised state of her government. There was no cohesion among the King's advisers, the members of the so-called General Directory. Moreover, the King preserved Frederick the Great's two habits of recourse to confidential secretaries as his chief advisers (his so-called *Kabinett*) and of dealing with each Province separately. To these faults we must add an enormous formality and rigidity and the young King's inability to provide energetic and purposeful direction.

It is the glory of Prussia that there were men in office who saw that radical change was necessary and were strong enough to make it. The purpose of all the changes was to bring the state and the people into organic relation and to give to the people a real interest in the success of the government. The ideal was by no means fully realised but enough was done to give a new cohesion to the Prussian state. The military reforms may be taken first. These were the work of three remarkable men: Scharnhorst, the organiser, Gneisenau, the soldier-idealist, and Clausewitz, the great theorist of military tactics. These men took advantage of Napoleon's having laid it down that the Prussian army must not exceed 42,000 men to make universal military conscription a reality from which there were no exemptions, and a pride rather than a burden. Men served for a short term in what became now a highly trained professional army and being quickly passed through its ranks became the source, by service in a *Landwehr* or militia, of a large reserve vastly in excess of 42,000 men, ready for action when the time came. An humane code of discipline; the opening of officers' commissions to the sons of burghers; the end of foreign recruitment; the reform of the supply system to eradicate jobbery: these were the chief other means of introducing a new professional pride in the army.

The political and social reorganisation of Prussia was more important. This was the work of vom Stein—one of the dispossessed imperial knights—and embodied in three great measures, the Emancipation Edict of October 9, 1807, the reorganisation of the government completed by the scheme of December 1808, the Edict for Local Institutions and the Town Edict, both also dated December 1808. The plan ascribed to him for some sort of central representative institution was not embodied in legislation before, under Napoleon's pressure, he was dismissed on November 24, 1808. But much had been done to make Prussia a more open society. The Emancipation Edict, in the first place, swept away at one stroke the rigid social hierarchy consolidated by Frederick the Great. It abolished all prohibitions upon burghers buying land, noblemen engaging in trade or peasants buying land traditionally cultivated by noblemen. Secondly, it abolished the legal status of serf. It did not create peasant proprietors or a race of tenant farmers since labour services remained, but they could be commuted for rent. It laid the foundations, therefore, for this change. Thirdly, there were important provisions to safeguard the peasants in their holdings against the consolidating ambitions of landowners. The reorganisation of government did away with the practice—it was to reappear later in the century—of *Kabinett* government; set up ministries of a modern kind for foreign affairs, war, finance, justice and internal affairs; provided for greater solidarity among the Ministers than existed among the advisers of the Crown when they had simply been members of the General Directory, by setting up a new institution, the Council of Ministers. It survived until 1918. Above the Council of Ministers was a larger body, the Council of State, which in the end only met occasionally and proved less important. The Edict for Local Government retained the old Provinces in the countryside, but did away with the so-called Chambers of War and Domains, replacing them by Boards, or committees, of officials each at the head of new and subordinate administrative units, the Governments (*Regierungen*). The Town Edict introduced representative government into the towns by means of elective town councils which varied in size according to the size of the population of the town. All citizens, as distinct from residents, were obliged to serve, if called upon, either in paid offices or as members of the Town Councils. Towns lost their variety of special privileges and individual organisations, but were more nearly self-governing communities. Another Minister, Hardenberg, was important for his skill in spreading taxation and in increasing its yield, but he was also responsible for diminishing the effectiveness of some of the safeguards against peasant eviction that had been important to Stein. Queen Louise, the wife of Frederick William III, intelligent and beautiful, came to be the symbol of Prussian, even German, resistance to the French.

These changes in organisation would not have availed much had they not been supported by a corresponding intellectual movement. This was the flowering period of German literature and philosophy. There was a large reading public and a large writing profession, so that it is not surprising that as great a contribution to the development of Germany's sense of nationhood was made by the political theorists as by the resentment of those who experienced French exactions, depredations and the consequences of the Continental System. Kant was as important in Germany as Rousseau was in France. Herder, Humboldt, Fichte and Hegel all made contributions to a vivid intellectual life that laid the foundations for the structure of liberalism and nationalism built after the fall of Napoleon. Herder had soberly assessed the French Revolution and called upon Germans to remember their own traditions of self-government rather than blindly to imitate the French Constitution. Kant had held out the ideal of a 'republican constitution', by which he meant a monarchical form of government but one where the monarch identified himself with the people and executed its will and where the law was supreme over both the king and his subjects. Wilhelm von Humboldt was the founder of German liberalism in that he rejected the paternalist, all-powerful autocracies of the eighteenth century and formulated a system which would give all possible opportunites for the individual's moral, religious, artistic and political development by restricting to the utmost the activity of the state. It was appropriate that he should be associated with the founding of the University of Berlin in 1810. Hegel, the philosopher of the all-powerful state, was chiefly important after this period. It was J. G. Fichte who was most important in this period in reviving Germany's national pride. During the winter of 1807–08 he delivered in Berlin a series of lectures, afterwards published as *Addresses to the German Nation*, in which he teased and flattered his audience into faith in the great cultural and moral qualities of the German nation. His lectures reached a wide public and for those whom they did not reach there were the patriotic songs of Ernst Moritz Arndt or the activities of Ludwig Jahn.

One other and most characteristic feature of Prussian reorganisation must be noted. The importance of education for the strength and even for the military strength of the State was a Prussian belief before it was accepted elsewhere in Europe. The chief stages in the advance of her power have been marked by the founding of Universities. Now, when, in the hour of her deepest humiliation, she was daring to hope for liberation and victory, as we have already seen, the University of Berlin was founded. Halle had hiterto been the chief University for the old Brandenburg lands, but Halle was now under Napoleonic influence, and its sessions had been for a time suspended. The new University attracted from the first men of outstanding distinction, and it was soon housed in a palace and received an adequate income from the State. It was of great importance in the nineteenth century.

Prussia would clearly have to be reckoned with. Napoleon had at first approved of Stein's appointment to the Prussian service, and apparently believed Prussia to be incapable of recovery. Later he realised the meaning and the danger of the movement in Prussia, and insisted on the dismissal of Stein and the confiscation of his property. Stein passed into the service of the Tsar and continued to work against Napoleon.

Long before Prussia was prepared to re-enter the war, Napoleon had to draw his sword against other and weaker Powers—against Spain and against Austria. And in these wars there is a quality which separates them from the earlier wars that the French Republic and Napoleon had waged. Napoleon has to fight now not merely against governments and official armies. The peoples themselves take a spontaneous part in them. There were signs of popular resistance all over Germany in 1809. Indeed, from 1808 onwards patriots spun a web of secret communications over a great part of north Germany. The first martyr in the movement of feeling against the French had been the bookseller, Johann Philipp Palm who in 1806 was shot as the alleged author of a pamphlet, *Germany in her deep Humiliation*, against the French. In 1809 there were no fewer than five attempts to overthrow the Kingdom of Wesphalia. Katt, Dörnberg and Schill are the best known among those patriots who waged individual wars against the French. A general insurrection was not yet possible. Most potential leaders looked to Austria for direction, not as yet to Prussia. But here there had been formed the *Tugendbund* or League of Virtue, which gained widespread adherence among those who saw hope for Germany in a moral revival. They were mostly landowners and notabilities in north Germany. It was not until 1813 that the armies of Napoleon in Germany were really to experience the dangers of moving about the countryside through a hostile population ready spontaneously to commit individual acts of war. In the valleys of Spain and the mountains of the Tyrol, however, they encountered already in 1809–10 a popular resistance that strained their powers to the utmost.

The war with Spain is in every way most notable and interesting. That France should receive there her first decisive check on land was quite beyond the bounds of probability. The corruption of her court, the slackness of her government and the absence of military valour in her armies meant that few were aware of the reserves of strength in the nation. We have seen the varying relations of Spain to France since the outbreak of the Revolution. After her withdrawal from the war against France in 1795, she had been drawn more and more into the orbit of France. After the rupture of the Peace of Amiens she had provided France with financial assistance, and had sent ships to the Battle of Trafalgar. We have already noticed the incapacity of the Bourbon King Charles IV (1788–1808) and the importance of his Minister Godoy, the paramour of the Queen. The hostility of the heir to the throne, Ferdinand, the Prince of Asturias, to this group sufficed to make him a kind of popular hero. A rallying-point to all the dissatisfaction with the Government was provided by Ferdinand, but there were not many overt signs of it. The reforming spirits in the public administration of Charles III's reign had been superseded; the ministerial system had broken up; court factions had become important and a favourite ruled. The strongest conscious sentiment of the people was probably its devotion to the Church, and from the Church it derived much of its strength and cohesion in the great struggle which was soon to break out. The Spanish Church was democratic, but its resources were ill-distributed and the Inquisition, 'an ineffective irritant', stood in the way of easy access to foreign books and new ideas. Yet there was a small but important section of the people interested in economic progress and ready to work for the parliamentary government and equality before the law now enjoyed by France.[1]

Napoleon believed that Spain would offer no greater resistance than Italy had done. 'I shall write upon my banner the words *Liberty, Freedom from Superstition, the Destruction of the Nobility*, and I shall be received as I was in Italy, and all the classes that have national spirit will be on my side.' So Napoleon believed, and much in the government of Spain favoured this view. The explanation of Napo-

---

[1] R. Carr, *Spain, 1808–1939* (1966), pp. 60–78, conveniently sums up the effects of the Spanish Enlightenment.

leon's failure and bitter disappointment in Spain is that he had confused the Government with the nation. He did not take into account the strong national cohesion of Spain. In spite of the robust local feeling in the provinces Spain was united and she was intensely proud. Spaniards would not submit to foreign rule.

Napoleon had every reason to despise the policy of the Spanish Government. The royal family could hardly have served Napoleon better if it had been their conscious object to betray Spain into the hands of France. As early as 1807 Prince Ferdinand had appealed to Napoleon to grant him his paternal protection and to open the eyes of 'my good and dearly loved parents.' The King and Queen, hearing of the appeal, had themselves requested the help of Napoleon to settle their family troubles. He felt that he held them in the hollow of his hand, and already dreamed of annexing the country. He forced Spain into a war against Portugal, the aim of which was to deprive the British of harbours, by means of which, in spite of the Berlin Decrees, their goods gained access to the markets of Europe. The campaign was successful, and allowed Napoleon to introduce considerable bodies of French troops into the country, under the pretext of supporting the war against Portugal. The Spaniards were already provoked into anti-French feeling but he did not see it; for the anger of the crowd was directed against Godoy. The King, frightened by the attitude of the people, signed a paper abdicating the throne in favour of Ferdinand, who was acclaimed by the whole country as the man who should regenerate and free Spain. But Charles, in a letter to the all-powerful Emperor of the French, repudiated his act of abdication and declared that it had been extorted from him by threats. Napoleon saw his opportunity and used it to the full. He induced Ferdinand to come to him at Bayonne by trickery and by force. Then the King and Queen and Godoy came thither too. Napoleon refused to recognise Ferdinand as king, and threatened him with prosecution for high treason. Charles signed a treaty whereby he resigned all his rights to the throne of Spain to the Emperor of the French. Napoleon could claim that he had thus come legitimately into possession of the throne of Spain. Napoleon was in the position of Louis XIV in 1700. Spain was in the power of France. 'The Pyrenees existed no longer.'

In fact Napoleon had committed his greatest blunder. He was met by the spontaneous resistance of the nation gathered in force behind its Church and the authorities of Provinces and cities. The little province of Asturias, with its half-million of inhabitants, declared formal war against him. It could not be subdued among its mountains and arid roadless plains. Great Britain at once promised assistance and was quick to send it. Napoleon had no idea of the severity of the task that awaited him. 'If I thought it would cost me 80,000 men I would not attempt it, but it will not cost more than 12,000,' he said. It cost him half a million men and perhaps his crown!

It is plain from the course of this war how completely Napoleon and his enemies had changed their weapons and the causes for which they fought. He had struck into Italy in 1796 in the name of liberty; he had offered freedom from Austria and from despotism; he had commanded a national army against armies of the old and really mercenary stamp. But it was Spain now that appealed to liberty and it was from Spain that the next most notable experiments in constitution-making came.

Napoleon showed that he regarded the deposition of the royal family as irrevocable by calling his brother Joseph from the throne of Naples and making him King of Spain. It was despotism establishing despotism, and the constitutional arrangements which he promised were never brought into action. The resistance of Spain, on the other hand, was at first carried on by local committees (*juntas*). From these in 1808 a central and supreme committee was formed. In 1810 the Cortes—the Parliament of Spain—were convoked under popular pressure, with a complete and liberal electoral system, at Cadiz. They formed themselves into a Constituent Assembly and drew up a form of government after the pattern of the first constitution of the French Revolution. The sovereignty of the people, and the liberty of the individual and of the press, were declared. Torture was suppressed; the finances were reformed. The legislative power was placed in the hands of the Cortes, which were to consist— and in this they went back to the French example of 1791—of a single chamber elected by a complicated method, which was, however, founded on manhood suffrage. The executive was in the hands of a monarchy hereditary in the family of the still beloved Ferdinand. This constitution of 1812 became the watchword of the Liberals of the next generation. There was no other constitution in Europe which declared honestly for manhood suffrage and a single chamber. On one point only—and that a most characteristic one—was the constitution of 1812 behind the general demands of Europe: the Catholic faith was declared to be the only true one, and to be the permanent religion of Spain. No other form of worship was to be allowed in the country.

The sword had to decide between the opposing policies. Great Britain gave her help from the first; but, before Wellington had begun his career of stubborn resistance which led to so complete a victory, the Spaniards unaided had inflicted on Napoleon's armies their first serious defeat. This was the famous Battle of Baylen, July 1808. The French General, Dupont, capitulated with his force of 20,000 men. Europe rang with the wonderful news that a General of Napoleon had laid down his arms before an army of the despised Spaniards. The situation was so dangerous that Napoleon came and took over the command himself. He re-established the prestige of the French arms. Madrid was reoccupied. Joseph, who had fled after the Battle of Baylen, was replaced on the throne, and gained the nominal allegiance of the capital. Sir John Moore and the British army had advanced into the neighbourhood, but turned towards the coast when the presence of Napoleon was known, and with difficulty escaped to Corunna. If Napoleon could have stayed in Spain with the bulk of his army all might have gone well; but his vast Empire demanded his attention, and events on the Danube soon drained away a large part of his forces.

With smaller forces Napoleon's Generals—the chief were Soult and Ney—found the task a terrible one. 'It is a country,' said King Joseph, 'like no other; we can find in it neither a spy nor a courier to carry messages'; and Marbot's *Memoirs* show at what risk detachments of the French army lived among a savagely hostile population. The Spaniards showed little inclination for the more formal operations of war, and their unpunctuality and the looseness of their organisation strained Wellington's temper at times to breaking-point. But they carried on irregular warfare with wonderful persistence and skill, and showed extraordinary endurance and fury in defence of their towns. The Siege of Saragossa is among the most heroic acts in the annals of Europe. The place seemed hardly defensible, but it was defended against the French armies by the citizens and soldiers, who held them at bay from June to August, when it was relieved. 'Flinty and indomitable,' Spain had often—from Roman times onwards—shown herself well adapted for irregular warfare. The help of the British was of the utmost possible value; the brunt of the more formal military operations fell upon them. But the resistance made by the Spanish themselves was greater than is sometimes recognised. Spain never showed, even in moments of depression or defeat, the least inclination to accept the Napoleonic system or Joseph as king. The Spanish War has been well called the cancer that drained away the strength of Napoleon. And the European situation demanded all his attention, and soon all his strength.

After the beginning of the Peninsular War in 1808 the futility of Napoleon's position became plain: every victory seemed to add to his difficulties and brought with it the occasion of another war. But at first two main ideas dominated his policy: war *à outrance* against Great Britain and an intimate alliance with Russia. The two were closely associated in his mind; for he believed the alliance with Russia might indirectly give him the victory over Britain. Russia, therefore, had priority and he arranged a conference with Tsar Alexander at Erfurt (September 27–October 14, 1808). It was the spectacular zenith of his career. France made parade there, not only of her military strength, but also of her scientific, literary, artistic and theatrical achievements. It was also an occasion of impressive homage to the French Emperor from the German princes and from some of Germany's intellectual leaders. Napoleon and Alexander found time to visit Goethe at Weimar and both he and Wieland were decorated with the Legion of Honour. But more serious business went less well. Alexander showed some response to Napoleon's talk of a joint attack upon Turkey and a partition of the Sultan's dominions. He showed no inclination for combined action against possible movements of resistance in Germany or on the part of Prussia and Austria. When the conference broke up relations cooled and a note of irritation and suspicion began to creep into Napoleon's correspondence with the Tsar. Moreover, at Erfurt Talleyrand had begun to give Napoleon ground to suspect treachery. He learnt enough of his relations with the Tsar to exclude him from his confidential service. Talleyrand was dismissed from the Foreign Office. But Napoleon also nourished suspicions against Fouché, his great Chief of Police. Even the Marshals, loaded with benefits at his hand, were ready to desert. Napoleon was beginning to lose his sureness of touch, for the forces that were entering the arena, forces of opinion and economic interest, were not to be measured with the mathematical exactness that was his most familiar tool. He had no longer 'the sense of the possible.'

Austria had by now undergone revival, not in her case a revival that struck deep into society, but a renewal of vigour in the Government and a patriotic movement among the aristocracy. Archduke Charles was the principal source of reform. He caused the establishment of a Council of Ministers to co-ordinate the work of the Chancery and the War Department; he was able to induce Hungary to increase its contribution to the army. Above all he gained the dismissal of old men and brought forward Count Philipp von Stadion. He gradually established his control; gave Austria drive and power. Wholly German by birth, education and outlook, he stimulated the growing anti-French feeling among the aristocracy and fitted Austria, deprived now of her Italian dominions, to give the lead expected of her to growing German resistance.

Napoleon anticipated the action of Austria by declaring war. He spoke of the coming struggle as of little importance, and of Austria and her armies with contempt. 'I will box her ears, and then she will thank me and ask what orders I have to give.' But his efforts to draw the Tsar into a hearty co-operation failed. The Tsar could not refuse to abide by the promise which he had given at Erfurt, but he let the Austrian leaders know that he would strike no hard blow.

The despised armies of Austria put up a resistance desperate beyond anything that Napoleon had yet encountered. It is true that the first part of the campaign in Bavaria went easily in favour of the French. The Austrians, though commanded by the Archduke Charles, who was later to show himself no unworthy opponent of Napoleon, were swept out of the country with heavy loss in what is known as 'the campaign of five days.' But it was different when Napoleon approached Vienna. His first effort to cross the Danube resulted in the stubborn and bloody Battle of Aspern, May 1809, and failed to achieve its purpose. The rumour spread like wildfire that it was another Battle of Baylen, and that this time the French had been defeated under the direction of Napoleon himself. But Napoleon studied the situation with the greatest care, extemporised boats and bridges, deceived the Austrians as to the point where he intended to cross, and passed the river in safety. Then followed the desperate Battle of Wagram, July 1809. It was a complete French victory, and has been thought by some to be the masterpiece of his tactical skill. But the slaughter was enormous on both sides. The enemy was more difficult to subdue after each victory. He was learning rapidly the methods of Napoleon himself. 'The brutes have learnt something,' said Napoleon when he saw the dispositions of the enemy at a later battle. In truth, the process of learning had already begun, and Napoleon was the one great schoolmaster of the soldiers of Europe. The French armies, too, had lost something of their old quality. They were no longer really French armies. Soldiers from the Confederation of the Rhine and from Italy were to be found in great numbers in the French ranks. They were efficient and courageous, but they lacked something of the spontaneity and dash that had distinguished the Emperor's troops in his early campaigns. It was Napoleon now who used troops essentially mercenary, and he encountered a resistance which became more and more national. The Tsar's alliance had not helped Napoleon at all; the Russian troops had abstained from real fighting.

The Austrians somewhat unexpectedly accepted a humiliating peace after the Battle of Wagram. Their aged statesman, Thugut, was consulted and advised surrender. 'Make peace at any price,' he is reported to have said. 'The existence of the Austrian Monarchy is at stake; the dissolution of the French Empire is not far off.' The Austrian Empire lost three million and a half of subjects; she had to reduce her army to 150,000 and to pay a considerable war indemnity. Most of what is now the coast of Yugoslavia was ceded to Napoleon under the title of 'the Illyrian Provinces.' The King of Saxony received the Duchy of Warsaw (Peace of Schoenbrunn, October 10, 1809). Austria's humiliation was as deep as that of Prussia; her revenge and her triumph would come at the same time.

Certain subordinate incidents illustrate the condition of Europe more clearly than the great battles. The Tyrolese war was an example of spontaneous insurrection. The Tyrol was a part of the dominions of Austria which had been ceded to Bavaria. When the war came the Tyrolese rose on behalf of their old Hapsburg rulers. It was the Spanish war in miniature. The peasants were inspired by a love of independence and by religious hatred of the French. Chief among their

Chapter 7

THE CATASTROPHE OF NAPOLEON

The military incidents at which we are now to glance form one of the most dramatic chapters in the military history of modern Europe. We must go to the career of Alexander the Great or of Hannibal for wars so full of personal, military, and national interest as those which saw the fall and the overthrow of Napoleon. But in accordance with the general purposes of this book the story of the fighting will be very lightly passed over. Our chief effort will be to gain some idea of the forces which were making for the overthrow of the great conqueror.

Napoleon did not deserve the title that was given to an early king of France; he was not 'well-served.' True, he had great servants both for peace and war in the earlier part of his career, and he showed himself jealous of the reputations of some of them. But as his career advanced, and every victory only increased the number of his enemies, many drew from his side and began to think of making terms with his opponents. We have already seen this in the careers of Talleyrand and Fouché, and the same tendency may be seen among his soldiers. One of the most determined of his later enemies was Bernadotte. He had been a soldier of the Republic and had not welcomed the rise of Napoleon to supreme power in the *coup d'état* of Brumaire; but he had accepted the new ruler of France and had served with distinction under him, and, though his conduct of campaigns had sometimes been sharply criticised, he had won wealth, glory, and title. After the Battle of Austerlitz he had been raised to the rank of prince. His destiny seemed closely linked to that of the Emperor.

A strange turn of fortune carried him to the throne of Sweden and made him the leader of the enemies of France. The Swedes had played a great part in the wars of Europe in the seventeenth and early eighteenth centuries. But they had overtaxed the resources of the nation, and the last quarter of a century had been full of domestic unrest. In 1789 there had been a sort of revolution which had reaffirmed the almost absolute authority of the Monarchy. But King

Gustavus III was murdered in 1792, and the reign of his son, Gustavus IV, saw nothing but failure at home and abroad. In 1809 came another revolution: the King was deposed. His uncle reigned in his place as Charles XIII; he had no children, and a successor was chosen in the royal house of Denmark.

The condition of the country was wretched. It had been forced by Napoleon to take part in the Continental System and was thus deprived of much trade in the Baltic, which legitimately belonged to it, and incurred at the same time the hostility of Great Britain. Finland had been handed over to Russia shortly after the Treaty of Tilsit. Norway was, as it had been for many generations, attached to the Crown of Denmark. When therefore the heir, so recently chosen, died in 1810, the Diet hoped to make a choice that should secure for them commercial and perhaps territorial advantages. If they chose one of Napoleon's Marshals they hoped—in strange error—that the Emperor might be induced to allow the relaxation of the Continental System in their interest. In any case, they looked forward to winning the favour of the one great military Power in Europe. So Bernadotte was approached and accepted the throne, and ultimately reigned as King Charles John, though we shall continue to call him Bernadotte.

The choice was a veritable 'comedy of errors.' The Continental System was the central point of the policy of Napoleon and would under no circumstances be voluntarily withdrawn. He was uncertain of the fidelity of Bernadotte and saw his elevation to a throne with jealousy. Sweden was brought by the election, not into friendship with France, but into bitter conflict.

To return to France and Napoleon. There was little trace in him now of the former armed champion of the Revolution, of the old leader of the national armies of France against the 'bloody standards of tyranny.' His armies were cosmopolitan and all served of necessity. He ruled without more than the dim shadow of constitutional liberty at home. He paraded his friendship and admiration for the autocratic Tsar. Further, after his last peace with Austria he had used his power to procure for himself an Austrian wife in place of Joséphine, whom he had recently divorced—not for personal but for political reasons, hoping in a new marriage to find an heir to the Empire and the support of Austria for his schemes. So the unfortunate Marie Louise came from Vienna to Paris, bore the Emperor a son, and soon saw the collapse of his fortunes. He became by this marriage the nephew of Marie Antoinette, the guillotined Queen of France.

The situation in Europe changed, but never became more favourable to Napoleon's hopes. The only chance of the permanence of Napoleon's 'European settlement' would have been the winning over of European opinion to the acceptance of a system that brought with it the triumph of the principles of the French Revolution. But there was no sign of that. Public opinion grew more and more hostile.

National sentiment grew stronger. The economic hardships and the
burden of conscription alienated even those who were best disposed.
The Spanish war still dragged on, and before Napoleon could turn
to it with all his forces and energy a much greater danger came in the
east.

The Russian alliance was the very foundation of his new policy
and an integral part of his schemes against Great Britain; and now
there came, instead of alliance with Russia, war. The relations of
Napoleon and Alexander had never been really cordial—not even
amidst the festivities of Erfurt. There was no principle of stability in
the alliance, no common aim.[1] At bottom Napoleon merely wanted
to use the Tsar for his own purposes and to strengthen his own
position in Europe. The Tsar, naturally, had different views, and
there were soon many causes of friction. During the last Austrian
war the Tsar had given no real help, when perhaps, if he had liked,
he might have prevented the war. The Tsar, too, showed no inclination to accept and co-operate in the blockade of Great Britain. On
the contrary, it was known that British commerce was secretly
admitted, while a high tariff was openly placed on French goods coming into Russia. Nor were the grievances of the Tsar against Napoleon fewer or smaller. His Austrian marriage seemed to show a
tendency to look away from Russia to Austria for support. He had
not considered the susceptibilities of Russia in more serious things.
When, in 1810, he had annexed Holland and the north-west of Germany, in order to bar that entrance against British commerce, the
Duchy of Oldenburg was one of the places occupied by the French
Emperor. The heir to the duchy was the brother-in-law of the Tsar,
and the Tsar was naturally offended. Nearer home there was a more
serious question. Napoleon had formed most of the Polish territories
which he had taken from Prussia and from Austria into the Duchy
of Warsaw. The Russian Government was always peculiarly sensitive
to what happened in Poland. She had many millions of Poles among
her own subjects, and the idea of independence might have an awkward effect on their imaginations. Napoleon had promised that the
name of Poland should not reappear on the map; but the Duchy of
Warsaw was Poland under a thin veil. The Tsar was profoundly discontented with Napoleon's Polish policy. Of all the causes of conflict between the two the Polish question was probably the most
important.

It was quite beyond the power of diplomacy or arbitration to prevent the collision. As irritation deepened into enmity both sides
worked feverishly to find alliance and military support. Fear kept the

---

[1] 'At bottom the great question is—who shall have Constantinople?' wrote Napoleon (May 31, 1808); and this was one of the reasons why he and Alexander could not
agree.

centre of Europe in Napoleon's train, but no one could be ignorant that Austria and Prussia would fall from him in the hour of defeat. Russia made offers to the Poles and hoped to win them from the side of France, but they were the only people who regarded the prospect of another French victory with enthusiasm; it would bring, they hoped, an independent Polish kingdom. Russia had better fortune with the northern Powers. Bernadotte, the new ruler of Sweden, was won over by the promise that he should be allowed to annex Norway. He counted henceforth as the bitterest of Napoleon's enemies, and brought to the Allies a valuable knowledge of the character and methods of the French army. Great Britain made a treaty with Sweden and Russia, and as usual provided subsidies. The Tsar had more valuable allies even than Sweden or Britain. The vast distance, the climate, the thin population, and the strong national feeling of Russia were enemies beyond the power of Napoleon to cope with.

At the end of June 1812 the Grand Army passed over the Niemen, in four main divisions, amounting in all to about 600,000 men, and the invasion of Russia began. It was a vast force, but not the largest ever gathered under a single command up to that time, and it has been immensely exceeded since then. The Russian commander, Barclay, had less than half the French force and he retreated before it. Napoleon marched as far as Vitebsk—about half of the 500 miles that separated the Niemen from Moscow—and had some thoughts of stopping there and trying to organise the vast district which had been abandoned to him. But there were dangers on all sides: he was lured on by the hope of settling all difficulties by a great victory and the surrender of the Tsar. So he pushed on towards Moscow; disease, desertion, and the need of establishing garrisons in the country he passed through had already reduced his army dangerously. The Russians had now determined to fight. Kutusov had displaced Barclay. The Russian army stood at bay on the banks of the Borodino (September 1812). The murderous battle that followed was a victory for Napoleon in that the Russian army retreated and left the road to Moscow open to him; but his losses had amounted to 40,000, and the Russians had lost fewer. A little later he was at the gates of Moscow, expecting a formal surrender. None came, and he entered an empty and abandoned city. Napoleon took up his quarters in the Kremlin—the ancient palace of the Tsars. It seemed the culmination of his career of triumph.

Napoleon knew how unreal the triumph was. No message came from St. Petersburg. A great fire broke out in Moscow—not accidentally—and consumed valuable provisions for men and horses. It would perhaps have been possible to remain in Moscow for the winter and to return to Europe when the spring had brought food and warmth. But that was dangerous in any case, and what would happen in Europe while Napoleon was away? It was clear that this was no war against armies and governments; it was the nation against which he had to fight. When the news came to Paris there was but one cry; 'It is another Spanish war!'

The retreat began on October 19. Napoleon hoped to force his way farther south and return by a route that would afford him provisions; but Kutusov blocked his way at Jaroslavetz and held it against the French attacks. Napoleon was forced back on to the route he had already swept clear of provisions on his march to Moscow. This sealed the destruction of the army. The Russian winter came on November 5. Already many thousands of soldiers had been lost by cold or disease or desertion. But the worst was yet to come. The Niemen was reached on December 13. Napoleon's losses are reckoned at 170,000 prisoners and 170,000 dead. That is all we can say of a tragedy almost without parallel in history.

Western Europe had read with incredulous amazement the news from Russia. But, as it became clear that Napoleon had suffered decisive defeat and crippling losses, there was a universal stirring which soon took the form of widespread resistance. The Russian armies, under the command of the Tsar himself, entered Germany. He had with him Stein, the Prussian reformer, who had been driven from Prussia by the orders of Napoleon and now preached the duty of national resistance. Napoleon had by no means given up hope of recovering from his Russian disaster. He called on France for immense efforts in men and money. There was by no means universal readiness to obey. There were stirrings of revolt in La Vendée and in some other parts of the country. There were many stories of men who broke out their teeth or cut off their thumbs in order to avoid military service. But the great danger that threatened France, and the pride of the country in the military triumphs of Napoleon, worked wonders. In 1813 he had again half a million men under his command. They were young and unequal to the veterans of the Grand Army; but both Ney and his master were loud in their praise of the courage and endurance of the young conscripts. Napoleon again dreamed of a peace enforced in Europe by complete victory. If he surrendered anything it would lead to the surrender of all. And victory would allow him to hold what he had and to regain what he had lost. He hoped by a show of strength to keep Prussia on his side. He believed himself secure of Austria through his marriage with Marie Louise and his understanding with Metternich, the crafty Chancellor who had ruled since 1810. He determined, therefore, to make no concessions—though large concessions might perhaps have kept Austria faithful to the French alliance—and to let the sword decide. He could not yet believe that the sword had broken in his hands. Yet he was himself not the old Napoleon: he had grown stout and was at times, and even at critical moments, overcome by fatigue. His power of will was as great as ever and his tactical and strategic skill is thought to have suffered no diminution. But he had lost much in elasticity of mind and had no longer his old quick sense of the realities of the situation.

Frederick William, the King of Prussia, was not so ready to rise as his people. He had had bitter experience of the weight of Napoleon's hand, and hesitated to challenge him again; but the country was full of enthusiasm. The League of Virtue (the *Tugendbund*) had won many adherents. The patriotic poems and songs of Arndt, Körner, and others did much to inflame the popular mind. There were, too, more serious forces in the background. The reforms of Stein had given new life to the body politic of Prussia and Scharnhorst's reform of the army gave her a force of 150,000 men.

The first movement in Prussia against the French came in spite of the King. Colonel Yorck was besieging the Russians in Riga as an ally of the French. When the news of the Russian catastrophe reached him, acting on his own responsibility, he refused to continue the siege against those whom he considered his allies, and made with them an agreement by which he declared his army to be neutral. Such neutrality did not really differ from hostility to the French. The King of Prussia was bound to repudiate his action, but he soon followed it. East Prussia had risen spontaneously as the Russian troops advanced. The Provincial Estates of East Prussia were summoned, and put all their forces at the disposal of the enemies of Napoleon. It was impossible for the King of Prussia to delay any longer. In January 1813 he signed with the Tsar the Treaty of Kalisch. The two sovereigns undertook not to make any separate peace, and the Tsar promised that Prussia should recover its ancient boundaries, and that Germany should be free. A little later it was declared that if any princes or peoples in Germany did not join the Allies they should lose their independence when the settlement came, and that their territories should be at the disposal of the allies. Austria came in to the same side, but more slowly and with more duplicity. Metternich assured the French Ambassador that the alliance with his master corresponded to the permanent interest of the two countries. But all the time he was negotiating with Prussia, and ultimately joined the Convention of Breslau. Napoleon was driven back to the west of the Elbe; and Hamburg and Dresden, both situated on that river, were soon occupied by the army of liberation. Nor was it only his allies who were falling from Napoleon. His own Generals were, many of them, on the edge of desertion. Bernadotte commanded already in the ranks of the enemy. Murat and Jomini were soon to pass over to that side, and the Marshals who remained with him were often critical, negligent, and depressed.

And yet Napoleon gained victories which would have been reckoned great if it were not for the disasters which so soon followed them. He defeated the allied Russians and Prussians, first at Lützen and then at Bautzen. They were unquestionable victories, and threw the enemy into great depression, but they were won at a terrible cost to the victors. The orders of Napoleon, moreover, were no longer carried out by his subordinates with the old eager loyalty. There was little that resembled Austerlitz and Jena in these obstinate struggles. The defeated allies, moreover, retreated eastward and had soon re-formed their armies and were ready for a further struggle.

It was at this juncture, moreover, that Austria threw in her lot openly with the Allies. Metternich played his cards with the most perfect skill and lack of scruple. He proposed to Napoleon an armistice which should last from June 4 to July 28, 1813; this period was to be used to prepare the ground for a general peace congress. Napoleon accepted the proposal and signed the armistice.

Was peace possible? Were the two chief negotiators in earnest? With whom lies the responsibility for the failure? It is clear that the situation did not admit of a peaceful solution of the problems, and that neither party sincerely desired the cessation of the war. Metternich was aware of the growing enthusiasm of Germany and of the rapidly accumulating forces against Napoleon. Napoleon on his side still hoped for a settlement through victory, and knew that only victory could secure his power either in Europe or in France. He is reported to have said to Metternich: 'Sovereigns who are born on the throne can be beaten twenty times and still go back to their capitals. But I can't, because I am a parvenu.' It is a sentence which reveals a permanent feature of Napoleon's position, and explains much of his policy. In a conference with Napoleon which took place at Dresden, Metternich suggested the abandonment by France of nearly all her territories beyond the Rhine. The interview between the two men was a very stormy one, and Napoleon talked at one time about going to Vienna again, at the head of his army, to settle the dispute. He consented, however, to prolong the armistice and to attend a Peace Congress at Prague. The Congress was never really constituted. Austria despatched an ultimatum. Napoleon disdained to reply to it, and Austria issued a declaration of war.

The Allies had nearly a million men under arms, and henceforth Napoleon was usually outnumbered. His enemies hoped to overwhelm him by a series of indecisive attacks and to defeat him in detail. Yet the campaign consisted of two great battles: one deserving to rank among his greatest victories; and the other his most serious, his one altogether irreparable defeat.

At Dresden he anticipated the attack of his enemies and gained a complete victory. Earlier in his career he would have followed it up with furious energy, and would perhaps have made it decisive of the campaign in Germany. But he seemed incapable of the continuous exertion which he had so often shown in his youth. His lieutenants, too, failed to support his plans. Five successive actions in which they were defeated neutralised the effects of the Battle of Dresden. Diplomacy gained important advantages against him. Metternich insisted on negotiations with the princes of the Confederation of the Rhine. They were offered a continuation of their powers and titles after the peace if they would join the Allies now. Stein deplored the offer as involving the sacrifice of all hopes of building up a united Germany at the peace. The offer was accepted by most. Bavaria came over to join the Allies. Saxony almost alone remained faithful to Napoleon.

Meanwhile Blücher and the Prussians had crossed the Elbe. Napoleon's position at Dresden was untenable. He fell back westward, and on October 16, 1813, began the Battle of Leipzig—'the battle of the Peoples', as it is called. There was fighting for three days, and it was not all favourable to the Allies. The losses amounted to some 130,000 men, and of these about 50,000 were French. The broken fragments of the French army escaped by the one route that was left open. With what troops he had left Napoleon made for the Rhine. An army of 50,000 men, chiefly Bavarians, tried to stop him at Hanau, but was easily brushed aside. The French army reached the Rhine at the beginning of December, and the ravages of disease were almost as fatal to it as the German sword had been. The garrisons that had been left behind in Germany—about 190,000 men— soon surrendered. East of the Rhine Napoleon's power had disappeared. The French armies had almost been withdrawn from Spain. Wellington entered France victoriously from the south.

France had now to face the horrors of invasion, which she had inflicted on so many lands but had not herself known since 1793. She was weary of war. Her dreams of world victory were all dissipated. She was exhausted in men; her commerce was destroyed or languishing. There had been during the last ten years singularly little political interest in the country. The movement of the armies had engrossed the attention of all men. But now, when the Emperor was coming back to France a beaten man, men's minds recurred to their old ideals. Some liberals dared to utter again the watchwords of the Revolution. The Royalists saw again a chance—after so many disappointments—of the return of the Bourbons. Louis XVIII, as all Royalists called the brother of Louis XVI, who had fought against the Revolution as the Comte de Provence, issued a proclamation urging the French to regard the invading allies as their friends and promising a diminution of taxes, a regard for acquired property, peace and pardon. The old nobility showed no hesitation about returning to France in the ranks of the invaders. The restoration of the Bourbons was openly advocated in France. Yet there was a good deal of enthusiasm still for the Emperor. He represented, at least to many, the cause of national defence. The Government was strong enough or popular enough to draw 350,000 soldiers from the country. Napoleon would not fall without a struggle.

The military genius of Napoleon as strategist was never shown more clearly than in the war for the soil of France. The invaders were perhaps taking things too easily, and assumed too readily that no further resistance was probable. It is quite possible, too, that the wisest and most patriotic course for Napoleon to pursue would have been to recognise the inevitability of defeat, and to have spared to France the sufferings, and to the Allies the exasperation, of a further campaign. But it is impossible not to admire the steady nerve, and the strength of will, which seemed at one time likely to turn defeat into victory. Twice over he defeated Blücher with heavy loss. The whole Allied army seemed for a time in real danger of destruction. They had lost confidence in the presence of the French and their great commander. An army with twice the numbers of the French refused battle. It might seem that the triumphs of Valmy were to be repeated on an immensely greater scale, and the Emperor was popular once more. The cruelties of the Prussian and Russian invaders made the task of defence all the more necessary in the eyes of the people, and the invading Allies encountered a genuinely popular resistance. The peasants in many districts, exasperated by the exactions and cruelties of the invaders, rose against them in a way which recalled the Vendean war. The coalition seemed really in danger of dissolution.

The diplomatists were active during these months as well as the soldiers. It is, however, very rare that a war in which the passions of the combatants have been violently roused can be settled by negotiation before a military decision has been reached. On two occasions there were negotiations with a view to a settlement. First, Metternich had interviewed a representative of Napoleon in November 1813. It was suggested that France should abandon all her conquests except Belgium and what lay within the limits of the Rhine and the Alps. There was probably little sincerity on either side, and as we have seen the war went on. Next, when Napoleon had shown how dangerous he could still be, a congress was held at Châtillon. Now it was proposed that Belgium should be abandoned and what France had won under the Revolution in the east and south. She was to return to her pre-revolutionary boundaries, and some hope was held out that Great Britain would restore some of the colonies which had been taken from her during the war. But all ended in smoke. The sword must decide.

In the final campaign Napoleon showed daring and hope. He gained some wonderful successes, and he was at times marvellously supported by his soldiers. But his whole position was undermined. His forces were exhausted, while the enemy could draw on an immense reservoir. His plans presupposed the resistance of Paris, and Paris was in no mood for resistance. When by a daring move Napoleon placed himself in the rear of the Allies, they determined at last that courage was safer than prudence and pushed on for Paris. The Emperor had foreseen the possibility of an attack on Paris, and he had sent orders for the Government to be moved to the Loire. But his orders in the hour of his weakness were no longer obeyed. The Empress was sent away with the child, who, it was hoped, was to carry on the glories of the Empire, but Napoleon's brother Joseph remained in the city. A battle was fought outside of Paris, stubbornly contested, and entailing great loss of life. Then the city capitulated. Napoleon had some thought of continuing the war outside of Paris, but he saw the impossibility of his plan. His Marshals were weary of fighting, and showed less readiness to obey than many of the common soldiers. At last, on April 6, he signed his abdication. 'As the Allied Powers have declared that the Emperor Napoleon is the only obstacle to the re-establishment of peace in Europe the Emperor Napoleon, obedient to the oaths that he has sworn, declares that he renounces for himself and for his heirs the thrones of France and Italy, because there is no personal sacrifice, even that of life itself, which he is not ready to make in the interests of France.' He is thought to have attempted suicide. A fortnight later he bade a touching farewell to his Old Guard and retired to the island of Elba, where he was to be allowed to maintain the empty name and ceremony of Empire.

The fall of Napoleon's power settled some questions, but brought forward others that proved very difficult. Who was to rule in France, and by what right and in what manner? What was to be done with the vast European territories over which Napoleon had ruled or in which he had exercised a decisive influence? As the flood subsided many of the old landmarks reappeared, but some had been swept away for ever. There were many concurrent forces deciding these issues; but there were two dominating personalities. Among the Allies there was no one to rival in influence Alexander of Russia, a strange and baffling character. He was the object of endless adulation from Frenchmen and foreigners, and he oscillated between humanitarian and religious ideals on the one hand and egoistic and Russian aims on the other. And on the French side there was Talleyrand, who, after his strange career as Jacobin and imperialist, as trusted agent of Napoleon's schemes and traitor to Napoleon even while he served him, was now the one man who seemed to exercise a prevailing influence with the hesitating politicians of France. For the moment Castlereagh, Wellington, and the British were of less account than these two men.

A regency on behalf of Napoleon's infant son; the transference of the Crown to one of his Marshals—these schemes were suggested and considered. But in the end the restoration of the Bourbon dynasty in the person of Louis XVIII was decided on. It was a solution founded on a principle—the principle of legitimacy—and it won the assent of all the Allies. The Senate, the impotent body which was nearly all that remained of the Constitution of Brumaire, and contained some members who had voted for the execution of Louis XVI, under Talleyrand's guidance declared that 'the French people freely call to the throne Louis-Stanislas-Xavier de France, brother of the late king'; and they added to their invitation certain constitutional articles guaranteeing the principles of the Revolution. It was twenty-two years since the Bourbons had disappeared from the soil of France, and the number of those who really cherished their memory was small. France as a whole had no hand in the matter. Paris accepted a decision which was really dictated by the armies of the Allies, and the affair was settled. Louis XVIII soon returned to Paris, and his awkward reserve, his assumption of Divine Right, and his faint expressions of gratitude to those who had restored him to the throne, especially his coldness to the Tsar, had a depressing effect. It is said that at his formal entry into Paris there were some of the troops who insisted on crying 'Vive l'Empereur!'

Louis XVIII, then, would reign—though already some were asking for how long—but by what right and within what frontiers? The first question was settled when Louis XVIII 'granted' a charter regulating the methods of government—that is to say, he insisted on his Divine Right and gave to the people only such liberties as he thought fit. The general settlement was adjourned to a congress which was to meet at once at Vienna; but before the plenipotentiaries met there it was agreed that France should have the frontiers of 1792—the frontiers, that is, which she possessed before the revolutionary wars had begun—with some small rectifications which were nearly all to her advantage. France was to be represented at Vienna. The Allies could not refuse to treat on terms of equality a king whom they had themselves established on the throne of France; but before the diplomatists met at Vienna they had procured from the French King a definite promise that he would accept all the decisions of the Allies.

The aims and intrigues and difficulties of the diplomatists of Vienna will be treated in the next chapter. They were working their way through passionate rivalries, that at one time threatened war, to some sort of solution when the news of Napoleon's return to France fell like a bombshell upon the Congress and threw everything into confusion. Napoleon had been encouraged to attempt his great adventure by the rumours of the dissensions of the Powers over the Saxon-Polish question. The news from France also made him think that his return would be welcome to many. The Government of Louis XVIII had hardly begun to function, but its general character was apparent. It was associated with the loss of the territories that Napoleon had conquered, and offended thus the pride of the French people. The *émigré* nobles were returning, and they clamoured for the restoration of their confiscated lands. The peasantry—always so important a force at the basis of the social fabric of France—believed themselves to be threatened in their possessions. Napoleon's soldiers too, whether still in the ranks of the army or dismissed from it, were bitterly discontented. Those who had been disbanded could in many cases find no employment. Dupont, whose surrender at Baylen had first shown that a Napoleonic army could be defeated, was made Minister of War, to the great irritation of the soldiers. There were thus mutterings of discontent, though there was nothing to indicate the miraculous success which awaited Napoleon on his arrival in France.

His banishment to Elba with an important title and a toy Court was an absurdity. It was impossible to keep him under supervision, and yet his position was one from which he inevitably wanted to escape. The income that had been promised to him was not paid, and its non-payment gave him the pretext that he needed. He slipped away from Elba and landed near Antibes on the south coast of France. He had no support of importance except his name and the memories of twenty years; but that proved more than sufficient. The new Government had struck no roots, and the Powers of Europe, who had defeated Napoleon, had not thought it necessary to provide for the support of the restored monarchy. The army deserted Louis XVIII almost *en masse*; the great majority of the people welcomed Napoleon. Ney, who had been sent out to resist him and had promised to bring him back to Paris 'in a cage,' came back as his supporter and general. The King and his brother and the emigrant nobility had once more to 'go on their travels,'

The iron dice of war fell, as we know, fatally for Napoleon, but it would be rash to assume from the event that he had no chance of success. He had a large and enthusiastic army, strengthened by the return of large numbers of prisoners from Russia. It had been clearly shown at the Congress of Vienna how strong were the antagonisms that underlay the official harmony of the Allies. If Napoleon had won a great victory he would probably have offered terms of studied moderation, and it is not impossible that they would have been accepted. But there were permanent features in the life of Europe which made the return of the days of Marengo and Austerlitz and Jena unthinkable. The nations of Europe were awake. The Governments were nowhere the mere lifeless machines that they had been before the French Revolution. They had a large enthusiastic popular support. Europe was fighting France with her own weapons. And, further, the support that Napoleon received in France was by no means untroubled by hesitations and suspicions. As soon as the first moment of delirium was past there were few indeed who were willing to support the idea of Napoleon reigning as he had reigned in 1805. He was sensitive to the condition of public opinion. He issued a decree instituting two Chambers for legislation, one of which was to be popularly elected; the press was to be free; Ministers were to be responsible to the Chambers. Then, though the organisation of the military force was occupying all his attention, he submitted this new Constitution to a plebiscite. Only a million and a half voters went to the poll, but the support of a large majority gave him the appearance of a constitutional position. Had he returned victoriously from Belgium the Constitution could hardly have lived unchanged. All turned on the decision of battle.

Napoleon was without an ally in Europe. Murat, King of Naples, had indeed raised an army and appealed for the support of Italian sentiment, knowing that he would be expelled from the throne of Naples by the Congress of Vienna. But Napoleon believed that Murat's action was prejudicial to his own chances, and the Italian movement was soon suppressed. Napoleon started for the front on June 12. He aimed at striking against the British and the Prussian armies before they could effect a concentration of their forces. He gained a considerable though a partial success against the Prussians at Ligny. Blücher, the Prussian commander, promised Wellington that he would join him at Mont St. Jean, and it was in reliance on this promise that Wellington accepted the Battle of Waterloo on June 18. At the end of the day Napoleon was beaten beyond possibility of recovery. Paris capitulated on July 3. Napoleon surrendered on July 9 and was sent to St. Helena.

The dramatic episode of the Hundred Days' Campaign had altered the outlook in Europe, and materially for the worse. In 1814, the Allies had been willing to maintain the view that they had been fighting against Napoleon, not against France, and they were prepared to give France fair if not generous terms, inflicting on her no war indemnity and insisting on no military occupation of her territory. At the Congress of Vienna, under the skilful management of Talleyrand, France had began to assume the rôle of an equal among the Great Powers of Europe. There were many who would have liked to punish her more severely; but on the whole the absence of bitterness was remarkable. After Waterloo, the attitude of the Powers was different. The welcome that the country had given to Napoleon seemed to show that it identified itself with him. France had now to pay an indemnity of 700 million francs and to submit to a military occupation by 150,000 men under the command of Wellington. The art treasures which had been brought to Paris from all parts of Europe by Napoleon were, quite justly, restored.

It was not certain at first that Louis XVIII would be restored. The regency for Napoleon's baby son, or a prince of the House of Orleans, were suggested as alternatives. But Louis was decided on in the end. The past utterances of the Allies and the difficulties that would be caused by any other settlement made him inevitable. The question of the frontiers of France was hotly disputed. All Germany would have liked to annex something on the eastern frontier of France. Prussia was the spokesman of the nation in demanding the cession to Germany of Alsace and Lorraine. But both Russia and Great Britain opposed the mutilation of France. The Tsar Alexander was the supreme figure in Europe for a time. He was moved to defend France by the sentiment of generosity which was powerful and genuine with him, and also by the feeling that a strong France was essential to Russia in the political combinations of Europe. Political and diplomatic considerations also moved Castlereagh and the British Government, though they, too, were by no means insensible to the appeal of justice. So, with small exceptions, the territory of France remained what it was before the Revolution began. The Germans were especially fierce against France and their demands were resisted with difficulty, but they were resisted. Alsace and Lorraine were not surrendered. The Pont de Jéna was not blown up. Their plundering of the provinces which they occupied was checked.

The declared intention of those who fought against France had been to resist the Revolution and its principles and to restore the old order which had been destroyed by Napoleon. It was assumed that the storm which had raged in Europe for nearly a quarter of a century would now pass off and the Continent would reassume its old life, aims, and methods. The diplomatists of 1814 and 1815 were in no mood to profit by the great opportunity afforded for social and political experiment and reconstruction. Liberty, equality, fraternity, democracy, progress, humanity, were words of dangerous associations. But it was soon seen that the forces identified with the French Revolution were not to be so easily controlled. The enthusiasms which they represented would, it was hoped, be suppressed and the Balance of Power restored, but despite the efforts of the statesmen of 1815 to restore the Old Europe, history dates the rise of a new Europe from these events.

Chapter 8

THE FAILURE OF INTERNATIONAL GOVERNMENT, 1814–25

The defeat of Napoleon was followed by a long period of peace among the Great Powers—a peace moreover that was only in part one of exhaustion. It opened with the attempt of the Great Powers of Europe to make a constructive agreement for peace, the greatest attempt ever made in the history of Europe to this date, an attempt of such importance that it may properly be regarded as beginning a new era of European relationships. The breakdown of this international experiment must not blind us to the magnitude of its results. There was no great war in Europe for a century and no major war until 1853; the territorial settlement remained the political basis of Europe for thirty years; the system of government by congress, destroyed before the end of the first decade, left as a tradition behind it the practice of international conferences, inherited by the twentieth century from the nineteenth.

The explanation of the breakdown is to be found in a combination of factors. A policy of reaction was pursued in varying forms by most of the governments in Europe; in Austria under Metternich, in Prussia, saved from the worst excesses by the results of her earlier reforms, and in Russia, most conspicuously after Nicholas I succeeded Alexander in 1825. In comparison with these governments the Tory administration in Britain seemed dangerously liberal, and the breach which developed between Britain and her three allies in the time of Canning was no mere matter of diplomacy; beneath the divergencies of policy at the Conference tables lay a fundamental difference of outlook. Britain as the exponent of constitutional monarchy had adherents in France, in the Netherlands, in Greece, Portugal and Spain, and contesting parties in all these countries provided opportunities for diplomatic rivalry. Deeper still in the body politic of Europe were the great forces of nationalism and revolutionary discontent, breaking out from time to time to the surface. In Italy and Spain, in Greece, Poland and Belgium, revolution was active, although only in Greece and Belgium was it successful. In Germany and Austria it was latent, showing itself in incidents and agitation rather than in open war, until the Year of Revolution gave a new turn to European development. The main responsibility for the failure of the attempt to bring a lasting peace by a combination of the Great Powers must be attributed first to those who acted as the High Priests of reaction, and in the second place to those who were led by their national and liberal fervour to seek redress by violence. Some responsibility must be given, too, to the successive statesmen of Britain who followed a policy which made impossible the maintenance of the unity of the Alliance.

The Four Great Powers, Austria, Britain, Prussia and Russia, had finally been brought into a great alliance by the Treaty of Chaumont (March 9, 1814). By this agreement the Signatory Powers undertook to unite in alliance for twenty years. They proposed first to overthrow Napoleon, next to prevent him or his dynasty from returning to France, lastly to guarantee the territorial settlement to be made by a concerted alliance for twenty years. Austria (Metternich) and Russia (Alexander) had quarrelled so much that they found agreement difficult, and it was due to Castlereagh's influence that this union and agreement were brought about. Its effects were immediate. By the end of March, as we have seen, the Allies had decided to restore the Bourbons to France and had occupied Paris. Napoleon abdicated for himself and his family in the first days of April, and the Allies sat down to mould the map of Europe anew, according to their hearts' desire. By May 30 the First Treaty of Paris was signed. France was treated with as much consideration as was possible under the circumstances, but it was not a consideration which could satisfy patriotic Frenchmen. She was not disarmed, nor was she called upon to pay a war indemnity, nor to restore the masterpieces of art which she had removed from Italy or Germany. Her boundaries in Europe were not to be those of 1789 but of 1792, and she even received certain extensions beyond this line. Malta, which Napoleon had conquered, but which Britain had taken from him, remained British. Outside Europe her treatment was less generous. She retained all her trading stations and commercial privileges in India, but was compelled to dismantle all fortresses. She ceded to Britain Mauritius, a naval station on the way to India. But the Powers returned to her the rich island of Guadeloupe and most of her other possessions in the West Indies. Tobago and St. Lucia (which had great strategic importance) were ceded to Britain, and part of San Domingo to Spain. France retained her Fishery Rights in the St. Lawrence and off Newfoundland. Her military advantages in her colonies were, therefore, lessened, but her commercial wealth remained practically unimpaired. Yet the Allies could have deprived her of every colony she possessed.

---

[1] The date given on the document, March 1, 1814, is fictitious.

In the published articles of the First Treaty of Paris, the Powers announced that they intended to restore Holland with increased territory; to form an independent German Federation; to recognise the independence of Switzerland; and to form a new Italy, composed of sovereign states, 'beyond the limits of those countries which are to revert to Austria.' This first sketch of the territorial arrangements of Vienna was defined in more detail in secret articles to the Treaty, which need not detain us here.

The Allies agreed to meet at a Congress at Vienna in the autumn to settle the rest of Europe (outside France) on an agreed basis. But they had reckoned without France. Redeemed, restored, forgiven, a monarchy again and akin to the old type of European states, France claimed a share in the discussions of Vienna. She was there to play for her own hand and to make mischief, and Talleyrand, her representative, was able greatly to trouble the waters. Russia and Prussia, on the one hand, quarrelled fiercely with Austria and Britain, on the other. Talleyrand held the balance and used it to the advantage of France. Finally, at the beginning of 1815, the differences at Vienna became so serious, that France, Austria and Britain formed a defensive alliance to resist the claims of Russia and Prussia.[1] This extreme step produced good results: Alexander gave way on some points, Prussia followed suit. All matters were really adjusted when the world was suddenly startled by the news that Napoleon had broken loose from Elba, that Louis XVIII was in flight, and that France had once again welcomed the Emperor, whose downfall the rest of Europe had decreed. The return from Elba and the campaign of Waterloo have been well described as 'the most wonderful adventure in history.' They have been recounted in the last chapter. Even had Napoleon won at Waterloo, he would probably have been crushed a little later by the Austro-Russian armies advancing from the east. And his defeat ended the matter. The French people showed no desire to cling to him after his disaster, and submitted once more to

---

[1] This extraordinary alliance was signed on January 3, 1815. Technically it was secret and not known either to Tsar Alexander or to the King of Prussia. But its substance was certainly known to them at the time and produced a very marked effect immediately on their policy. The point, on which the Russo-Prussian group was opposed to the Anglo-Franco-Austrian group, was simple: Prussia desired to annex the whole of Saxony in exchange for the large amount of Polish territory she was surrendering to Russia, and Alexander 'backed up' Prussia to the limit. Metternich refused to allow Prussia so large an extension of territory contiguous to Austria, and Castlereagh (and ultimately Talleyrand) stood with him. The difference went right up to the brink of war and it was only when Alexander was convinced that the other group would fight that he gave way. Ultimately, Prussia secured only about half of Saxony. Talleyrand's part in the matter has been somewhat exaggerated. He did not create the differences between the Allies, which were fundamental, but he inflamed and exploited those difficulties to the advantage of France. Much, however, of what he gained for France was thrown away by Napoleon's intervention. See C. K. Webster, *The Congress of Vienna, 1814–15*(1934), pp. 106 ff.

the return and the rule of the gouty and uninspiring Bourbon. Napoleon's adventure has only importance in that it brought further misfortunes on France. The terms imposed on France by Europe were sterner. She was now compelled to pay a war indemnity, to restore the works of art, to submit to being garrisoned by an Allied army until 1818. Her boundaries in Europe were further reduced from the line of 1792 to that of 1790, and certain places of strategic importance on the frontier were now taken from her.[1] Indeed, had it not been for the moderating counsels of Castlereagh and Wellington, she might have been compelled to cede Alsace and Lorraine.

Setting aside the more drastic terms imposed upon France, the Vienna settlement was not materially altered by the return from Elba. The Treaty of Vienna was actually signed on June 9, before the decisive day of Waterloo. Its provisions fell into several great groups. The first of these may be best indicated by describing it as the settlement of the Balance of Power. The principle was that each Great Power was to obtain the territory or its equivalent that it had held in 1805. Except in the case of Russia, this was fairly carried out. Russia negotiated with the sword in her hand and obtained more than the other Allies liked. She got a large part of Poland, including Warsaw the capital, which she recovered from Prussia, and promised to form a national kingdom of Poland and to endow her with a constitution. In the opinion of both Castlereagh and Metternich this accession of power and population was too great, and upset the Balance of Power. Alarm was increased by the fact that Alexander maintained an army of nearly a million men, which was about twice the number that good judges thought necessary.

As regards Germany, the balancing of power was fairly carried out. Prussia complained that she got less than the 1805 standard, and this was true. But she had had a great deal of Polish territory in 1805, and she exchanged this for half of Saxony and for the Rhine Province, German in blood and speech. It is singular that Prussia at the time showed no special desire for this last acquisition, which made her ultimately the national champion of Germany against France.

Austria adjusted the balance against Prussia in Germany by preventing her from annexing all Saxony as she had desired. Further, the territorial strength and independence of the Grand Duke of Baden, the Kings of Württemberg and Bavaria and the Grand Duke of Hesse Darmstadt, which had been assured by the treaties with which Metternich in 1813 had detached them from the Confederation of the Rhine and the French alliance, were confirmed at Vienna. When, in 1813, the Kingdom of Westphalia fell into its component parts, Brunswick, Hesse Cassel and Hanover, the latter severed from

---

[1] These stiffened terms were embodied in the Second Treaty of Paris, signed November 20, 1815.

its British connection, obtained a good acession of territory. This, too, Vienna confirmed. A good deal of common sense was shown in rounding off territories and in settling old-time differences, and the total number of German states included in the new Federation was reduced to thirty-nine. Austria retained, in effect, the headship of Germany, though Prussia was not far behind her in authority.

The fact is Austria did not aim at gains in Germany, but in Italy. She acquired Venetia and recovered Lombardy. All the other states in Italy were really satellites in her train. Piedmont acquired Genoa, and was helped by this acquisition to defend the North against France. The Duchies of Tuscany, Parma and Modena and the Papal States were restored, and Naples, with Sicily, was again set up as a kingdom under a Bourbon. By a secret treaty, made (with Castlereagh's approval) between Metternich and the King of Naples, the latter promised not to grant a constitution without Austria's consent.

The next important phase of the settlement concerned Holland and Belgium. These were united into one kingdom, again with the idea of strengthening the resisting power of small states against France. Castlereagh further restored to the United Kingdom of the Netherlands the enormously rich Dutch colony of Java, and lent her two million pounds to fortify her frontier against France. This policy has been described as 'wise but unsuccessful.' It certainly was unsuccessful, for the Belgians separated from the Dutch in half a generation. But Castlereagh doubtless thought that his generous economic concessions would reconcile the two peoples.

Switzerland was recognised as independent and was guaranteed by all the Powers. Spain and Portugal recovered their old boundaries in Europe. Denmark was deprived of Norway, which was handed to Sweden. This settlement caused heartburnings, as Castlereagh had to threaten Norway with a blockade before she gave way. But, though this incident was an unpleasant one, it was not one for which practical diplomats will blame Castlereagh. At a critical moment, Sweden refused to join the coalition against Napoleon unless Norway was promised to her, and Castlereagh was compelled to pay the price.[1]

Certain other settlements were made by, or in consequence of, the Treaty of Vienna. The property claims of individuals who had suffered by the war were fairly met. The vexatious disputes as to diplomatic etiquette and precedence were finally settled. A doctrine as to international rivers was laid down, which was important for the future. The slave trade was declared inhuman and it was abolished

---

[1] An almost exact parallel is afforded by the secret Treaty of London (April 26, 1915) in which Italy obtained great concessions from France, Britain and Russia as the price of entering the war. Castlereagh's treaty was, however, discussed in the Commons before Norway was coerced.

by France, Spain, Holland, and Sweden, and promised to be abolished by Portugal. This great concession to humane ideas was almost solely due to Castlereagh, and to the British popular agitation behind him.

It has been customary to denounce the peacemakers of Vienna as reactionary and illiberal in the extreme. It is indeed true that they represented the old régime and were, to a large extent, untouched by the new ideas. But they represented the best and not the worst of the old régime, and their settlement averted any major war in Europe for forty years. According to their lights the settlement was a fair one. France was treated with leniency, and the adjustments of the Balance of Power and territory were carried out with the scrupulous nicety of a grocer weighing out his wares, or of a banker balancing his accounts. Russia alone gained more than her fair share, and this was because she had an undue proportion of armed force. The settlement disregarded national claims, forced 'unnatural unions' on Norway and Sweden, on Belgium and Holland. But in each case the ally and the stronger partner (Sweden and Holland) demanded it, and the Allies did not see their way to resist the demand. A more serious critcism was the disrespect paid to the views of smaller Powers. Though the settlement was supposed to be in favour of the old order and existing rights, the smaller states were ruthlessly sacrificed for the benefit of the larger. For this side of the activities of the peacemakers there is little excuse, and it is the gravest criticism of their actions.

The work of Vienna, interrupted by Napoleon, was completed by two treaties, signed at Paris on November 20, 1815. Of these, one, the Second Treaty of Paris, bound France to carry out the new arrangements imposed in consequence of the return of Napoleon, to submit to the frontiers of 1790, to pay an indemnity, and to return the works of art to foreign capitals. The second treaty was the Quadruple Alliance between the Four Great Powers. They bound themselves to maintain the arrangements of Chaumont, Vienna, and Paris by armed force for twenty years, both as regards the territorial boundaries now fixed and as regards the perpetual exclusion of Bonaparte and his dynasty from the throne of France. Finally, by Article VI, they agreed to 'renew their meetings at fixed periods' to discuss matters 'of common interest.' In the last article lay the germ of future international government.

The germ of its destruction lay in a solemn declaration by which Alexander sought to bind all monarchs together in a Christian union of charity, peace, and love, issued on September 26, 1815. It was to be signed by kings alone. The Regent of Great Britain was unable to sign it, though he sent a private letter to Alexander, expressing his sympathy with the sentiments. With this exception it was signed by every king in Europe and by the President of the Swiss Republic.[1] Its importance was, in a sense, fortuitous, for it came to be regarded by European liberals as a hateful compact of despots against the liberties of mankind. It was not that, nor had it any diplomatic or binding force. Charity and love are not capable of being defined in diplomatic terms, and no one except Alexander thought seriously of the Treaty. Castlereagh called it a 'piece of sublime mysticism and nonsense.' Metternich made profane jests about Christianity in connection with it. Neither regarded himself as in any way bound by it.[2]

The bond which Castlereagh and Metternich did recognise was that of the Quadruple Alliance. But they differed greatly about its interpretation. According to Castlereagh, Britain was bound to defend the territorial limits laid down at Vienna for twenty years. She was bound also to meet periodically in congresses with her Allies, but she was not bound to interfere in case of internal revolution in any country (other than an attempt to restore Napoleon). Metternich argued that the Quadruple Alliance did commit its members to armed interference to suppress internal revolution in any country, if the Congress thought it advisable. In the end these two views were bound to come into conflict.

International control worked well for a time. The chief statesmen

---

[1] It was originally signed by the three rulers of Austria, Russia and Prussia. The Sultan was not asked to sign; Alexander thought at one time of asking the President of the United States to do so.

[2] Two quotations may here be profitably contrasted (E. Hertslet, *Map of Europe by Treaty* (1875), vol. I. pp. 318, 375):

Article II of the Holy Alliance Declaration, September 26, 1815	*Article VI of the Quadruple Alliance of Paris, November 20, 1815.*
'In consequence, the sole principle of force, whether between the said Governments or between their Subjects, shall be that of doing each other reciprocal service, and of testifying by unalterable good will the mutual affection with which they ought to be animated, to consider themselves all as members of one and the same Christian nation; the three allied Princes looking on themselves as merely delegated by Providence to govern three branches of the One family, namely, Austria, Prussia, and Russia, thus confessing that the Christian world, of which they and their people form a part, has in reality no other Sovereign than Him to whom alone power really belongs,' etc.	'To facilitate and to secure the execution of the present Treaty, and to consolidate the connections which at the present moment so closely unite the Four Sovereigns for the happiness of the world, the High Contracting Parties have agreed to renew their Meetings at fixed periods, either under the immediate auspices of the Sovereigns themselves, or by their respective Ministers, for the purpose of consulting upon their common interests, and for the consideration of the measures which at each of these periods shall be considered the most salutary for the repose and prosperity of Nations, and for the maintenance of the Peace of Europe.

Does one not see in the first quotation the warm, vague mysticism of Alexander, and in the second the cold practicality of Castereagh?

of Europe knew one another personally, and they were all interested in seeing that France remained quiet and paid her debts. At the first 'periodic reunion' in 1818, at Aix-la-Chapelle, it was agreed that French conduct had been satisfactory, and that the allied armies should evacuate her soil at once. France was once more forgiven and restored and readmitted to the rank of a Great Power. She was admitted into a new quintuple combination (consisting of herself and the Four Great Powers), and invited to take part in any further periodic reunions. The Quadruple Alliance was, however, strictly maintained, for the Allies thought it might still be necessary to act against France.

Alexander now came forward, flourishing the Treaty of the Holy Alliance and demanding a general union of sovereigns against revolution. He wanted, among other things, to send an armed allied force to help the Spanish king to subdue his revolted colonies in America. Castlereagh strongly opposed this project and prevailed on the Congress to disclaim the use of force in any such attempt. Alexander pressed on with his doctrine of general intervention, but was again resisted by Castlereagh, who was now joined by Metternich. Eventually, the two contented Alexander by agreeing to a vague formula about moral solidarity, which meant very little to them but a good deal to him.

For two years longer the 'moral union' endured, and then in 1820 came a thunderclap. A military revolution broke out in Spain, which demanded the very democratic constitution of 1812 (above, p. 116). The king's life was in peril, and he eventually gave way to all demands. He adopted the constitution and professed to be a complete and liberal constitutional monarch. Alexander was horrified at the news. He feared the army and he feared democracy, and both had been triumphant in Spain. If these movements spread elsewhere no monarch would be safe and the Christian union would be dissolved. He issued a circular saying that it was clearly the duty of other monarchs to assemble at once in Congress, to denounce the Spanish Constitution of 1812, and, if necessary, to send an allied army to repress it by force. All this, he claimed, had already been admitted by the Great Powers in the formula to which they had subscribed in the Holy Alliance and at Aix-la-Chapelle.

This extravagant extension of the obligations of Vienna obliged Castlereagh to declare himself. On May 5, 1820, he issued a lengthy State paper, which was the foundation of British foreign policy in the nineteenth century.[1] He said that Britain was committed only to pre-

---

[1] Full text was for the first time printed in *Cambridge History of British Foreign Policy* (1923), vol. II, pp. 623–633. Cp. also H. Temperley and L. Penson: *Foundations of British Foreign Policy*, pp. 48–63 (1938). A few extracts are given here. 'It [the Alliance of the Great Powers] was an Union for the re-conquest and liberation

venting the return of Napoleon or his dynasty to France, and to maintaining the territorial arrangements of Vienna by armed force for twenty years. He regarded the Spanish revolution as an internal affair not dangerous to other countries, and he did not think Britain would be justified in sanctioning any attempt to suppress it by force. Britain, he explained to the diplomats of the Continent, owed her present dynasty and constitution to an internal revolution. She could not, therefore, deny to other countries the same right of changing their form of government. Moreover, the British Government could not act without the support of its Parliament and people. Neither had been informed that any obligations, other than those he had explained, had been contracted at Vienna. Britain would fulfil those obligations, but no others.

At first the Continental diplomats thought that Britain was not in earnest. Moreover, further democratic revolutions broke out in Naples, Piedmont and Portugal. The Constitution of 1812 was demanded in each case. Metternich was affected by the first two, and now accepted the idea of a Congress. Castlereagh was still reluctant to attend one, and so sent only subordinate officials to represent Britain.

of a great proportion of the Continent of Europe from the military dominion of France; and having subdued the Conqueror, it took the State of Possession, as established by the Peace, under the protection of the Alliance.—It never was, however, intended as an Union for the Government of the World, or for the Superintendence of the Internal Affairs of other States.

'It provided specifically against an infraction on the part of France of the state of possession then created: It provided against the Return of the Usurper [Napoleon] or any of his Family to the throne: It further designated the Revolutionary Power which had convulsed France and desolated Europe, as an object of its constant solicitude, but it was the Revolutionary power more particularly in its Military Character actual and existent within France against which it intended to take Precautions, rather than against the Democratic Principles, then as now, but too generally spread throughout Europe . . .

'. . . Nothing could be more injurious to the Continental Powers than to have their affairs made matter of daily Discussion in our Parliament, which nevertheless must be the consequence of Their precipitately mixing themselves in the affairs of other States, if We should consent to proceed pari passu with them in such interferences . . .

'. . . The fact is that we do not, and cannot feel alike upon all subjects. Our Position, our Institutions, the Habits of thinking, and the prejudice of our People, render us essentially different . . .

'. . . No Country having a Representative System of Gov[ernmen]t could act upon it [the principle of one state interfering by force in the internal affairs of another], – and the sooner such a Doctrine shall be distinctly abjured as forming in any Degree the Basis of our Alliance, the better . . .

'. . . We [England] shall be found in our Place when actual danger menaces the [territorial] System of Europe; but this Country cannot, and will not, act upon abstract and speculative Principles of Precaution . . . ' In one word, as Castlereagh writes, keep the Alliance "within its *commonsense* limits". [His own italics.]

The Congress met towards the end of 1820 at Troppau. Alexander drove furiously and induced Metternich and Prussia to concur in a circular, which asserted that the Three Powers would never recognise the right of a people to circumscribe the power of their kings. The three monarchs of Eastern Europe threatened, in fact, to make war on revolution, in the interest of kings, wherever it raised its head. Castlereagh, as soon as these sentiments became known, published a despatch (January 1821), in which he repeated the sentiments of May 5, 1820. In Parliament he declared that the Troppau Circular was 'destitute of common sense.'

The breach between the Allies was now widening. But Alexander went on. He issued further circulars full of 'high-flying sentiments.' A third Congress at Laibach (Ljubljana) in 1821 commissioned Metternich, as the instrument of the Alliance, to suppress revolution and constitutions in Naples and Piedmont. The Austrian armies moved into Italy in March 1821, destroyed the constitutions of Piedmont and Naples, and set up the Kings once more upon their old thrones. Castlereagh openly declined to have anything to do with such proceedings.

Most people would now have said that the period of international government was at an end; but this was not yet the case. In March 1821 a revolt broke out in Greece agaist the Turks. It was not really a democratic revolt or a demand for a constitution at all; it was a national revolt, a movement of Greek Christians to overthrow an abominable alien tyrant. Metternich, however, recognised no difference between Sultan Mahmud of Turkey and King Ferdinand of Naples or of Spain. The cause of monarchy was, he thought, equally endangered, the support of the moral union equally necessary; and this view might be used to counter the possibility that Alexander would declare war against the Turk at once in the interests of his co-religionists in Greece. To avert this peril was an evident necessity. Metternich and Castlereagh met one another at Hanover towards the end of 1821, patched over their difficulties and agreed to summon one more Congress, where they hoped to prevent Alexander from taking any active measures against Turkey.

The Congress was summoned for the autumn of 1822, but, before it met, two events happened. The disturbances in Spain became so serious in July that France began to talk of interference there; and, on August 3, Castlereagh, whose mind had given way, took his own life. In his later years Castlereagh had shown some objections to the Congress System; he was succeeded by Canning, who destroyed it.

The Congress at Verona was soon occupied with Spain rather than with Greece, for at the beginning of the meeting France asked the Alliance if it would support her in the invasion of Spain. Canning, who regarded Congresses with suspicion, sent the instruction that, if there was a determined project to interfere by force or by menace, then, *come what may*, Britain would not be a party. This instruction was communicated by Wellington to the Congress on October 30, 1822. It was a bombshell and prevented the Alliance as a whole from acting by armed force in Spain, though France took separate action.[1]

Canning's attitude in 1822 had damaged the 'moral solidarity' of Europe, and injured the Congress System. But the system was not yet extinguished. In December 1823 the King of Spain, now restored to his throne, summoned the Allies to a Congress on Spanish America. To the astonishment of Europe, Canning flatly declined to send a British representative (January 30, 1824). The result was that the attempted Congress was a failure. Later, in 1824, Alexander attempted to call a Congress over the question of Turkey and Greece. Canning finally refused to attend this, on behalf of Britain, in November 1824. The other Four Great Powers, however, met at St. Petersburg in January 1825, although they broke up in May on very bad terms and without having decided anything. To all intents and purposes this was the end of the Congress System.

Canning's objections to this project of international government may be stated as follows. Congresses, he said, were all very well to settle a Treaty. But a system of 'periodic reunions' of Powers was highly dangerous. In the first place, the people of Britain did not like their delegate, who represented a parliamentary state, to commune in secret with despotic powers. Britain, too, was liable to be outvoted. In the second place, the Congress System tended to establish the system of general intervention by force in the internal affairs of different countries, a system which Britain, by the very nature of its government, was bound to oppose. In the third place, small Powers were not represented and their rights were apt to be disregarded or overridden. Canning would have had no objection to a Congress, limited to a policy of 'moral solidarity,' consulting the wishes of small Powers, and disclaiming the use of force. But the Congress System, as it had developed by 1822, did none of these things, and Canning thought it better to oppose it altogether. And in this opposition he was entirely successful. From 1825 onwards the Congress System was discredited; and the policy for Europe was defined by Canning as 'Every nation for itself, and God for us all!'

It is not fair, however, to dismiss this first serious experiment in international government without pointing out some of its merits. The idea of personal conference and mutual confidence between rulers was excellent. Castlereagh was sincere in promoting the reunions, and so was Metternich, up to a point. But Alexander went too far and too fast for both. After 1820 the Congress System became in effect a trade union of Kings for suppressing the liberties of peoples.

---

[1] France eventually invaded Spain on her own responsibility in April 1823, restored King Ferdinand, and abolished the Spanish Constitution.

To the continuance of that system, parliamentary Britain could not consent and parliamentary France only shared in it with reluctance. The smaller Powers, who did not share in it at all, were naturally opposed to it. In the thirties there were European Congresses again which did much good. But, though the Great Powers still took the lead, there was no collective attempt to revive the doctrines of absolutism, to condemn revolution as such, or to proclaim a general policy of intervention by force. Parliamentary Britain and parliamentary France were, therefore, able to enter freely into conference with the three despotic monarchies of East Europe. The conference which settled the independence of Belgium is a good example of how Great Powers can meet without embarrassment and effect lasting good, because each respected the institutions and difficulties of the other.

It is worth while comparing the period of Congressional Government with the second great attempt to create an international organisation, that which gave birth to the League of Nations in 1919. The Holy Alliance Declaration had really nothing to do with the Treaty of Vienna, while the Covenant of the League was a vital part, indeed obviously the most vital part, of the Treaty of Versailles. Congressional Government failed because it attempted first to promote, and then to enforce, the monarchical principle upon the different states of Europe. In the League there were monarchies, despotic and constitutional, and republics, and semi-sovereign communities. Members were not, as in the Holy Alliance, 'members of one and the same Christian nation'; they were members of a League of Nations, Buddhist, Mussulman and Christian. Congressional Government was attacked by Canning because it infringed the rights of small states; on the Council of the League of Nations small states could outvote the Great Powers, while any small Power could express its views in the Assembly. The Congress system died because despotism was not reconcilable with the opposed system of parliamentary freedom; the League of Nations survived until it was destroyed in a world at war. Both were dangerously weakened by the fact that they were never universal; in neither case did the Powers learn the secret of reconciling national interests with the common good. It is too soon yet to judge whether the secret has been found by the makers of the third great experiment in international organisation.

Chapter 9

AUTOCRACY, CONSTITIONALISM AND REVOLUTION, 1815–48

The German Confederation, established by the Powers in 1815, was intended to hand over Germany to the management of Austria and Prussia. Metternich quickly assumed the lead. His aims, though concealed with much art beneath a cloud of pompous phrases, were simply and brutally realistic. He believed that the one necessity was to crush Liberalism, Constitutionalism and Parliamentarism in Germany. Prussia was militaristic (Canning at any rate called her 'a downright grenadier, with no politics but the drumhead and cat-o'-nine-tails'). So long, therefore, as Austria pursued this reactionary policy, Prussia would be obliged to follow in her wake. Metternich trusted to win her gratitude and support by discouraging the spreading of the vigorous constitutional movement in the south German states. Nassau, Baden, Württemberg, Bavaria and Saxe-Weimar acquired parliaments though not, of course, parliamentary government. He was to prove completely successful. No more parliaments were set up.

The Conference of German Princes which met at Carlsbad in 1819, endorsed Metternich's policy. Regulations for controlling the press, for intimidating the universities and for curbing the full expression of opinion throughout Germany, were adopted with unanimity. Metternich thus became possessed of a powerful police instrument, which he used without mercy. For a time he was quite successful. During 1820–21 the revolutions in other parts of Europe did not affect Germany, where Metternich's iron rod kept Liberals in awe. The revolutionary wave of 1830 caused some slight disturbances in German states; it would have caused more but for Metternich. But, from that time forward, his power declined. He had nothing to offer young Germany but repression, intimidation, and a police régime. His rule was barren and sterile and unimaginative. It was impossible for the rising tide in Germany to be bound within this narrow dyke. Hence, in 1848 the wave, which for a moment overthrew all old institutions in Germany, had gathered force from the repression itself. *Après moi le déluge* was repeated when Metternich and Old Austria vanished together in 1848.

Old Austria really did vanish in 1848, because it was feudal, archaic, despotic and despised. Old Prussia did not vanish then because, Old Prussia had already been replaced by a new one born in the period of reform after Jena, in the bitterness and humiliation of Napoleon's colossal triumph. It is true that the parliamentary movement died out in Prussia and, since with her Saxon and Rhenish acquisitions she ruled a third of Germany, this was important. Frederick William had promised an elective parliament in 1810 and his Minister, Hardenberg, in 1817 renewed assurances that it would be granted, and there were serious considerations of a constitution in 1820 and 1823, but after that interest waned. It is also true that after the departure of Hardenberg and Humboldt, Frederick William III had no minister capable of resisting the domination of Metternich. But if politically Prussia surrendered her independence to Austria, economically she advanced to the leadership of Germany. There were three main reasons for this. First, the part of Saxony and the Prussian Rhine Province acquired in 1815 were far ahead of the rest of Germany in resources, communications and technical development. Second, especially in the Rhine Province, she had the advantage of old-established business families, an adequate labour supply and freedom from antiquated restrictions. This meant that her business classes were open-minded to the ideas of economists like Friedrich List and Friedrich Harkort; ready to adopt new methods in banking and economic organisation (the joint stock company) and in industrial production (mechanisation). Third, she had a good tradition in the bureaucratic encouragement of private industrial enterprise, by state subventions, by state aid to technical schools, by state-aided missions abroad to capture foreign inventions.

Prussia stepped forward most seriously to the economic leadership of Germany by her foundation of the Zollverein. The roots of this Customs Union were in the economic distress immediately after the conclusion of peace. The years 1816–17 were years of hardship and shortage, caused among other things by the closing of the French markets exploited when the Rhineland had been part of France, by the reopening of the continent to the flood of textile and metal goods produced by the mechanised industries of Britain, and by the tariff walls erected by Austria, Russia, Holland and Britain. Another root was the agitation for so-called free trade by List and his followers. The supporters of national unification encouraged public opinion to be favourable to the action which the German Governments took for economic reasons or for reasons of local policy. Thus the most important root of the Zollverein was the Prussian tariff of May 26, 1818. This was a frontier tariff erected all round the Prussian Kingdom, so that after 1821 no duties were levied on goods entering the towns or crossing the frontiers of enclave territories. At the outside frontier raw materials for manufacture were admitted free of duty, but import duties were levied on industrial and agricultural products. Prussia had an effective means of pressure on her neighbours when she levied high duties on goods in transit, that is goods going through Prussia for consumption elsewhere. This sent prices up in the nine small states on Prussia's borders. Between 1819 and 1831 they negotiated arrangements for admission to the Prussian tariff system as if they were Prussian territory. The Customs Union that thus grew up was no more than one of several Customs Unions that the same economic motives, which had impelled Prussia to action, produced elsewhere. But the south German states responded to the new Prussian system by making a Customs Union of their own. When this failed Hesse Darmstadt negotiated her admission to the Prussian system (1828) while Bavaria and Württemberg, later joined by Baden, made their own union. In 1828 Saxony, the five Saxon Duchies in Thuringia, Hesse Cassel and Nassau made a Middle German Union. But both the Bavaria-Württemberg and the Middle German Union failed, and, one by one, these negotiated their admission to the Prussian system. On January 1, 1834, the fully constituted Zollverein came into being. It included all Germany except the three north German maritime states, Hanover, Brunswick and Oldenburg, and, of course, the Austrian Empire.

Moreover, the Prussian army, reformed by Scharnhorst and Gneisenau, had shown its power under Blücher in the campaigns of 1813, 1814 and 1815 and had recovered its importance. Between 1815 and 1840, when Frederick William III was succeeded by a man of a different calibre, the army was, as in the eighteenth century, the most important factor in the development of the State. Only second in importance to the army was the bureaucracy. It was at once honest and efficient. It reformed the finances, organised the localities, and governed with increasing skill. Prussians were well-educated, hard-working, law-abiding and prosperous.

Frederick William IV, who came to the throne in 1840 and ruled until his mind failed in 1858, was a gifted king, perhaps with more weight of intellectual powers than his character could support; for there were many vacillations in his policy. The treatment of the Poles in Prussia, for example, was not handled with ability. Sometimes they were cajoled, sometimes they were overawed. And though the Poles might have been conciliated by the one conduct or intimidated by the other, they came to despise and counterwork a Government which could not make up its mind to be either benevolent or harsh.

To two things Frederick William IV set his mind with some consistency. One was the constitutional reform of Prussia. A distinction was developed in Prussia between a constitution and a parliament. Frederick William wished to take a middle course between an elective parliament with legislative powers and a mere revival of the Provincial Estates or mediaeval Diets. The word 'constitution' would describe whatever new arrangement was constituted. But his ideas mystified his ministers. He schemed in 1841 for a meeting of all the Provincial Estates together in a United Diet, in 1842 for a combined meeting of standing committees of the Provincial Estates, in 1844 for a reorganisation of the Provincial Estates so that they might give financial advice without acquiring legislative powers. All three schemes failed. The King did just enough to educate his subjects in parliamentary ideas, and yet not enough to satisfy any political aspirations. In February 1847 with no preliminary warning he suddenly summoned the United Diet. It seemed restless meddling rather than consistent policy and the King's want of steadiness accounts for much of the confusion and turbulence in Prussia in 1848–49.

The second thing to which the King set his mind was the reform of the German Confederation. There were those in Germany who hoped to give the Confederation a central executive and an elective parliament instead of the assembly of diplomatic representatives of the member states which sat in Frankfurt and was called the Federal Diet. Others hoped to make a reality of clauses in the Federal Act which provided for a common German army and a common judiciary. Frederick William IV, with the advice of General von Radowitz, resolved to give life to the Confederation in its military aspect. Prussia prepared a strategic plan for the defence of Germany and took the lead in organising under three commands the ten Army Corps to which the states were bound by the Federal Act to contribute contingents. In 1840 there was a scare of war with France and already then it had been Prussia and not Austria who took the lead in negotiating with the Governments to mobilise this army. Radowitz contributed much to the standardisation and co-ordination of military practice among the German states. In 1847 there was much canvassing of reform of the Confederation and not only in Prussia. Frederick William and Radowitz took up these projects but with little sympathy for any wide sharing of political power. It was this interest, as well as the power of Prussia, which lead to Frederick William's being offered the crown of Germany in 1849. He was to refuse it.

In 1814 France began the experiment of a Constitutional Monarchy. Alexander had insisted that the Bourbons should not return till a Charter was granted and the constitutional experiment begun (above, page 131). Louis XVIII tried to retain as much power as he could. The result was that he had to take the blame for things not of his doing, except that he was incurably indolent. In the south there was the White Terror when adherents of Napoleon, supposed or real, were massacred. The first elections, to everyone's surprise, filled the Chamber with young and zealous royalists. It was a Chamber the King could never have expected to find. He called it *La Chambre*

Introuvable. His first ministers had some success in foreign affairs and finance. But they showed unwisdom in other ways, by cutting down the army and intimidating the press and making mistakes in detail, as when they abolished the tricolour. After Napoleon's defeat at Waterloo they shot Marshal Ney. Frenchmen were indignant that a man who was a heroic soldier but no politician should have been condemned by dubious methods and shot under circumstances of peculiar atrocity. When the Government tried to put a brake on repression the cohesion of the royalists collapsed. Fresh elections in 1816 produced a less pliable Chamber but enabled the Government to experiment with a middle-of-the-road policy until 1820.

The Government did nothing when the *émigrés* attempted to regain their property or the Church recover control of secondary education. Its policy, therefore, suggested to the common man that the Bourbons meant to take from the peasant his land and upset the Revolution. Despite every effort the opposition in Parliament increased. In 1823 the Government took a bold plunge and went to war with Spain, which had forced a Bourbon king to accept a democratic constitution. The enterprise was brilliantly successful, the king was freed and the constitution abolished. But everyone knew that the Bourbon General in command was without experience and that the Marshal of Napoleon, who had accompanied him, had won the laurels which he wore. These tinsel glories only awakened the anger or contempt of the veterans of Napoleon.

Louis XVIII died in 1824, and the last restraint of wisdom was removed. Charles X began well by announcing his attachment to parliamentary institutions and by appealing to the French love of ceremonial. But he soon became unpopular. He was ultra-reactionary and clerical to the core. The indemnity he granted to the *émigrés* was intended to quiet their claims and give security to the peasants. His law against sacrilege, unenforceable anyhow, was intended as a manifesto against the secularisation of the State. Both were misinterpreted. Villèle, Prime Minister since 1822, continued to strengthen the financial administration and French prosperity increased, but he put a low, utilitarian stamp on all he did. France became bored, and the boredom of the people is dangerous to the rulers of France. In 1827 the opposition in Parliament got worse; the National Guard could not be trusted, and had to be disbanded; finally Villèle was dismissed. He was succeeded, after an interval, by Polignac, an intriguing diplomat wholly unfitted for the post. He was Chauvinist, which was bad; ultra-clerical, which was worse; and an enemy of Parliament, which was fatal. He offered 'a spirited' foreign policy and promoted the conquest of Algiers, but he could not work with the Chamber which successive elections had made more and more liberal. Finally he induced the King to issue four Ordinances dissolving Parliament, altering the electoral law, and gagging the press.

In July 1830 Charles X fell, overthrown by a public opinion whose force Polignac in entire ignorance had let loose. The revolution which occurred was due largely to Lafayette and to Talleyrand, two men who were not often found in agreement, and their agreement on this occasion is suggestive. Their plan was a Constitutional Monarchy of the British type, with Louis Philippe (the Orleanist Bourbon) as a good solid bourgeois and constitutional king. With comparatively little difficulty the public was persuaded to try the experiment, and to accept Louis Philippe as their ruler. The choice was not a bad one, and the event impressed Europe a good deal. A revolution in France had been bloodless and it had set up a solid constitutional monarchy. It seemed to correspond, indeed, with changes in French society. During the thirties and forties the old families in France retract in political importance in both local and central government. Their sons engage in careers and marry into the *haute bourgeoisie*. Political power was in the hands of financiers, bankers and wealthy capitalists in the distributive trades—with Guizot in the forties in the hands of a Protestant, historian and man of letters. Their power was backed by the old families. Even so at the end of Louis Philippe's reign it is the men with their daily bread to earn, professional men and journalists, who are to the fore. One should also notice that, though the reign was a period of prosperity for the business classes, it was one of increasing poverty for the growing working class in the cities.

Louis Philippe had many qualifications for his task. He was shrewd though not scrupulous, and fully conscious that he must never forget his rôle of constitutional king. He was tolerant in religious matters, whereas his predecessors had been bigoted. He took pains to divest himself of any character of Divine Right. He sent his sons to the ordinary schools, he walked about the streets with an umbrella under his arm, he lived in the Tuileries and appeared readily to bow from the balcony when there was any applause in the streets. He was anxious to represent himself as the heir of all the historic tendencies of France. As a Bourbon he claimed to embody the historic past, as the son of Egalité and the soldier of Jemappes he claimed to have shared in the glories of the Revolution. He restored the tricolour and the National Guard. He did not even refuse to recognise Napoleon. During his reign, the body of the great Conqueror was brought from St. Helena by a son of the royal house and laid in the most magnificent of resting places at the Invalides. He filled the Palace of Versailles with pictures of all the battles of French history and solemnly dedicated it 'to all the glories of France.'

At first sight it is difficult to see how any ruler could have done more to conciliate his subjects. He did much, but he did not do enough. It may be that the Revolution or Napoleon had drawn too deep a trench between Bourbonist France and the France which succeeded it. Now there were no Declarations of Liberty and Equality, no colossal victories over kings, no dazzling or splendid personalities. At any rate the Bourbons had been hopelessly discredited, and Louis Philippe could not deny that he was a Bourbon. His aim was peace and commerce, and these had no brilliance, none of that *éclat* so dear to French minds. Perhaps the Revolution of 1848 would not have been caused by the *ennui* of France, though Lamartine has written that it was. There was something deeper than the resentment of Paris at the tedium of his rule. Parliament was an assembly of businessmen and bourgeois, it was manipulated by bribery and by tricks, and in this manipulation Louis Philippe had a full share. A king who excelled in shuffling the parliamentary cards, and was suspected of marking them, could not be the ideal of France.

Louis Philippe's reign was unfortunate in result and in France, but it was not without benefits in Europe. At the very outset he lent great aid to the cause of constitutionalism and to peace. Neither was wholly to his own advantage.

As a direct result of the July Revolution in France, a revolution in Belgium broke out in August. The great experiment of a Dutch-Belgian reunion, the reunion, that is to say, of the Seventeen Provinces of the sixteenth century, might well have succeeded. William I, indeed, seemed to be succeeding between 1825 and 1828. He made no attempt to 'dutchify' the south. Indeed, some have said that Holland's fault was that she was not prepared to play the part Prussia played in Germany or Sardinia in Italy. But he pursued policies that were Belgian through a bureaucracy that was chiefly Dutch. Moreover, he became entangled in Belgian domestic disputes, particularly over the control of schools by the Catholic Church, and so incurred the wrath of one section of Belgian opinion. Finally the dynamic classes in Belgium, the manufacturers and a new working class, were affected by the liberal ideas and disliked William's policy of economic control. The supporters of the reunion were the quieter classes, writers, scholars, historians, classicists. The disorders of 1830 probably signalised a struggle for power, but it came to be expressed in the language of national antagonism. A Belgian Deputation laid their grievances before the Dutch King at The Hague. At first they demanded only an administrative separation from Holland, and were ready to accept the Prince of Orange as a Viceroy. The King insisted, before complying with these demands, that Dutch troops should occupy Brussels, and their entry into the Belgian capital produced three days of street fighting (end of September 1830). At the end of that time they were expelled. All Belgium now rose, and the Dutch troops were confined within the walls of Antwerp and Maestricht. A provisional Government was appointed, a National Convention summoned, and it was proclaimed that 'the Belgian Provinces, detached by force from Holland, shall form an independent State.'

The Dutch King now took the judicious step of appealing to the

Five Great Powers to intervene, on the ground that the territorial settlement of Vienna was threatened. He was right. The Quadruple Alliance had guaranteed to maintain by force the territorial limits imposed at Vienna for twenty years. France had agreed to these limits, and, if Louis Philippe broke this agreement, the four other Great Powers had the right to make war upon him. Louis Philippe's position was, therefore, peculiarly delicate. Many Frenchmen wanted to annex Belgium or part of it, and he was still insecure on the throne. If he surrendered to the patriots of France, he risked war with Europe; if he surrendered to Europe, he risked dethronement in France.

The position for the four Allies was difficult too. The first breach was thus threatened in the fabric of Vienna. Were they to permit it or not? Fortunately the three great despotic monarchies of the East were not prepared to act at once in the matter. While they hesitated, in November 1830, before negotiations had got very far, Palmerston came into the Foreign Office in Britain. He was quite resolved not to let France gain any influence over Belgium, but he was not equally resolved to maintain the settlements of Vienna. After all, treaties had to come to an end sometime, and he did not think highly of this particular arrangement at Vienna. Being a disciple of Canning, he sympathised with nationality and, provided Belgium could be formed into a nation, he thought that she could be turned into a good bulwark against France. He had the sense to see that a restless Belgium, attached to Holland, would invite French attacks, while a free Belgium would be more likely to repel them. He was, moreover, not unwilling to consider the possibility of a self-governing Belgium under a separate Dutch ruler.

The Belgian National Congress met at Brussels on November 10, 1830. Feeling was in favour of France, and, but for the fear of Britain, a French prince would probably have been proposed for the throne. As it was, the Congress declared the House of Orange deposed, the throne vacant, and the future form of government a limited and hereditary monarchy. The Five Powers now intimated to the Belgian Congress that they should maintain the House of Orange, and that, if they did not, Allied armies might occupy the country. The Belgian Congress haughtily refused to yield. Most fortunately for them a revolution broke out in Poland at the end of November. This attracted the direct attention of the Tsar, and indirectly concerned both Austria and Prussia, whose Polish subjects were in sympathy with the rising. Hence the attention of the three Eastern Powers was drawn elsewhere, and Palmerston was left to face Louis Philippe.

Talleyrand was sent by Louis Philippe to London to see if he could not secure advantages from Palmerston. The veteran diplomat, however, found his match. He had the worst cards, and Palmerston was not afraid of playing his trumps. Talleyrand first demanded

Luxembourg, and next Philippeville and Marienburg, for France. Palmerston showed no sign of yielding, so that Talleyrand was compelled to collapse. The solution, which saved the face of France, was to announce the perpetual neutrality of Belgium and to guarantee it by the word of the Five Powers. This decision was announced in January 1831. The French Government blustered and talked of disavowing Talleyrand, but eventually accepted the terms, as did the King of Holland. The Belgian Congress refused to do so, and the proposal for a French prince remained a posibility. On February 3 they chose the second son of Louis Philippe, the Duc de Nemours, as their king. The Five Powers now sent Belgium an ultimatum, embodying their demand for neutrality and thus excluding the Duc de Nemours. This expired on June 1. On June 4 the Congress gave way, revoked its previous decision and elected Leopold of Saxe-Coburg-Gotha as their king.

Leopold had been the husband of Princess Charlotte, and after her death he had continued to reside in England. He was a liberal in principle, and a most able, prudent, and sagacious man. By infinite tact and patience Leopold succeeded in working out a settlement, known as the Eighteen Articles, which he persuaded the Five Powers to accept. After much trouble the Belgian Congress also accepted them, but the King of Holland refused to do so. He sent his troops again into Belgium in August, and Louis Philippe promptly replied by marching in French troops who occupied Brussels. The settlement seemed as far off, and the French danger as great, as ever.

Palmerston, however, now again took a strong line. The Polish revolution was over, and the Tsar and the King of Prussia both offered to send troops to expel the French. Palmerston bluntly told France that she must evacuate Belgium 'in a few days,' and in September France consented to do so. The settlement was really arrived at in the Five-Power Treaty with Belgium of November 15, 1831. But infinite difficulties and delays appeared. The three Great Eastern Powers were unwilling to ratify the treaty, and the Dutch King refused to accept it or evacuate Antwerp. Eventually, a French army and a Franco-British fleet operated against him and expelled the Dutch finally from Belgium (1832–33). It took six years more before a definitive treaty satisfying all parties was signed by the Five Great Powers (April 19, 1839). This treaty, which finally established the independence of Belgium, is the famous 'scrap of paper' torn up by Germany when she invaded Belgium in 1914.

It has been right to dwell at some length on this Belgian incident for two reasons. It illustrates the difficulties of Louis Philippe, anxious for peace yet afraid of his Chauvinists, and compelled to shuffle and balance between Europe and France. More important than all this, it exhibits a breach made in the Treaty of Vienna in the name of national independence. It marks the triumph of parliamentarism and constitutionalism, alike in France, Belgium, and Britain. For Belgium the results were entirely good. She obtained an ideal constitutional king and was able to draw up a constitution remarkable for its liberality and breadth. Behind the guarantee she built up her national life and characteristics, her art, her literature, her patriotism, her individuality. It is doubtful whether Belgium was a nation in 1830; it is certain that she was eighty years later. And she owed her life to Palmerston and her marvellous development to her sagacious ruler.

In the matter of Belgium, Palmerston achieved decisive success in promulgating the cause of limited and constitutional monarchy throughout Europe. That was because the Belgians were fitted by nature to be free and orderly, ready to obey the law and to enjoy the gift of liberty. For a precisely opposite reason he was to fail in bringing the lessons of liberty to Portugal and to Spain. And, in the result, he was involved in disagreeable controversy with Louis Philippe. The situation was simple, though the details are complex. During the early thirties, Portugal and Spain were both ruled by child-queens whose advisers professed to be constitutional, and opposed by Absolutist pretenders who raised rebellions against them. Palmerston sided with the constitutionalists in each case, and finally offered an alliance to both Portuguese and Spanish Queens to expel their pretenders. It was accepted, and being joined also by France (April 22, 1834), was known as the Quadruple Alliance. The Portuguese Pretender was easily expelled (1834) but it needed some years to get rid of Don Carlos in Spain (1839). Palmerston had hoped by this arrangement to erect a constitutional *bloc* in West Europe, which would balance the three despotic monarchies in the East. He thought that Britain would keep the lead, and that Portugal and Spain could be used to persuade France to follow. Nothing of the sort happened. Portugal and Spain were no more important as constitutional states than as despotic monarchies. They might, with perfect safety, have been left to conclude their sordid and futile quarrels without help from outside. They proved no aid to either Britain or France; on the contrary, the Spanish question involved both countries in a serious quarrel, which contributed to the overthrow of Louis Philippe.

The Louis Philippe period, despite several serious incidents, was marked, during most of its time, by increasing co-operation between Britain and France. Royal visits took place and a species of *entente cordiale* was established which seemed complete by 1845. It was not only a memorable epoch in the history of the two countries, but an immense support to Louis Philippe in France. The rupture, which took place in 1846 over Spain, was, therefore, doubly unfortunate. It turned on the question of the marriage of the young Queen Isabella and her sister. Louis Philippe finally brought it about that Francisco, Duke of Cadiz, should marry the Queen, and her sister should marry the Duc de Montpensier. These arrangements, celebrated on October 10, 1846, concealed a mean trick. The French Government had promised the British that the Queen's sister should not marry a French prince until Isabella *was married and had had children*. The marriages were now simultaneous, and the Duke of Cadiz *was incapable of having children*.[1] It was believed by Britain that Louis Philippe thought that he had secured the reversion of the Spanish throne to his son, though it cannot be proved that this was in fact the French motive.

Palmerston's wrath was great. He protested violently against the 'indirect influence' and 'illegitimate methods' of France with regard to Spain. War did not follow, but hostility did. Louis Philippe had lost his best friend in Europe and ruined the *entente cordiale*. He had no more to hope from Britain, and the continuance of his throne and dynasty depended henceforth upon France and upon himself.

Even so late as 1846 many people thought that France had at last learnt Britain's ways and was modelling herself on her Parliament and Constitution. They little knew France who said that. From all sides came mutterings of the storm. The French papers were scathing in their comments on the trickery shown both in the home and in the foreign policy of the Government. The transport of the body of Napoleon to the Invalides revived Bonapartism and Napoleon-worship in all its fervour. While Thiers was writing lyrical raptures about imperialism, Lamartine revived the sentimental enthusiasm for a republic by the eloquence of his *History of the Girondins*.[2] Louis Philippe and Guizot, his Foreign Minister, saw well enough that France wanted something. But the small remedies and concessions they were prepared to offer were taken as signs of weakness by their opponents.

The Orleans Monarchy was based on a definite theory. It had rejected Divine Right and established the reign of 'pure reason.' It had thrown over the Catholic party and the Bourbon Legitimists, but it had made no effort to come to terms with the revolutionists or the democrats. It attempted to establish the rule of the bourgeois, the middle class, as a 'golden mean' between Ultraism and Republicanism. Citizens who paid 500 francs in taxes were eligible for election as deputies to Parliament; those who paid 200 francs were eligible

---

[1] The children Isabella eventually bore were apparently those of someone not her husband. The Duc de Montpensier was the son of Louis Philippe. The view here given is that of Palmerston, Public Record Office, F.O. 96/21, minute of September 30, 1846. The belief of the British Government and diplomatic service, as well as possible other motives for the French policy, is fully documented in R. Bullen, *Palmerston, Guizot, and the Collapse of the Entente Cordiale* (1970), Ch. V, especially p. 150.

[2] Published 1847. Lamartine's remark, 'My book required a conclusion: it is you who are making it,' came fortuitously true, when the Constitutional Monarchy was succeeded by the Second Republic and then the Second Empire, cp. D. Johnson, *Guizot* (1963), p. 244.

as voters. No one else had any rights whatever. But the poorer bourgeois had an important privilege. They formed the National Guard, a body which performed (inefficiently and irregularly) the functions of gendarmes and of soldiers. They thus possessed considerable power. But they were expected blindly to obey the dictates of the Parliament and the press and on the public platform which fanned showed lack of discipline on parade. The King was obliged to discontinue reviewing them because they uttered hostile cries when they saw him. In Parliament, through what was termed the 'fatal dexterity' of Guizot in manipulating the instruments of corruption, Louis Philippe was secure. There was, indeed, a formidable opposition led by Thiers, but this opposition in itself would not have been disastrous, for Thiers wished to return to power and his methods were, on the whole, constitutional. But there was much angry talk both in the Parliament and the press and on the public platform which fanned and excited the wilder revolutionary elements without.

The situation at the end of 1847, therefore, was that Louis Philippe had a majority but also a formidable opposition in Parliament, and that the poorer bourgeois in the National Guard were discontented and uncertain. Outside, the agitation both of the Right and of the Left was extreme. The Ultra-Right demanded the Legitimist Bourbons, the White Flag and Catholic education in the schools. The Left was moved by two strong currents. Lamartine was proclaiming the glories of the old Republic, free, conquering, and enlightened. Louis Blanc led a party which added the propaganda of socialism to the already formidable elements of democratic unrest. To the rights of man, to universal suffrage and political equality, he added national workshops, a social policy and a class warfare. Moreover, the secret society (*Société des Saisons* from the names of the seasons given to its sections) led by Blanqui and Barbès kept Baboeuf's ideas alive and from a German branch of it the Communist League of the forties and fifties traced its ancestry. What made these attacks from all quarters so effective against Louis Philippe was that all the different elements of opposition agreed on two points. Whatever the merits of Louis Philippe, his home policy was sordid and corrupt, and his foreign policy had ended by provoking the hostility of Britain. Louis Philippe had counted on Britain to raise him from the condition of a parvenu monarch by acting as 'sponsor' for him in the Courts of Europe. This policy, at one time successful, had now totally failed. The bourgeois monarchy had no longer a *raison d'être*. It had no longer a consistent or intelligible policy. Nothing shows this fact more clearly than that Catholics and Republicans began to approach one another, to concert an attack on the Government.

Guizot, in an unwise speech at the beginning of 1848, denounced the 'blind and hostile passions' which aimed at destroying existing institutions. The opposition, Catholic as well as Republican, decided, since political meetings were illegal, to hold a great banquet in Paris as a protest against Guizot's utterance. The Government threatened to prohibit the banquet, which had been fixed for February 22, 1848. This firm attitude for a moment dismayed the ill-assorted coalition of Catholic Ultras, Democratic Republicans, and of Socialists. But, on the night of February 21–22, the Paris mob intervened, and the result was the fall of Constitutional Monarchy in France (February 25), and the flight of the King and his family to England.

It was the destiny of Louis Philippe to prove that France had no love for Constitutional Monarchy of the British type. Balances of power, limitations of demoncracy, compromises of ideal, were not favoured in France. She liked least of all Louis Philippe's compromise, which was not the rule of a religious idea as under Legitimist Bourbons, nor of a strong man like Napoleon, nor of a democracy like the Republic of 1793. Put in another way, the Monarchy had so developed after the mid thirties as to have only the narrowest basis of support, that of the business classes, and that support proved passive. And so, in 1848, France overthrew Louis Philippe and once more tried first the Republican, and then the Napoleonic, experiment.

During this period Germany, outside Austria, was shifting slowly away from reactionary conservatism towards reform. Belgium successfully established constitutionalism, and France made a prolonged experiment in the same direction, which was feebly imitated by Portugal and by Spain. Elsewhere the resentment of two nations against alien rule fanned hotter passions and led direct to revolution. These two nations had each been partitioned and divided by several powers. Poland was split into three parts, Italy into seven.

When Alexander obtained the larger part of Poland in 1815 he gave it a constitution and declared his intention of governing it as a National Kingdom. He was sincere in his aim and was supported for a time by many patriotic Poles, notably by the noble Czartoryski. But the Russian oil and the Polish vinegar declined to mix. The Poles, the subjected race, felt themselves superior in everything but force. They prided themselves on their Latin culture, aristocratic equality and Catholic religion. It made little difference that Alexander granted them a liberal and progressive constitution. A gift from a Russian ruler, however gracious, was an object of suspicion to most patriotic Poles. The first Diet opened in 1818, but a severe press censorship was established in 1819. Though the Diet met again in 1820, Alexander soon dismissed it, and did not summon another for five years. Secret societies had begun to grow, and Alexander, on opening the third Diet in 1825, so restricted its powers as practically to suppress the constitution.

When Alexander died at the end of 1825 there occurred the

Decembrist rising among Russian liberals, in which Poles were involved. The young Tsar Nicholas was an autocrat. He was deeply incensed by the attitude of Poland, and although it was probably at this time that he resolved to suppress such liberties as remained to Poland, he concealed his purpose. After five years he summoned the fourth and (as it proved) the last Diet. The session was short, and suspicion was evident on both sides. The French Revolution of July 1830 greatly excited the Poles, and secret societies developed even among the officers of the army. The preparations which Nicholas now made to suppress revolution in France and in Belgium provoked an insurrection in Warsaw (November 29). An interim government was formed by the end of the year, which was pro-national and anti-Russian.

The Poles showed great indecision. Their army numbered over 50,000 men and the Tsar was caught unprepared; but they wasted time in futile negotiation. At the same time they made the breach inevitable by deposing the Tsar (January 1831). The Russians, who had now concentrated their troops, entered the kingdom in February in overwhelming numbers. The first battles were indecisive, and the Poles held their own till May. But the end was only delayed till September. The Russians then entered Warsaw and destroyed the constitutional kingdom and liberties of Poland at a blow. For a quarter of a century an iron rule was imposed upon her. She lost all separate and orginic life, and was governed purely by the sword of Russia.

The chivalrous character of the Poles, their revolutionary zeal and their gallant resistance awakened great sympathy in Europe. It was kept alive by the presence, for instance, in London and Paris of large numbers of Polish refugees. Polish national feeling was alike too intense to permit co-operation with Russia and too strong to be subdued even by the harsh and brutal measures of repression which Russia now applied. Moreover, though separated into three parts, Poland preserved her ideal of national unity. She remained, wrote Maitland, 'three undigested fragments in three stomachs.' And the Poles under Austrian, and even at times under Prussian, rule had some chance of expressing their nationality. The annexation of Cracow by Austria in 1846 proved a real aid to a Polish resurrection. For Austria allowed the Poles of Galicia something like 'home rule,' and under her mild sway the national feeling developed. Cracow became the centre of Polish culture, art, literature, and national propaganda. And the nucleus of national aspiration formed there was eventually to expand over all Poland.

We have already seen how French rule in Italy stimulated Italian political liberalism and national feeling, already developing at the end of the eighteenth century. On the one hand hatred of foreign invasion and the flow of money and art treasures to Paris and resentment at the tribute of men for the French armies were common national sentiments shared by all Italians. On the other hand, the part played by Italians in the early Republics—Melzi d'Eril in the Cisalpine and Mario Pagano in the Parthenopian—rationalising administration, modernising finances, introducing public primary education and establishing equality before the law, stimulated liberal and patriotic ideas. In a new generation of dramatists (Alfieri and Niccolini), poets (Ugo Foscolo and Giacomo Leopardi), novelists and historians (Alessandro Manzoni), there was a fresh flowering of Italian literature and an awakening sense of pride in the long series of great historical events that had happened in the peninsula and in the great cultural achievements of Italians in the past. Moreover, during the Napoleonic period a good deal of political cohesion had in fact occurred. After the French annexation of Savoy and Nice and later Piedmont, at the very end of the Napoleonic period, there were only three units in Italy: the Kingdom of Italy, the Papal States, and the Kingdom of Naples. The Kingdom of Naples fell to the vigorous and dashing Murat, who finally conceived the bold scheme of uniting all Italy under his rule. During 1814 and 1815 Murat put his plan into practice and finally proclaimed the Union of Italy. He was defeated and eventually shot, but his rash action was symptomatic of the way many men were thinking at that time. These were the facts of life in 1815: Risorgimento, which means resurrection or revival, was happening in the vigorous intellectual life of Milan, Florence, even Rome; assimilation was taking place among the various Italian States.

The Italian States had been restored, as we have seen, by the Treaty of Vienna. But life within them was much changed since 1789. In Lombardy, where Austrian rule held back the expression of political ideas, there was a vigorous interest in education and economics and there were journals such as the *Politechnico* and then the *Annali di Statistica* in which writers like G. D. Romagnosi and C. Cattaneo, later to play a part in the Milan insurrection, expressed their ideas. In Piedmont a political opposition to the autocratic methods of the King raised the standard of liberal constitutionalism. The insurrection of 1821 in which the heir to the throne, Charles Albert, was involved, failed but it created a legend. Silvio Pellico's account of his imprisonment after it was a powerful literary weapon against Austria who had helped with her army to quell the rising. Three Piedmontese writers, V. Gioberti, Cesare Balbo and Massimo d'Azeglio, not only contributed to the great histories written during the Risorgimento but by their discussion, in books written during the forties, of the forms which a united Italy might take, performed an excellent work of propaganda. Venice was distinctive. Ruled by Austria, her aim was self-government. She was anxious to make the institutions, known as the congregations, established by Austria into genuine instruments of 'home rule'. In Tuscany, and even in Rome between 1816 and 1823 and again after 1846, there was a reforming movement, utilitarian and materialist it is true and derived from the eighteenth-century Enlightenment as well as from Napoleonic paternalism, but none the less real for that. Tuscany's capital, Florence, was the home of G. P. Vieusseux and his monthly periodical, *Antologia*, and after its suppression in 1833 the *Archivio Storico Italiano*. These were focal points of the Italian cultural revival. Secret societies had existed throughout the Revolutionary and Napoleonic periods and they continued. The Federati had prompted the rising in Turin in 1821. The best known of them, the Carbonari, prompted a rising in Naples in 1820. The King was made to swear to a democratic constitution. It was soon suppressed by the Austrian army. Naples and Sicily were both better and worse off than in 1789. They were better off in that entails and feudal tenures had been abolished and their societies were more open. They were worse off in that the peasants were now vulnerable to victimisation by a new gentry seeking to making profits out of their estates. Thus regionalism was strong in Italy between 1815 and 1840 but each region was making its distinct contribution to a common Italian national awareness.

In 1833 the Republican Giuseppe Mazzini, an exile for alleged implication in the rising of 1821, dissatisfied with the Federati and Carbonari, had founded Young Italy. The new society abandoned secrecy except for the names of its members, published its programme and was highly organised on a national basis. It was organised not for conspiracy, but for a real seizure of power. The old secret societies had been aristocratic. This had a large popular element. In two years it numbered 60,000 members. 'Ideas,' Mazzini said, 'grow quickly when watered by the blood of martyrs.' And the blood was not wanting. In 1844 the brothers Bandiera deserted from the Austrian Navy and went to head a revolt in Calabria. They and their followers were quickly surrounded by the troops of Ferdinand of Naples and captured. Nine of them were shot by his soldiers, while the cry 'Long live Italy!' still echoed on their lips. The martyrdom was a symbolic one, for the victims came from all parts of Italy. The Bandiera brothers were Venetians; others who suffered with them came from the Romagna, from Modena and from Perugia. If Italians could not live, they could at least die, together.

Two events, which occurred just before 1848, lent great strength to the surprising movement in favour of national unity which then electrified all Italy. Charles Albert succeeded to the throne of Piedmont in 1831. He had been discredited by the failure of the constitutional movement in 1821; he was clerical and therefore suspected of being anti-national; and his early measures were repressive. But, though timid and hesitating, he was sincere. Those about him gradually recognised that he had the cause of Italy at heart, and dreamed that one day she might be free. Charles Albert indicated some sympathy with these ideas in private, and began to be recognised as a possible leader for the future. The second event was that a Cardinal was elected Pope who seemed a liberal, a nationalist and patriot. The new Pope elected in 1846 was Pius IX. He is said to have imbibed patriotism from the Carbonari in his youth. It is certain that when a Cardinal at Imola in 1840, he openly expressed his disgust at Austrian police methods, sentences, imprisonments, exiles and executions. But the great position which he held, his authority over Catholics everywhere meant that he could never be only Italian. Yet the first measures which he took gave an extraordinary impulse to national aspirations. One of his first measures was to proclaim an amnesty in the Papal States, and to pardon all political offenders and suspects. The effect of this step was quite indescribable. By one act he became famous, and the appearance of a liberty-loving Pope was hailed as a miracle from heaven. Metternich was astounded. 'We were prepared for everything,' he said, 'but a Liberal Pope. Now we have got one there is no answering for anything.' The 'Revolution,' wrote a keen observer to Charles Albert, 'wants no making. It is made already.' Metternich began to contemplate the use of force in 1847, and the inevitable revolution began early in 1848. In January Sicily rose against Naples. Charles Albert granted a constitution on February 8, and on February 10 Pius IX published his allocution which contained the famous phrase 'God bless Italy!' The next day he used the same words in addressing the crowd from the balcony of the Quirinal, and evoked the most frantic enthusiasm. With a liberal Pope at Rome and a constitutional king at Turin, Italy was already revolution-ripe. Mazzini, for a moment obscured, was soon to be in the forefront, and Garibaldi was already at hand to command the army of 'Young Italy.'

The period 1815–48 opens with an attempt by the diplomats of Europe to bridle the forces unloosed by the Revolution and by Napoleon. The settlements of Vienna were made to adjust the territorial ambitions of Great Powers, not to satisfy the claims of nationalities. But, so far as the Great Powers were concerned, the territorial settlement was successful and kept Europe out of wars on the grand scale for forty years. The more ambitious experiment in international or congressional government, which lasted from 1815 to 1825, ended in disaster. It turned into a 'Trade Union of Kings' with a mutual insurance policy, and failed to take account of the needs and desires of a strongly popular and parliamentary government like that of Britain. Canning render a service not only to Britain, but to Europe, in ending this hazardous experiment.

The Metternich policy, both in Austria and in Germany, was a similar attempt, which failed for similar reasons. Metternich aimed at imposing a uniform system of repression on a series of peoples or states, which objected to being denied the aspirations of self-government or national cohesion. The peoples of the Austrian Empire and the states of Germany struggled against the Metternichian strait-waistcoat and burst it asunder in 1848. And the success of this revolution was permanent. Neither the Germany nor the Austria which Metternich had known was restored after the convulsions of 1848.

In Prussia, on the other hand, a series of able men anticipated liberalism and revolution by a wise and intelligent policy of education and reform, and by imposing on the State a system of military discipline, which proved the strongest security of law and order. The system was suited to the people, who valued intelligence and strong government accompanied, as it was, by economic prosperity. Hence the waves of 1848, which turned Metternich's castles into sand heaps, broke fiercely but vainly upon the solid rock of the Prussian State.

Louis Philippe had tried to be a constitutional monarch and was the first to fall in 1848. But the system which he applied was unsuited to the French nation. It took no account of equality and the rights of man, which were the most enduring legacies of the Revolution of 1789. It had nothing of the splendour and enlightenment of the Napoleonic régime. A government based on a narrow franchise, dull and not brilliant, pacific and not military, oligarchic and not democratic, was bound to fail. In Belgium or in Piedmont or in Britain, the masses were content at this time to accept the rule of the middle class; in France they were not. So Constitutional Monarchy succeeded in other lands just for the reason that it failed in France. While it averted or tranquillised revolution elsewhere, it produced or enforced it in France. To leave it here is to ignore a working-class dynamism which was being stored up below the surface. The ideas of Baboeuf were not dead either in France or Italy. The writings of Saint-Simon, Fourier and Proudhon which will be discussed in the next chapter, had given new channels to ideas of social reconstruction.

Poland and Italy differed both from revolutionary France and from the Constitutional countries, for they showed themselves more ardent for national independence than for democracy, and more ardent for democracy than for constitutionalism. Their hatred of the foreigner made them plunge into revolutionary courses, and too soon for success to be achieved. The failure of Poland was evident in 1831, that of Italy in 1849. But the strength and force of their effort, the enthusiasm evoked by their heroism and devotion, did not perish altogether. Italy had made a revolution, but at the same time she had made a nation; and the failure of the one caused the success of the other. Italy was to succeed in 1860, Poland to fail again 1863. But, though it took much longer, Poland won her national independence, in so far as she still has independence, by self-sacrifice as truly as Italy had done.

Looking, however, actually at the results we may say that autocracy and revolution fared badly, and constitutionalism well, during this period. The autocratic powers, by trying to repress and not to moderate or assimilate the expansive force of the new ideas, produced the explosion of 1848. And it was then that the advantages of constitutionalism were seen. The world was not 'revolution-ripe' in 1848, but it was 'made safe' for Limited Monarchy. Everywhere—except in France—the results of that upheaval tended in favour of Palmerstonian liberalism and of Constitutional Monarchy

Chapter 10

THE FRENCH REVOLUTION OF 1848 AND THE ESTABLISHMENT OF THE EMPIRE

The French Revolution of 1848 was the work of Paris alone, and of only a small part of the population of Paris. There had been agitation in the provinces against the narrow character of the franchise, but in the movement which sent the Orleanist monarchy 'on its travels' the provinces had taken no part. It can hardly be doubted that the great majority of Frenchmen were opposed to what happened.

Louis Philippe had hoped that his dynasty might be continued in the person of his grandson, under the regency of the Duchess of Orleans. But the Chamber was in no mood to adopt that solution, and the Paris crowd soon invaded its precincts. The session was closed, but the members who remained behind, supported by the crowd, acclaimed as a provisional government a list of names which were suggested to them by Lamartine. The list had already been drawn up by the *National* newspaper; this revolution in Paris marks the very zenith of the direct political influence of newspapers. The list contained seven names; all were well-known reformers and republicans. The most notable among them were Lamartine, Ledru-Rollin, and Garnier-Pagès. But while this was going on in the Assembly hall another government had been drawn up in the offices of the *Réforme*, a paper of strong socialist opinions. The men on the *National* list were on this too, but it also contained some other names, especially that of Louis Blanc, the one great representative of socialism to his generation. The two were merged together, and thus was formed the 'Provisional Government.' They owed their powers entirely to revolution and had no constitutional standing.

From the first there were sharp divisions among them. The socialist section had been accepted very unwillingly by the moderate middle-class republicans, of whom Lamartine was the eloquent spokesman, and who were contented with a republic and an extended suffrage. They regarded Louis Blanc almost as an enemy, and were far from ready to give loyal support to his schemes. Certain important steps were taken immediately. Universal suffrage was declared. The new electors, over nine million in number, were at an early date to elect an Assembly which was to settle the constitution. The National Guard, which had long been restricted to the middle class and regarded as primarily a safeguard for property, was declared to be thrown open to all citizens. Louis Blanc had also, in appearance at least, gained a great victory for his favourite idea. He had declared to a body of petitioners that the Government undertook to guarantee to all Frenchmen sufficient work to support life, and a decree at once declared the establishment of 'National Workshops.' This last was a decision of the utmost importance for the future of the Republic.

The course of a revolution, when once it has broken out, inevitably follows the impulse of the ideas of the time. Paris before 1848, and to a smaller extent France, had been full of political and social speculation. The chief influence came from Saint-Simon, who had died in 1825. This strange man and powerful thinker had thrown out a great mass of ideas, partly scientific and partly Utopian. His proposals rested on a general view of human history. Critical and constructive epochs had, he believed, alternated, and the French Revolution of 1789 had marked the end of the last epoch of criticism and destruction. The task before the world, and especially before France, was to build up a new order. The chief aim of that order was to procure a better life for the industrial classes. It was to be carried out under the direction of a new religion, which was vaguely theistic in character, but which was to possess an elaborate organisation of savants and priests. Social industry was to take the place of private enterprise, but the new order was to be substituted for the old without violence or confiscation. Many of the details of his schemes, as of his life, lend themselves to ridicule; but he exercised a great influence on thinkers and politicians of the next generation. Fourier (1772–1837) and Proudhon (1809–65) also attracted much attention from their contemporaries. Victor Considérant was a good propagandist for their ideas. The proposition from which these men started was that property determined the character, the justice or injustice of relations between men in society. Fourier's system was one in which production and consumption were organised in common without equality of property. It was achieved by the constant repartition of goods taking into account the contribution each made to production under three headings, capital, skill, work-time. The right to bequeath property would be abolished. He did not consider it necessary to abolish the family, but children were to be educated all together and equality among them preserved by limiting what they learned. In order for all this to be done it would be necessary to limit the size of communities. So families were to live together in phalansteries. Each phalanx would have land, from which all that was necessary to maintain the community could be produced, and a building (phalanstery) where all the members, some 1000 to 2000 souls, would reside. The apartments of families would vary in size and amenities according to what each had earned in the repartition. The allocation of work and constant change of work were key elements in the system. For both he relied on 'desire' which he believed, if untrammelled, would allow each to do what he wanted, all the time, and all the work still to be done. Fourier's ideas were formulated in the twenties and gained a hearing in the forties after the decline of Saint-Simonianism.

Proudhon's two books, *Qu'est-ce-que la Propriété?* (1840) and *Système des contradictions économiques* (1846), expounded a system designed to abolish property altogether, not to replace it by common property or equal private property. Goods produced (including, say, the cure of an illness) were to have attached to them a named value; each kind of work in the production of a commodity was similarly to be assigned a value. The essential principle on which social relations should be based could then be applied. This principle was the complete equality in the work demanded from each and in the return on that work. Separate possession continued, but solely as return on work. The rule of man over man would be abolished and government consist in the mechanical tasks of evaluating goods, allocating work and evaluating it, and relating the two values in the distribution of goods. In the perfect society order would be assured through the responsible self-control of the fully developed and free individual. Each man would be a law unto himself, but part of the law he prescribed to himself was his right relationship to other men.

The young Karl Marx (1818–83), who came from the upper bourgeoisie and was linked by marriage to the aristocracy (his brother-in-law was von Westphalen, the Prussian Minister), had already developed his materialist explanation of history in Paris and Brussels between 1844 and 1845. He had been educated in Bonn and Berlin Universities and at Berlin had come under the influence of the followers of Hegel. He worked with one of them on the *Rheinische Zeitung* before he moved to Paris. By 1846 he had begun to mark off his position from those of Bakunin and Proudhon. In February 1848 he published the *Communist Manifesto* which has been called his literary masterpiece. It was, however, less immediately important than the socialist practices of the followers of Louis Blanc. Louis Blanc was an immensely voluminous writer on political and economic subjects. He had written with passion of the condition of the industrial classes in Paris and elsewhere, and he called upon the State to make the remedying of their condition its chief concern. His own schemes were many, and are characterised by a good deal of vagueness and sentimentalism. In his view the history of mankind revealed three stages: first, a stage of authority in politics and religion; then, a period of individualism represented by the Protestant revolution and by such writers as Montaigne; then, lastly, there would come a period of association and fraternity. There had been strivings after this in all periods, but it had culminated in the great French Revolution, with its immortal formula 'Liberty, Equality, and Fraternity.' The task before mankind now was to organise life on a basis of association and fraternity. He was sure of victory, for he believed in the essential goodness of human nature, and he believed that the transformation to the final stage would come easily and without bloodshed. 'All that is necessary is to provide workmen with money, form a co-operative workshop, and success will come inevitably.' There was thus something Utopian in his outlook; but his scheme was a wide and general one and he had his plans for every part of life and government. Public opinion had seized on one point only, and had misrepresented that—the right to work. 'We will work and live or we will fight and die' was the watchword of those who thought themselves Louis Blanc's followers. We have seen how he was carried into the Provisional Government by popular support, and how he had declared that work would be provided for all. The majority of his colleagues disliked his ideas, but an attempt would have to be made to put them into practice. Many of Louis Blanc's colleagues hoped that the scheme would fail, and did their best to make it fail. He proposed also the formation of a Ministry of 'Progress.' This very vague title did not commend itself to the Provisional Government, and they established instead a 'Government Commission for Workmen,' which was to consider all questions relative to their welfare.

Was the failure of the National Workshops due to some intrinsic fault in the scheme, or was it caused by the lukewarm support or actual disloyalty of Blanc's colleagues? Modern socialists have with one accord declared against the idea of providing work for the unemployed, unless it can be made really useful and remunerative. The failure of Louis Blanc's scheme is at any rate certain. The promise of constant work at a fair wage drew to the workshops all the casual labour of Paris, and soon great numbers from the provinces as well. In two months the numbers of those who drew a wage—we cannot say who worked—rose from 25,000 to 66,000. Then only two days' work was provided each week; on the other days the unemployed received a dole (called *un salaire d'inactivité*) of one franc per day. The scheme had taken a turn quite different from what Louis Blanc had imagined; he had hoped to provide genuine and productive work in ordinary workshops by means of State subvention. On every ground, economic or moral, the actual scheme adopted was a failure.

The National or Constituent Assembly, elected by manhood suffrage to draw up a constitution, came together on May 4. Every effort had been employed to produce a republican majority, and of the 900 members there were hardly any open monarchists. But the great majority of the members were unknown, and they showed their attitude to the social question, which interested Paris so deeply, when they established an executive Government consisting of Arago, Garnier-Pagès, Lamartine, and Ledru-Rollin; but without Louis Blanc. Paris and France were not in accord on great questions of policy. It is the beginning of that opposition between the country and the capital which is one of the prominent features and factors of French political life for the next twenty-five years.

Paris was angry with the Government for its reactionary tone; angry with it too for its refusal to lend help to the Poles in their resistance to Russia. A great popular demonstration invaded the Assembly, and tried to dissolve the Government and substitute another with Louis Blanc at its head. But the attempt failed; the hall was cleared by the National Guard; Louis Blanc retired into exile. The victorious Assembly then turned to the workshops, in which they saw the great support of the socialist opposition. An inquiry was held, and the workshops were declared closed on June 22. A mass of misery was thrown on the streets of Paris without resource or hope. But the socialist party had its organisation, its clubs, and its newspapers, and it took up the challenge. Barricades were drawn across the narrow and tortuous streets of Paris. The Assembly was declared dissolved and the workshops re-established. It was civil war, for much the same motives and of much the same kind as that which was to desolate the capital in the days of the Commune of 1871.

General Cavaignac was given sole power, and he carried war into the enemy's camp with great vigour. There were four days of desperate fighting, during which each side charged the other with treason and massacre. On June 26 the Assembly was again master of the city. But this terrible incident left behind bitter hatreds and suspicions, and made the task of finding some basis of national unity far harder during the following years. The middle and propertied classes had been much frightened, and demanded a Government strong enough to save them from further danger of insurrection.

The Assembly could now go on with its work of constitution-making. There were some points on which there was no doubt. They began with a vague Declaration of Rights in the traditional French manner. They accepted universal, or rather manhood, suffrage. They gave the legislative power to a single Assembly of 750 representatives. The future of France was closely bound up with their decision as to the form of the executive. Monarchy and Empire were not considered. France was to be a Republic and was to have a President. But what sort of President? A figure-head or a real ruler? A President after the fashion of the President of the United States, who is the real head of the executive Government, or a powerless official such as the President of the Swiss Confederation? It was really a difficult problem. The decision that was taken proved fatal to the existence of the Republic, but it is not certain that it was not under most circumstances the wisest course. The legislators were influenced by two main considerations. First, they held, as Frenchmen had for long held—being led to that conclusion by the teaching of Montesquieu among others—that the executive should be separate from the legislative, and that therefore the executive should not proceed from the legislative and depend upon it; and, secondly, they stood for the sovereignty of the people. Why, therefore, should not the people appoint the executive head of the State as well as the legislators? Was it not as important that he who carried on the work of the State should do so in the interest of the people as that the laws should be made by men who were appointed by popular election? By a large majority the Assembly declared that the President should be elected by manhood suffrage, should hold office for four years, and should not be re-eligible. Some have held that constitutional forms are not of real importance, and that 'whate'er is best administered is best.' A clearer refutation of this view could hardly be found than this. The decision of the Assembly led swiftly to the Second Empire, to a period when the military glory of France seemed restored, and then to Sedan and the Commune. The history of Europe still bears the traces of that vote of the Assembly.

Louis Bonaparte, the son of the King of Holland and nephew of the great Napoleon, was the eldest representative of the Napoleonic family. The world had heard a good deal of him already. He had lived in Switzerland, in Italy, in England, and in America. He had mixed with revolutionists in Italy, and had moved in the higher ranks of society in London. He had always taken himself seriously and believed himself reserved for a high destiny. In 1836 he had struck into France from Strassburg and had raised the imperial flag, but the attempt had ended in a fiasco, and he had been captured and sent to America. Then, in 1840, when the bones of his uncle were being brought to their stately resting-place in Paris, he had tried again. He had landed at Boulogne with much dramatic preparation, and again had come to swift ruin. This time he was sent to the fortress of Ham on the northern frontier of France, and there was kept for some time in very easy confinement. He saw friends, wrote much, and finally escaped without much difficulty. The fall of the House of Orleans allowed him to return to Paris, and he was elected to the Assembly.

What had he in his favour? He had ideas, but they were as yet hardly known. He had not a striking presence, but he had great tact and pleasant manners and the power of keeping silence impressively. But, above all, he was a Napoleon. France had forgotten the suffering and the humiliation that Napoleon had brought upon her. She remembered only the glory, the victories, the prestige of France. Thiers had recently written about him in volumes that were widely read. Though not wholly composed in the spirit of hero-worship, they had fired the imagination of France. The successes, such as they were, of the Orleanist régime seemed drab in comparison. But

Napoleon seemed to offer France something beside glory. He seemed to offer security and stability under a strong Government. The days of the barricades had left a deep impression on the mind of France. They wanted a ruler with a strong hand and will, who would prevent that horror from reappearing. The popularity of Louis Bonaparte had already been shown during the elections to the Assembly. When he became a candidate for the Presidency the country was swept by a fire of enthusiasm that destroyed the chances of every other candidate. Cavaignac, who had suppressed the rising, received a million and a half of votes; Ledru-Rollin, the faithful radical, some 370,000; Lamartine, who at one time had seemed to sway Paris by his eloquence, had only 17,000 supporters. Louis Napoleon had five and a half million of votes. He assumed the office of President in December 1848 and took the oath: 'I shall regard as enemies of the fatherland all those who attempt by illegal means to change what France has established.'

The new President was no ordinary man. He was a man of ideas, and he dreamed dreams, some of which have become realities. The Suez and the Panama canals were foreseen by him, and he contributed to the ultimate completion of both. He had none of the temperament of a soldier, but he had written suggestively on the use of artillery. He regarded European diplomacy with a comprehensive imagination, which allowed him sometimes to anticipate the future. He had clear and interesting ideas on politics. It seemed to him that the time of Parliaments was passing, and that they could not again play the all-important part that had been played by the British Parliament in the past. They belonged to a time before means of communication were fully developed. Now, the executive Government could come into direct touch with the people and need no longer rely on a great Assembly to such an extent as formerly. In his view there were two essentials in the life of the State: manhood suffrage and a Government resting directly on it. That he was a Napoleon was at once the cause of his triumph and the fatality of his whole career. It pushed him on irresistibly towards military adventure, and in war he showed no talents, and through war he came to his catastrophic fall.

It was no easy post that the President of the Republic had accepted. He had difficulties at once with the Constituent Assembly, which differed from him in foreign policy, especially with regard to Italy, and seemed to desire to prolong its sessions unduly. The position was hardly easier when the Constituent gave way in 1849 to the Legislative Assembly, elected under the new constitution. The moderate republicans of the Constituent had sunk to an insignificant handful. There was a larger group—some 180—of revolutionary republicans who still cherished the ideals that seemed to have been suppressed in the days of the barricades. Much the largest party was 'the party of order,' Catholics and monarchists who saw in the 'extreme left' the great danger to their ideals and to France. Louis Bonaparte was personally popular in the country, but there was hardly a sign of a Bonapartist party in the Legislature.

Fear of revolution was the dominant passion of the Assembly. Yet the danger does not seem really to have been great. An armed demonstration against the Italian policy of the President led by Ledru-Rollin was beaten down with the greatest ease. A number of members were expelled from the Assembly. But men of the same opinions were sent by the constituencies to take their places. The Assembly in alarm determined to purge (*épurer*) the suffrage. Universal suffrage was the very base of the constitution and it was not attacked in name; but conditions were attached to its exercise—especially three years' residence in one place—which reduced the number of voters on the register by about three million. Those excluded belonged very largely to the shifting industrial population of the great towns.

The 'red peril' was thus banished. But the result was that the tension between the Assembly and the President became much greater. They had accepted him as an ally against revolution, and now that danger seemed removed. The majority were monarchists, and he could not be anything but hostile to their aims. The monarchists were themselves divided: some—the legitimists—desiring the restoration of the Bourbons in the person of the Count de Chambord, who for them was King Henry V; while others looked to some member of the Orleanist house. This far-reaching difference now led to the establishment of the Empire, as it later led to the Third Republic.

It must be admitted that Louis Bonaparte displayed none of the fairness and openness that should characterise the head of a state. His attitude towards the grave situation was that of an adventurer and a conspirator; not that of a President or a patriot. He saw the chance of seizing an imperial crown, and all other considerations were swept aside by the consuming passion of ambition. And yet it is not difficult to make out a case for his policy. The days of the barricades were near. France still feared the recurrence of the 'red peril.' The bitter hostility of the parties threatened the very existence of the Republic. The demagogic conspiracy of which the President spoke in one of his addresses was a reality, and the monarchists were inevitably enemies of the constitution. He was personally popular, as the plebiscite was soon to show. Parliamentary institutions had struck no deep roots in the country. France needed a strong hand to maintain order until the people had really made up their minds as to the form of government they desired. The situation has many clear points of resemblance with that which Napoleon I had dealt with in the days of Brumaire (1799). His nephew had the thought of his uncle's career constantly before him; and like his uncle he thought much of France, but more of himself and the personal position which the crisis would enable him to win.

His four years' tenure of office would soon be at an end. Was he to obey the law and sink into the obscurity and comparative poverty of private life? He was determined to secure a prolongation of his power, and he hoped—as Napoleon I had hoped at the Revolution of Brumaire—to secure his aims by constitutional means. The constitution allowed an alteration of its articles if three-quarters of the Assembly voted in favour of revision. In July 1851 the proposal was made that the President should be allowed a second term of office: 446 voted for it and 270 against it. That was not the required three-quarters majority. It would be necessary for him, as it had been for his uncle, to draw the sword. He would appear as the champion of the people and of order. He had not protested against the Bill that had limited the franchise when it was passed, but now he demanded its repeal in the name of the sovereignty of the people. The Assembly refused, and gave him the chance of posing as the champion of outraged democracy. His schemes had been penetrated by many. Saint-Arnaud, his most trusted confederate, had been brought home from Algiers and given the command of the home army. In January 1851 Thiers had said: 'The Empire is already in existence.'

His plan was to dissolve the Assembly and to appeal directly to the people to vote a new constitution which should give him large personal powers. On December 2, 1851, the blow was struck. In the night the walls were placarded with a proclamation to the French people. The Assembly was declared dissolved; a new constitution was to be submitted in outline to the vote of the whole people. If they did not support him he would retire. 'But if you think that the cause of which my name is the symbol—that is, France regenerated by the Revolution and organised by the Empire—is also yours, proclaim it to the world by granting me the powers that I ask for.' The Palais Bourbon—the hall of the Assembly—was occupied. Several prominent members were arrested: Thiers, Cavaignac, and Changarnier among them. So far there had been no bloodshed. Perhaps there need have been none. But there came a rising in the streets of Paris; 'the barricades' again on a small scale. It was beaten down easily, and perhaps a conflict might have been avoided altogether. The bloodshed of those days was never forgotten, and Victor Hugo put his eloquent pen at the service of the enemies of the future Emperor, and branded him as the criminal who had shed innocent blood in order to overthrow a constitution which he had sworn to defend. There were some 800 victims, and a greater number were subsequently deported to Cayenne and Algeria.

The new constitution was soon placed before the voters. The President was to hold office for ten years and was to nominate all the Ministers. There was to be a Council of State—nominated, of course, by the President—which was to prepare the laws. A legislative Assembly elected by universal suffrage was to vote on the laws and the budget. Lastly, there was to be a nominated Senate which was to 'guard the fundamental pact and the public liberties.' Much in all this was very vague; but it was clear that all the reality of power would rest with the President, and that the Assembly would have at most a power of veto on such measures as were submitted to it. A few days later all the voters of France were called to vote 'Yes' or 'No' on the following resolution: 'The people desires the maintenance of the authority of Napoleon Bonaparte, and delegates to him the necessary powers to establish a constitution on the basis proposed in his proclamation of December 2.' Every effort was made by the Government to secure a favourable verdict, and the means employed were often unfair. Yet when every deduction has been made, the answer showed an overwhelming encouragement to the President in his new task. There were 7,439,000 who voted Yes, and only 640,000 Noes.[1]

Louis Bonaparte became President on those terms on December 21, 1851. In less than a year he exchanged the Presidential for an Imperial title. Again there was much intrigue and corruption used to bring about the result; but again we cannot doubt that there was much real popular enthusiasm for the restoration of the glorious title of Empire. It was one of the things always remembered against him that he said at Bordeaux: 'It seems that France is inclined to return to the Empire; well, the Empire means Peace.' The proposal that the hereditary Empire should be conferred on him came from the obsequious Senate. It was submitted to a plebiscite, and 7,824,000 were returned as saying 'Yes', while only 253,000 said 'No'! Napoleon reigned at once as the Emperor Napoleon III; for to all true imperialists Napoleon's son, the Duke of Reichstadt, who had died in 1832, was Napoleon II, though he had died uncrowned.

The new Empire that thus came into being was in theory the ideal of paternal monarchy. It contained all that was best in the principles of the great Revolution, and all that was most efficient in the organisation of the first Napoleon. In his proclamation after his election as President, Napoleon had said that 'he had searched the past for the best examples to follow; that he preferred the principles of genius to the specious doctrines of men of abstract ideas'; and that, as France for the last fifty years owed her progress to the administrative

---

[1] F. A. Simpson, *Louis Napoleon and the Recovery of France* (2nd ed., 1930), p. 162, says that the authenticity of the figures is now generally admitted, and that official pressure did not create but merely exaggerated Louis Napoleon's majority. Incidentally (pp. 163–76) he makes out a strong case for the *coup d'état*. For a more recent assessment of the support of Louis Napoleon see T. Zeldin, *France 1848–1945* (1973), vol. I, pp. 512 ff.

organisation of the Consulate of Napoleon, he had thought it best to adopt also the political institutions of the Consulate. The Emperor was to be in constant and close touch with his people; he was to be their true representative and to interpret their will, securing liberty, relieving poverty, putting at the disposal of the nation the best intelligence of the nation in his Council of State, and avoiding always the dangers and delays of party strife. The *most* characteristic Napoleonic institution was the plebiscite. It was the supposed instrument for bringing the Emperor into direct contact with his subjects individually. Hardly less characteristic was the Council of State, already mentioned. It comprised the men of talent and expert knowledge whom the Emperor had chosen—not that he, therefore, controlled them. On the contrary, he found it difficult to make his ideas overcome the specialist's innate conservatism. Napoleon's personal power and his dependence on the Council of State of course reduced the importance of the Ministers. Together with these two characteristic institutions we must reckon a third: the notable. The Napoleonic formula of confidence from below, power from above, translated into practice, meant the presence in the Legislative Assembly of local notabilities selected on a property qualification. Universal manhood suffrage was maintained but the Government removed names from the electoral roll and assured the election of 'suitable' men, not only by the property qualification, but also by the control of elections through the mayors (appointed by the Government), who acted as returning officers, through 'official candidates' put up with the backing of the Prefects, and through the manipulation of constituency boundaries. The function of the notable was to bring forward the opinion of his locality to the Government and to take back to his locality, and make it understood and acceptable, the policy of the Government. Thus the powers of the Legislative Assembly were much diminished. It could not initiate measures; it could not amend the budget; it voted secretly and could be overruled by the Senate. Its diminished importance was reflected in the shortness of its sessions: it sat for only three months in the year.

Though it is unfair to describe the Napoleonic Empire as a police state there was certainly an increase in the vigour and the effectiveness of the censorship and the control of opinion. Napoleon had realised that a public opinion influenced or dominated by men of literature, by those in charge of education, and by journalists, might be a dangerous enemy. It was impossible to control literature. Napoleon found writers to support his régime; but, in exile, Louis Blanc and Victor Hugo and many others never ceased to attack him in books and pamphlets of all kinds. The pen of Victor Hugo was an enemy whose attacks never ceased or slackened, and for nearly all the period of the Empire his was the most powerful voice among the writers of Europe. Education, on the other hand, could be and was controlled by the Minister of Public Instruction acting in the interests of the Government. The professors of the University were brought under the direct control of the Minister; they were ordered to dress neatly and not to let their beards grow 'that the last traces of anarchy may disappear.' In the Normal Schools—where teachers were trained—no history or philosophy was to be taught. Private schools, especially those in the hands of the clergy, were encouraged. All were carefully watched in the interest of the Government. Newspapers were rigorously supervised and controlled. None could be started without permission from the Government. There was a heavy stamp duty. For writing contrary to the wishes of the Government, journals could be easily suspended or suppressed. The printing of books was hardly freer. The right of association and of public meeting was so closely limited as almost to be 'destroyed. In contrast the status of the army and its place in society was raised.

What did France think of all this? Napoleon never won the great towns to his side. Paris, in spite of all he did for its buildings and its *boulevards* and the trade of the city, was always his bitter opponent. The country districts were, however, always friendly, and the plebiscites, which supported his different appeals, cannot be interpreted except as signs of this approval. Some eminent historians have thought that if he could have maintained peace he might have made his régime durable; but the history of France does not encourage us to think that a régime could last long, if it did not satisfy the desire for glory, neglected liberty, and denied freedom of thought.

The road of conspiracy and adventure by which Napoleon had made his way to the Empire fatally limited his choice of agents. Republicans such as Cavaignac, Orleanists such as Thiers, would not take service under him, and there were many others on whose loyalty he could not rely. He was forced to accept the services of men who were to a greater or smaller extent his fellow-conspirators. His most trusted supporters and agents were Persigny, Walewski, Morny, and Saint-Arnaud. As an adventurer, too, he could not procure the alliance of one of the reigning families of Europe. Napoleon's marriage to Marie Louise was a warning here. Yet a marriage was necessary to complete the imperial establishment. In January 1853 he married Eugénie de Montijo, Countess of Teba, a beautiful Spaniard with some Scottish blood in her veins. Her presence added great charm to the life of the Court, and she played her part with wonderful success. It was policy as well as inclination which made Napoleon inaugurate a series of balls and receptions. It was not only the Court but Paris also which plunged into a round of gaiety that soon made the city, what it had not previously been, the great centre for the pleasure-seekers of Europe. The city was rebuilt under the direction of the Prefect Haussmann. Its narrow streets gave way to wide thoroughfares, and the health and amenities of the city were much

Chapter 11

THE REVOLUTION OF 1848–49 IN GERMANY, IN THE AUSTRIAN EMPIRE, AND IN HUNGARY

Metternich had said that Austria was suffering from a mortal disease in October 1847. It was so, and the disease had been accelerated by his own policy. Not only in Austria but in Germany and in Europe as a whole, a policy of pure repression, anti-national and anti-liberal, ended, as it was bound to end, in inanition. The Germany and Austria of the Metternichian régime died in 1848. The reaction of 1849 could not return to the past: it could only improvise for the future.

The character of the revolution assumed different forms in the various parts of Central Europe. In Germany the movement was based on a strong desire for national unity linked to a strong belief that liberalism (i.e. representative governments and constitutions) would achieve this end. These impulses united professors and students, who dreamed of unity, to the workers who wished for the suffrage and to peasants who wished to abolish feudal rights. In the German part of Austria the movement was similar, but the population, as a whole, was liberal rather than national in its outlook. In Hungary and the non-German parts of the Austrian Empire the impulse, though sometimes liberal on the surface, was in essence always national. A wholly different set of forces was there put in motion. The Czechs of Bohemia, sturdy patriots from the days of Huss, fought fiercely for their rights against the hated Austrian. The Magyars, proud of an old constitution and a parliament, struggled to free themselves altogether from Austrian rule, but they struggled equally to place under their own racial domination a mass of Slavs and Rumans, who formed more than half of their population, and were fiercely insistent on their own rights. The paradox therefore emerged in Hungary that Serbs, Croats, and Rumans ultimately fought for Austria against Hungary to secure their national rights. And, greater paradox still, the Tsar of Russia came to their assistance. Thus Austria was saved partly by the division of her enemies, partly by aid from outside. And the recovery of Austria brought with it the success of reaction in Germany. The course of events was indeed exceedingly dramatic. In March 1848 revolution was everywhere triumphant. Before the end of the year the prospects of revolution were dark, and in 1849 reaction again prevailed everywhere.

There had been a rising in Cracow in 1846. It was suppressed by Austria and the Free City, losing its autonomy, was incorporated in the Austrian Empire. Because of this incident Tsar Nicholas feared a rising in Poland and was not, therefore, inclined to interfere in Germany. The French Republic had disclaimed war and proclaimed a policy of national egoism. There was to be no repetition of the European policy of the First Republic. The battle for political freedom in Germany was not then to be interrupted from outside. It was later to be traversed by the battle of nationalities with each other and later still by the battle of the fourth estate, the wage-earning poor, for social rights. But in March 1848 there was simply a marvellous transformation scene suddenly displayed in Germany. But victory in the battle for freedom was only revolutionary in a limited sense. It is true there were peasant risings and some tumultuous scenes, but Crowns were nowhere in danger in Germany. Armies remained loyal to the Governments. There were changes of Ministers but Governments everywhere functioned without interruption. The characteristic starting-point had been an orderly public meeting and a petition to the King, Grand Duke or Duke for the so-called March demands. These were everywhere granted. Everywhere liberal Ministers were appointed, more power given to parliaments where they existed and parliaments set up where they did not exist, juries introduced into the courts, restrictions on the press lifted and citizen militias founded. Most important, everywhere the ruler promised to co-operate in the summoning of a national parliament. On March 20, 1848, indeed, the King of Bavaria abdicated in favour of his son, but this was due to special causes and did not affect the general character of events. The co-operation of the rulers enabled elections for the national parliament to take place. The initiative lay with a small self-constituted committee of fifty-one liberals, many of them members of the parliaments of the south German states which had existed for some thirty years, The committee met at Heidelberg and invited other known liberals to a *Vorparlament* to plan the electoral law. The *Vorparlament* sat from March 31 to April 3 in Frankfurt. It determined that the National Assembly should be elected by universal manhood suffrage and direct elections and meet in Frankfurt in May. In the event, since the elections depended on the co-operation of the Governments of the several states it was elected on a variety of franchises and mostly by indirect election.

The success of the revolution was assured, however, as much by what happened in Austria as by what happened in Germany. In Vienna four groups had suddenly coalesced: the court opposition to Metternich, the political opposition in the Estates, due to meet on

March 13, the liberal bourgeoisie, and the students. The Emperor hesitated. The students petitioned. The crowd, mostly well-to-do citizens assembled. *Pereat Metternich* was the cry. Before the end of the afternoon Metternich's resignation was offered and accepted. He fled the country, exclaiming, so they say, that a deluge would follow him. Almost casually a régime had fallen. The flight of Metternich was of immense typical significance. It marked the era of the revolution's glory. The strongest symbol of reaction had fallen at the first touch of the revolution's hand. A man, who for thirty years had gagged the press, cowed or destroyed the parliaments, and imprisoned the revolutionaries of Central Europe, was hunted from his capital and the Continent amid the scorn and execration of the world.

On March 15, the Emperor issued an Edict at Vienna, which promised a liberal constitution, freedom of the press, and a Parliament (*Reichstag*). The constitution was published on April 25. The Reichstag was elected and met on July 22. A National Guard (the symbol of the power of the bourgeoisie) was also to be established. This showed that revolution had prevailed even in the arch-capital of reaction. The day before (the 14th), the revolution had triumphed at Budapest, and the Hungarians demanded that, in accordance with their old constitution, the Ministers should become responsible to the majority in the Lower House. This demand was granted (March 17) by the Emperor in his capacity of King of Hungary. On the 15th, the revolution at Budapest had also demanded freedom of the press and the establishment of a National Guard, and these demands were ultimately also conceded, together with an admission of the autonomy of Hungary. What had in fact happened in Budapest was quite different from what had happened in Vienna. In the latter capital a liberal and popular movement had prevailed, but in Budapest an intensely anti-German and anti-Hapsburg national Hungarian Government had taken charge.

In Berlin on March 18, Frederick William had proclaimed a new German policy: the transformation of the German Confederation from a league of states into a truly Federal State by the combined action of rulers and people. He had already in 1847, as we have seen, convened the United Diet—a meeting of all the Provincial Estates together. When it reassembled for the second session in March 1848, it made arrangements for the summoning of an elected Prussian parliament. Known confusingly as the Prussian National Assembly, it met in Berlin on May 22 and set about making a constitution for Prussia. There need then have been no serious trouble in Berlin. But Frederick William provoked it by muddled-headedness. There had been a demonstration in Berlin and the throwing up of barricades on March 18. The King called out the troops. This led to street-fighting and the raising of the black-red-gold national standard. But the barricades had crumbled and Frederick William, with the courage of desperation, threw himself on the loyalty of his subjects and sent the troops back to barracks. The King opened his arsenal and supplied the Berliners with arms, and saluted a procession which carried before him the bodies of civilians slain by his own soldiers. On the 21st the King, who had appointed a Liberal Ministry, issued a proclamation that Prussia was merged in Germany. He rode round the capital wearing a black, red, and gold armlet stopping on the way to address students and speak to the people. The next day his heir, the Prince of Prussia, who was hated as a reactionary, was smuggled out of the capital and fled to England. The Prince (who was to be William I) shared with Bismarck the honour of being the most unpopular man in that Germany which they were in twenty years to unite and to rule with brilliant and popular success.

Meanwhile the German Confederation had set about reforming itself and was engaged in considering a variety of schemes when in May the National Assembly met. It was simply ignored. The National Parliament, when it met in Frankfurt on May 18, consisted chiefly of the middle class, the bourgeoisie, the patriotic class; the landed interest and 'big business' were inadequately represented, and labour hardly at all. The Assembly was deeply influenced by the professors, lawyers, and literary men who sat in it. After a preliminary struggle the Austrian interest won a victory over the Prussian, and the Archduke John, a liberal and popular Hapsburg, was appointed *Reichsverweser* (Imperial Vicar). An executive which ignored the separate governments had thus been created, and an Austrian and a prince was at its head. This policy ignored alike the prejudices of conservatives who favoured separate governments and of radicals who objected to a prince. But neither the Governments nor the radicals were strong enough to protest at the moment.

Almost the first act of the Assembly produced a humiliating rebuff. The *Vorparlament* had tried to liberate Schleswig-Holstein from Danish rule. Prussia, which had sent troops to occupy these two Duchies, had been defeated by the Danes, and a truce favourable to Denmark concluded. This truce the Assembly, after suffering much humiliation, was compelled to accept. When this became known, the members of the Assembly were hustled and intimidated by the mob at Frankfurt Order was finally restored (September 18) by the arrival of Prussian and Austrian troops, but not before two blameless and popular deputies had been murdered. Thus, even in the autumn of 1848, it seemed clear that the revolutionary element was getting out of hand and that the historic Governments alone could keep order.

We must now see how far the Government at Vienna had been able to settle its own affairs by September 1848. The Austrian Reichstag achieved a complex piece of land legislation, dated September 7, which abolished serfdom, or peasant subjection as it was called, and all dues and labour services connected with it and gave moderate compensation to the landowners. Thus it succeeded both in releasing the peasants into the economy as consumers and in modernising the social structure of the Empire. It sealed the fate of the Reichstag which had contained many peasants who, satisfied, now withdrew. When the Government recovered enough confidence to do so it banished the Reichstag to Kremsier and soon afterwards, in 1849, dissolved it. The Hungarians under the lead of Kossuth went far on the way to separation, abolishing feudalism and giving the land to the peasantry. At the same time he made it quite clear that the Hungarians (Magyars) would give no racial privileges to the Serbs, Croats, or Rumans within their kingdom. Thus, at the very moment that Austrian authority was crumbling at Vienna, Kossuth, by his own folly, was finding allies for it and against himself among the non-Magyar subjects of the Hungarian Crown.

In Vienna in May a second revolution had shown the impotence of the Government. Student demonstrations on May 3 brought down the Minister who had succeeded Metternich. On May 17 the Emperor and Court had fled secretly to Innsbruck. On May 26 there were further demonstrations by armed students and citizens. The immediate result was to unloose further nationalistic aspirations. On June 13 the Czechs rose in Prague. But, after some weakness on the part of Windischgrätz, the Austrian commander, the Czech revolutionaries were bombarded in their capital and forced to surrender (June 17). Windischgrätz thus achieved the first victory of reaction in Austria, or indeed in Europe, and all the supporters of the old régime again raised their heads. This first success was soon followed by the news that Radetzky had beaten the Sardinians in Italy (July 25) and reoccupied Milan (August 6). Thus the generals were gaining victories and the morale of their troops was being strengthened. The fact that further reaction was expected was clearly shown when the Emperor returned to Vienna (August 12).

The Court returned to Vienna just at the moment that a conflict with Hungary had become inevitable. This conflict was due largely to two men—to Kossuth, the revolutionary leader of Hungary, and to Jellačić, the artful Ban or Governor of Croatia. Kossuth had been working steadily for the independence of Hungary and had been openly arming to crush the rebellious Serbs and Croats. Jellačić, appointed Ban of Croatia in June, had used his power to forward the Croat National Movement and to stir up both Serbs and Croats against Hungary. Jellačić, at once an adroit intriguer and a bold gambler, played his cards well. He was suspended from his office, but he visited the Emperor at Innsbruck, pointed out to him the advantage of conciliating the Slavs, and was finally restored to power (September 4). He lost no time and, summoning both Croats and Serbs to his aid, he crossed the Drave and invaded Hungary with an army (September 17). His military venture was not successful, but it had one important effect. Crossing the Drave was 'Crossing the Rubicon,' not only for Jellačić, but for the Austrian Court. The Hapsburg Crown was now irrevocably committed to war against Hungary, and an actual declaration of war was issued by the Austrian Government on October 3.

One hope, however, remained. The revolutionary leaders at Vienna might coerce the Government and join hands with those at Budapest to make the revolution triumph in both capitals. Kossuth promised to send Hungarian forces to the aid of his brother revolutionaries in Vienna. In September yet a third revolution had occurred in Vienna. There were liberal bourgeoisie demonstrations against war with Hungary. There were working-class riots arising from poverty and unemployment. The Austrian Minister of War was murdered. The Emperor and Court fled a second time to Innsbruck (October 7). But this time the Austrian Government was to be saved by its generals. On October 13 Jellačić and his army were close to Vienna, and on the 17th Windischgrätz and a still larger force appeared from the direction of Prague. Windischgrätz decided to offer no terms and refused to negotiate with rebels. He simply demanded disarmament and unconditional surrender. There was a chance that the Hungarian forces might liberate their brother revolutionaries, for they were nearing Vienna; but on October 30 they were defeated by Jellačić within sight of the capital, and all hope was gone. This ended the resistance of the city, and Windischgrätz entered it as a conqueror the next day. Like Jellačić he had often acted without, or in defiance of, the orders of the Court and had saved the dynasty despite itself.

So far as Austria was concerned the revolution ended with the fall of Vienna. Windischgrätz appointed his brother-in-law, Prince Felix Schwarzenberg, as Chief Minister, a man of iron will and great ability, who governed as an autocrat and coolly disregarded the revolutionary Ministry and the Austrian Reichstag. On December 2 the incapable Emperor abdicated in favour of his eighteen-year-old nephew, Francis Joseph. Schwarzenberg remained the real ruler of Austria with the programme of an indivisible Austrian Monarchy, ruled by a bureaucracy. He disdained the constitution drafted by the Reichstag and contemptuously superseded it, and dissolved the Reichstag in the early days of March 1849.

Liberalism had been scotched in Prussia in November 1848, about a fortnight after it had been suppressed in Austria. Frederick William had long vacillated between unworthy deference to popular pressure and absurd insistence on his Divine Right. At length, however, he made up his mind, and summoned Count Brandenburg and Otto von Manteuffel to his councils (November 1). They acted quickly, and announced (November 9) that the Prussian National Assembly would be transferred from Berlin to Brandenburg. Troops entered the capital on the 10th and rendered the Assembly's attempt to combine with a new democratic movement hopeless. The Assembly was dissolved on December 5. On the same day, however, the King published a constitution 'granted by his own free will'. Under this parliamentary system with the alterations of 1849, introducing the three-class franchise, and of 1850, Prussia was governed until 1918. The two greatest German Powers had again asserted their authority in their own capitals. Experience had shown that the strong hand availed and that the troops could be trusted. Prussia was entirely able to keep order. Austria, now secure in its own hereditary provinces, still had to suppress revolution in Hungary and in Italy.

While the end of 1848 portended the victory of reaction in Germany and Austria, it was still possible for the revolution to be successful elsewhere. In Italy the cause of national unity was not yet hopeless, and Hungary was to amaze the world by her vitality. Her resistance was even more remarkable than appears at first sight. For Hungary had not only to improvise an army and to fight regulars superior in numbers, equipment, and organisation, but she had also to meet irregular levies of Serbs, Rumans, and Slovaks within her own demesne. Even so, it is doubtful if Austria would have prevailed had not she summoned to her aid the armies of Russia. Hungary was fortunate in possessing a governing class of conspicuous political gifts, but she owed most to the enthusiasm aroused by Kossuth and to the great military ability displayed by Görgei, the most prominent of the Hungarian commanders. Unfortunately, Kossuth was as militarily ignorant as Görgei was politically inept, and the two men were always at variance. Owing to these jealousies and discords it was not until March 1849 that Görgei really obtained control of the Hungarian army.

During the winter of 1848–49 Hungary owed its safety to the slowness with which Windischgrätz moved. He was influenced partly by political considerations, but was, in general, cautious to the verge of cowardice. He held Budapest as well as Vienna, but made little attempt to harass his opponents, and least of all to pursue Görgei into the mountainous districts in which he was reorganising his army. Early in April Görgei moved swiftly upon him, caught him unprepared at Isaszeg (April 6, 1849) and defeated him heavily. Görgei followed up this success by relieving Komárom, the strongest fortress of Hungary, forcing one Austrian army back on Vienna, and another under Jellačić back on Zagreb. The military success was startling. Görgei had dispersed and divided the Austrian armies, and his recovery of Budapest was only a question of time.

The changes in the situation were marked by three signs. The Austrian Government recalled Windischgrätz from command in the field; they appealed to Russia for help; and drove Kossuth into open rebellion. The latter, holding his Parliament at Debreczen, felt strong enough to depose the Hapsburg (April 14), to declare the Monarchy suspended, to proclaim himself governor, and to issue a Hungarian declaration of independence.[1] So strong was Hungary's position that even the utter defeat of the King of Sardinia at Novara (March 23) did not shake her. Kossuth even urged Görgei to advance on Vienna, though Görgei for military reasons declined to undertake this hazardous measure. Early in May he moved on Budapest and, after some weeks, captured the place. On June 6 Kossuth triumphantly entered Budapest, and for a few weeks enjoyed the glittering semblance of power. In realty his position was precarious. Görgei well knew his military weakness, due both to inferior numbers and to paucity of supplies. But there were grave political weaknesses as well. Görgei and the army believed in constitutional monarchy, Kossuth in sentimental revolution. The magnates and the wealthier classes were alarmed at the revolutionary excesses of Kossuth, and the revolutionary paper currency was dropping in value every day. Görgei was probably right in thinking that only a military dictatorship could save the country. But, though he was the only possible candidate, he was not endowed with any political insight, and Kossuth was determined to retain the whole civil power as long as he could. So there were delays over this most vital matter until the step, when taken, was too late to save the situation.

In point of fact the issue was already decided. On May 1 it was known that the Tsar of Russia had answered Austria's call for aid, and was about to send a fully equipped and independent army into Hungary under Field-Marshal Paskiévić. This intervention was ultimately to be decisive. The motives of the Tsar have been much debated, but they seem, in reality, to have been simple. Numbers of Poles had fought in the Hungarian army, and several of them had been eminent as generals at the head of it. In March, Russian troops had entered Transylvania and been expelled by the Hungarian forces, and a Hungarian division had been stationed near the Galician frontier expressly to encourage the Poles to revolt against Austria. The Tsar was particularly sensitive about the Poles, and considered that all sovereigns ought to unite against revolutionaries. He intervened partly to suppress the Polish revolt in the bud, partly to aid the Divine Right of a brother ruler against revolutionaries. Both objects were congenial to Nicholas, and both were to be attained. The two sovereigns met at Warsaw on May 21 and there settled upon the plan of campaign.[2]

---

[1] This was erroneously dated the 19th March.

[2] Nicholas, after he had quarrelled with Austria in 1854, asked her ambassador whether he knew who had been the two stupidest Kings of Poland. He answered his own question thus: 'The first was King John Sobieski, who liberated Vienna (1683) from the siege laid by the Turks, the second am I. For both of us . . . saved the House of Hapsburg.' J. Redlich, *Emperor Francis Joseph of Austria* (1929), p. 156.

Hungary was to be invaded from three sides—by Haynau, the new Austrian commander, from Vienna, by Jellačić from Zagreb, and by Paskiévić, who was to cross the Carpathians and take the Hungarians in the rear. Görgei was in a bad position, hopelessly outnumbered and hampered by the political necessity of defending Komárom and Budapest. By July 14 Jellačić, though he had met with reverses, contrived to join hands with Haynau, and on the 18th the combined Austrian army entered Budapest. Operations were then transferred to the Theiss (Tisza). Görgei skilfully avoided contact with the Russians of Paskiévić, but Haynau caught up with the southern Hungarian army and utterly routed it at Temesvár (August 9).

Görgei had anticipated defeat, and informed Kossuth at Arad on August 10 that he would surrender if Haynau were victorious at Temesvár. Kossuth dramatically answered that, in such case, he would commit suicide. On the 11th the news of the Temesvár disaster arrived. Thereupon Görgei prepared to surrender and asked Kossuth to abdicate, in order to relieve the political head of responsibility for surrender. There is much mystery about these negotiations and Kossuth subsequently asserted that Görgei had been ordered to insist on the autonomy of Hungary and accused him of deliberately betraying her to the enemy. The charge is absurd, and was probably put forward merely as a popular explanation of Hungarian disaster. For Kossuth knew quite as well as Görgei that resistance was impossible.[1] Even if Görgei had demanded the autonomy of Hungary, neither Haynau nor Paskiévić would have admitted any terms but those of unconditional surrender on a military basis. On August 13 Görgei therefore led over 23,000 troops to the Russians at Világos and laid down his arms. He was the most remarkable of revolutionary soldiers produced by the upheavals of 1848.

'Hungary lies at the feet of Your Majesty,' wrote the triumphant Paskiévić to the Tsar. But, in fact, Görgei's army and the settlement of Hungary were both handed over to Haynau. That worthy proceeded to punish the rebels. Owing to the intervention of the Tsar, Görgei's own life was spared, but thirteen of his generals ('The martyrs of Arad') were shot or hanged, and nearly 400 officers were imprisoned. Batthyány, who had been Prime Minister of Hungary, and over a hundred politicians were executed. Kossuth himself, Count Julius Andrássy, and seventy-four others were hanged in effigy. Cruelties of all kinds took place, and the atrocities of Slav and

---

[1] Kossuth made the charge of treachery in a moment of great excitement when fleeing from Hungary. He never repudiated it, but it is no longer sustained by serious writers. The main charge is that Kossuth stipulated that, in case of surrender, the autonomy of Hungary should be reserved. Even if this is true (which it probably is not), Kossuth was insisting on a condition which Görgei could not have possibly obtained. Cp. C. A. Macartney, *The Hapsburg Empire, 1790–1918* (1968), pp. 428–31.

Ruman guerrillas passed wholly unpunished. Haynau's ruthless rule earned for him the nickname of 'Hyena' and brought him a severe punishment at the generous hands of the draymen of Messrs Barclay and Perkins when he visited England some years later. On October 28 Haynau was at last checked, but his proceedings had already earned Austria a name for wicked brutality.

Kossuth had not committed suicide when surrender came, as he said he would. On August 17 he buried the Hungarian crown near the border town of Orsova and fled to Turkey from Hungary, which he never saw again. He became an eloquent voice in the wilderness, displaying both in Britain and in the United States that marvellous gift of exciting human emotion which had made him the first man in Hungary. He lived for nearly fifty years and remained irreconcilably anti-Hapsburg. In 1902 his bones were brought back to rest in his own land amid scenes of emotion such as Hungary had never witnessed. He had indeed exercised a volcanic and incalculable power. For conservative forces had been strong in Hungary, and without Kossuth there would have been no revolution.

The course of revolution was fairly run by the summer of 1849. For, though there remained much unrest, there was no longer any doubt that the constituted authorities would ultimately prevail over the revolutionaries. The revolution had been like a wave or like a charge of cavalry, sweeping over a vast surface resistlessly for a moment, but unable to hold for long the ground thus gained. It had been beaten back everywhere by material force. The first blow to revolution was the capture of Prague on June 17; the second the fall of Vienna at the end of October, the third the reassertion of the King of Prussia's authority in Berlin in November. The last and most stubborn resistance, that of the Hungarians, where national patriotism stimulated revolution, was only ended by calling in a foreign and a Russian army. In every case revolution had begun without bloodshed; in every case reaction triumphed by violence and by militarism. Sentimental liberalism, rose-water revolutions, even national uprisings, had failed before the iron hand and naked force of authority. What was now to be seen was whether the revolutions had been altogether in vain, and whether reaction could be permanent.

Chapter 12

REACTION IN GERMANY, AUSTRIA, AND HUNGARY, 1849–60

The year 1849 opened in singular obscurity. Prussia had restored her kingly power, Austria had restored order in her German provinces: so the two greatest states in Germany were again in existence. But the German National Parliament remained with a Central Executive and *Reichsverweser* (Imperial Vicar) as the living symbol of German unity, as the body which might hope still to realise the dreams of so many and to make Germany no longer a name but a nation. There were too many of the smaller states committed to its policy, there was too much public opinion still in its favour, for it to be flouted altogether or at once. It was therefore in a position to force, and did force, upon Austria a great decision as to the future. After long debate the members of the National Assembly had decided not to exclude Austria from the proposed Federation (or Empire, as it was often called), but they equally declined to include any non-German part of Austria in the new German union. So they offered Austria a place in the new German Empire, but stipulated that her non-German parts (Hungary, etc.) should stand aside. Schwarzenberg replied to this offer on December 13, 1848, by saying that Austria and all its parts would, in future, be one single, organic centralised state, and, as such, must enter the Confederation (*Bund*). He rejected the new German Empire altogether, and proposed to revive the old *Bund* with a stronger executive.

His reply gave Prussia a great chance for obtaining the leadership in Germany. For the National Assembly, affronted by the Schwarzenberg proposal, turned to Prussia for sympathy and aid. After further insults from Schwarzenberg, the National Assembly completed their constitution and chose the King of Prussia as German Emperor (March 27–8, 1849). Had Frederick William been a great ruler, as he admitted he was not, Prussia might have obtained the leadership of Germany. After much hesitation Frederick William refused the offered crown (April 3),[1] and so threw away the prize which his successor was one day to enjoy.

---

[1] It would be more correct to say he adjourned the question *sine die*.

The refusal of the King of Prussia was a great blow. But the popular support and the serious differences between Austria and Prussia still permitted the possibility of a united Germany, for twenty-eight states had solemnly signified their assent to the resolutions of the National Assembly which established the new constitution and the German Emperor (April 4). The day after this assent was signified Austria withdrew her representatives from Frankfurt. The National Assembly replied by reaffirming the constitution. Then, on May 4, Prussia denied the authority of the Assembly and withdrew her deputies. This step was decisive. The shadow of an Assembly continued to exist, transferred from Frankfurt to Stuttgart. But, on September 30, 1849, Austria and Prussia took over the functions of the Central German Power, and thus ended the power, if not the existence, of the Frankfurt Assembly. And the constitution fell with it. It was not at all like the German constitution which was produced by the German victories of 1870; but in many respects it was not unlike that one which was produced by the German defeats of 1918. It contained the same assertion of the rights of the Empire against those of the states; it had a strong popular element in the Upper House; it made a real attempt to introduce popular representation; and it sought to establish personal liberty as the fundamental right of a German citizen.

In April and May 1849 democratic insurrections or military mutinies occurred at Baden, in the Rhenish Palatinate (part of Bavaria), and in Saxony. Prussian troops were at once sent to restore order in Saxony, and were also used to suppress some fresh but not dangerous disorders in Prussia herself. Prussian forces also moved into Baden, into the Bavarian Palatinate, and into Württemberg. Prussia was at the same time negotiating with Bavaria, Saxony, Hanover, Württemberg and some of the smaller states to bring her own form of national unity into being, the so-called Erfurt Union. Austria became highly suspicious. If Prussia solved the German problem Austria would no longer be the first Power in Germany. Schwarzenberg was quite ruthless and quite determined. He meant to restore the old *Bund*, to reassert the Austrian hegemony in Germany, and to brush aside all other schemes as idle. And he could not do this without a spectacular humiliation of Prussia.

Late in 1850, disturbances in Hesse Cassel put a match to the powder magazine. Schwarzenberg was not going to have Prussia gaining any more prestige by a restoration of order there. He determined that Austria should play that part, and prepared to move on Hesse-Cassel with an Austrian army of 200,000 men (reinforced by contingents from Bavaria and Württemberg). Prussia mobilised in reply, and a collision actually took place between Prussian and Bavarian troops. But, as always happened at a crisis, Frederick William tottered and gave way. At Olmütz the iron Schwarzenberg dictated to Prussia a settlement of the Hesse affair. which left all the honours in the hands of Austria, and also provided for the abandonment of the Erfurt Union (November 28, 1850). Before the end of the year Schwarzenberg carried the restoration of the old Confederation (*Bund*) intact, of course with Austria at the head of it as of old. To all appearance Austria was stronger than ever, and reaction in his person was dominant and supreme.

The pitiable humiliation of Olmütz marked the lowest point of Prussia's timidity and surrender. Schwarzenberg seemed a greater Metternich, and Prussia appeared to be brought as low in the dust as after Jena. And there was a further degradation now. When Prussia had been vanquished by Napoleon she had at least been true to the idea of German unity. Now she had begun by promising to champion that cause, had betrayed those who supported it, and acquiesced in the haughty demands of Austria. Germany seemed as feeble, as disunited, as nerveless as ever. Prussia had had the chance of being the first Power in Germany, and her King that of wearing an Imperial crown. All she had done was to rivet still tighter the chains which bound Germany at the feet of Schwarzenberg. The 'humiliation of Olmütz' seemed to put the union of Germany at a more distant date than ever, and permanently to disqualify Prussia as its champion.

This way of looking at things was in reality very fallacious. Schwarzenberg's strong will and ruthless energy had indeed enabled him to achieve diplomatic victories without and order within. But the plan for the future settlement of the Hapsburg dominions was doomed to failure from the start. Schwarzenberg was right to try something new, but what he actually tried had already been condemned by experience. His idea, in brief, was to treat all the Austrian Empire as a mass of molten metal—to run it out in one mould, and to stamp it with one die—to make it speak one language, have one law and one Government, and obey one master. It was to be unified, centralised, and bureaucratised. The scheme ran counter to the nature of things, and had already been attempted in vain by Joseph II under far more favourable circumstances. Even if the lessons of history could have been dismissed and the aspirations of a dozen races[1] could have been trodden out, there was no possibility of the plan succeeding unless there were at least twenty years of uninterrupted peace. And, within eighteen years, Austria met two crushing defeats at the hands of a conqueror. The second of those conquerors was Prussia, which, in a campaign of six weeks, reversed the verdict of Olmütz.

As a matter of fact, Schwarzenberg had it in his power to conciliate different races in Austria, and to reduce the Magyars to impotence

---

[1] In addition to Germans, there were seven Slav races, Czechs, Poles, Ruthenes, Croats, Serbs, Slovaks, Slovenes; three Latin, Ruman, Ladin, and Italian; two Ugrian, Magyar and Szekler.

in the Kingdom of Hungary. His best plan would probably have been to extend a system of thorough devolution of self-government to different races.[1] By this means he could have confined the five million Magyars within the territory they inhabited, and separated from their body politic five million Slavs and two million Rumans. Valuable economic resources and strong alien populations would have been cut off from Hungary and would then have been at the disposal of the Hapsburgs. Schwarzenberg's determination to crush Magyars and Slavs alike beneath a common yoke was recognised by the former as a great blunder. 'What is given to us,' sneered the Magyars, 'as a punishment, is given to you [the Slavs] as a reward.' A golden opportunity of fashioning the Austrian state anew on the basis of liberal and moderate self-government was thus lost. The course Schwarzenberg took led not only to disaster abroad, but to the *Ausgleich* (1867) within; it involved ultimately a dual system (Austria-Hungary) in which the Magyars became in reality the more powerful element, a result which a judicious policy could easily have averted.

Throughout the decade 1849–60 the centralising measures, initiated by Schwarzenberg and continued by Bach, worked steadily for the destruction of the Hapsburg monarchy. Nationalistic tendencies, everywhere repressed in 1849, were in fact restored and revived by the excesses of reaction. In Austrian Italy the hatred of the Hapsburg burnt strongest, but it flamed hardly less fiercely among Magyars and Czechs. When Austrian armies were in the field in 1859 and in 1866 neither Slavs nor Magyars showed any readiness to fight for the Hapsburg. And it could only have been a very stupid policy which brought Magyars and Slavs into agreement.

Austria then was doomed when she adopted a centralising policy at home, for that was certain in the end to lead to disasters abroad. Also, a close observer would have noted that, despite the brilliant triumph of Olmütz, Austrian policy had met with virtual defeat even in Germany. Prussia had indeed been momentarily humiliated, but Austria had been unable to realise the wider programme of Schwarzenberg. She had not obtained inclusion of her whole territory as a unified state in the *Bund* as he had wished. She had failed also to break up the Prussian Zollverein, or to substitute for it a more general customs union in which she was included. So, though temporarily triumphant, Austria's position was really dangerous and unstable.

It may be well at this point to sum up the results of 1848–49. An unparalleled outpouring of human emotions had deluged Central Europe. And, though the tide appeared to ebb, its marks were every-

---

[1] It is exceedingly interesting that this plan is substantially that which Franz Ferdinand is known to have adopted in 1914. He was convinced that the way for the Hapsburg Empire to continue to exist was to upset the dual system and to make all nations equal under the House of Austria.

where, and were often ineffaceable. In Austria and in Hungary the servitude of the peasant had ended. So, even the revival of political tyranny in its acutest form was accompanied by a large measure of economic freedom.

German liberals never recovered from the display of the impurities in their idealism which they had made at Frankfurt. They showed there that they would refuse to other nationalities, to the Poles and the Czechs, the realisation of the aspirations they claimed for themselves. They also showed themselves too ready to come to terms with established authority. The liberalism, so much in evidence everywhere, had been primarily a bourgeois movement. It was of the sentimental and romantic order. Its leaders were generally men without political experience or organisation, and the movement appeared to have been crushed by the heavy-handed policemanship of Berlin and Vienna. But all the German rulers had granted or liberalised constitutions, and these led to some restraint on the power of rulers and to the growth of real parliamentary life in different degrees in all the states including Prussia.

As to German nationalism, through the failure of the Frankfurt Assembly it became clear, perhaps dangerously so, that it could develop independently of liberalism. Yet at Frankfurt there had assembled a veritable aristocracy of the intelligence of the nation, gathered in from all the states. It did much to break down barriers and these would never be rebuilt. There had been a German Parliament and executive; most men felt that they would see both again. Yet the internal weaknesses and alien populations of Austria made it difficult to suppose that she would ever lead the way in that direction. To a keen observer, indeed, the peril of Austria lay in her repression of nationalistic tendencies in her own lands. Palmerston held the view in 1848 that her Italian possessions were a weakness of which she would be well rid, and that Hungary could be conciliated by liberal self-government. He was right in both respects, but, had he the knowledge we have to-day, he could have gone further. He might have pointed out that the Czechs would never be satisfied until their national aspirations were fulfilled, and that even obscure races, like the Slovenes, the Croats, and the Serbs, needed to be conciliated by Austria, if she was to survive. Certainly no one would have dreamed in 1848 that the Hapsburgs would have to fight Serbia in 1914, because the aspirations of Yugoslavs were incompatible with the existence of Austria. But the nationalistic leaven set to work in 1848 was to leaven the whole of Central Europe, and ultimately to produce a ferment which only a universal war could allay.

Finally the events of 1848–49 had made men aware of, indeed had helped to create a third force. The force of democratic, even socialist, idealism had asserted itself for the first time: in Vienna in September 1848, in Berlin in November 1848, in Saxony, where Bakunin had been to the fore, in the Spring of 1849. The names of known leaders are few, but the massed meetings they addressed, the clubs they formed are known and were to be important for the future. They were men who were making or learning their doctrines almost from day to day, but as we saw in a previous chapter, they had important writings upon which to draw.

Chapter 13

REVOLUTIONARY MOVEMENTS IN ITALY

We have already seen that there was a fermentation of opinion in Italy very dangerous to all the governments established there. National sentiment and the feeling that Italy, which had once been the great home of centralisation, should achieve unity and centralisation again, had taken possession of the minds of a large part of the educated classes and had vaguely permeated also the rest of the population. Balbo, in his history of Italy, had shown how the land had been enslaved to the barbarian, and had held up the hope of liberation. Gioberti, in his remarkable book, *Del Primato morale e civile degli Italiani* (1843), had pointed to the Papacy as the power which had given a special character to Italy's place in Europe and by reorganising the states in a Confederation might lead her once again to primacy in Europe; and Mazzini had preached nationalism in alliance with democracy in a manner which made him feared as a revolutionary force, dangerous to the constitution of society as well as to the established governments. There was, however, no sign of any great change. Metternich ruled in Italy as completely as in Vienna, and there seemed little likelihood that the country would cease to be that 'geographical expression' which he had called it in 1815. Yet the first step in the movement of revolution came from this land of despotism, and from the part of it which seemed most wedded to the ideas of the past—the Papacy itself.

In June 1846 Cardinal Mastai-Ferretti was elected Pope, and took the title of Pius the Ninth. Though at the time of his election he was little known outside a restricted circle, he became for the next two years the most prominent of European leaders and the centre of the hopes of the liberals of Europe. He was eulogised as few statesmen in modern times have ever been eulogised. Then there came disappointments and reaction; and he was regarded as an arch-traitor and the enemy of the progress of mankind. The man himself was simple and well-intentioned. His love of Italy and his dislike of the Austrian dominion were perfectly genuine. With the best intentions he struck a match to light a candle, and discovered to his horror that he was in a powder magazine. So neither eulogy nor blame was justified. The Papacy even in its temporal capacity could not lead a national movement whose destination was war and that not even a defensive war and one anyhow against Catholic Austria. Moreover, Pius IX entertained a notion of government as a personal trust. Fully to share it with an elective parliament was to shirk the responsibility and betray the trust. Finally, his values were spiritual and liberalism ultimately implied the secularisation of the state or, at least, its release from identification with any Church.

Nevertheless, his reforms were all in the desired direction. After the amnesty referred to in chapter 9, came a modification of the censorship of the press. The entirely authoritarian and ecclesiastical character of the Government was modified. A Council of State was established in April 1847, chosen by the Pope from the names submitted to him by the governors of the provinces. A Council of Ministers was appointed in June to discuss, but not to control, the action of the Papal Government. The Jews were released from their Ghetto at Rome. Men believed that there was much more behind these moderate changes, and that they were carried out by the will of the Pope alone, in opposition to his reactionary surroundings.

All Italy caught fire from these events in Rome. Metternich was much alarmed. He had foreseen everything, he said, except a liberal Pope. Liberalism—for that name at this epoch was applied even to violent revolutionary opinions—raised its head all over Italy; in Sicily, in Naples, in Tuscany, in Parma, in Milan, in Venice, and even in Savoy. Everywhere it was the mark of a liberal to applaud the Pope, and in some states it was forbidden to cheer the name of Pius IX under heavy penalties. But all this enthusiasm and this hope of an early victory for liberal nationalism rested on illusion. The changes that had been introduced in Rome were far from revolutionary. As we have seen, the Pope's task would have been impossible of solution even to a much more powerful intellect and will. It is clear that in the long run nothing would satisfy the logical demands of Italian nationalism short of the abdication of the Papacy from its temporal power; and Pius could not even contemplate that. When he ceased to be carried along by the tide of popularity he turned again to the Austrian power to rescue and support him.

It will be well to follow Pius to the end of his liberal phase, though before that came to an end important movements had begun in other parts of Italy; these had a decisive influence on events in Rome, which soon ceased to occupy the centre of the Italian stage. Some progress was made with the promised reforms. A municipal council was established for Rome. Some of the public buildings of Rome were put in its power, and the famous letters SPQR[1] were again to be seen on the walls of Rome. The enthusiastic demonstrations which welcomed these acts showed no diminution in the popularity of the Pope. Even the men of extreme views were in some instances swept away by it, and Mazzini wrote a public letter expressing approval of what the Pope had done, 'because it will shorten the way, and spare us dangers, bloodshed, and disasters, and because Italy will be at one stroke placed at the head of European progress.' The Pope used language which might have warned men that he was not willing to go all the way that the revolutionaries desired, for in a public speech he spoke of his determination to maintain the rights of the Sacred College of Cardinals and warned his hearers against dreaming of a Utopia incompatible with the sovereignty of the Pope. In truth the Pope was growing seriously alarmed by the consequences of his action, as seen in the revolutions that were breaking out in all parts of Italy. He began to withdraw himself from public applause and to dream of reaction.

Yet for a short time the progress of the liberal movement in Rome continued. The revolutions that were happening elsewhere—in Sicily, in Naples, in Milan, in France—which frightened the Pope so much, made it impossible for him to stop. It was fear now, not enthusiasm, that drove him on. He appointed a Ministry consisting mainly of laymen, and then hastily, in March 1848, promulgated a constitution. It was warmly but uncritically welcomed, for it maintained the Sacred College of Cardinals as a dominant part of the political constitution, and declared that no law could be accepted which conflicted with the canons or customs of the Church. But it was a constitution, and 'constitution' was almost a magical word at this epoch.

The rest of the history of the Pope's constitutional schemes depends directly on the war against Austria waged by northern Italy, to which we must turn in a moment. The Pope declared against any idea of participating in the struggle, and lost at once the support of the nationalists everywhere.[2] He still hoped to work the constitution that he had promulgated, but the fiercer spirits were rapidly gaining the upper hand in Rome. The Pope's chief Minister was Rossi, who sympathised with many phases of liberalism. In November 1848, as he went to the Assembly of Deputies, he was assassinated, probably by the anarchical section of the revolutionaries. Rome was in turmoil and the Pope, now terribly alarmed, abandoned all ideas of working

---

[1] Senatus Populusque Romanus: the Senate and People of Rome.

[2] The Pope issued an Allocution on April 29 disavowing all participation in a war against Austria, but declaring that his troops would defend the integrity of the Roman State. At that moment the Papal forces were in Venetia.

with the constitution in a liberal spirit. Fearing that he might be forced to further concessions, he left Rome and took refuge at Gaeta in Neapolitan territory. Through weakness rather than through cowardice he had refused the part that the liberals pressed upon him. He had no further influence on the contest for Italian liberty and unity; nor was Rome any longer the centre of the struggle.

Italy was well prepared for the spread of the revolutionary movement. The society of Young Italy had enrolled many members throughout the country, and the Risorgimento was widely supported among the younger nobility, the educated classes and to some extent by the artisans of the cities. The initiative everywhere rested with the ruling classes or those just below; the peasants, except in Sicily, did not rise. It was surprising that the first rising, after the tobacco riots in Milan in January 1848, should have been in Sicily. Yet Sicily had once before had a parliament—during the English occupation in 1812—and she rose against Naples whom she hated, while the peasants seized the landlords' land. In January 1848, a manifesto was issued in Palermo demanding 'reforms in agreement with the progress of the age and in accordance with the wishes of Europe, Italy, and France.' The insurrection was announced for January 12, and it actually broke out on that day. From January 12 to January 29 the Sicilians fought the Neapolitan army in the name of independence and an Italian confederation. Ferdinand II, King of Naples and Sicily, granted a constitution to his Kingdom as a unit and recovered control. Ferdinand yielded out of fear and his motives deceived no one.

Ferdinand's constitution had a direct effect in inducing the Pope to grant the constitution for the Papal States which we have already noticed. It excited the nationalists of Tuscany to action. The Government of the Grand Duke Leopold II was not one of the most oppressive in Italy, and Florence was a centre of the Risorgimento already, as we have seen. The Grand Duke made small concessions at first, but these were far from contenting the population of Florence, Leghorn, and the other towns of Tuscany; and, in February 1848, he issued a constitution on the model of the Neapolitan one.

What happened in Tuscany was not of much importance, for she could rarely pursue a really independent policy. The future of Italy turned mainly on one point: could the power of Austria be shaken in the north of the peninsula? The fate of Italy, therefore, was decided in Piedmont (the real basis of the Kingdom of Sardinia), and in Lombardy, where Austria maintained an authority which the inhabitants never ceased to regard as foreign and oppressive. Sardinia was the least Italian of all the Italian States. Its King, Charles Albert, preferred to speak French instead of Italian, and its population had very incomplete racial affinities with the people of the south. The House of Savoy, which held the crown of the Sardinian kingdom, stood to Italy very closely in the relation in which the House of Hohenzollern in Prussia stood to Germany. Half non-Italian though it was, its population was far more military than any other within the borders of Italy, and its royal family were energetic and ambitious. It was military strength, good statesmanship and a certain honesty which allowed the House of Savoy to be recognised as the representative of the national aspirations of Italy; much the same qualities produced an analogous result for the Hohenzollerns in Germany. The King, Charles Albert, was already favourably known for his decided opposition to the House of Austria. He had declared his hope that all Italy would join to expel the foreigner: he was brave, with a real touch of heroism in his character; but his policy was so hesitating that he was called *Re tentenna*; his policy was declared to be the policy of seesaw. The explanation of his hesitations and changes is to be found partly in his temperament; partly in his strong devotion to the Catholic Church; but above all in the fact that he distrusted liberalism as endangering the unity of the State.

The eyes of Italian patriots were already fixed on Charles Albert. His declaration in favour of a united Italy had been outspoken. Journalism was freer in Turin than elsewhere in Italy, and patriots driven from their own states found an asylum there. Foremost among the writers in the journals was the Count of Cavour. He wrote about railways, education and free trade. He was editor of *Il Risorgimento*, and it was he who, at a meeting of editors to consider the situation, urged them frankly to demand a constitution; all other reforms which they desired, he said, would either flow from this or were contained in it. Their opinion was forwarded to the King, but received no immediate answer. Yet in February 1848 he issued an edict announcing the early grant of a constitution, which followed a few days later. It led him to war, to disaster, to exile, and to death; but it led his son to the throne of a United Italy. It established a limited and parliamentary monarchy, on the English model. It served not only for the Kingdom of Sardinia, but for the Kingdom of Italy, which was soon to come into being; and with slight changes it was the constitution of Italy till Mussolini came.

Not only Italy, but all Europe was ablaze with revolution now. In February 1848 the monarchy of Louis Philippe fell in France. And in March the fall of Metternich released serious revolutionary forces in Italy. When the news reached Milan battle was soon joined. It was fought between the Austrian Deputy Governor (the Viceroy was away), the City Council, which eventually went over to the patriots, and the Austrian garrison, on one side, and on the other side, eager young noblemen and writers, such as Carlo Cattaneo, who raised a makeshift army, a few Mazzinians and the street crowds who manned the barricades. The revolt assumed definite form and organisation, and after five days of hard fighting, March 17–22, the Austrian troops were driven off and the patriots were left in possesssion of the great city. About the same time the Governments were driven from Parma and Modena. By the end of the month Milan, Parma and Modena had declared themselves part of Sardinia. More important was the rising of Venice against her Austrian masters. The patriotic leader, Daniel Manin, was released from prison, and he at once assumed the leadership of the movement. A civic guard was organised and the Austrian garrison found itself hopelessly outnumbered. The governor determined to withdraw his men from the city, and their departure was greeted with cheers for Saint Mark, Italy, and Pius IX. The Pope's name would soon cease to be associated with the national hopes!

War was inevitable, for Austria would certainly not accept as final her humiliating surrender to the despised Italians. Nor could Venice and Lombardy by themselves hope to resist the reinforced armies of Austria. All turned on Charles Albert and the Kingdom of Sardinia. He had less hesitation about making war than about granting a constitution. On March 23 he issued a proclamation to the peoples of Lombardy and Venice declaring that his people sympathised with the heroic struggles of their neighbours against their oppressors, and that they were coming to give them that assistance which a brother expects from a brother, and a friend from a friend. The Sardinian army, mainly consisting of Piedmontese soldiers, at once crossed the Ticino. The sword must now decide the fate of Italy; and the sword of Austria proved the heavier and the sharper.

The war was a great disappointment to the patriots. In truth they had little to which they could trust except the genuine enthusiasm and devotion which actuated most of those who fought in the Italian ranks. Outside Piedmont there was little organisation, and the help that came from the states of the centre and the south was of little consequence. Charles Albert's heart was in the struggle, as he clearly showed when disaster came, and his physical courage was beyond reproach, but he had little military skill and he found no generals to distinguish themselves in the war. The Austrians—in spite of the troubles that were shaking the State at home—were more favourably situated. Though forced to retire before the first attack of the Italians, they held in the famous quadrilateral (Verona, Peschiera, Legnago and Mantua) places of great strength which gave to the Austrian army a sure road by which it could maintain its connections with Austria and receive reinforcements. In Radetzky, though he was over eighty years of age, they had a commander whose energy and skill were recognised by his bitterest opponents,[1] and the general discipline and skill of the Austrian armies were far above those of their

---

[1] The famous phrase 'In Ihrem Lager liegt Oesterreich' (Austria lies in *your* camp), applied to Radetzky, shows alike the desperate situation of Austria and her dependence on military success.

opponents. Only the complete collapse of the Austrian power north of the Alps could probably have saved the Italians from complete defeat.

There was no real union among the Italian states. There was strong local feeling in Milan, in Venice, in the duchies of the centre, and above all in Naples and Sicily. Until the fortunes of the war threatened to turn against them they were for the most part unwilling to subordinate themselves to the kingdom of Sardinia. There was friction between Milan and Venice, and in all the states there was strife between the republicans and the royalists. Beneath the surface there were anarchical groups working equally against both the republicans and the royalists. There was talk of an Italian league, but it was never a favourite idea with Charles Albert, and it came to nothing. There was even a constituent assembly sitting in Rome made up of deputies from several Italian parliaments.

The Austrians had already been driven out of Milan. They withdrew still further to the east. The Italian troops showed at times great courage and could claim victories. Their greatest was the capture of the important fortress of Peschiera. But when Radetzky was ready for the counter-attack the end soon came. On July 25, 1848, the Italians were heavily defeated on the twice fatal field of Custozza. Charles Albert was driven back on Milan. The Milanese were of course angry at the failure of their hopes. The friction with the Piedmontese was increased by defeat, and Charles Albert was accused of having betrayed the national cause, when he failed to defend Milan. The Austrians entered Milan again. Charles Albert and the Sardinian army were allowed to withdraw beyond the frontier.

It remains to consider briefly the behaviour of the rulers of the various Italian states during this time of hope and confusion; for in their behaviour is to be found the explanation of the fact that when at last the Italian victory was won Italian unity was secured not by any scheme of federation, such as was adopted in Germany—where the local differences in language, race, and character were not nearly so great as in Italy—but by the incorporation of the whole of Italy in the kingdom of Sardinia. No ruler of Italy, with the single exception of Charles Albert, showed any real devotion to the national cause; and the national cause, therefore, when it triumphed could make no use of any other of them.

We have already traced the fortunes of Pius IX as far as his flight to Gaeta. His name disappeared from the hatbands, the standards, and the battle-cries of Italian soldiers henceforth. The King of Naples had never had any of the real belief which animated Pius IX in the cause of Italy and constitutionalism, and took the first opportunity of joining the cause of reaction. The national movement threatened indeed his dominions with disruption, for Sicily showed no inclination to be satisfied with equal rights in the constitution of Naples. The inhabitants had thrown down the statues of the Bourbon kings and had declared that Sicily was henceforward an independent State. The rebellion mastered the whole island, and the crown was offered to the second son of Charles Albert, who, however, thought it wise to refuse it. Ferdinand's acceptance of the constitution had from the first been hypocritical, and the denunciation of the war by the Pope induced him to throw away all pretence. He declared indeed at first that it was his 'firm and immutable will' to maintain the constitution, but he withdrew the troops that he had sent to the help of the national cause in the north of Italy. Then, disorders in Naples, which were easily suppressed, gave him an excuse for dismissing his Parliament and in fact withdrawing the constitution. Sicily was now invaded. Messina was taken and cruelly punished. The intervention of the French and British fleets stopped further military operations; but it was clear that the old régime would be restored in both parts of the Neapolitan monarchy.

Leopold, the Grand Duke of Tuscany, was not of such base metal as Ferdinand of Naples, and we have seen how easily the constitution had been established in Tuscany. The Parliament was organised; a popular Ministry was appointed. The Grand Duke even sent representatives to the constituent assembly in Rome. Soon afterwards, however, it was denounced by the Pope. The opposition of the Pope was the cause or the excuse for Leopold to abandon not only the constituent assembly, but also the national cause as a whole. He went first to Siena and then escaped to Gaeta and joined the Pope in the territory of the King of Naples. There was therefore, ten years later, no place for the Grand Duke of Tuscany in the free Italy that was then established. The smaller dukes played no better part, and Modena and Parma readily accepted the rule of Austria which they had for the moment thrown off.

The behaviour of Sardinia was very different, and she had her reward. The truce which had been signed after the Austrian occupation of Milan was no settlement of the problem of the future of Italy. The Parliament at Turin demanded the renewal of the war and Genoa threatened a republic if the Austrian terms were accepted. Charles Albert therefore led out again the discouraged troops to face their victorious opponents. At Novara (on March 23, 1849) the Piedmontese army (for the Sardinian army had its main support in Piedmontese soldiers) was completely defeated, with some suspicion of treason among the commanders. Charles Albert declared that he had sacrificed everything for the cause of Italy; that he had not been able to find death on the battlefield; and that as he was now the chief obstacle to peace he would resign the crown. His son Victor Emmanuel became king; Charles Albert retired to Portugal and died there a few months later.

Victor Emmanuel could not foresee that fate had in store for him the glorious throne of a United Italy. But in the first days of his reign he did much to secure it. He was urged, in the negotiations which followed the battle of Novara, to abandon the constitution and better terms were offered him if he would consent; but he steadily refused. In his first proclamation to the people he pointed to the enemies, both internal and external, which threatened the constitution; but declared himself its determined defender. Alone among the princes of Italy he nailed the flag of liberty to his mast.

The Revolution now only held its own at two points on Italian soil: at Rome and Venice. These two romantic chapters of Italian history must be very briefly summarised. The flight of the Pope had left the Eternal City in great confusion. The Pope in vain tried to rule from his place of exile. The extremer spirits of the nationalist movement came to Rome, and among them Mazzini. A revolutionary republic was set up and the government was placed in the hands of a triumvirate (consisting of Mazzini, Saffi and Armellini); but in fact it was Mazzini who directed the whole policy of the republic. Garibaldi—already the chosen hero of Italy—came and placed his sword at the disposal of the triumvirate. Together Mazzini and Garibaldi challenged the power of Austria and of the Papacy in the name of God and the People.

The contest was in any case a hopeless one, for the republic would soon have been crushed between the forces of Naples and of Austria. But another Power entered the arena and decided the issue. France was still a republic and its president was Bonaparte, soon to be Napoleon III, who knew something of Italian revolutions and had some sympathy with them. He needed, however, the support of the clergy, and he feared the establishment of the power of Austria in Rome. He decided, therefore, to interfere, and he despatched a French army to Civita Vecchia to overthrow the republic and restore the government of the Pope. Oudinot, the French commander, underrated at first the power of Garibaldi, and was sharply checked on his first advance. But then reinforcements were brought up. The Neapolitans gave some assistance to the foreign invader. On June 30 the city fell into the hands of the French. Garibaldi decided to withdraw into the mountains before the French entered, and appealed for volunteers to follow him. 'I offer neither pay nor quarters not provisions; I offer hunger, thirst, forced marches, battles and death. Let him who loves his country in his heart and not with his lips only follow me'. A number of volunteers responded to the heroic challenge. They were pursued and dispersed, and Garibaldi only escaped at last after much suffering; but many of those who went out of Rome with him lived to play a part in the triumph of ten years later.

Venice had shaken off the lethargy of centuries to take a part in the national movement. We have seen how the news of the revolution at Milan had stirred her to a similar movement. Manin proved a great

leader. Venice declared herself an independent republic and co-operated with the movement in Milan. Later, when fortune was turning
against the national cause, the Venetians consented to a close union
with Milan and Piedmont under the leadership of Charles Albert.
But, as we have seen, the Austrian arms pressed on to victory. Even
after Custozza and Novara, however, the Venetians fought on. But
Venice was no longer the impregnable city that she had been in the
days before long-distance artillery had been invented. The Austrians
bombarded the city and did great damage. Cholera came to intensify
the sufferings of the population. At last, on August 24, Manin recognised that further resistance was impossible. He retired into exile and
the city passed again into the power of the Austrians.

So ended in entire failure the attempt of Italy to win her independence from Austria. What enthusiasm and a few great leaders
could do had been nobly done. But discipline and unity in leadership
and in organisation had been notably and fatally absent. Italy, moreover, had found no help from any outside power. Charles Albert had
proudly declared that Italy could save herself (*Italia farà da sé*).
Count Cavour, the soberest and wisest brain among the statesmen
of Italy, was among his supporters. He doubted Italy's power of settling her own fate without foreign help. He saw that the sword of
France must if possible be thrown into the scale against the sword
of Austria, and it was the constant effort of his statecraft to bring
about that result. The Risorgimento was over. The next phase of the
Italian story would be a sterner one. It would be political unification
made by war with the leadership and organisation which the patriots
lacked in 1848–49, made above all by diplomacy which gained the
help of a foreign ally. But blood had been shed in 1848–49 and this
did as much to root the movement for national unity in the whole
country as ever the cultural revival of the first half of the century had
done. Below the surface in Italy too a third force was fermenting. It
found fumbling expression in the crowds of Leghorn and Rome and
clearer voicing in Carlo Pisacane, the first Italian socialist.

Chapter 14

THE EASTERN QUESTION AND THE CRIMEAN WAR

At the end of the eighteenth century the Eastern question assumed its modern form. Three factors determined it: the growing weakness of the Turk at Constantinople, the rise of small, vigorous Christian nationalities in the Balkan peninsula, and the effect of both on the policy of the Great Powers. Between the years 1788 and 1791 Austria and Russia attacked Turkey in concert, and Russia, asserting that she was the protector of Christians in the Turkish Empire, advanced as far as the port of Oczakov on the Black Sea. The younger Pitt, speaking for Britain, denounced the danger of the Russian advance and the menace to Turkey's integrity. Parliament did not support him over this incident, but he had set the fashion for his successors; for almost ninety years to come they followed a pro-Turkish and anti-Russian policy. Austria, too, showed a moderate attitude to Turkey in 1791. She returned nearly all her conquests to Turkey and henceforth sought to protect her. For, by 1791, both Britain and Austria had recognised that Turkey was a menace, not because of her strength, but because of her weakness.

At the dawn of the nineteenth century, then, Russia began to creep south down the Black Sea coast, her eyes always on Constantinople as an ultimate goal. Austria crouched on Russia's flank, a suspicious hound threatening to spring when Russia was once engaged with Turkey. Britain watched from afar, resolved to protect the commerce of the East Mediterranean and to defend Constantinople itself against attack. The disturbances always began by the attempts of small Balkan nationalities to assert their independence of Turkey, and the Great Powers then interfered to regulate or to improve their status. The Turkish attitude was always the same. For Christian subjects (*rayahs* as they were called) to rebel was an unspeakable presumption. Sometimes the Turk tried to anticipate such plans by massacre, and his massacres increased as his power grew weaker. At other times the Turk, though forced to grant some status or privileges to Christian individuals or races, attempted to evade or delay the execution of the provisions. Reform or concession was never granted to a Turkish subject except under pressure of the Great Powers. If granted in theory it was always, as far as possible, withdrawn in practice. Much ingenuity was shown in setting the Great Powers by the ears. The three several elements of the problem then are, first, an Oriental Government established in Europe, misgoverning millions of Christians, and slowly disintegrating in power. Next, there is a collection of Great Powers, of which Russia alone generally seeks to accelerate Turkish disintegration. Last, a collection of small subject Christian nationalities all gradually organising, educating and strengthening themselves to throw off the Turkish yoke. This situation produced, during the nineteenth century, endless rebellions of subjects against the Sultan, three Russo-Turkish wars, and two wars in which France and Britain, as well as Russia, took a part for or against Turkey. Of these subject nationalities the Rumanians inhabited the provinces of Moldavia and Wallachia (modern Rumania).[1] They had always been ruled as separate principalities with native governors and a quasi-independent status. The chief racial areas, inhabited respectively by Serbs, Bulgars and Greeks, correspond roughly to the boundaries of their respective territories in 1913. Serbia and Greece were more dependent on Constantinople than Moldavia and Wallachia, but no large Turkish population lived in either. Both the district and population of Bulgaria adjoined Constantinople, and hence the emancipation of Bulgaria lagged behind that of Serbia or Greece.

It was the Serbs, and not the Greeks, who struck the first blow for Balkan freedom. The revolt began in 1804 under Kara (Black) George, the ancestor of the Karageorgević dynasty of Serbia. It was a story of heroic fights and bloody massacres on both sides. But after eight years Kara George maintained his position, and in the Russo-Turkish Treaty of 1812 obtained a promise of autonomy. He was defeated in 1813, and fled the country. Then in 1815 his rival, enemy and ultimate murderer, Miloš Obrenović, raised another revolt. He was successful in asserting the *de facto* independence of Serbia at once and, after many and very tedious delays, secured a constitution and, by 1829, the recognition of himself as Prince of Serbia.

The obscure struggle of peasant heroes against Turkish armies thrice their size attracted little attention in Europe. But all the Great Powers became stirred when the Greeks rebelled in 1820. Russia was excited by the execution of the Patriarch of Constantinople and by massacres of Greek Christians, and it was feared that she would at

---

[1] Rumania, as constituted in 1913, included Moldavia and Wallachia and part of the Dobrudja, about 7–8 millions in all. After the war of 1914–18 she doubled her population and added Bessarabia, the Bukovina, Transylvania and part of Hungary. After the war of 1939–45 she lost Bessarabia and northern Bukovina to the U.S.S.R. but retained Transylvania.

once attack Turkey. Austria and Britain at once took measures to avert this danger. For some years Canning and Metternich were in agreement in principle. The struggle between Turkey and her Greek rebels was nobody else's affair. The duty of the Great Powers was to 'hold the ring' and to permit none of their number to use force. For, if Russia tried to settle the quarrel by war, Canning believed she would 'gobble Greece at one mouthful and Turkey at the next!' This situation lasted from 1820 till the end of 1825. Then a striking change occurred. The Sultan appealed for aid to Mehemet Ali, Pasha of Egypt, and Mehemet sent his son Ibrahim and a disciplined army to the Morea. His success was so great that Russia declared she must intervene to save the Greeks from extinction.

Canning decided that the only way of averting war was for Britain to act with Russia in putting pressure on Turkey. Austria declined to do this and stood aloof. Britain and Russia signed an agreement to this effect on April 4, 1826. Turkey was to be urged to make an armistice with the Greeks and to grant to them a measure of 'home rule.' But even so, force was not actually proposed, and it was not until July 6, 1827 (and after France had joined as a third party), that the Allies signed a definite treaty to employ force towards Turkey, in case of her refusal to listen to the Allies' proposal to accept an armistice and give autonomy to Greece. This led, just after Canning's death (August 12, 1827), to the Battle of Navarino. There, the joint British, French, and Russian squadrons destroyed the Turkish and Egyptian fleets. This great catastrophe to Turkey rendered not only the autonomy, but the independence, of Greece inevitable, though the death of Canning probably made a great difference to the form it assumed.

Early in 1828 Russia took exactly the step which Canning had tried to prevent, and declared war upon Turkey direct and alone.[1] But, though British and French remonstrances were little heeded by Tsar Nicholas, it does not seem that at this time he intended the destruction of the Turkish Empire, or even the immediate annexation of large parts of it.

After preliminary reverses the Russian army reached Adrianople in the summer of 1829. Diebitsch, the commanding general, despite the smallness and demoralisation of his army, assumed the airs of a conqueror and summoned the Turks to make peace. The Sultan was cowed and the Treaty of Adrianople was promptly signed (September 14, 1829). Territory was indeed acquired in Asia at Turkey's expense, which resulted in an advance in the Caucasus area. But

---

[1] As is well known, the Allies had maintained that the battle of Navarino was 'an untoward event' and Britain refused throughout to consider herself at war with Turkey. So did France, though she took the strong step in 1828 of sending troops to compel the evacuation of the Morea. The fact is that the Treaty of London of July 6, 1827, was Canning's work, and not approved by his successor Wellington or by France.

nothing similar was acquired, or attempted to be acquired, in Europe. Russia's boundary with Turkey was still the river Pruth, far to the north of Moldavia. Her policy in Europe was not annexation but peaceful penetration.

France and Britain were very much afraid that Greece would become a vassal state dependent on Russia. Wellington, therefore, proposed to divide her into two halves so as to make her as small and weak as possible. Aberdeen even went further, and propsed to 'trisect' her. Happily Wellington and Aberdeen were turned out, and wiser counsels prevailed under Palmerston and Grey. The boundaries of Greece were enlarged to include Arta and Volo; she was declared independent, and guaranteed a loan and a monarchy (1832). The recognition by Russia, France and Britain of her independence, to which Russia consented with extreme reluctance, was an important landmark in Balkan history. The experience of the later nineteenth century showed that Balkan states which became independent were zealous to remain so. They regarded their own interests first, and those did not usually coincide with Russia's or with those of any other Great Power. To recognise a Balkan state as independent of Turkey was really a way of helping her to become independent of Russia. And Greece got rid of Russian influence at once. In the Principalities Russia was by no means successful in asserting her influence; the Rumanians already cherished, and for long maintained, a bitter hatred of Russia. In Serbia the reigning Prince (Miloš Obrenović) managed to use Russia as a catspaw in his frequent bickerings with the Turks.

In relation to Turkey herself the experience of Russia was wholly different. For her the Tsar Nicholas soon won what seemed to be a great and startling triumph. The policy of Russia after 1829 was, for at least ten years, a singular reversal of her traditional aim to press on to Constantinople, annexing as much territory as possible on the way. A committee of Russian statesmen was appointed by Tsar Nicholas in 1829 to examine the results of the probable break-up of the Turkish Empire. They reported, contrary to Russian traditional policy, that it was desirable to preserve the integrity of the Turkish Empire. If Turkey dissolved further, they said, with a good deal of prophetic insight, strong small Balkan states would be formed, and Russia would prove unable to influence them. On the other hand, she already had treaty rights and influence in Turkey as it was, which she could increase by economic control and peaceful penetration. If Russia was to seek territory it should be in the direction of Armenia or Baghdad, not Constantinople. Nicholas grumbled but accepted the report, and his policy was for ten years the *status quo* and the integrity of Turkey.

Nicholas communicated his ideas to Austria, and obtained Metternich's support for a decade. But he was too proud to explain his policy to Britain, and Palmerston continued to oppose Russia and to believe that she intended to annex Constantinople and to seize the Dardanelles. Palmerston believed quite wrongly, that the convention of Müchengrätz which Russia signed with Austria on September 18, 1833 was a partition of Turkey by Austria and Russia. It was, in fact, not Russia but France which was active in a policy of dismembering Turkey during the period 1830–41. This is the time when she secured Algiers; it is the period also when she favoured the revolt of Egypt against Turkey, and sought by this means to secure help for her own Mediterranean schemes. Britain, on the other hand, was as anxious as ever to preserve the Turkish Empire, and therefore naturally opposed the French scheme.

The real trouble lay in Egypt. There, Mehemet Ali, the bold and ambitious Pasha, had long been in only nominal subordination to the Sultan, but had sent troops to assist the Sultan in subduing Greece. He had already become Pasha of Crete, and hoped to add the pash-aliks of Syria and Damascus to that of Egypt. The Sultan showed himself jealous and suspicious, and listened to advisers who were the personal enemies of Mehemet. That bold Pasha thought himself, and perhaps actually was, in danger, and decided to avert any possible design to expel him from Egypt by attacking the Sultan and seizing Damascus and Syria. So Mehemet Ali called on his warlike son Ibrahim, and instructed him to start a 'preventive war' against the Sultan.

In November 1831 Ibrahim invaded Palestine by sea and land with a small but well-disciplined army. His march was as successful as Allenby's in 1918. Jaffa, Gaza, and Jerusalem fell in rapid succession; he was delayed, like Napoleon, at Acre, but ultimately captured the city (May 1832). Damascus fell in June, Aleppo in July, and Ibrahim actually crossed the Taurus mountain range, winning another victory in the Beylan Pass, before the end of the month. He was equally successful in diplomacy, posing as a liberal and a loyal subject of the Sultan at the same time. In December 1832 Sultan Mahmud sent his last army against Ibrahim. That great warrior utterly routed it at Koniah. The Sultan was thus at the mercy of his victorious and rebellious vassal.

The Sultan had already been imploring Britain for aid, but while Russia seemed quiescent Palmerston was unwilling to bring Britain to the aid of Turkey, a policy at once very bold and very dangerous. At the moment of the disaster of Koniah a Russian mission arrived at Constantinople and the Sultan, in despair, turned to the hereditary enemy for help. 'A drowning man,' said one of his advisers, 'clings to a serpent [for aid]'; and the Sultan clung to Russia. The Tsar, like the Sultan, hated 'rebels,' and a bargain was ultimately struck. In February 1833 the 'drowning man' formally demanded assistance from 'the serpent.' On February 20 a Russian naval squadron anchored off Constantinople, the only time one ever appeared there with Turkish consent. In April six thousand Russian troops landed on the Asiatic shore opposite Constantinople. The Sultan was thus safe, and meanwhile France and Britain both put pressure on Turkey to make concessions to Mehemet Ali. As a result, by the end of April 1833, the Sultan ceded to him Palestine, Syria, Aleppo, Damascus, with permission to occupy the seaports of Adana, and Ibrahim withdrew to Syria. The crisis seemed ended.

The Russian troops also began to withdraw from Asia, but, before they did so, the Turkish Sultan was made to sign a secret treaty with Russia. The Treaty of Unkiar Skelessi (July 8, 1833) was in reality an offensive and defensive alliance between the two Powers. By a secret article, which only gradually leaked out, Russia waived her rights for Turkish military aid, and Turkey agreed in return to close the Dardanelles to all warships *au besoin* (and *au besoin* meant at the demand of Russia). Had this treaty ever become operative Turkey would have been, in every sense, a vassal of Russia. Nicholas seemed to have the practical, if unavowed, control of the Straits, of Constantinople, and of the Sultan.[1] But the victory was too complete, the obstacles too great. The entry of Russia's warships into the Straits would have meant war with Britain, and France had strong reasons for supporting Egypt against Turkey. Palmerston was all for the integrity of the Turk as against Egypt, and therefore high in favour with the Sultan. If he was able to avert the Egyptian danger, the Sultan would lean in future on Britain and not on Russia. His dependence on the latter Power was veiled, so he need not be embarrassed when evading the obligations of Unkiar Skelessi.

Sultan Mahmud was prepared to be just as treacherous towards Egypt as he intended to be to Russia. And he had a chance of success against Ibrahim, for that professed liberal had speedily alienated his Syrian subjects by his tyranny. Sultan Mahmud realised that, if his generals struck Ibrahim on the flank, the Syrians might rise against him. The Sultan undoubtedly gave the provocation, for in April 1839 he sent a Turkish army to Bir on the Euphrates and made it cross from the left to the right bank, thus enabling it to strike at Ibrahim's communications between Palestine and the Adana ports. The Great Powers at once got alarmed, and it was agreed to send a joint Franco-British squadron to the Bosphorus, in case the Russians entered Turkey. It was too late: the last act of the dying Sultan was to tell his general to attack Ibrahim. The Turks moved against Ibrahim early in June. Three severe blows followed in relentless succession. On the 24th Ibrahim utterly routed the Turks at Nezib, capturing 15,000

---

[1] The meaning of this secret article is still disputed. But it is noticeable that the Strait of the Dardanelles is at the western end of the Sea of Marmora and that the article makes no reference to the strait at the eastern end, *i.e.* the Bosphorus.

prisoners and all their guns and stores. On July 1 old Mahmud died, and was succeeded by Abdul Mejid, an ignorant boy of sixteen. Immediately afterwards the Ottoman fleet sailed off to Alexandria and surrendered to Mehemet Ali, alleging as a pretext that Constantinople was sold to the Russians. Mehemet Ali, proud of the triumphs of his son and of Egyptian arms, was intoxicated, and thought he could retain his prizes and his power. But he had gravely miscalculated. Turkey, or even Europe, he might defy, but there was one person he could not defy, and that was Palmerston.

If Palmerston had hesitated in 1832, he acted at once in 1839. The boy-Sultan alternated between bombast and panic, France was secretly supporting Egypt, Nicholas was playing his own game, Austria was timid and doubtful. But Palmerston had two assets: his own resolution and British sea power. A British blockade of Alexandria at once began, though the French refused to co-operate. Palmerston replied by proposing a Conference of the Great Powers at Vienna. Negotiations dragged on, Russia intervened, and France procrastinated. Palmerston drove on the European team with the fury of Jehu, and Egypt and France were crushed beneath his wheels.

What happened was this. Finding reason to suspect France of favouring Egypt, Palmerston signed a Convention in London on July 15, 1840, with Austria, Prussia, and Russia. The terms were that Mehemet Ali was to become hereditary Pasha of Egypt and Pasha of Acre for life. If he did not evacuate all other conquests and accept these terms within ten days, he was henceforth to be confined to Egypt alone.[1] There were two difficulties in this Convention. It was signed without France and force would be necessary to make it effective against Mehemet Ali. Palmerston soon showed that he was equal to both emergencies and was prepared, in cheerful and characteristic fashion, to 'call' both 'bluffs.'

Guizot, to whom he communicated the news of the Convention, told him that exclusion of France was 'a mortal affront.' Thiers, the Prime Minister, declared that the good relations with England were shattered, and pushed on military preparations; the whole French press screamed with rage. Palmerston never had believed that France would make war on him, and in this case he was right in his belief. The wrath of France evaporated soon after the fiery words had been uttered. Brave old Soult, who became French Prime Minister in October, knew that war with Britain would risk the dynasty. Meanwhile, Palmerston secured a great triumph over his other opponent.

Mehemet Ali allowed the ten days prescibed in the terms of the Great Powers to pass without any formal notice, but a British and Austrian squadron appeared off Beirut and demanded the Egyptian

---

[1] Austria, as well as Great Britain, definitely promised to give naval aid to Turkey (Art. 2) if Mehemet Ali refused the terms.

evacuation of Syria (August 11). On September 9 Admiral Stopford bombarded the town and landed a Turkish force. On October 9 he captured Beirut. Syria at once rose in revolt against Ibrahim, and the British squadron moved on to Acre. That city had defied the Crusaders for two years, Ibrahim for six months, and Napoleon for two. On November 3 Admiral Stopford destroyed it in three hours! For the second time a British Admiral had made Ibrahim miss his destiny.[1]

Ibrahim knew well enough the value of sea power and the danger to his communications, and prepared hastily to evacuate Syria. Egypt itself was now in danger. The boy-Sultan had plucked up courage to depose Mehemet Ali.[2] That worthy received the news with calmness. This, he said, was his fourth deposition. He hoped to get over it as well as he had done the other three, with the help of God and the Prophet! But he changed his tune when Admiral Napier appeared before Alexandria and threatened to address him with the iron lips of cannon. He capitulated at once, and signed a Convention (November 27) promising to submit and to evacuate Syria, provided that he was guaranteed as the hereditary Pasha of Egypt. The Sultan and the Great Powers demurred to this conclusion. But Britain had her way, and triumphed over all opponents. Mehemet Ali survived his fourth deposition, but was confined in future to Egypt. The solution was a permanent one. Men began to see what they had previously forgotten, that the conquests of one Eastern potentate over the other, of Amurath over Amurath, are essentially fleeting. The Syrians, who had welcomed Ibrahim as a deliverer, revolted against him as a tyrant. Mehemet Ali had once threatened Constantinople: neither he nor his son ever again even threatened Palestine. Egypt, which Mehemet Ali and Ibrahim had made greater than Turkey, actually became weaker than it in the space of fourteen years. Deprived of its leaders, overburdened with debt, and distracted by internal disputes, it was the feeblest of the provinces of the Turkish Empire. In 1854 France, which had aimed at giving Syria to Egypt or to herself, was discredited, and Palmerston earned the undying gratitude of the Sultan.

The British triumph was completed by the signing of a Convention on July 13, 1841, whereby the Great Powers and the Sultan pledged themselves not to permit 'vessels of war belonging to foreign powers' to enter the Dardanelles and the Bosphorus. Russia still believed that the principles of the Treaty of Unkiar Skelessi could be maintained, and was inclined to be quite friendly to Britain, whom she

---

[1] Sir E. Codrington, by destroying the Turkish and Egyptian fleet at Navarino, prevented Ibrahim from conquering Greece in 1827.

[2] This was a distinct blunder and contrary to the terms of the Allied Convention of July 15, 1840.

regarded as a dupe. In fact, the Tsar was wholly mistaken. The Sultan regarded him as an interested bully, to whose menaces he had been compelled to submit while in danger, but against whom he could now invoke the disinterested Britain. Quite unaware of all this Nicholas sought a *rapprochement* with Britain, and an understanding as to the future, in the famous conversation he had with Lord Aberdeen in 1844.[1] There is no doubt about what he said. Tsar Nicholas expressed the view that the Turk was 'a dying man,' that his Empire was disintegrating, and that it was well to make provision beforehand. He meant to have Constantinople and, in return, Britain was to have Egypt or Crete as well if she liked. That, said Nicholas, would show that he was ready to observe the Balance of Power and to give a fair compensation to Britain. The proposition was much misrepresented during the Crimean War, when Tsar Nicholas figured in the Jingo press as 'a giant liar,' and Britain as a Crusader protecting the right. But it is singular to note that this suggestion of Nicholas was actually adopted in 1915. Grey then agreed to Russia having Constantinople, and his reason is obvious. Cyprus and Egypt had by then been declared British possessions. There was, therefore, no reason why we should not favour Russia's claims on Constantinople. The reason Britain did not had already been brusquely and brutally expressed by Palmerston in 1839. 'All that we hear every day of the week about the decay of the Turkish Empire, and its being a dead body or a sapless trunk, and so forth, is pure and unadulterated nonsense.'[2] No compromise was possible when the Tsar said the Turk was 'a dying man' and Palmerston answered 'Nonsense!' Therein lay the germ of the Crimean War.

THE CRIMEAN WAR

The Crimean War occupies a peculiar place in the history of Europe in the nineteenth century. The military methods resemble rather those of the Napoleonic age than of the period soon to be opened by Moltke and the military system of Prussia. Steam vessels were used, but they were still built of wood. The Paixhans shell was used by Russia with devastating effect on the Turkish wooden ships at Sinope, but armament generally was traditional. The telegraph had been brought to Vienna and was thence extended, but only when a

[1] In 1841 the Whigs went out and were succeeded by Peel, with Aberdeen as Foreign Secretary. For the conversation of 1844 see text in K. Bourne, *The Foreign Policy of Victorian England 1830–1902* (1970), pp. 258–61.

[2] P. Guedalla, *Palmerston* (1926), pp. 212–13; cp. C. K. Webster, *The Foreign Policy of Palmerston* (1951), Vol. II, p. 657.

sea cable was laid in 1855 from Balaclava to Varna could news be telegraphed from the Crimea. Many modernised medical and other services resulted from the war, but when it began, since auxiliary services developed during the Napoleonic Wars had beem disbanded, feeding and sanitation for the armies was almost mediæval in character. It was the last war on a large scale in which cavalry was able to play its traditional rôle; it was the last war in which the railway played no operational part. And if its methods and instruments are strange to the modern student, its aims and its diplomacy seem still more so. Ecclesiastical questions that might belong to the time of the Crusades play a part in the causes of the war. The victors in the struggle gained little if anything from it. The integrity of Turkey was in fact not maintained. The advance of Russia was not permanently checked. In the war of 1914–18 France and Britain spent many thousands of lives and many millions of money in the effort to undo some of the consequences of their victory in the Crimean War, which had been won with so much loss of blood and treasure. Yet the war is in many ways very interesting. It provides us especially with a singularly instructive illustration of the way in which wars are brought about, and the procedure of some of the actors in the story is seen without the concealment and the allegation of false motives behind which diplomatists have usually liked to work.

There were for this war, as for all wars, many converging causes. But of all these causes the condition of the Balkan peninsula was the most important. The Turkish power extended over the whole of it with the exception of the free kingdom of Greece. Few even among European diplomatists of that epoch had any clear idea of the network of races and religions and languages that filled up the peninsula. The Turkish rule was not intentionally cruel, nor actually so except when its authority was dangerously challenged, or, which was not always the same thing, thought by the Turks to be so challenged. It was everywhere little more than a garrison of occupation—maintaining, not very effectively, a sort of order, raising taxes, and for the rest letting the subject populations go their own way and follow their own ideas in social life and religion. But without question the Turkish power was growing weaker, less effective militarily, and more corrupt. It was little influenced by the progress of science and industry which had so changed the character of Western Europe, and for political liberty and the participation of the people in the administration of the government it had a deep-seated aversion. As Turkey grew weaker, and partly because it grew weaker, the subject nationalities and religions grew more self-conscious. The Greeks had already broken away and established an independent power. Their example produced inevitably stirrings among the other races. Beyond the Danube, in the Principalities of Moldavia and Wallachia, there was, in accordance with recent treaties, a large measure of self-government, and the people—not yet known as Rumanians—were eager for more. The Serbians were conscious of their great past and dissatisfied with the considerable amount of self-government which they had already won. The Montenegrins still maintained their practical independence behind their mountain fortresses. The Bulgarians, Albanians, and Macedonians were as yet hardly conscious of any separate existence, but their lands were full of disturbances resulting from a sense of the differences which separated them from their rulers. Religion was a potent element of the ferment of the country. There were many Mohammedans among the conquered peoples; but the Orthodox or Greek form of Christianity persisted among most, and of the Orthodox Church the Russian Tsar was the admitted head. Religion in the Balkans was always apt to assume a strong political character, as has so often been the case in countries where open political action has been impossible.

The position in the Balkans was obviously unstable. A revolution might at any time occur in one of its districts which would seriously upset the Balance of Power; and the Great Powers to the north of the Danube watched events with anxiety in which ambition and fear both played a part. The Empire of Austria owed its origin to the necessity of barring the way against an invader from the lower course of the Danube, and its whole life was closely bound up with resistance to the Turkish power. Fear of the Turkish power had indeed now passed away; but that fear had been followed by another—the fear of the power which might take Turkey's place in the Balkan peninsula. Austria desired influence, if not territory, there for herself, and she feared the designs and ambitions of Russia. Of the nature of these ambitions there could hardly be any doubt. Russia was the great Slav state, and the majority of the population of the Balkans spoke Slavonic tongues. Even the Bulgarians, though not wholly Slavonic, had adopted a Slavonic language. Moreover, Russia, as we have already said, had religious grounds for interference on behalf of the members of the Orthodox Church. She claimed also that she possessed treaty rights of interference as well; and it was a constant matter of dispute as to how far these rights extended. In the Treaty of Kutchuck Kainarji, which was drawn up in 1774 between Russia and Turkey, there were two clauses which bear upon the controversy. By one article (14) Russia was allowed to build a Christian Church in Galata—a part of Constantinople—and to keep it always under her protection. By another article (7) Turkey promised to protect the Christian Church and religion within her dominions and to allow the Russian Ambassadors to make representations on behalf of the Church in Galata. On the ground of these articles the Russians claimed a right to represent and protect the Christian communities of the Balkans. This would have meant a perpetual danger of interference (think what it would have meant if the French had had the right in the eighteenth century to 'protect' the Catholics of Ireland), and the right claimed by Russia had never been admitted by Turkey.[1]

There was nothing necessarily evil or mean in Russia's ambitions. It doubtless seemed to the Tsar a religious and national duty to do his best for those who belonged to the same religious communion and spoke the same tongue as his own Russian people. There could at any rate be no doubt about them. In January 1853 the Tsar Nicholas had had a conversation with the British Ambassador which became famous. The Tsar was an old friend of Lord Aberdeen, the British Prime Minister, and was on very friendly terms with Sir Hamilton Seymour. In this conversation, which had at once been reported to London and was published when the Crimean War broke out, the Tsar spoke of Turkey as a country that 'seemed to be falling to pieces.' The Turk was, he said, 'a very sick man' who might suddenly die on their hands. It was very important to make up their minds as to what should be done with his territories before that event occurred. Britain and Russia between them could settle it without war. Then he hinted pretty plainly at the settlement that he desired. The Balkan states were to be independent under Russian protection. Russia was to occupy Constantinople but not to annex it. Great Britain was to lay hands on Egypt. It was a partition of Turkish territories that he suggested between Great Britain and Russia, with France left out of the deal.[2] Great Britain showed no inclination to fall in with this scheme. The maintenance of the integrity of Turkey was the traditional British policy and there was no desire to alter it. The conversation created a deep distrust of the designs of Russia, perhaps unjustly.

Then arose the question of the Holy Places. This was in itself a serious matter, or rather the passions which it aroused were serious. It concerned the management of the places of pilgrimage at Jerusalem and especially the Church of the Nativity at Bethlehem. The Turkish Government kept order between the rival claims of the Latins or Roman Catholics and the Orthodox or Greek and Russian Christians. The French Government had a traditional right—running back to the times of the Crusades—to be considered the protector

[1] But the other Great Powers (e.g. Austria and Great Britain) had long admitted Russia had *some* right in the matter. In 1823 Metternich admitted this, and Canning stated that Russia had a special right of friendly advice on behalf of Christians in Turkey in peace time. He qualified this by saying he doubted whether this 'right extended to interference on behalf of subjects of the Party who had thrown off their allegiance.' See H. Temperley, *The Foreign Policy of Canning* (1925), p. 325.

[2] The Tsar was in fact only repeating a conversation he had had with Aberdeen at Windsor in 1844 (p. 213 and notes)—and seems to have thought the latter agreed with him. For further material on Nicholas's ideas *see The New Cambridge Modern History* (1960), Vol. X, pp. 471–2.

of the Christians in the East, but since the development of the power of Russia the Tsars had begun to put forward their own claims. Genuine religious feeling came to strengthen national rivalry and political ambition, and furious passions were aroused by the question of the custody of the keys of the church at Bethlehem and the placing of a star in the grotto of the Sacred Manger.

Yet these questions were settled before war fever gripped Russians or Turks. The situation became grave only when the Tsar sent to Constantinople Prince Menschikov—one of the most prominent figures at the Russian Court—to demand not merely concessions on these points, but also a treaty guaranteeing for the future the Russian claim to be accepted as the protector of the Christians of the Balkan peninsula. The chief part on the other side was played by Lord Stratford de Redcliffe (this title had been conferred on Stratford Canning in 1852). He feared and disliked Russia, and though he saw the weak points of Turkey very clearly, he was nevertheless determined to uphold her integrity and independence even at the risk of war. He took much responsibility upon himself. Communication with London took a long time, for the telegraph had not yet been brought to Constantinople. He persuaded the Sultan to make concessions on the comparatively trivial question of the 'Holy Places,' but to stand firm against guarantees for the future and the Russian protectorate of the Balkan Christians. Both were derogations of sovereign rights. In May 1853 Menschikov left Constantinople in protest against this decision, and it was clear that war was dangerously threatening. The view that wars are always fought for economic interests finds little support in the origins of the Crimean War. National ambition, rivalry and fear are the motives which impelled the nations to what proved a severe struggle.

The withdrawal of Menschikov from Constantinople was a serious step; and the war that threatened all but came when a Russian army in July 1853 crossed the Pruth and occupied Moldavia and Wallachia. The action of Russia could be represented as falling short of actual war, for she had certain treaty rights in the Principalities; and diplomacy made a last attempt to avoid the outbreak of hostilities. Austria regarded the course of affairs with great interest, for the contest was close to her frontiers, and on lands in which she had ambitions if not claims. A conference was called at Vienna and a declaration was drawn up which aimed at protecting the Christian population of the Balkans without admitting the right of Russia to interfere. There was hope that peace might be preserved. Turkey refused to accept the declaration in its simple form; Russia accepted but gave a dangerous interpretation of it. Passion was growing hot in both countries, and on October 4, 1853, a nationalist, excited Turkey declared war against Russia. Lord Stratford de Redcliffe had perhaps tried to restrain her at the last moment.[1]

Who would be the combatants? The nations of Europe would not allow the war to be fought out as a duel between Turkey and Russia, for the interests involved were too great. Austria watched the contest with close attention; seemed again and again on the point of interfering, but never interfered. Prussia was sore, but she had lost confidence in herself through her failures during the revolutionary period. Some of her statesmen, including the rising Bismarck, saw in a situation which occupied the forces of Russia and the attention of Austria an opportunity for Prussia to play an important and decisive part. But the Prussian King was immovably disinclined to adventure, and Prussian influence was hardly perceptible during the course of the war. The actual combatants came from a further distance. Support of Turkey and jealousy of Russia were traditional in the foreign policy of Britain. The spread of Russian power into the Mediterranean would, it was thought, threaten Egypt and the road to India. The war fever developed under the influence of Palmerston and the press. In France under the régime of the new Empire public opinion played a much less important part. All rested with Napoleon III, and he had declared in words never to be forgotten that 'The Empire means peace.' Strong forces, however, pushed him into war; the desire to maintain the prestige of France in the East, his dependence on the Catholic and Clerical party in France, above all the need which he instinctively felt to give the country what it expected from a Napoleon—glory and victory. At the end of October 1853 the joint French and British fleets passed the Dardanelles to give their moral support to Turkey. While they were in the neighbourhood of Constantinople a Russian fleet attacked and destroyed a Turkish squadron near Sinope. This quite natural act of war seemed an insult to the two great Western Powers; and open war came on apace. It was declared by France and Britain in March 1854.

This marked two great changes in European politics. There had been war between Russia and Turkey roughly once every twenty years for nearly two centuries. But never before had Turkey had military allies from the West. The Crimean War was a war to assert that the future of Turkey concerned all Europe. There had been wars between Britain and France for an even longer period. This was their first alliance in war for many centuries.

The Russians were in the Principalities. The first object of the Allies was to drive them out. This was soon accomplished—too soon to allow it to seem a great triumph and a reason for ending the war. The Russians had laid siege to Silistria, through which they thought

---

[1] Stratford's conduct is a source of much dispute. Aberdeen complained of his 'dishonesty,' and it has been asserted that, while formally trying to restrain the Sultan, he was secretly urging him on to war. It is not certain that all of his secret papers are extant, but the reluctance of Stratford to order up the fleet is in his favour.

to pass to a crossing of the Balkans and to a march on Constantinople. But the defence of the place was unexpectedly stubborn. The attitude of Austria, while Russia remained on the Danube, was menacing. The siege was abandoned and the Russians withdrew altogether from the Principalities, into which Austria sent a garrison. This was to hold them until the peace, when they were to be handed over to Turkey. If it had not been for the passions that had been aroused by the war peace might perhaps have come. But it would have seemed a tame ending to such great preparations. After an interchange of communications with Austria, Four Points were agreed on as summarising the programme of the war: (1) the abolition of the Russian Protectorate of the Danubian provinces; (2) the freedom of the navigation of the Danube; (3) the revision of the Straits Convention of 1841 and the introduction of Turkey into 'the European equilibrium'; (4) the renunication by Russia of her exclusive patronage of the Balkan Christians.

The war then must go on, but in what theatre? As often before, it proved difficult to discover a vulnerable point in Russia's wide territories, loosely organised as they were. Cholera had already shown itself with appalling deadliness in the ranks of the Allies, and the French and British armies were in many ways unprepared for a great enterprise. The choice of the Crimea was a sea Power's choice. It was believed that it would be easy to attack the Russian naval station of Sebastopol. The naval power of the Allies could be brought into use, and it would lead to the destruction of the Russian preponderance in the Black Sea, which was one of the declared objects of the war.

In September of the year 1854 the Allies—Turks, French and British—landed on the beaches of Eupatoria, north of Sebastopol. Saint-Arnaud and Raglan then began their march on to the city itself. On September 20 they met the Russian commander, Menschikov, posted on the northern side of the river Alma. After hard fighting, in which the rapid dash of the French *zouaves* contrasted with the more deliberate methods of the British, the Russians were completely defeated, and the road to Sebastopol was open. The Allies probably made here the greatest of the many mistakes during the campaign. They did not attack the city at once, though the Russian commander, Todleben, held that such an attack could not have been resisted; and they made no attempt to establish any blockade on the north side of the river on which Sebastopol stands. Instead, they undertook a long and difficult march round to the south of the city and established their camp there. The interval thus allowed was brilliantly used by Todleben to throw up the fortifications which held the besiegers at bay from September 1854 to September 1855.

The great siege had some peculiar features. It was never a blockade. No serious attempt was made to cut off the city from communication with Russia. Stores and reinforcements were often attacked, but all through the siege men and supplies were thrown into Sebastopol after a long journey from Russia. Prince Menschikov commanded a considerable army in the hilly region to the east of the city, and from thence he constantly threatened the besieging armies and sometimes attacked them and inflicted serious loss. The plan of the Allies was to capture Sebastopol not by starvation but by bombardment and direct assault. The supremacy of the Allied navies was the very basis on which the whole siege depended; but the direct action of the navy was small. Neither in the Baltic nor in the Black Sea were the navies of the Allies able to inflict on the Russians really serious loss. The Russian fleet was sunk in the mouth of Sebastopol harbour. The Allied fleets could not enter and their guns could not reach the city from the outside. The Allies pounded with their artillery Todleben's fortifications from the south and then attacked the shattered fortresses. Menschikov watched and attempted to interrupt the siege from the outside. The one all-important question was whether the Allies could force their way in or not.

Their military superiority was unquestionable. When Menschikov on October 25 endeavoured to break the communications with their naval base at Balaclava he was driven off, though important redoubts fell into his hands and a new road had to be adopted and built. When on November 5 he attacked the British at Inkerman he was in the end driven off by the British and their French Allies. On August 16, 1855, he attacked the French and the Sardinians (we shall see shortly how they came to enter the war), and was again driven off after heavy fighting. But these attacks had not been by any means without their result. They had seriously embarrassed, and sometimes postponed, the attack on the city.

The attack encountered difficulties of various kinds. No great soldier appeared on the side of the Allies. Raglan commanded the British forces until his death in June 1855. He had fought at Waterloo and was perhaps too old for the novel circumstances of the war. He was succeeded by General Simpson, who had not won so good a reputation as his predecessor. The French were at first commanded by Saint-Arnaud, who had played an important part in the *coup d'état*. When cholera had carried him off in September 1854 he was succeeded first by Canrobert and then by Pélissier. The difficulties of the command were increased by occasional divergence of aim between the French and British; but none of the Allied commanders showed originality or genius. Todleben, the Russian engineer of German origin, is the one soldier on either side who won for himself high admiration. The others had to struggle against enemies that seemed at one time more difficult to overcome than the Russians—namely, against disease and the climate. Cholera had shown itself in the early stages of the war and had been alleged as a reason against going to the Crimea at all. It attacked the camps before Sebastopol with terrible fury, and was hardly less fatal in the base camps and the hospitals. The way in which the dread enemy was attacked and subdued by Miss Florence Nightingale is among the heroic chapters of British history. The ravages of the disease reduced the numbers of the attacking force to a dangerous extent and weakened the morale of the troops that were not touched by it. Then there was the winter—against which no precautions had been taken. Even the War of 1914–18 produced no picture of misery more depressing than what was afforded by the cholera-haunted, frozen trenches and miserable tents on the heights before Sebastopol. It seemed at one time as though the siege might be made impossible by the double curse of cold and cholera. The British effectives were at one time reduced to 11,000. The Russians suffered as great or greater hardships. Their courage and endurance won the ungrudging admiration of their enemies.

Amidst all these difficulties the approaches to Sebastopol were made far more slowly than had been expected. There was a heavy bombardment from the 17th to the 30th October 1854; but the hold of the Russians was not shaken, and then for the first time it became plain that the armies 'were there for the winter.'

During the winter, diplomacy was active and eager to bring more Allies into the field against Russia. Austria would yield to no inducements. A conference was held at Vienna which lasted from March till May 1855. The Russian Tsar Nicholas had died during the course of the siege and had been succeeded by Alexander II, who sent a representative to Vienna. The 'Four Points' were accepted by Russia as a basis of negotiation. It appeared at one time as if peace might really come. But when war has once begun diplomacy has rarely availed to bring hostilities to an end before some decisive blow has been struck, and so it proved here. Austria judged that the Russian concessions were sufficient, and refused to join in the war. France, Britain and Turkey determined to struggle on. The military needs of the allies and the political needs of Sardinia had brought her into the war as their ally. Sardinia had no direct interest in the Crimean struggle. But the King and his Minister, Cavour, understood that to send Sardinian troops to the Crimea would vindicate the claim of Sardinia to rank with the Great Powers; would set up a claim to the support of France, and give the representative of Sardinia a place at the Conference table when the terms of peace were settled. So 15,000 Italian troops landed in the Crimea.

Soon after the winter had relaxed its hold the attack on the fortresses was renewed. Some successes were gained, though the joint attack arranged for the anniversary of the Battle of Waterloo (June 18) was a costly failure. The death of Raglan and the attack on the Allied lines which resulted in the Battle of the Tchernaya postponed the final attack. On September 5 there was a heavy bombardment (during the War of 1914–18 it would not have been called heavy!) for three days. The attack was launched on the 8th. The British failed in the attack on the fortress of the Redan; but the French under MacMahon seized the Malakov and could not be driven out, and the Malakov commanded the city. The Russian army marched out and joined the forces of Menschikov. The Allies marched in and possessed themselves of the forts and the harbour, of a vast quantity of guns, and of hospitals where were heaped under horrifying conditions a mass of wounded and sick Russian soldiers who could not be removed (September 8, 1855).

There was nothing necessarily in the loss of Sebastopol to bring the war to an end. The war went on indeed for some little time yet; and the Russians ended with a success when they captured the fortress of Kars in Asia Minor from the Turks and the British officers who commanded them. But the losses of Russia and her financial exhaustion made peace most desirable.[1] The new Tsar was anxious to give his country peace, and through the mediation of Austria a conference was called at Paris.

The relations between Great Britain and France had stood the strain of the war very well. There had been differences of opinion as to the conduct of operations, and some criticism of policy, but nothing serious. At the Peace Congress in Paris, however, the French Emperor seemed to be cooling in his relations with Britain, and to be turning towards his late enemies the Russians with sympathy and admiration. The value of a Russian alliance to France was presenting itself to his mind. The Congress sat for nearly eight weeks from February 25 to April 16, 1856.

We may look first—though quite out of chronological order—at some points not directly connected with the Eastern Question. On the proposal of Lord Clarendon, the Powers expressed a 'wish' that before having recourse to arms States 'should have recourse to the good offices of a friendly Power.' A very hesitating and quite fruitless approach to the greatest of European problems! It deserves notice as being one of the signs that the problem of international organisation and the wisdom of arbitration to prevent war was forcing itself on the attention of Europe.

On April 16 came the Declaration respecting Maritime Law and the management of a naval war, whereby Great Britain at last consented to conditions which she had long resisted. The points are highly technical. Privateering was abolished. Enemy goods could not henceforth be seized on a neutral vessel unless they came under the

---

[1] It is an interesting contrast to the War of 1914–18 that the Russian Government went on paying British bondholders their interest on the Russian Debt throughout the war. The attempt of Hungary to pay interest in 1915 to British bondholders was prohibited by the British Government on the ground that it was 'trading with the enemy.'

category of 'contraband of war.' Neutral goods carried by an enemy could not henceforth be seized. Blockades 'to be binding must be effective'; such a general blockade as was declared by Britain against Napoleon could no longer be used. It was an honourable attempt to regulate and humanise naval warfare. But 'contraband of war' proved an elastic term, and the Wars of 1914 and 1939 have made the world sceptical about the possibility of humanising what is essentially inhuman.

The real business of the Conference was to decide the future of Turkey, and (what was the same thing from another point of view) to check the advance of Russia. Here much was achieved, although the sum of the achievement did not amount to a final settlement. The Black Sea was neutralised: no 'flag of war' could appear in it; no military or naval establishment could be made in it; the Straits were closed to foreign warships. The independence of Turkey was affirmed: no Power had the right to interfere between the Sultan and his subjects; the privileges of Moldavia, Wallachia, and Serbia were guaranteed, but always under the suzerainty of Turkey; 'the generous intentions' of the Sultan towards his subjects 'without distinction of religion or of race' were recognised, as was the 'high value' of the proposals he had made in a recent Firman. Russia ceded south Bessarabia to Turkey and it was incoporated in Moldavia.

So the war was ended, and Turkey was saved from destruction. Henceforth there was to be (if diplomacy and treaties availed to produce it) a Turkey, united, independent, tolerant, progressive; a Turkey that would rapidly come into line with the constitutional life of the West, that would abandon massacre and corruption, and become an equal member of the comity of nations.[1] Let us look into the next few years and see the results of all these schemes.

The hopes of Turkish reforms were all disappointed. The Turks did not believe in them, and in the mass of the population there was an entire absence of the mutual consideration and self-restraint which alone make free institutions workable. Religious equality struck at the basis on which Muslim life had rested since the time of Mohammed. Among the reforms promised was equal admissibility to military service. But most of the Christian populations disliked military service and preferred to pay a tax, and the Turks infinitely preferred their money to their service.[2] It was declared a few years later that the only result of the promise of reforms was the creation of a few more officials. Protests and complaints produced only

[1] The admission of Turkey into the 'comity of nations' was a new unprecedented action. It was clearly due to the desire of France, Great Britain and Austria to emancipate Turkey from the religious control or interference of Russia [see p. 216, n. 1]. Yet, in fact, the Powers as a whole found it necessary to make elaborare provisions for the protection of their own national interests within the Turkish Empire

[2] In 1869 recruiting was again openly restricted in the Turkish Empire to Muslims.

expressions of good will and promises of inquiry. In 1861 Abdul Aziz succeeded to the Turkish throne. He promised many reforms. He would reduce expenses; suppress corruption; have only one wife. But little, if anything, was done; a harem of 900 wives was soon re-established with a correspondingly large court expenditure. Lord Stratford de Redcliffe had said 'Turkey cannot float; she must either sink or swim,' but the Sultan seemed of the opposite opinion.

While Turkey floated on to destruction, the subject nationalities were showing a stirring vigour which was often uncomfortable to their subjects and neighbours as well as to their rulers. Greece had enjoyed twenty years and more of 'liberty,' but she had disappointed many of the hopes that had been founded on her. Many things were against her. Her territories were small; her frontiers were dangerous; her past and her position as representative of all those who called themselves Greeks, attracted her towards dangerous ambitions. Her King, Otto, was most sincerely devoted to the well-being of the country, but he failed to win the loyal support of the nation. During the Crimean War the general opinion of Greece was favourable to the Russians rather than the Allies, and Otto became unpopular for refusing to take part in some wild escapade for an insurrection in Turkish territory. In 1862 a revolution broke out, and though the first movements were suppressed Otto found it necessary to abdicate. The next King, George, was of Danish blood, and Great Britain made the propects of his reign brighter by ceding the Ionian Islands to Greece. Yet the task of the new King was exceedingly difficult. The armies were in an almost constant condition of mutiny; there was no stability in the political life of the country; and the popular sentiment was always profoundly stirred by the news of resistance to the Sultan in different parts of his dominions. It is to these that we must now turn.

In the north-west—in Serbia and in Montenegro—the native population made considerable advances towards independence. The right of Serbia to self-government under the suzerainty of Turkey had been guaranteed by the Treaty of Paris, and there were Turkish garrisons in the forts at Belgrade and elsewhere and a certain number of Turks living under the protection of the forts. But the Serbians were determined to increase the liberties which they had already won. They were for the most part a vigorous peasant population and they formed a military material capable of all acts of daring and heroism. Their effectiveness was weakened by their sharp local feuds, their readiness to prosecute family quarrels in the spirit of a vendetta, and the rivalry of two families for the headship of the State. These were the Obrenović and the Karageorgević, something of whose fortunes has already been told. Alexander Karageorgević was ruling Serbia at the time of the Crimean War, and he seemed to many of his people to have played a tame game, when circumstances would have allowed him to play a bold one. He had also great difficulties with his people as to the introduction of forms of constitutional liberty. In 1859 the situation became impossible for him and he abdicated; and the Skupshtina—the very turbulent Parliament of Serbia—asked Miloš Obrenović, who had been driven from the throne twenty years before, to return. He came with approval of Turkey, but he showed his independence of Turkey by declaring his authority to be hereditary, against the will of the Sultan, and when he died in 1860 he was succeeded by his son Michael. There have been more heroic and romantic figures on the Serbian throne, but none more successful. He organised the Government and the army and gave to Serbia the appearance of a civilised European State. Much was done for the culture and the education of the Serbians. The language was purified; the legends were carefully collected and became a great source of pride and patriotic inspiration to the people. But for our purposes it is more important to notice that his people made a great advance towards independence by securing the withdrawal of the Turkish garrisons. The murder of individual Serbians by Turkish soldiers and the bombardment of the town of Belgrade by the Turks in the citadel brought the matter to a head. Michael was supported by the Great Powers, and in the end all the Turkish troops were withdrawn, and nothing was left of the Turkish power in Serbia except the stipulation that the Turkish flag should fly by the side of the Serbian on the ramparts of Belgrade. It would clearly not be long before a further step was taken. Some diplomatists thought it might be incorporation with Austria or with Russia; but the Serbs themselves were in no mood to exchange one suzerainty for another.

The Principality of Montenegro was inhabited by a people closely akin in race and language to the Serbians. The little mountain state had always maintained its independence of Turkey, though the Turks had never admitted that independence as a right. In 1858 the Turks endeavoured to force their claims on the Montenegrins, but they were defeated among the mountains at Grahovo with immense loss, in a battle that deserves to rank along with Marathon and Morgarten as one of the most heroic deeds of men defending their freedom against the invasion of a tyrant. But the Turkish danger remained, and Michael of Serbia was aiming at some closer union between Serbia and Montenegro when he was assassinated in 1868. Michael was a man both of ability and ambition, and his plans extended beyond Montenegro and Serbia to the formation of a sort of Balkan League against Turkey. He had a secret treaty with the representatives of the downtrodden Bulgarian subjects of the Turk, and close diplomatic relations with Rumania and Greece. So much can be said with certainty and more can be inferred, but the death of Michael brought these far-reaching plans to nought.

In Serbia and Montenegro the Turkish power ebbed, as it ebbed everywhere, now slowly, now rapidly, down to the time of the War of 1914–18. The rule of Turkey was even weaker in 'the Principalities' than in Serbia and Montenegro, and it suffered an equally obvious rebuff. By the Treaty of Paris the protectorate of the two principalities—with some intentional emphasis on the word 'two'—had been transferred from Turkey to the Great Powers collectively. The object of the diplomatists was that the principalities should be kept separate and therefore weak, and that they should not challenge the suzerainty of Turkey. But the sense of nationality was strong in this strange Ruman people despite its varied composition and its marked social cleavage. Town was in sharp contrast with country; the native Rumanians with the large minority of Jews. But all spoke the Latin tongue which had been so strangely preserved during the Middle Ages; all were proud of their Latin civilisation, and thought of themselves as the representatives of Western culture amidst Slavonic barbarism, following as far as they could the fashions of Paris in social and political ideas. By the Treaty of Paris there were to be two States with separate constitutions, and the Sultan refused the demand of Moldavia and Wallachia that they should be allowed to unite under the name of Rumania. The utmost concession that could be won was that they should be known as the 'United Principalities' and that affairs which concerned them both should be regulated by a joint Commission. But the Rumanians adroitly won their way against the wishes of Turkey and of Europe. Each principality had to choose its head or 'hospodar.' They both chose the same man, a Moldavian nobleman, who took the title of 'Alexander the First, Prince of Rumania.' He declared that the Rumanian nation was founded, and united the two Parliaments. Europe had other problems to attend to, and the accomplished fact was accepted. Bucharest became the capital of united Rumania. The new ruler proved one of the most remarkable of Balkan rulers. He watched events in the West, and especially in France, very closely, and his policy was clearly founded on that of Napoleon III, and the methods by which he carried it through had some likeness to the *coup d'état*. Three great measures are associated with his name. He found a large proportion of the land of Rumania in possession of the monasteries. By a series of measures he transferred nearly the whole of these lands to secular uses, and at the same time gave to Rumania a large measure of religious independence. Then came his measures connected with land tenure. The Parliament resisted his first suggestions. He expelled the members by force and asked the people to choose by plebiscite between him and the Parliament. They supported him by the suspiciously large majority of 682,000 against 1000. Then he created a vast system of peasant proprietorships, and at the same time freed the peasants from the 'feudal' burdens which they had hitherto paid. It was the work of the French Revolution carried out without bloodshed. His last law established free and compulsory education. Modern Rumania still rests on the foundation which he laid.

But the towns disliked what seemed his devotion to agricultural interests. The nobility were bitterly angry at the destruction of their privileges. The clergy regarded his high-handed treatment of ecclesiastical questions as sacrilege. A revolution was plotted against him—they were made with a facility in the Balkans hardly to be paralleled elsewhere—and finding himself deserted by his troops he abdicated. The conspirators looked round for a foreign prince, and found one in Prince Charles of Hohenzollern-Sigmaringen. He belonged to the family of the King of Prussia, but he was also related to Napoleon III and was supported by him.[1] On the advice of Bismarck he accepted the offer, and it was announced that in the plebiscite 685,000 had voted for him and only 224 against him. The presence of a Hohenzollern on the throne of Rumania was important during the war of 1866, and it may be well to say here that it was his brother Leopold who figured so prominently in the events which led to the Franco-Prussian War of 1870. We need not follow Balkan events any further, but it is clear that there was little probability of Turkey becoming again the accepted suzerain of the Peninsula in any real sense. One district after another detached itself from the rule of the Turk; and their example proved infectious to other races and districts outside of the Balkan Peninsula.

[1] Alexander 1 (Cuza) was deposed in February 1866, and Charles elected in May.

Chapter 15

THE UNION OF ITALY

Napoleon III's claim that the Empire meant peace was soon submitted to another test. And again the ideas and personal interests of the Emperor were largely responsible for hostilities which took French armies once more to the well-known battle-ground of North Italy. The new war was in many ways a great contrast to the Crimean War. It was settled by two important battles, and produced nothing like the long agonies of the trench war round Sebastopol. It was, moreover, the first war clearly fought for that principle of nationality which was the one great and novel feature of the international difficulties of the nineteenth century. Nationality was the enthusiasm, almost the superstition, of the time. It was the continuation of the process that had been going on ever since the Reformation. As all agencies of human unity fell into the background or were destroyed—the Empire had disappeared, the Church had lost its old political influence—the State had become the all-important unit of organisation. It recognised no superior and admitted no control. But the more important and powerful the State became the more important was it to consider on what basis the power of the State rested. The movement towards constitutionalism which had been led by England was more than two hundred years old and had achieved great victories. It was widely claimed and often granted that the State should be identified with the people and that Government and people should be in active partnership. Now another question arose behind that. Who were the people that should form a state? Was any collection of individuals equally well adapted for state life? Men awoke with a new clearness and self-consciousness to the sense of nationality. This new sense appeared most strongly not among those nations which had already won a large measure of national independence and unity, not among the French or the English or the Spaniards; but among those who were still without a national state, and who, as a result of historical development, found themselves mixed up with other nationalities in the same state.

National feeling had shown itself strong though often vague in the Balkan Peninsula. It was a religious passion with large numbers of Poles. It had contributed to the failure of the union of Holland and Belgium. But the two countries where it produced the most striking political and military results were Germany and Italy. Germany since the Middle Ages had been divided and subdivided, and her vague constitution, which embraced Czechs, some Poles, and other non-German elements, gave no satisfaction to the national desire for unity. In Italy a sense of common nationality was rooted in the eighteenth-century Enlightenment and the cultural revival after 1775 and was stimulated by Napoleonic reorganisation. But since 1815 her seven separate states had been restored and Lombardy-Venetia annexed by Austria. We have seen how the Risorgimento (the word means resurrection and is properly applied to the period before political unification) was deepened by the failure of the revolutionary year, 1848. Italianism had been awakened in classes not normally politically alive. There were indeed differences of origin and temperament in the peninsula. The Lombard and the Sicilian were separated from one another by a wide difference of language and of historic development. But nationality, it is now clear to us, is rather a question of feeling than of objective fact. And the past greatness of the peoples of Italy, the dim memories of the Roman Empire, the poems of Dante, the art and science of the Renaissance, all served to keep alive the feeling that the Italians were a single and a great people. Moreover the large and powerful state had come to seem more attractive than the sturdy regionalism that chiefly marked the period before the revolutions of 1848. Mazzini had always an important influence on the Italian mind. To him and to his followers the claim of Italian nationality was not only a matter of history and pride but of passionate and almost religious belief. Italy united, free, democratic and republican was the one absorbing passion of his life; an ideal to be pursued at all costs and by all means. He held by each element of his programme. It was as important to him that Italy should be democratic and republican as that it should be united and free. He could not bring himself to accept the gift of unity and freedom at the hand of the Emperor of the French or of the King of Sardinia. We must add that he was able to look beyond nationality, and dreamed of the free nations of Europe voluntarily organising themselves into a greater association for peaceful co-operation.

In 1848–49 classes had been touched in Genoa, Leghorn, Rome and above all Sicily, which had social grievances. But aspirations for social change took the form of fumbling protest rather than a strongly led popular movement. Such hopes had little chance of success with Austrian influence re-established in the peninsula. Lombardy, it is true, continued the most economically progressive state. In 1857 the younger brother of the Emperor Francis Joseph, Maximilian, later to play so tragic a part in Mexico, was appointed governor of Lombardy and reformed its administration. But financial and military pressure on Lombardy and Venetia became heavier and nothing could assuage the hatred for Austria. Aspirations for social change were to appear again in 1859–61. They were never established during unification, far less satisfied. Free and United Italy was born of the Kingdom of Sardinia. It was a state only in part Italian, and had in the past pursued a narrow dynastic policy. Until the revolution of 1848 there was nothing in the history of the state or the royal family to mark it out as the standard-bearer of Italian liberty and unity; but in 1848 it had laid the foundations of its future greatness by joining with Milan in resistance to Austria, and above all by granting to its own people a really liberal constitution. Its policy under Victor Emmanuel was still Sardinian first and Italian second. But as its achievements opened new possibilities so its policy widened. That this was so was almost wholly due to Cavour with whom Victor Emmanuel's name will always be closely associated.

Cavour began his 'Great Ministry' in the year 1852. Count Cavour was the son of a Piedmontese nobleman devoted to absolutist ideals, and was intended for the army. But the young man at an early date had adopted advanced liberal opinions and had left the army. He had travelled widely and had studied the political life of France and of Britain with particular care. He had gambled and he had lost much of his inheritance. For a time he had seemed inclined to throw up all ideas of a political career and devote himself to the cultivation of his father's estates. But then the call to political service had come again. As a member of the Sardinian Parliament he had shown wide knowledge of the politics of Europe, and great hopefulness for the future of Piedmont and of Italy. His approach was economic and his hope was in railways, schools and free trade. Yet he pointed with approval to the concessions made by the statesmen of Britain to the demands of the people, and urged confidence in the people as the safest policy. Before Cavour was in office measures had been taken against the legal and financial privileges of the Church in Piedmont. He held subordinate office in 1850 before becoming Prime Minister in 1852. One of his first measures had been the dissolution of the monasteries. He had made himself known as a liberal in the sense in which the word was then used, and his liberalism was genuine. His programme of internal reform, with its great financial and administrative improvements, should not be obscured by the greater renown of his foreign policy. He was first a Sardinian minister with Sardinian aims. His policy became Italian when he associated his Sardinian aims with the national movement, but he did not draw out the latent political and social possibilities of the national movement. He worked in the direction things were going, but he did not anticipate the future. This is why in the end unification left important classes alienated and why it disappointed the idealists. His realism and unscrupulous diplomacy incurred already the hostility of Mazzini. Mazzini did not believe even in Cavour's honesty. He called him the 'ministerial liberator who taught his master how to prevent the union of Italy.' He disbelieved in the practicability of his schemes, and even if they were practicable they seemed a substitution of materialism for idealism and religion, treason for democracy, and a dragging down of the whole movement to a lower plane. Success when it came did not conciliate him. He had dreamed of a new earth and Cavour only gave him a rearrangement of the old one.

The Crimean War had provided Cavour with the opportunity for one of his skilful diplomatic strokes and he signed an alliance with Britain and France. There is, however, reason to think that the policy originated with the King and not Cavour. Sardinia, if she came in, would appear as one of the important Powers of Europe; she would claim a seat at the Congress which settled terms for peace and which would perhaps rearrange the map of Europe. So the Sardinian soldiers went to the Crimea, fought at the Battle of the Tchernaya with distinguished success, and showed that the failure of the Italian arms at the Battle of Novara did not spring from any incapacity of Italians for military effort. 'Out of this mud' (the mud of the Sebastopol trenches), said a Piedmontese soldier, 'Italy will be made'; but Cavour went more slowly. At the Paris Congress he got the opportunity he wanted of ventilating the grievances of Italy. He was warmly supported by Clarendon, the British Foreign Minister, and the Conference listened to a formal statement of the misgovernment of Italy both in the south and the north and of the international dangers which sprang from it. Sardinia now was a recognised part of the diplomatic web of Europe. Cavour had courageously used his opportunity.

This success opened up the possibility of a more general alliance with France. Napoleon III in his youth had known something of the revolutionary movement in Italy. Real sympathy with the doctrine of nationality, which he sincerely preached, drew him to the side of Cavour. But it needed all Cavour's astuteness and strength to turn his vague sentiment into action and to prevent him from turning back when the dangers of the enterprise made themselves felt.

In January 1858, as Napoleon and the Empress were going to the opera, bombs were thrown at them. The imperial party escaped, but there were many killed and wounded. Several Italians were arrested, and the chief agent in the plot was discovered to be an Italian, Orsini. He had at one time been in close touch with Mazzini, though no sympathy with his attempt at assassination could be brought home to Mazzini. Orsini declared that what he had done had sprung from his belief that Napoleon had betrayed the cause of Italy. From his prison he wrote two letters to Napoleon appealing to him to free

Italy, and on the scaffold of the guillotine his last cry was 'Long live Italy!' The effect of these events was—strangely—not to drive Napoleon from the cause of Italy, but to draw him nearer to it. He took what was the really decisive step in June 1858.

Napoleon liked to keep the conduct of foreign affairs largely in his own hands and sometimes to act without the knowledge of his own responsible Ministers. He sent a message to Cavour through a private source that he was going to spend the summer in Plombières, and that he would be glad to see Cavour there. Cavour realised the opportunity that this simple-looking invitation offered. 'The drama,' he wrote to a friend, 'approaches its crisis.' He met the Emperor on July 21–2, and had a long discussion with him, first in his residence and then in a long drive outside the town while Napoleon himself held the reins. The aim of the two conspirators (for they were that, however ideal their aims) was war. France promised to support Sardinia in a war with Austria on condition that Cavour provided a pretext, which would justify France's action in the eyes of Europe. The Austrians were to be driven out of Italy. The north was to form a kingdom of Italy under Victor Emmanuel; then all Italy was to be united in a federal bond under the presidency of the Pope. This, Cavour well knew, could only be won by the sword of France and Napoleon. And what pay would he require? There can be no doubt that he would be glad to serve a cause in which he sincerely believed. The prestige which he would win and the consequent strengthening of his throne would be of the utmost value to him. But he demanded also tangible reward. Savoy and Nice were to be ceded to France— Savoy the cradle of the royal house and of the Sardinia State, Nice the birthplace of Garibaldi—and Victor Emmanuel was to consent to the marriage of his sixteen-year-old daughter to Napoleon's cousin, Jerome. The future was to show how unwise it was in Napoleon to insist on these or any terms. The catastrophe of 1870 might perhaps have been avoided if Napoleon had not alienated the sympathies of the Italians to whose freedom he contributed so much. But it must be remembered that he had to justify his action to the French as well as to the Italians.

Cavour had, without planning it, now the chance to conquer northern Italy for Sardinia. It was his business to bring about the war in such a way that it should seem to be an aggressive action on the part of Austria; and in the pursuit of this end he had often to complain of his imperial fellow-conspirator. With Napoleon the cold fit was always apt to follow the hot. Up to the end of the year 1858 all went well for his plans; in December of that year the secret Treaty between France and Sardinia was drawn up. It was called a defensive alliance. In case of war France was to provide 200,000 men and Austria was to be driven out of Italy. Cavour was confident. 'We have Austria in a cleft stick,' he wrote, 'and she cannot get out of it without firing the cannon.' The people of northern Italy were excited. They cheered Victor Emmanuel and the Kingdom of Italy, and cried 'Long live the war!'

Yet during the following months there were times when it seemed as though the war might slip through Cavour's fingers after all. Napoleon had told the Austrian Ambassador on New Year's Day that he regretted 'that his relations to the Austrian Empire were not so good as they had formerly been.' A pamphlet had been issued with his approval on 'Napoleon and Italy,' preaching anew the doctrine of Nationality and pointing out that it was applicable to Germany as well as to Italy. But there seemed little eagerness for the war in France, except perhaps in the army itself. Great Britain, and to a lesser extent Russia, urged the possibility of settling the Italian trouble by means of a European Congress. That was also one of Napoleon's 'ideas' and he could not refuse to consider it. His will was so unstable that Cavour was in despair. Peace seemed for a moment certain. 'Nothing remains for me but to put a bullet through my head,' he said. Then came an incident never quite fully explained. Perhaps Austria was weary of the long delays; perhaps she was encouraged by addresses of loyalty from various parts of her dominions. She despatched to Turin an ultimatum demanding disarmament 'within three days,' and sent her troops into Piedmont on April 29, 1859. No military adventurer or despot has ever welcomed war with greater ardour than was shown by Cavour at this moment, and yet he was a civilian and a parliamentary statesman. The moment marks his conscious association with the national movement—a movement below the level of courts and cabinets. The Austrian Emperor declared he was fighting for 'the rights of all peoples and states and for the most sacred blessings of mankind.' But the general feeling was that it was he who had broken the peace. Victor Emmanuel was declared Dictator by the Piedmontese Parliament, and the war began.

The Italian War interested nearly every Great Power in Europe, and there was much talk of intervention. Men asked with anxiety, what would Great Britain do, what would Russia do? But the action of Germany and of Prussia was really the most critical question. Austria, despite her mixed population, counted primarily as a German Power, and she was at the head of the German Confederation. Prussia, despite her grievances against Austria, would not see unmoved the defeat of the Austrian armies by French and Italian forces. The federal army and the Prussian army were both put on a war footing. Austrian diplomacy could not induce them to go further at first; but the thought of German or Prussian intervention was always in the mind of Napoleon III and was a chief influence on his actions.

The Austrian armies, however, had to bear the attack of their enemies without allies. The soldiers showed themselves brave, and one general, Benedek, gained a high reputation from his management of the campaign. But the different national elements in his army had no interest in the issue of the campaign and the higher ranks were confined to the nobles. The French armies were later than was expected in entering Italy, but the situation there was highly favourable to the national cause. There were spontaneous risings all over the north of Italy. There were risings in Modenese territory. Parma, like Modena, expelled its ruler. In Tuscany and in its capital, Florence, there were movements of the utmost importance. There were great popular meetings in Florence which cheered for 'war, independence and Victor Emmanuel.' The King of Sardinia was asked to undertake the military dictatorship of Tuscany. Royal commissioners were soon installed to govern all three duchies. Yet we may see now the first hint of those difficulties which later ruined the popularity of Napoleon III in the eyes of the Italians. Perhaps he was misunderstood; but the suspicion arose that he was not anxious to see Tuscany absorbed in the Kingdom of Sardinia; that he had other designs for the country; and that he hoped to see Jerome succeeding in some way to the Duchy. The enthusiasm for the national cause spread further south, as soon as the Allies had won their first victories. In the Romagna and the Legations the Papal troops were driven out; the popular cry was for union with Italy and Victor Emmanuel and a royal commissioner took over here too. There was no hope now that Pius IX would join the national cause, but there was an effort made to bring in Naples. There Ferdinand II had just died and had been succeeded by his son Francis II. The attempt to win him over failed entirely. There was some sympathy among his Ministers and in the population; but the young King, who was married to the sister of the Austrian Empress, held by his father's policy.

Napoleon III had consulted Jomini—a General of the great Napoleon—as to his plan of campaign; but his schemes were far from settled when he arrived, and he is not judged to have shown any conspicuous talent in his management of the campaign. The Austrians were equally undecided. Their troops came in slowly. Count Gyulai held the supreme command and was thought to have owed his promotion over the heads of abler men to Court influences. On the Italian side public attention was chiefly given to the 'Hunters of the Alps'—a fine body of irregular troops collected from the most enthusiastic elements of the patriots of Italy and commanded by Garibaldi, who already was regarded by public opinion as the incarnation of the romance, of the daring and the poetry of the national cause. Napoleon had no love for him, and perhaps might have made fuller use of his great talents. As the allied forces advanced into the Milanese territory Garibaldi acted on the left flank among the foothills of the Alps. But the brunt of the fighting fell on the French troops, and, without disparaging the great courage and devotion of the Italian army, it is plain that it would have gone hard with the national cause if it had not had the support of the armies of France. Perhaps the Austrians would have been wiser if they had followed the suggestion of standing on the defensive under cover of the fortresses of the 'Quadrilateral.' But they decided to defend the Milanese, and the issue was decided in two battles. On June 4 was fought the Battle of Magenta, and after heavy fighting, which fell almost entirely on the French, the Austrians were defeated. They were defeated, but not broken, and retreated towards the 'Quadrilateral.' Bolder counsels, however, prevailed; and a greater battle than Magenta was fought at Solferino, just to the south of Lake Garda, on June 24. It was a long-drawn-out and murderous encounter. In the centre and on the right the French and Italians gained a complete victory. The Austrians held their own under Benedek on their right with obstinate courage and only withdrew when the battle had been lost in other parts of the field. The losses on both sides reached many thousands, and the impression of horror was very much increased by the reports of the insufficiency of the medical services. The idea of the Red Cross organisation sprang from the impression produced by the spectacle of the battle.

The Battle of Solferino was a very heavy defeat for Austria, but it was not so overwhelming a blow as to appear decisive of the whole campaign. Yet through the action of Napoleon III the whole campaign ended here. What were his motives?

The war had been a great triumph for him. The year 1859 marks the very zenith of his power and reputation in Europe. He was credited by many with extraordinary diplomatic subtlety and was thought likely to establish a power in Europe as great as that of the first Napoleon. In the Crimean War he had turned back the power of Russia and re-established Turkey. Now he had crushed Austria and called a free Italy into being. When he entered Milan after the Battle of Magenta he was welcomed with an adoring rapture such as has fallen to the lot of few conquerors. 'Our liberator, our saviour, our benefactor,' the enthusiastic crowd called him. His way was strewn with flowers by the women of Milan. His words raised this enthusiasm still higher. He would do nothing, he said, 'to force his will on the people of Italy.' 'Use the good fortune that presents itself to you. Your dream of independence will be realised if you show yourself worthy of it. Unite in one great effort for the liberation of the country.'

Napoleon had snuffed up all this incense with unconcealed delight. And yet soon the enthusiasm of the Italians gave way to suspicion and their gratitude turned to resentment. Napoleon was always an adventurer and a dreamer. The 'sense of the possible,' that most necessary gift of the statesman, was not his. His imagination conjured up splendid scenes and glorious triumphs, but never showed him a firm road to his goal. We may see him, his whole life through, starting and turning back; desiring the end but frightened of the inevitable means.

Amidst the glories of the Italian campaign there was much to alarm him. Glory had to be paid for. The slaughter and the torture of the Solferino battlefield had profoundly impressed his imagination. The Italians, too, showed themselves by no means so malleable as he had hoped. Whatever schemes he had for the future of Tuscany broke down before the determination of the Tuscans to be masters of their own destiny. Was it, indeed, politic to call into existence a powerful, independent Italian state on France's frontier? Moreover, despite his name, he was no soldier. His powers lay in another direction—in unexpected diplomatic combinations and in his power of appeal to the imagination of men. These were good reasons for desiring to be done with the war. But there was a more powerful one in the storm that now clearly threatened from the side of Germany. Prussia had her own bitter quarrel with Austria, but she could not see with pleasure the humiliation of a German power by France and Italy. Her army had already been placed on a war footing; she now prepared her whole forces and proposed that she should be given the command of the German army. It was clear that the French forces might soon be wanted to protect the Rhine frontier.

Napoleon determined to bring the war to an end; and in pursuit of this end he acted—as he was accustomed to do—rather as a conspirator than a statesman. Everyone expected a renewal of the fighting, when Napoleon despatched General Fleury on a private mission to the headquarters of Francis Joseph, the Austrian Emperor, suggesting an armistice with a view to peace. The Austrian ruler was quite ready to receive the overtures. The defeats that his army had suffered were serious, but they were not the only ground. Hungary was threatening revolt and troops were wanted to suppress it. The prospect of Prussian intervention by no means suited Austrian diplomacy, for it would be accompanied by concessions to Prussia in Germany, which Francis Joseph was by no means willing to make. So he met Napoleon at Villafranca, and soon arranged the preliminaries of peace.[1] Lombardy was to be handed over to Napoleon, who would then transfer it to Victor Emmanuel. Both France and Austria would then support the formation of an Italian federation under the titular presidency of the Pope. Venice was to remain with Austria, but was to form part of the Italian Confederation. The rulers of Modena, Parma and Tuscany were to return. The Pope was to be urged to introduce reforms into his state. A meeting of the representatives of

---

[1] An armistice was signed on July 8, and the preliminaries at Villafranca on July 11, Sardinia not being consulted.

all the states concerned was to be held to ratify and develop these suggestions.

We know that this was the beginning of Italian independence and unity; and that the completion of the structure came with great rapidity. But to many Italians, and above all to Cavour, it seemed treason to the cause, the ruin of their hopes, the very negation of the liberty and unity that they aimed at. Cavour was full of despair. 'Nothing can come of this peace,' he said. 'I will turn conspirator and revolutionary, but this treaty shall not be carried out.' After a violent scene with his King he resigned his post as Prime Minister. But soon hope dawned on him again; for events in the centre of Italy took a surprising turn.

In Tuscany, Modena, Parma and the Romagna the inhabitants were in no mood to allow the two Emperors to hand them back to their old rulers. A representative Assembly in Florence declared unanimously 'that Tuscany desired to become a part of a strong Italy under the constitutional rule of Victor Emmanuel' (August 1859). Parma and Modena and Bologna demanded equally strongly union with the kingdom of Victor Emmanuel. It may be true that Sardinia helped in making the return of their rulers impossible to Modena, Parma, Tuscany and the Romagna. It is certainly true that Ricasoli in Tuscany and Farini in the Romagna—they were royal commissioners and Farini a close friend of Cavour—made diligent and successful propaganda among the peasants for union with Sardinia. Officially Victor Emmanuel could only express sympathy, and a proposal to appoint a prince of the House of Savoy Regent over the central Italian lands was defeated by the opposition of Napoleon.

The final peace treaty, signed at Zürich on November 10, 1859, contained no provision for the return of their rulers to the central Italian states. Lombardy was annexed to Sardinia, but the Pope had shown not the least inclination to play his part in the formation of an Italian Confederation. It was proposed to refer the final organisation of Italy to a Congress, which should consist of the signatories of the Peace of Vienna and should meet at Paris. But the Congress never came together. It was forestalled by the settlement which Italy made for herself.

Cavour had not remained out of office long. He was Prime Minister again in January 1860, and before that he had exercised a great influence on the course of affairs. He aimed at the settlement of the central Italian question by direct secret negotiations with Napoleon. It will be remembered that Napoleon had originally claimed Savoy and Nice as the price of his alliance with Sardinia. He had not claimed his payment, because he had not fulfilled his part of the contract. But now if the central duchies went to Victor Emmanuel he might claim it. The cession of Savoy and Nice was a terrible blow to Italian feeling, but Cavour determined that it must be done. Napoleon's favourite method of a plebiscite was to be employed both in the case of Italy and of France. An enormous majority in Tuscany and an almost unanimous vote in the other lands declared for union with the kingdom of Victor Emmanuel. The official name of the kingdom was still Sardinia, but it was generally known as Italy and was determined to deserve the name. Then came the voting in Savoy and Nice. The victory of annexation was suspiciously complete. Savoy by 130,538 vote to 235, Nice by 24,448 to 160, declared for union with the Empire of France. Napoleon's triumph seemed for the moment greater than Cavour's. But he had lost the gratitude of the Italians; they felt that he had been paid, and well paid, for the services which he had rendered. The whole movement for incorporation in a United Italy (for Sardinia was clearly but a first stage to Italy) had been carried out in the central provinces with calm, self-restraint, and dignity, in spite of the passionate enthusiasm that had been everywhere manifested.

Cavour had achieved the annexation of the central states, not by seeing in advance how the national movement would develop, but by taking advantage of the way it had developed during the rule of the royal commissioners. It is important also to recognise that he had achieved it at the cost of losing some elements in the movement: old Tuscan families who cherished the tradition of Tuscan detestation of Sardinia; the 'fusionists', so-called, who wanted to make united Italy from below by a spontaneous fusion of peoples circumventing the governments; and, overlapping with the last group, Mazzinian republicans, idealists and others who wanted social change.

This wonderful series of events had won for a United Italy a firm basis in the north and centre of the peninsula. But hardly more than half of the whole peninsula had been won. There remained Venice, Rome, and the kingdom of Naples to be added to the territories of free Italy before the long-dreamed-of national unity would be accomplished. Pope Pius IX had now no vestige of his old liberalism; the population of the Papal States was restless, and a large proportion of it sympathised with the ideas that had triumphed in the north. At Naples Francis II (as already mentioned) had succeeded in 1859. He was not a cruel tyrant, nor quite without sympathy with new ideas, but he inherited a task that was probably beyond the powers of any ruler to accomplish. It is particularly difficult to appreciate the condition of the Neapolitan and Sicilian kingdom; the popular temperament was divided from that of northern Europe by such great differences. The mass of the peasants was uneducated and illiterate, and took little interest in the political revolution which swept over the country. The power of the Church was very great, and the people were sincerely though not intellectually attached to its observances and beliefs. The secret societies—especially the famous Camorra— were a constant source of danger, impeding the establishment of a

law-abiding society. But there was a section of the population as full
of enthusiasm for Italian liberty as any that could be found in Lombardy or Tuscany. It was, however, for some time very doubtful what
interpretation the Sicilians would wish to give to liberty and unity.
It was not at all certain that they would be willing to merge the
independence of Naples and Sicily in the Kingdom of Sardinia, even
if it assumed the name of Italy, and there was a strong party that
desired some form of autonomy.

Conspiracy and insurrection were almost continuous in the southern kingdom, and were powerfully stimulated by the success of the
patriots in the north. King Francis was aware of his danger and considered whether it might not be possible to adopt reforms which
would satisfy the national sentiment of his people. But before anything serious had been done Garibaldi had landed in Sicily, and the
greatest and most successful adventure of nineteenth-century Europe
had begun. For anything like it we have to go back to the adventures
of Robert Guiscard, the Norman, in much the same lands, or the
expedition of Cortes to Mexico in the beginning of the sixteenth century. It is an amazing story of heroism and of intrigue. Garibaldi held
the eyes of all Europe and he holds the attention of all who read the
history of the period. His courage and his skill as a leader of irregular
forces; his sublime enthusiasm for the cause of Italy; the simplicity
and nobility of his character—these are as clearly written on the
events of those years as his political incapacity and his ignorance of
many of the forces which dominated the European world at that time.
In loose association with him was Mazzini, who saw a chance in these
southern movements to establish a free and united Italy on a different
basis from that constitutional and monarchical one which had
triumphed in the north. He hoped to see the banner of 'God and the
People' raised against that of Italy and Victor Emmanuel, and to
establish at least the beginnings of a republican régime in the south.
When the triumph of Italian unity came it was in a form so different
from what Mazzini desired that he declared 'I shall have no more joy
in Italy; the country with its contempt for all ideals has killed the soul
within me.' Garibaldi's bright sword attracted all men's attention,
and they hardly noted at the time the all-importance of the action of
Cavour and the Government of the Kingdom of Sardinia (for such
was still its official title). Yet the annexation of Naples and Sicily
depended as much on Cavour as on Garibaldi. He knew of it before
it took place; he told Garibaldi that 'when it is a question of under-
takings of that kind, however bold they may be, Count Cavour will
be second to none.' Cavour never worked easily with Garibaldi and
was thoroughly distrusted and even hated by him; but his support
was necessary at every turn of the great drama. The support was
given courageously and quite unscrupulously. Never did diplomacy
employ with more skill the *double entendre*, the half-truth, and even

the lie direct. The union of Italy of which Dante had dreamed was accomplished; but it was carried through, especially in its last phase, in the spirit of Machiavelli.[1]

The story begins with the rising in Sicily on April 4, 1860. This was not a liberal or nationalist insurrection, but a protest of the hungry, the lawless and the oppressed peasant. It was also Garibaldi's opportunity.

On May 5, 1860, Garibaldi left Genoa with two vessels and 1136 volunteers, to whom were distributed on the passage the famous red shirts. They landed at Marsala on the 11th. The little band was of course utterly unequal to the defeat of the royal garrisons of Sicily. All depended on the reckless courage of Garibaldi. This was the quality which Garibaldi possessed in full measure. He advanced on Palermo, the chief military seat of the Government of Naples. The skill of his leadership, the courage of his troops, the support of the Sicilians and the miserable weakness of Lanza, the commander of the garrison at Palermo, along with some amazing good fortune, account for the wonderful victory won outside Palermo and the subsequent capture of the city itself. This first triumph decided the issue of the campaign in Sicily, and soon King Francis had no supporters in Sicily outside the fortress of Messina. But now Garibaldi determined on an even bolder stroke. The events in Sicily had set in motion similar movements in Naples, and the nationalists appealed to Garibaldi for help. Victor Emmanuel forbade him to pass the Straits, and at the same time suggested to him the language in which he should refuse. He landed at the extreme south of Italy and marched on Naples through country excellently adapted for resistance, but there was no resistance. King Francis was betrayed by many of his Ministers and soldiers and loyally served by hardly any. The King left Naples for Gaeta on September 6 and Garibaldi entered the next day. The enthusiasm of the people was almost delirious. The triumph of the red-shirted Liberator was amazing, and it was borne with great modesty and simplicity.

Towards the expedition Cavour showed that ability to face two ways which to the idealists always seemed dishonesty. Evidence, for instance, respecting his attitude to its departure from Genoa can be interpreted to prove either that he pretended to hinder it while secretly helping it or that he seriously hindered it while pretending to help. Indeed, he could not be frank for he did not know whether it would fail or succeed. He had seen with mingled delight and alarm what had happened in Sicily and Naples. He was delighted that the

---

[1] In 1870 the Spanish statesman Castelar congratulated Rattazzi, Cavour's successor, on having accomplished the union of Italy, which 'Savonarola could not achieve by giving himself to God, nor Machiavelli by giving himself to the Devil'. Cavour made the best of both worlds.

throne of the Bourbon King was overthrown, but he was anxious to know what was to take its place. Garibaldi had always declared that he was acting in the name of Italy and Victor Emmanuel; but it was by no means certain what practical meaning he was prepared to give to that watchword. He had refused simply to declare Sicily annexed to the Kingdom of Sardinia, and was probably justified by military considerations. The future was still quite uncertain. Mazzini and his followers were working for a republic. There was a strong party who wanted to give to Naples and Sicily some separate and independent standing in a free and united Italy. Sicily especially wished for autonomy. The recovery of the supporters of the Bourbon monarchy could not be quite ruled out of the possible events of the future, for King Francis was holding out at Gaeta, and the inevitable disappointment with the results of liberty was bringing him some support. It seemed to Cavour that the time had fully come for his royal master to take an open part in a drama in which he had all along been a most important though concealed influence. He had no confidence in the intellectual capacity of Garibaldi to deal with the situation.

He saw, too, an opportunity of not only completing the settlement of Naples but also of adding to the territories of Italy some part at least of the long-coveted Papal lands.

Pius IX knew of the impending danger. There were stirrings of revolution in the Marches and in Umbria. The Papal Government had entirely failed to win the support of the population since the events of 1849. The Papal army had, however, been considerably increased and improved. It consisted of men drawn from various countries, and especially from France, Ireland, and Belgium. The Papal Government was recognised as a part of the State system of Europe, and it was difficult to find an excuse for attacking it. Cavour declared in a despatch to Piux IX that the King of Sardinia felt himself bound 'in the cause of humanity' to prevent the Papal troops from suppressing with violence the popular movements in Umbria! ('If we did for ourselves,' said Cavour on another occasion, 'what we do for our country, what rascals we should be!') On this pretext the Sardinian army entered the Papal States and defeated the Papal army at Castelfidardo. The forces of Victor Emmanuel then pushed on into Neapolitan territory and took over the authority which had been hitherto exercised by Garibaldi as Dictator. Garibaldi at first declared that he had no confidence in Cavour and that he would not declare annexation to the kingdom of Victor Emmanuel until Rome had been conquered. There seemed some danger of a collision between the red-shirts and the regulars; but the danger passed. King Francis was forced to abandon Gaeta and retired to Rome. Garibaldi met the King, and was warmly thanked by him for what he had done. He refused, however, all rewards with almost unexampled unselfishness, and retired to his island home in Caprera. Plebiscites were

taken in Naples, in Sicily, and in the newly conquered Papal territories. By the usual overwhelming majorities the population declared
for immediate annexation to 'the constitutional monarchy of Victor
Emmanuel.'

The first Italian Parliament met in Turin in February 1861. In
March a new constitutional decree containing a single article was
promulgated: 'Victor Emmanuel II assumes for himself and his successors the title of King of Italy.' We shall see later how in 1866
Venice and in 1870 Rome were joined to the territories of Italy.

Cavour equivocated to the end. He twice promised autonomy
to Sicily, for instance, only to outbid his own agents, La Farina,
Depretis and Crispi in succession, for the support of the Sicilians.[1]
He stimulated the hostility of Garibaldi, for he could use it to appease
Napoleon III and Pius IX. The policy of centralisation pursued after
annexation seemed a breach of faith despite the plebiscites. The
Church, supporters of the old régime in Naples and the Papal States,
Sicilian federalists and Sicilian autonomists all tended to hold aloof
after unification. And nothing had been done for land-hungry peasants or the poor. Something of the promise of the Risorgimento had
been lost in its political outcome. But the dream of European Liberals had been turned into reality.

---

[1] For the struggle for power in Sicily see D. Mack Smith, *Cavour and Garibaldi*
(1953).

Chapter 16

THE DEVELOPMENT OF THE FRENCH EMPIRE

In speaking of the Crimean War and of Italian events it has been necessary to say a good deal of Napoleon III and of his foreign policy. Here we shall attempt to trace the development of the internal history of France as far as January 1870.

Napoleon III was an adventurer who had seized power by violence and in breach of the constitution to which he had sworn loyalty. The memory of the *coup d'état* clung to him always 'like an iron weight attached to the leg of a convict.' But he had erected the machinery of personal government. During the fifties he ruled through ministers chosen at his pleasure, the knowledgeable and able men in the Council of State, in the civil service and the prefectures. His Legislative Assembly of notabilities and his Senate of celebrities were submissive. The masses had expressed their approval in the plebiscites. His régime during these years really was supported by large and strong elements in French society. The agricultural population gave him its constant support right down to the time of his fall. The moneyed classes—industry, commerce, and the stock exchange—saw in him their defence against socialism and the red terror. The Catholic party—a strong element in French life—regarded him at first with decided favour. Had his system been permanently successful it would have had a great effect on political opinion in Europe and on the development of political forms.

Yet few men had an *active interest* in the survival of his régime at all costs, perhaps only his fellow-conspirators of the *coup d'état*, Morny, Persigny, Walewski and a few others. He could count on very little spontaneous loyalty. Thus successes of a striking character would be necessary to him. Despite his claim that the 'Empire means Peace' he was constantly pushed by his name and the Napoleonic tradition into a policy of demonstration and adventure. France would forgive him much or all if he gave her glory and prosperity; but failure of any sort would be fatal to him.

Of the members of the family of the great Napoleon he was in touch only with the ex-King Jerome and his two children, Mathilde and a son called Jerome. But from this group Napoleon III could hope for little help. The younger Jerome posed as a democrat and as an anti-clerical, and was a continual source of trouble to the Emperor. Napoleon III had been given the right to appoint his own successor, but he looked to a marriage and the birth of an heir to strengthen his position and to assure its continuance. It has been already related how he married in 1853 Eugénie de Montijo, a beautiful Spanish lady, of noble but not of princely birth. She behaved in the position to which she was so unexpectedly raised with grace and dignity. She was a strong Catholic and a decided opponent of liberal views, and when a son—the Prince Imperial – was born to her she looked at the policy of France largely in its bearing on her son's destiny; but her evil influence on the fate of the Empire, except perhaps in 1870, has been much exaggerated.

There was at first very little formal opposition. The proscriptions which had followed the *coup d'état* had shown the danger of opposition. The Assembly was powerless; the press was closely watched and quickly suppressed if it ventured to criticise the new régime. But the calm would not last long, and the Emperor was well aware of the forces of opposition hidden just under the surface. There were the royalists in their two groups: the legitimists who upheld the Bourbons; and the Orleanists who desired the return of the family that had been driven off by the Revolution of 1848. The Comte de Chambord was the representative of the older line. He was a rigid and perfectly honest man to whom monarchy was a part of religion, who had no personal desire for a throne and would not attempt to win it by compromise or concession. He lived at Frohsdorf in Austria, and his party was for the present nearly negligible. The Orleanists had a much stronger following both in France and outside of it; and the princes of this house declared themselves in sympathy with much of the liberal thought of the time. The republican opposition was the really dangerous force. It could not show itself in the Assembly and could make little figure in the press; but it had the support of the populations of the great towns and especially of Paris. Napoleon's greatest failure was with the cities of France. All his efforts failed to win them to his side or even to abate their hostility. The intellectual leaders of France were also for the most part in opposition. The novelist and historian, Prosper Mérimée, and the historian Duruy supported the Emperor; Lamartine did not oppose him; but they were a feeble force to oppose to the names ranged against him—Thiers, Michelet, Louis Blanc, Renan, Georges Sand, and above all Victor Hugo. Victor Hugo refused to take advantage of the act of amnesty, and from his exile in the Channel Islands or in Belgium attacked Napoleon in writings which were of European importance.

In the general election of 1857 the imperial system worked successfully. The result of the Crimean War doubtless made the Napoleonic régime really popular with many, and in any case the scales were weighted so heavily against all opponents that it is difficult to see how the opposition came to send any representatives at all to the Assembly. A group of five—of which the chief names are Émile Ollivier and Jules Favre—represented the opposition and did their best to criticise the measures of the Government.

His Italian policy struck the first serious blow against Napoleon's position; for it bitterly offended the clericals, who had hitherto supported him with enthusiasm. These now saw the hated House of Savoy raised by the support of France to a position which soon led it to the Italian throne. When the Pope's troops were defeated at Castelfidardo, and when his territories were reduced to an extent insufficient to support his power, it was Napoleon III almost as much as Cavour who was responsible for this. The clerical press—the chief paper was *L'Univers*—became as bitter as the republicans in its opposition to the policy of the Emperor. From the clericals Napoleon never again received wholehearted support. But, if Napoleon's Italian policy had lost him the support of the clericals, it had not won him the support either of the national party in Italy or of the liberals at home. We have seen that the Italians charged him with having deserted them and with breaking the word which he had given to Cavour at Plombières. The French liberals, on the other hand, did not forgive him for still upholding the power of the Pope, and their opposition was all the greater when, in 1862, Garibaldi was repulsed and captured at Aspromonte, in his effort to reach the Papal States and rally them to the national cause.

The moneyed classes were also alienated and, more than all, the manufacturing class. The Free Trade movement had triumphed in Britain, and Napoleon had much sympathy with its economic conclusions and its social aims. In 1860 Cobden went to Paris to discuss with him the wisdom of a commercial treaty which should lower the tariffs on British goods coming into France. Cobden thought highly of the Emperor's 'straightforwardness and fairness' and believed him to be genuinely interested in relieving the condition of the poor. Napoleon determined on the treaty without considering French opinion, and Cobden believed that the people of France were overwhelmingly against the project. Napoleon hoped by this measure to establish more friendly relations with Great Britain, to which he always attached the greatest importance. He did not succeed in that object, and he alienated the moneyed classes, who had given him hitherto their warm support as their defender against the forces of disorder.

Here too we will note, though a little out of chronological order, his great Mexican adventure, which contributed so much to the failure of his system of government. There is no incident more characteristic of the man and his methods; of his brilliant but uncontrolled imagination; of his way of confusing fancy and fact; of his habit of taking up a project with enthusiasm and then dropping it with disgust, when the first difficulties showed themselves.

Mexico was plunged in great disorder. Since her independence had been achieved in 1823 she had found little stable government, but early in 1861 Juárez had made himself President. Mexico owed money to creditors of many nationalities, but especially to the French, Spanish, and British. When President Juárez in 1861 suspended the payment of interest for two years the creditors appealed to their Governments for help.

The situation so far was simple, but Napoleon's imagination saw great possibilities behind it. The United States of America were disabled by their great civil war from enforcing the Monroe doctrine, by which they claimed a monopoly of influence in the American World. It might be possible to establish in Mexico a state under the control of some European Power, which would act as a bulwark against the Anglo-Saxons, 'this aggressive people which, if it be not stopped, will cover all America and then the whole world.' Even if this state were not in French hands it might be used to win valuable alliances for France. A new chapter in the history of the world might open!

A joint French, Spanish, and British expedition sailed for Vera Cruz, hoping to exercise pressure which would produce the payment of the required interest on the Mexican debt. But it turned out that it would be necessary to enter the country, and then, on different grounds, Great Britain and Spain withdrew, leaving France to go on alone, as her ruler was quite willing to do. The task, however, proved more difficult than was expected. Puebla offered a successful resistance to the invader, and the city of Mexico was only reached in the summer of 1863.

Napoleon now had the brilliant idea of offering the throne of the Mexican 'Empire'—for such was to be the title of the new state—to Maximilian, the brother of the Austrian Emperor, Francis Joseph. Maximilian was a traveller and a scientist of distinction and was believed to hold liberal views on politics. Among other great results, which were hoped for from this move, were the friendship and perhaps the alliance of Austria. Maximilian accepted the offer after some delay and against the advice of Francis Joseph and of Great Britain. He was supported by a French army of 23,000 men. He was received with an appearance of enthusiasm in the city of Mexico.

But then this gorgeous 'palace in the air' dissolved quickly and tragically. Maximilian's supporters were divided and his opponents were determined. The North was now clearly gaining the upper hand in the American Civil War, and refused to recognise the new régime in Mexico. Napoleon too, in characteristic fashion, was as weary of the project as he had once been enthusiastic, for it was bringing constant disappointment and expense. He determined to withdraw the French forces and leave Maximilian, hoping that he would see the wisdom of retiring (February 1867). Maximilian refused, and struggled a little longer courageously against his enemies. The end came in June 1867, when he was forced to surrender to the native forces at Querétaro, and was shot in the courtyard of that town. The blow to Napoleon's prestige was irreparable.

This narrative has anticipated by several years the course of events in France. On November 24, 1860, Napoleon modified the absolute character of his rule. The Senate and the Legislative Assembly were to be allowed to discuss the policy of the Government once in the year. Ministers 'without portfolio'—that is, without definite administrative tasks—were given a seat in the Assembly in order to explain and defend the policy of the Government. By later decrees the debates in the Assembly were to be freely reported and published, and the press censorship was relaxed.

It is not true that the Liberal Empire resulted from concession to public pressure. Nor is the contrary opinion true that it was a premeditated operation put into effect when the Emperor judged it time 'to crown the edifice.' There is some truth in both views. Successive elections increased the number of republicans from five in 1857 to thirty-five in 1863 and the number of men elected without being official candidates had also increased, so that much pressure existed and concession to it was politic. The Emperor had said that he intended his régime to be authoritarian only for a period and he prided himself on his liberal views, his capacity to move with the times. But some importance should be given to factors which have nothing to do with either of these views. It has been argued, first, that the Liberal Empire was implicit in the system from the beginning. One cannot expect an Assembly of notabilities—real notabilities most with careers outside politics and each with a power base of his own in his own locality—not to wish sooner or later for real discussion and effective power. Second, the Legislative Assembly, re-elected every five years, really did reflect public opinion and it could only strengthen the Government if it had opportunity to comment more systematically on its policy. Similarly, and in the third place, the Legislative Assembly having acquired much experience, its debates would be a valuable aid to the Government—there were good debates on Italy and on Mexico. Finally, it could only strengthen the Government if Ministers sat in the Legislature. They had, indeed, found it inconvenient to be excluded. It is plain that November 24, 1860 represented a real change of system from the ministerial changes that Napoleon made at the same time.[1]

[1] The whole subject is discussed in T. Zeldin, *The Political System of Napoleon III* (1958).

After the elections of 1863 the Legislature contained a frankly republican group with such leaders as Berryer, Jules Simon, Favre and, above all, Thiers, who again entered the parliamentary arena. The opposition pressed for Ministers responsible not to the Emperor but to the Legislature and attacked the financial administration of the Empire. Two prominent members made noteworthy approaches to Napoleon. Thiers was the greatest and most observed statesman in France. In a much-quoted speech he demanded for France what he called the 'necessary liberties'—of the press, of the person, of elections, of representation, of majority Government. In return he would support the Empire though he would never take service under it. The action of Émile Ollivier was of even more immediate importance. He was by tradition attached to the Liberal party. His father had suffered exile for his opinions, and he had been one of the most eloquent of those 'Five' who for some time had been the sole representatives of opposition in the Assembly. But he was essentially moderate and conservative in his temper, and when Napoleon brought forward a proposal for legalising certain 'coalitions' of workmen—contrary to the tradition of France since the great Revolution—Ollivier determined to assist him. He did not hold, he said, by the maxim 'all or nothing,' which he considered a dangerous one. He was content to take a little every day.

Napoleon affected to make light of the astounding triumphs of Prussia in the wars against Denmark and Austria. In an official *communiqué* he expounded his doctrine of nationality, but he also stated that France would increase her armaments and would see to it that Germany remained divided in the future. The first proposition was contradicted by the second, and the third revealed either the insecurity or the warlike spirit of France. But French feeling refused to be comforted. Thiers declared that Sadowa was a great defeat, as serious for France as the Battle of Pavia had been nearly three and a half centuries before. Many were undoubtedly found to agree with him.

The victory of the Prussian national army produced many heart-searchings in France. It has been customary to compare it with the French system, which was based on conscription (the casting of lots, that is, among all who were eligible and the entire exemption from all military burdens of those on whom the lot did not fall) and then on strict professional training for seven years; and to maintain that the Prussians were mere amateurs compared with the French soldiers and that they would prove on the field of battle little more than 'improved national guards.' But Sadowa had changed all that! It was patent to all that the French army must be increased and the French system altered. Some, among whom the chief was Trochu (afterwards commander of Paris in the great siege of 1870), were anxious to adopt the Prussian system of universal military service; but French opinion was not ready for that. In the end, the term of service was lengthened and a new reserve—the 'garde mobile'—was planned. But these changes were not fully introduced when the storm of 1870 broke over France.

The political system was more thoroughly reconstructed. There was urgent need to do something. Moreover, it had become clear that to stop half-way between personal rule and parliamentary rule was impossible. The press used the greater freedom which it had been granted to attack Napoleon with the utmost bitterness. Henri Rochefort displayed in *La Lanterne* all his unscrupulous wit and Delescluze was hardly less bitter than Marat had been. Gambetta revealed his extraordinary powers as orator and agitator in his defence of Delescluze when prosecuted by the Government. The ideas and passions of the Paris Commune were fermenting just below the surface. In 1869 Napoleon had withdrawn some of the measures by which he had hitherto tried to control the elections. The rural districts stood firm in his support, but some of his bitterest opponents were elected in the great cities. His supporters had a large majority in the Chamber, but three million votes had been recorded against him. The foundations of his system were slipping away.

He determined to take a bold step and initiate an entirely new system which he announced in opening the session of the new Assembly. A large step was taken towards that parliamentary system which Napoleon had at one time regarded as outworn. The Chamber was to be allowed to legislate freely and to control the budget in all its details. Members of the legislature might be Ministers. The system of a Ministry resting on the support of a majority in the Assembly seemed on the point of adoption. The functions of the Senate were to be enlarged. A clause was added which might mean little or much: the Emperor reserved to himself the prerogatives which the people had conferred upon him and which were essential for the preservation of order and of society. In January 1870 Émile Ollivier, once so ardent a liberal, was asked to form a Ministry. He induced Napoleon to submit his new system to a popular vote as he had submitted his earlier proposals. All the electors of France were called on to vote 'Yes' or 'No' to a declaration that they approved the liberal reforms introduced into the constitution by the Emperor with the assistance of the chief constitutional bodies in the State. Ollivier regarded the result with the greatest satisfaction. True, the great cities abated nothing of their determined opposition. In Paris 184,000 voted 'No' and only 138,000 'Yes'. Lyons, Marseilles, Toulouse were all against the Government, but in France generally 7,358,000 approved and only 1,571,000 disapproved. The abstentions were more numerous than the votes of dissent, but on the whole Ollivier was justified in regarding the result as a great triumph for what was now called the 'Constitutional Empire'. If there had been a few years of peace and calm it is at least possible that the new system might have led France peacefully into constitutional parliamentary life, with or without a Napoleon at the head of the State. But, before France got to understand the new system or how to work it, came the deluge!

We must pass soon to an examination of the position in Central Europe, which is the background of the Franco-Prussian War, but first we will glance at the relations between Napoleon and Italy, which are an important side-stream to the main current. Napoleon was destined, it seemed, never to derive any advantage for himself or France from all his Italian policy, well meaning though it had been and often of great advantage to Italy. By the Convention of September 1864, Napoleon had promised that the French garrison should evacuate Rome, and the King of Italy had given an assurance that Florence and not Rome should be adopted as the capital of the new Italian State. The French troops actually left in December 1866; and at once a movement started, with the connivance of Garibaldi, for the invasion and conquest of Rome. Clearly the Papal *zouaves* were quite unequal to the emergency. The French garrison was still at Marseilles. It was re-embarked, and reached Italy in time to join the Papal troops and defeat the Garibaldians at Mentana. The Italian liberals denounced Napoleon more bitterly than ever. De Failly, the general in command, reported that the new French rifle, the chassepot, 'had done wonders,' and something specially brutal was found in this remark. France in her hour of need would not find the Italian kingdom which she had done so much to create ready to help her.[1]

The last months of the Empire were much occupied with a new Roman question. The Pope had summoned a new Ecumenical Council for 1869. He had already declared his opposition to modern liberal and democratic ideas in no doubtful terms. It was certain that the new council would issue decrees that would offend liberal opinion, whether in Italy or elsewhere, and many held that France should use the influence of her exceptional position to prevent the council from assembling. But Ollivier overruled these views, and the Council met. Just at the moment when the relations between France and Germany were leading to the great war the Ecumenical Council was debating the question of papal infallibility, and the war had already begun when, on July 18, 1870, the council declared that the Pope was infallible 'when in the exercise of his mission as supreme teacher of all Christians he defines by his apostolic authority that which should be held by the Universal Church in the matter of faith or morals.'

[1] On December 4, 1867, M. Rouher, when interpellated in the Assembly, declared for the Government that they would *never* (jamais) permit Italian occupation of Rome. As Bismarck did not take this line, the French parliamentary utterance inclined Italy to Prussia rather than to France, and prevented her paying any real heed to the negotiations for a Franco-Austro-Italian alliance, which Napoleon pursued from 1868 onwards.

Chapter 17

GERMANY TO THE SEVEN WEEKS' WAR, 1848–66

The Revolutions of 1848 and 1849 had been a great disappointment to all liberals in Germany and Europe. Nothing of what liberalism desired had been won. Austria still ruled over her variegated populations with despotic sway. In Germany no approximation had been made to national unity nor to a central elective parliament. United Germany, like united Italy, was to be made by war and diplomacy and not by the spontaneous initiative of the liberal nationalist movement. Political interest was reconcentrated in the official and ruling classes and the rest of Germany retired from politics.

When Germany withdrew from politics it might be said with some accuracy that she retreated into economics; for this was the decade in which the industrial revolution came to the German states. The general intensification of economic effort industrialised Germany virtually within a generation. The chief industrial centres were in the Ruhr and Saar valleys, in Berlin, north-west Saxony and Silesia—all Prussian territory, be it noted. Gradual mechanisation in the textile and heavy industries which began in the thirties had been financed by foreign capital or state subventions: the new spate of rapid mechanisation was paid for by domestic capital either through public companies of shareholders or—more important as machines and buildings became more expensive—through the banks which greatly developed in size and importance. Capital was channelled into industries and railway building. Labour was released for industry and communications by the completion everywhere of the land legislation of the Napoleonic period. The Bavarian (1848) and the Prussian (1850) laws were the most important laws. The indirect effect of this legislation was to bring land on to the market and so to enable new men, some of them with business ability and ideas, to intrude into the class of aristocratic landowners and a new class of landless labourers to form among the peasants. Both helped to make agriculture work more like a food-producing industry. The raw materials of heavy industry, coal and iron, zinc and lead, were exploited as never before because old restrictions were removed and technology had much advanced. But the cotton industry became Germany's leading industry at first and she could import all the raw cotton she needed. On its demand side the new railways, the new single federal currency, the Prussian Thaler, replacing the confusion of coins hitherto current in Germany, and the low tariff imposed by the Zollverein were the chief stimulants of the economy. The Zollverein was enlarged to include Hanover and in 1853 was renewed for twelve years.

In Austria the régime was thoroughly despotic. The decade of absolutism, called the Bach era after Schwarzenberg's Minister of the Interior, was one of real personal autocracy. After Schwarzenberg's death in 1852 the young Emperor dispensed even with a Prime Minister. Though he had a Foreign Minister he conducted both foreign policy and defence policy himself. The Reichstag of 1848 had been first banished from Vienna to Kremsier and then dissolved; a constitution had been published on March 4, 1849, and a start made in carrying out its provisions. On December 31, 1852, it was cancelled. Moreover, it was Schwarzenberg's policy, as it had been Joseph II's, to achieve 'the unification of the lands and races under the Monarchy in one body politic.' He succeeded in relation to those gains of the Revolutionary Year which survived. Equality before the law and the disappearance of the landowners' courts (patrimonial justice) were distinct gains and they remained. A new hierarchy of courts separating the judiciary from the executive was set up for the whole Monarchy. Administrative reform accompanied by the establishment of language equality (allowing people to communicate with the administration in their mother tongue and to expect a reply in it, for example), while retaining German as the language of government, was another result of the Revolutionary Year. It was not universally thought of as a gain: to the nationalists it seemed part of a policy of Germanising. Thirdly, the emancipation of the peasants and the land reform was carried out over the Empire as a while though with modifications to suit each individual *Land*. It too was a distinct gain from the Revolutionary Year. Peasant proprietorship and the release of landlords from old obligations was a powerful impulse to the conduct of agriculture as a business enterprise. During the decade, as usual, the economically weak became weaker and the economically strong became stronger and those who took advantage of the new opportunities were perhaps not as many as those who became victims of them. But it was economically that the Empire was most rapidly modernised during the decade. The building of railways, the introduction of new industries, the development of mining and heavy industry also drew the Empire together. The policy of treating it as a fiscal unit by, for instance, abolishing the trade tariff between Austria and Hungary, and of establishing a single frontier tariff with low duties for the whole Empire, was the most successful manifestation of Schwarzenberg's policy as well as the most economically stimulating gain from the Revolutionary Year.

No change in principle was made until the Italian War of 1859, but then the character of the Government was completely altered. A military form of Government is inevitably shaken by military defeat. Yet financial difficulties and social changes meant a wider sharing of power sooner or later. There was one great problem. Should the constitution be centralist or federal? This was really the problem of how to accommodate Hungary. Centralisation was in fact abandoned and Hungary was enabled to return to the constitutional position that she had had before 1848. The details of the changes deserve closer scrutiny. They were introduced by the imperial decree called the October Diploma (1860) and extended by the March Patent (1861). The outcome was that the Austrian Empire had a bicameral legislature called the *Reichsrat*. Its consent was necessary for new taxation and for legislation relating to certain matters which concerned the whole Empire. The Emperor could still legislate by decree when it was not in session. The Upper House was composed of the Archdukes, princes of the Church, heads of aristocratic families and some life members nominated by the Emperor. The Lower House was composed of 343 delegates from the *Landtage*. *Landtage* were set up in the several lands of the Empire. The *Landtag* for Hungary was virtually the old Diet that she had had before 1848. The *Landtage* were elected by the so-called curial system. Each of four social categories was assembled into a curia to elect so many representatives. The landowners formed the first curia, men with wealth from a source other than land the second, urban and rural communes the third and fourth. The system thus begun was by no means Parliamentary Government: ministers were still the Emperor's nominees and his advisers. But it did recognise the new balance of social forces in the Empire.

The German element welcomed the new system; especially that part of it which allowed a much freer press. (It was at this time that the era of newspapers began for Austria.) The non-German elements in the state nowhere gave the new constitution a hearty welcome, and the Hungarians were not reconciled. Then came the war of 1866, and Austria had to turn for a time from experiments in government to the task of defence.

The driving force in Central Europe was not be found in Austria, but in Prussia and Germany, and it is to Prussia that we must turn with more careful attention. Prussia, under the constitution of December 5, 1848 (see above, p. 185), had a parliament (*Landtag*) but ministers were appointed by the King and responsible to him. The franchise was narrow and ensured the preponderant influence of the wealthy conservative classes. The powers of the hereditary Upper House were considerable. Newspapers were closely supervised and the Government exercised direct control over many of them.

One institution dear to the German revolutionaries and destined later to arouse the liveliest hopes in the German mind did not survive the reaction. A German fleet had been one of the creations of the shortlived German revolution. A fleet came into being and lay in Bremerhaven; a symbol, so it seemed to many, of a new opening for German energies. With the failure of the nationalist movement in the revolution, the enthusiasm for a German fleet died down. The federal Diet declared the dissolution of the fleet, and it was sold by auction.

In 1858 the intelligence of the Prussian King was definitely obscured, and his brother William succeeded, first as Regent in 1858, and then as King on his brother's death in 1861. Some had imagined that he was less reactionary than his predecessor. He was indeed more direct, clear-sighted, and capable though he was not a liberal. He appointed new Ministers and announced 'a new era'. He had some sympathy with German aspirations towards national unity, and the newly founded 'National Association,' with its motto drawn from Schiller, 'Be united, united!' met with no opposition from him. His real enthusiasm was for the army. He looked at all problems with the eyes of a soldier, and his support for the army soon brought him into conflict with the Prussian Parliament.

The army reform that was now proposed was in its first part sensible and practical. There had been a great increase of population in Prussia so that the arrangements made in 1815 for calling up army conscripts had become quite unfair. The annual intake which had been calculated for a population of 10 million must be raised from 40,000 to nearly 70,000 to make it proportionately heavy on a population of 18 million. The bill that was introduced into the Prussian Parliament proposed to increase it to 63,000. The rest of the plan, however, outraged not only the liberals but a sizeable majority of all shades of opinion. It was argued by the Government that the independent militia of 1813 was out of date. The bill, therefore, proposed to put the new levy into a strong professional army—it was to be doubled in size—to reduce the duties of the militia to garrison service and to end its independence; to increase the term of service due from conscripts to three years in the professional army, two in the reserve and a period in the militia. More than nine and a half million Thaler were needed to meet the cost of the full programme. This the Parliament refused. It was dissolved (1861). In the new Parliament the liberal opposition had increased in numbers and moved well to the left. Yet in Prussia and in the nineteenth century it was impossible for Parliament to win new powers by withholding supplies: people continued to pay taxes and the Government found means to carry through part of the army programme. On the other hand, it was also impossible for the Government to do without Parliament: it was needed for other legislation than the army bill. The deadlock was complete by September 1862. General Manteuffel had plans for civil war and Roon, the War Minister, for whom the army represented not only force but morals and religion too, stiffened the Government's will to fight. The King announced that he preferred abdication to surrender. Parliament rejected the whole military budget at once by 308 votes to 11. Roon cut the knot by telegraphing to Bismarck to come at once to Berlia. 'There is danger in delay.' It was September 18. Bismarck was at once appointed Minister President. He came to power as the strong man, clever enough to find a course of action which would neither surrender the army programme nor defeat the Parliament. Balancing on the knife edge between extremes was to be his policy until he fell in 1890 after twenty-eight years of power.

The constitutional conflict was not over until December 1866. For four years taxation was levied illegally, though Bismarck found a constitutional doctrine to give it a specious legality. In 1866 Parliament in the indemnity law condoned the illegality. The parliamentary opposition submitted because Bismarck had given it one-half of what it wanted, and that perhaps the half most passionately desired. For the liberal movement strove not only for parliamentary government, but also for national unity. Bismarck induced Germany to forgo the first by giving her the second in full measure, and coupling it with the intoxicating draught of military glory.

Bismarck was a well-known man in governmental circles when he received the appointment of President of the Ministry. In 1862 he was first ambassador in St Petersburg and then in Paris. He had represented Prussia at the Frankfurt Diet when a strong man was wanted who would not give way to the Austrian assumption of superiority over all other German states; and stories, perhaps half legendary, were told of his coolness and success in that capacity. He had seen with bitter regret the capitulation of the monarchy in the days of the 1848 rising, and had told the King in a private letter that he could rely on the army and that the popular forces were not as strong as they seemed to be. Certain characteristics of Bismarck are sometimes forgotten. In the first place his views and impulses rested on a basis of deeply-felt religious conviction. 'If I were not a Christian I should be a republican,' he is reported to have said. And in the next place he owed little or nothing to the academic training to which modern Germany owed so much. He had been at the University of Göttingen, but did not regret his neglect of his studies there. He spoke strongly of the cramping effect of university education and its tendency to check originality. His outlook on European politics was always Prussian rather than German. 'Prussians we are and Prussians we will remain,' he said. German unity was for him an extension of Prussian power. The spring of action in Bismarck was the sense of his own capacity to exercise power and to discharge its responsibilities. He gained power for himself, great power for Prussia with which he identified himself and great power for Germany with which he identified Prussia.

A difficult question soon came up for solution. Austria made herself the spokesman of German liberalism, and invited Prussia to a Congress of German Princes to discuss a scheme for a German federal union. The proposals were interesting. There was to be a 'directory' consisting of the representatives of six states, and Prussia, Austria and Bavaria were always to be of the number. There was to be a federal council and a federal assembly. The King, always anxious to work with Austria, was for accepting the invitation, and if we look at the issue from a 'European' point of view we can hardly doubt that he was right. But the new constitution would curb the action of Prussia, and Bismarck refused compliance. His will was usually stronger than his master's, and after a long struggle, which left both of them exhausted, the King agreed to abstain. The refusal of Prussia to co-operate brought down the whole proposal. The rivalry of Prussia and Austria for the leadership of Germany was a patent fact, and many saw that the sword must in the end decide.

Next came the Polish question. The country had not resigned itself to the measures of repression that had been undertaken after the rising of 1848. Dreams of national independence had never ceased to haunt the minds of the enlightened classes among the Poles. They saw their own past through a haze of romance and regret, and thought that whatever had been Poland in the sixteenth century should be Poland again. There was much that was well-intentioned in the treatment of Poland by Tsar Alexander II. He desired to emancipate the serfs and to establish a peasantry that should recognise its debt to Russia and repay it by loyalty to the Russian connection. Unfortunately, he joined to these measures some that directly attacked the middle and upper classes of Poland; and, especially, he enforced his military levy against them. While the peasants were to be left upon their lands, the classes associated with the national movement were to be swept into the Russian army. There followed a Polish insurrection, which gained some success at first and advanced beyond the boundaries of Poland on to territories which were thoroughly Russian. But the victory of Russia was certain unless Europe interfered.

European interference did not seem impossible; for Poland was a word that inflamed the imagination of all liberals of that age. There was great excitement in Paris and the feeling of Britain was decidedly in favour of Poland. Had Prussia shown any inclination to co-operate with the Western Powers Russia would have been faced with the prospect of a very dangerous coalition. But Bismarck was wholly against any support of rebels. He had a strong feeling that the friendship of Russia would be a necessity for Prussia in the contests which awaited her. He paid no attention to the protests of German liberals and the Prussian Parliament, nor even to the representations of the Prussian Crown Prince. He assured the Tsar of Prussian sympathy and Prussian support, and the Polish revolt was beaten down. The understanding with Russia that was thus established was one of the pillars of Prussian policy while Bismarck remained in charge of it; and the Tsar did not show himself ungrateful for what Bismarck had done.

The Prussian Parliament stormed and threatened. German liberal opinion regarded Bismarck as the great enemy. It was difficult to see how he could carry his policy through to victory in the face of general Prussian opposition. He was saved by the Schleswig-Holstein question, which led up to two wars.

The Schleswig-Holstein question has become a byword for obscurity. It is like some intricate trial at law where the opinion of the onlooker changes with the addresses of the different advocates. Denmark was an ancient and honoured monarchy connected with many of the greatest royal families of Europe. Her population was for industry, intelligence, and character on a level with the most advanced populations of Europe. Her southern frontier had, however, for long presented difficulties which had of late years become more acute. There lay the two Duchies of Schleswig and Holstein, which were admittedly no part of Denmark but which had been for long attached to the crown of Denmark. Schleswig was predominantly Danish in character and had been given a separate Diet of her own. Holstein was very largely German. It had formed part of the Holy Roman Empire of which Germans were beginning to think now with romantic regret, and it had been recognised as a member of the German Confederation by the Treaty of Vienna. It was separate from Schleswig, but had a common Ministry with it. As the strong sense of German nationality developed in Germany the hope grew that some means might be found to incorporate *both* the Duchies in the German State. The troubles of 1848 have already been touched on. The effort of the Duchies to break away from Denmark had been crushed and the whole Danish question had been, it was hoped, settled by the Treaty of London in 1852. This treaty laid down first that the present childless King of Denmark should be succeeded by the husband of his niece, Christian, Prince of Glücksburg, in all his dominions, and that these dominions included the two Duchies. Another clause declared that the relation of Holstein to the German Confederation was in no way altered by the treaty. The Great Powers – France, Prussia, Austria, Russia, Great Britain – signed the treaty, but it was not accepted by the Diet of Frankfurt, the organ of the German Confederation, nor by Frederick of Augustenburg, the rival claimant to the Danish throne. But the Diet was not taken seriously, and a personal claimant was not likely to throw Europe into war, if the signatories to the treaty stood firm.

The new King of Denmark, Christian IX, succeeded in 1863, and one of his first acts was to ratify an arrangement already made by his predecessor for the issue of a new Constitution, unifying his dominions and thus disregarding the traditional autonomy of the Duchies. The fact that Holstein was a member of the German Confederation was one of the reasons for the disastrous results of this measure. It provided the necessary *casus belli* to a Germany which was peculiarly sensitive to what happened in the Duchies. So Frederick of Augustenburg claimed the monarchy of Denmark and his claims were supported by the Diet at Frankfurt.

Apart then from the immediate occasion for the war the position was simple. There was a disputed claim to the Danish throne; and there was a dispute between Denmark and the German Confederation as to the Duchies. In the issue Denmark lost, but the Confederation did not gain. The gains went by an ironic stroke of fate to Prussia and to Austria, both of which had signed the Treaty of London and had recognised the right of Prince Christian to the succession to the Duchies. Yet the explanation of this strange turn is not hard to find. When weaker Powers quarrel it is often the strong that profit. The decisive factor in the confusion that so puzzled Europe was the strength of Prussia and the determination and skill of Bismarck.

On the death of the Danish King, Frederick of Augustenburg, as we have said, protested against the succession of Prince Christian and claimed the throne. The German Diet considered the matter and decided to support him. The Diet had never accepted the Treaty of London and its hands were quite free. 'Federal execution' was ordered—that is, the Diet determined to support its decision by the weak army which was at its disposal. Denmark could perhaps have held its ground against them. But mightier combatants entered the arena. Prussia convinced Austria that they should not leave these great decisions in the hands of the Confederation. Bismarck had used his opportunity to readjust Prussia's relations with Austria so that Prussia led and Austria followed. Prussia and Austria made a hasty alliance; and then declared themselves the executants of the will of the Diet. They had signed the Treaty of London, but they had not guaranteed it. They held themselves free to act according to what they conceived to be their interests in the new situation that had arisen. So the federal army was withdrawn and a joint Austrian and Prussian army entered the territory of Denmark.

Europe saw the step with alarm and with general sympathy for the small Power that was attacked by two large ones. The two invaders would hardly have persisted in their action in face of any general European protest. But Europe did not exist except as a geographical and cultural unit. The idea of the European Concert which had grown up in the earlier nineteenth century had become ineffective, except, and this only to a limited extent, in relation to Turkey. The ideas of the twentieth century, expressed first in the League of Nations and then in the United Nations, were not yet born. Nor was there any Power or group of Powers ready to interfere. Norway and Sweden looked on with sympathy, but much to Ibsen's indignation took no action. An ill-judged British intervention failed and was soon dropped. Napoleon III had the difficult Mexican affair on his hands and was not at this moment on good terms with Great Britain. Moreover, he had made himself the champion of the principle of nationality, and the action of the German Powers was defended as being a movement towards German national unity. What he had done and said in the case of Italy made it difficult for him to resist Prussia and Austria in Germany. There remained Russia, but Bismarck had secured the neutrality of Russia by his action in the Polish rising.

So the war of 1864 went on to a rapid end. The Austrian troops were supposed to have shown greater skill than the Prussians. When the Danish defeat was certain a conference was called in London; but the victors' terms were too hard to allow of settlement. The war continued. The Danish government was driven from the mainland, and had to accept the terms that the victorious enemy dictated. The terms were surprising. Prussia and Austria had been acting as executants for the German Federation and apparently for Frederick of Augustenburg. But their clients got nothing, and they took all for themselves. The interests of Europe and the rules of international right were openly flouted. In the Treaty of Peace which was hurried through by Bismarck, who always feared above all things the interference of a European Congress, it was declared that the King of Denmark 'renounces all his rights over the Duchies of Schleswig, Holstein, and Lauenburg in favour of their Majesties the King of Prussia and the Emperor of Austria.'[1] The German Confederation was completely ignored. The bungling efforts of Britain and France to interfere in the settlement were swept aside. The Duke of Augustenburg, on whose behalf Prussia and Austria had seemed to interfere, was treated with complete cynicism. An inquiry was held in Berlin as to the legal position of the Danish succession. It was declared that Christian IX was the only rightful heir both to the Dan-

---

[1] Treaty of Vienna, Art. 3, of October 30, 1864, between Austria, Prussia, and Denmark. The Convention of Gastein, August 14, 1865, gave Schleswig to Prussia and Holstein to Austria, but only to administer. The Treaty of Prague, August 23, 1866, by Article 5 transferred all Austrian rights to Prussia but arranged for a plebiscite in North Schleswig to decide whether the area should be returned to Denmark. Bismarck kept deferring the holding of this plebiscite, and nothing was done till 1919. The Articles 109–114 of the Treaty of Versailles provided for this plebiscite. It was held and the northern area of Schleswig declared in favour of, and was returned to, Denmark.

ish crown and to the Duchies. He had therefore full right to cede them in the treaty. Thus Austria and Prussia had to render account to no one for their occupation of the Duchies.

In these tangled events lie the beginnings of that condition of things in Europe which led at once to two major European wars and then forty years later to the first World War. 'England failed France and France failed England and both failed Europe. The triumph lay with Bismarck alone. He had laid his hand on the heart of France and detected its weakened movement. He had calculated the inertia of England. He held Russia by the memories of the Polish question.'

Schleswig and Holstein thus lay helplessly in the hands of Austria and Prussia. The two partners had from the first regarded each other with suspicion and hostility. The joint occupation of the Duchies had in it no principle of permanence, and in less than two years it led to a greater war between Prussia and Austria. The condition of Europe was restless and there were several questions out of which war might have come. But the driving force to war was without much doubt the ambition and power of Prussia and of her strong Minister. Germany dominated and united by Prussia – that was the dream that never ceased to occupy Bismarck's imagination; and the traditions and claims of Austria lay right across the road to its realisation.

The next question which contributed to the fulfilment of Bismarck's plans arose at the other end of the central block of European territory. South of the Alps the Italian Government, in spite of the many difficulties which it found in the management of its recently acquired territories, was anxious for more. Rome was the city and land most desired, but the road to Rome was decisively blocked by the action of France. In September 1864 Italy had signed a convention with France by which she had promised not to attack Rome and to adopt Florence as her capital, and on these conditions France promised to withdraw her garrison from Rome. But, if Rome was forbidden, Venice was not. True, Venice was in many ways separate, both in history and character, from the rest of Italy; but she desired incorporation with Italy, and Italy felt herself manifestly incomplete while Venice remained under Hapsburg rule. Bismarck, conscious of the coming struggle with Austria, made overtures to Italy, and after some difficulty made an agreement: that in the event of an Austrian war both Prussia and Italy were to throw all their forces into the contest; and that Prussia was not to make peace until the possession of Venice was secured to Italy. But what of France? She might exercise a decisive influence, and Napoleon III still aspired to be the arbiter of peace and war in Europe. In October 1865 Bismarck paid a famous visit to him at Biarritz, and there, amidst much apparent light-hearted gaiety, he managed to secure the good will of France. Napoleon lived in a world of dreams. 'Prussia and France are the two nations of Europe whose interests are most nearly identical,' he said; and yet Sedan was less than five years off!

It seemed at one time that war would have come in 1865, for the partnership in the Duchies led to many difficult problems. But in August the Convention of Gastein 'plastered over the cracks' and the partners divided their spoil. Prussia was to administer Schleswig, the more northerly Duchy, and Austria Holstein, the more thoroughly German. The situation was difficult, but with a strong desire for peace it was not incapable of a pacific solution.

The political situation in Prussia contributed something to the unlikelihood of a policy of peace. The liberal opposition had not ceased to oppose Bismarck and all his works, though there was some satisfaction to be gained from the Danish settlement – for the two Duchies would henceforth be in German hands. There was a new crisis in February 1866. War with Austria—provided, of course, that it was victorious—would complete the work of the Danish war in bringing the liberal opposition to heel. Paradoxically, political unrest at home strengthened rather than diminished the determination of Bismarck.

The rupture with Austria came over the supposed favour shown by Austria to the claims of Frederick of Augustenburg. In the administration of the two provinces Prussia and Austria had pursued widely different policies. The Austrian representative had done his utmost to conciliate the people of Holstein and had spoken of the claims of Frederick of Augustenburg as still valid. Prussia, on the contrary, had begun at once to Prussianise Schleswig. When, therefore, a meeting was held in Altona – in the neighbourhood of Hamburg and in the territory controlled by Austria – in favour of the claims of Augustenburg this was regarded by Prussia as an unfriendly act, and as a sufficient excuse for the war, which had been foreseen and desired for some time by the leaders of Prussian policy. For there can be no doubt on this point. It is true that no war springs from a single cause or from the action of one man. There are always many contributing and supporting causes. But it is certain that in 1865 Bismarck, Moltke and Roon desired a war with Austria and believed it necessary in the interests of Prussia and of the German policy, which was identified with Prussia. The domestic difficulty too, and the violent resistance of the Parliamentary opposition, could only, it seemed, be met in this way. Moltke said later that 'it was a war which was foreseen long before, which was prepared with deliberation and recognised as necessary by the Ministry, not in order to obtain territorial aggrandisement but in order to secure the establishment of Prussian hegemony in Germany.' Bismarck, too, realised clearly that his own personal position depended on the issue of the contest. 'Had I failed,' he said, 'the old women would have swept me with a curse with their besoms into the gutter.'

The fate of Schleswig and of Holstein was of great importance;

but it soon fell into the background. A war between two great military Powers was clearly threatening and the statesmen of Europe considered with feverish anxiety the problems that arose from the situation. The Powers not directly concerned abounded in well-meant schemes for avoiding the contest, and at the same time planned how to win for themselves some gain in territory or prestige, if the war really came about. The atmosphere was one of rivalry, suspicion, and above all of fear, which made all peace efforts very difficult. The German Diet at Frankfurt had some claim to be regarded as an umpire in the dispute, but neither Prussia nor Austria was inclined to accept interference from this quarter. Bismarck never wavered in his belief that the sword alone could cut the Gordian knot, and in his desire to bring about that solution. King William only gradually yielded to his Minister's strong will.

Amidst all the uncertainty one thing was clear. Whatever happened Italy would gain Venice. Prussia had promised not to make peace except on that condition, and Austria, anxious above all things to win the neutrality, or if possible the support, of France, declared herself willing to surrender Venice, even if the war went in her favour in Italy and Germany. A scruple of military honour kept her from handing over the territory at once to Italy and so preventing her from taking any part in the coming war.

It was the French Emperor who seemed to hold the balance in his hands, and the negotiations between him and Austria, Prussia and Italy were unceasing. The action of France, despite Bismarck's famous interview with Napoleon at Biarritz, was quite uncertain up to the last. The Emperor was ill of the disease which, it seems, diminished his energy and his will power from this time until his death. In marked contrast with Bismarck he saw nothing clearly, was not sure of his own wishes, and lived in a world of cloudy and half-realised schemes. One dream was that out of the war he might gain something for France, if possible, on the Rhine frontier. He believed that the forces of Prussia and Austria were about equally matched; that the war would be a long and indecisive one; and that in the end the sword of France would be thrown into the scale to decide the issue. Just before the outbreak of war he was moving decisively to the side of Austria. In June 1866 he signed an agreement whereby France promised her own neutrality and that she would use her best efforts to keep Italy neutral; while Austria promised to hand over Venice to Italy at the end of the war whatever its course, and to take France into her confidence with regard to any alterations in the German Constitution or in the Balance of Power among its members.

The Frankfurt Diet was the scene of the last diplomatic struggles. The sympathy of the smaller German States had been alienated from both Austria and Prussia by the Gastein Convention. But they exercised little influence on the course of events. The decision, as

Treitschke saw with delight, had passed from ideas and votes to power; and the Danish war had shown how small was the power in the hands of the Diet. Prussia had for some time played with the idea of a reform of the constitution of Germany. Now, in June 1866, she brought forward a definite proposal that the present Diet should be dissolved and the constitution abolished; that a new National Assembly should be elected to decide on a national constitution; and that Austria and the Austrian lands should have no share in this constitution. Austria answered by declaring that Prussia had broken the Treaty of Vienna and the Gastein Convention, and called for the mobilisation of the federal army against her. Nine votes supported the Austrian proposal, while six were given against it. Bavaria, Saxony, Hanover, and Baden were among the supporters of Austria. The Prussian representative, Savigny, solemnly protested against the action of Austria as unconstitutional; once more declared the existing constitution at an end and that Prussia was ready to co-operate in the formation of a new one. But all this was idle talk until a military decision had been reached. That came with a rapidity and a decisiveness altogether unexpected.

Chapter 18

THE DEFEAT OF AUSTRIA AND THE COMING OF THE FRANCO-GERMAN WAR

Europe looked on with amazement at the struggle between Prussia and Austria. The general opinion was that Austria had the better chance. The Prussian military system was untried; her short-service soldiers, it was thought, would prove to be little more than a 'national guard' against the Austrian troops with their long military training and traditions. Napoleon III hoped that an evenly balanced struggle would give him an opportuinty of intervention and allow him to appear again as the bringer of victory and peace.

The actual spectacle afforded by the war was something very different. The Prussian machine worked with fatal precision. Prussia took the offensive from the very beginning. She used the railways (their first use in this way) to deploy her armies in an arc, 270 miles long, from the Saxon frontier eastwards to the Prussian – Silesian frontier with Austrian Bohemia. Moltke's strategy was extremely bold; for he had exposed his forces to destruction by a rapid and dynamic opponent, but the Austrian Commander, Benedek, who had not wished for the command, knowing himself unfitted for it, was not that. The breech-loading needle-gun used by the Prussians proved a better weapon than the muzzle-loading rifle used by the Austrians.

The final scene in the German Diet produced war on June 14. Prussia had to deal with two enemy forces. There was the Austrian army in Bohemia, and there was the Hanoverian army whose aim was to join with the Bavarians and south Germans. On June 28— just a fortnight after the declaration of hostilities—the Hanoverian army was caught and crushed at Langensalza. Five days later, on July 3, the Austrian army was encountered by Moltke on the battlefield called by the Austrians Sadowa, by the Germans Königgrätz and by Czechs Hradec Kralove. The Austrians fought skilfully and stubbornly, and there were moments when Bismarck watched Moltke's face with great anxiety to see if he could read there any indication of the fortunes of the day. The arrival of the Prussian Crown Prince on the right of the Austrian army, after a famous march, decided the fate of the day and gave victory to the Prussians.

Austria had been forced by the alliance of Italy with Prussia to maintain a large force south of the Alps which would have been of priceless value at Sadowa. Against Archduke Albrecht in the Lombard plain the Italians showed little skill and were heavily defeated. On June 24 they were crushed at Custozza—already once fatal to Italian patriotic hopes. The Italian fleet too, whose superiority over the Austrian fleet was thought to be certain, was heavily defeated at the Battle of Lissa. If Italy had stood alone the work of 1859 might have been undone. But Bismarck had promised that he would make no peace which did not give Venice to Italy, and the victory of Sadowa completed the work of Magenta and Solferino.

It was not certain that the war would end after Sadowa. The defeats of the Italians and the military aspirations of Moltke and the King of Prussia pointed rather to a continuation of the fighting and a march on to Vienna. That the fighting came to an end, and that negotiations for peace were undertaken after the Prussian armies had advanced a little further towards their goal, was almost entirely the work of Bismarck. He never showed himself a greater master of diplomacy than during the four years between 1866 and 1870; and it is not merely diplomatic skill that he exhibited but also real statesmanship. The unity of Germany under Prussia was the idea always uppermost in his thoughts. That could not be secured by military success against armies that were mainly German. The conciliation of the South Germans was essential, and Austria must be so treated that she would not regard Prussia with a hatred that would efface all other considerations. There was also another fear in Bismarck's mind—the interference of the French Emperor. True, the struggle was far removed from the even balance that Napoleon had hoped for; but he was anxious to be accepted as mediator, and sent Benedetti, the French Ambassador, to the Prussian headquarters at Nikolsburg. Bismarck has told us in a chapter of exceptional interest in his *Reflections and Reminiscences* what were his reasons for insisting on peace.[1] The centre of his thought was 'We must finish off rapidly, before France has time to bring diplomatic action to bear on Austria.' So he forced the King, sorely against his inclination, to forgo the march on Vienna and to content himself with terms which had seemed at first entirely inadequate.

The Treaty of Prague was signed on August 23, 1866. Venice with the adjacent territory went to Italy. Austria handed it over to Napoleon, who was gratified by this opportunity of playing some part in the great drama, and Napoleon gave it to Italy. The procedure bitterly hurt Italian pride, and is one more instance of Napoleon's failure to win Italian support by all that he did for Italy. Article 4

[1] Chapter XX (Eng. translation 1898).

declared that Austria would no longer claim any share in the organisation of Germany. A North German Confederation was to be formed; and also an association 'with an independent international existence' of the states of Southern Germany. Schleswig and Holstein were to go to Prussia, though a clause, never acted on, declared that part of Schleswig was to return to Denmark if it expressed its wish by plebiscite to do so. The soldiers came back in triumph to Berlin. Moltke had shown his genius as a soldier, and King William a certain greatness of character; but the master mind had been Bismarck's throughout.

The feeling of Europe about these great happenings naturally varied from country to country. In Great Britain, where foreign policy was watchful but somewhat aloof, there was general satisfaction. In France, on the contrary, the triumph of Prussia was felt to be a great disaster. The supremacy of France in Europe disappeared at Sadowa. 'It is France that was beaten at Sadowa,' said Marshal Randon. 'What has happened,' said Thiers, 'is for France, the greatest disaster that she has suffered for four hundred years'—since the end, that is, of the Hundred Years' War. Napoleon III no doubt felt the deepest chagrin at the triumph of Prussia; but he tried to cover it by declaring that it was a victory for the doctrine of nationality which he had always so eagerly championed. He added somewhat inconsistently that Germany was divided into three independent parts and each part was smaller than France, and declared openly that France would prevent any further union of these sections and reorganise her military system. He hoped, too, to gain for France some compensation for the great increase in the power of Prussia in accordance with the idea of the Balance of Power. He was already so ill that much of the French diplomacy had to be carried on by his Ministers. Its course shows the extraordinary superiority of Bismarck in all departments of the game. He knew what he wanted and had made up his mind how it was to be got. In force and in finesse, in honesty and in duplicity, he was the assured master of the French diplomatists whom he encountered, and who were made to appear as amateurs fighting against a master of fence.

First, before peace was concluded between Prussia and Austria, Napoleon put forward through his Ambassador in Prussia, Benedetti, the idea that France might be induced to accept the annexations which Prussia proposed for herself in Germany on condition that France should advance her frontier up to the Rhine and even lay hands on Mainz. This would have meant the French annexation of territories that were thoroughly German in origin and character. Part of them, moreover, belonged to Bavaria, the leader of the South Germans, whose favour France was particularly anxious to win. Bismarck was careful not to show at first all the hostility which he felt to these proposals. He induced Benedetti to make a formal statement of the French claims. No sooner were they made than they were decisively rejected. The King of Prussia declared that under no circumstances would he abandon a single German village; he would rather risk another war. The French Emperor had to withdraw his proposals, for he was not prepared to enforce them by arms. It was a humiliating check for French diplomacy, and it did not end there. Bismarck communicated the French proposals to the correspondent of a French newspaper, *Le Siècle*, and they became known to all the world. The Southern Germans were thus taught to see in Napoleon a false friend and in Prussia the champion of German integrity, even of the integrity of those states against whom she was fighting.[1] Nor could Napoleon's action this time be justified by his favourite doctrine of nationality.

France had failed to get compensation on the eastern frontier; might she have better luck on the north? Bismarck had warned her off from German territory; would he be as strict a guardian of the lands of Belgium? To advance her frontier farther to the north had been for centuries the dream of the statesmen of France. Much of Belgium spoke French. The state was a comparatively recent creation of European diplomacy. Bismarck had used words which seemed to imply that he would not regard French occupation of Belgium as necessarily hostile to Prussia. Benedetti was instructed to bring this new idea before Bismarck. Out of Benedetti's conversations with Bismarck at Nikolsburg there emerged a draft treaty of Franco-Prussian alliance which included provision for the French annexation of Belgium. During their last conversation on August 31 Benedetti handed a copy of this (he had first put it on paper on August 23), with proposed French amendments, to Bismarck for submission to King William.[2] But the situation in Europe was constantly becoming more favourable to Prussia and French help of less importance. Bismarck rejected the idea of a French advance in Belgium as decisively as he had rejected compensation on the Rhine frontier. He kept Benedetti's draft proposal by him and used it four years later with decisive effect at a critical moment. For when in 1870 the war had broken out between France and Germany and there was fear that British opinion might veer to the side of France he communicated the document first to Gladstone and then to the editor of *The Times*.

---

[1] The Prussian treaties with Württemberg, Baden and Bavaria were signed on August 13, 17 and 22, i.e. *before* the Peace of Prague. In that treaty Article 4 provided that the new North German Confederation should be 'north of the line of the (river) Main.' The treaties with the Southern States provided for the extension of Prussian influence south of that river. Thus, to use a paradox, Art. 4 of the Prague Treaty was violated before it was signed.

[2] Mysteries once surrounding the negotiation have been solved: see W. A. Fletcher, *The Mission of Vincent Benedetti to Berlin 1864–1870* (1965), pp. 129–36 and appendices.

When it was published British readers saw that the French Emperor had actually proposed to violate the neutrality of those Belgian lands whose independence had always seemed so necessary to British interests; and a revulsion of feeling followed in favour of Germany.

The Rhine frontier was forbidden; Belgium was forbidden. But what of Luxembourg? It would be a great triumph to annex that tiny state, and perhaps it might be done without incurring the opposition of the great statesman of Prussia. The Grand Duchy of Luxembourg was indeed a strange bundle of contradictions. It was recognised as an independent state, and the King of Holland was the hereditary Grand Duke. But it was also a member of the German Confederation and of the Zollverein, and ever since 1815 a Prussian garrison had held its strong fortress as a protection against a French attack upon Germany.

The French Foreign Minister, De Moustier, undertook the delicate negotiation. The King of Holland was in financial difficulties and derived no real advantage from his nominal rule over this French-speaking population of 200,000. A sum was offered him by way of indemnity. He demanded more; Napoleon demurred, but eventually gave way. The proposal might have gone through; and Prussia and Europe would have been presented with an accomplished fact if Napoleon had not haggled about the terms, and if the King of Holland had not thought it necessary to inform the Powers, who had signed the guarantee of the neutrality of Luxembourg in 1839, of what was proposed. Prussia was among these, and thus the affair, which was already known to Bismarck in his private capacity, came before the official Government of Prussia. German national sentiment, immensely inflamed and strengthened by the victory over Austria, now blazed out against this proposal to cede what might be regarded as German territory to the great rival. Prussia refused her consent to the proposed arrangement and the affair fell to the ground. It seemed as though it might easily have led to war, which a large party in Germany and the Prussian war chiefs would have welcomed. Conciliatory voices, however, made themselves heard. Queen Victoria wrote to the Prussian King. Russia also used her influence in favour of peace. Bismarck himself was not for war. So a settlement was made in Luxembourg; only the Prussian garrison, which had clearly now lost all justification, was withdrawn. But war had seemed near. 'Nothing could have been more welcome than war,' said Moltke, 'and after all it must come.' Both German and French feeling had become embittered and hostile.

While France was thus making embarrassed and unsuccessful efforts to recover her position and prestige in Europe, Prussia advanced from strength to strength and was building the road along which in four years from the Battle of Sadowa she would advance to unity in Germany and supremacy in Europe.

The Peace of Prague had spoken of a federal constitution for North Germany. Prussia was absolute master there. She annexed outright Hanover, Hesse Cassel, Nassau and Frankfurt. The other states of North Germany, such as Oldenburg, and the Mecklenburgs, Brunswick, Anhalt, the five Thuringian Duchies and Saxony were powerless to resist in the least detail the will of Prussia. If Bismarck had wished to annex them all there could have been no effective resistance, and some advised that a centralised German state and not a federal league should be the form of the new Germany. This would, however, have conflicted with the words of the Treaty of Prague, and the supremacy of Prussia was so great that no real rivalry could be feared. It would also have made more difficult that union of Northern and Southern Germany on which Bismarck's hopes were set.

There was much speculation as to the form which the new constitution would take. Many brains were at work on it, but the decisive influence was with Bismarck. The result was something new in the constitutional history of Europe, a federal state of a kind which had in reality no precedent in Europe. Certain objects were clearly kept in sight throughout. There was to be a new State, and not merely a union or league of states already in existence, and in this new State Prussia must be supreme. There was to be no central executive except that provided by the Prussian Government. Above all, if the southern states wished at any time to join their brethren of the north there must be no constitutional difficulty in the way. The work was accomplished rapidly and a constitution was adopted in July 1867, which made possible the fulfilment of all Bismarck's aims.

The King of Prussia was hereditary head of the Confederation. The Chancellor was the only federal Minister and he depended wholly upon the King, who appointed him. It was as inevitable that the first Chancellor should be Bismarck as that the first President of the Confederation should be King William of Prussia.

The Council of the Confederation (*Bundesrat*) consisted of the representatives of the different states of the Confederation. They represented the Governments, not the peoples, of the various states. The number of votes possessed by each was determined by the size of its population. Prussia had seventeen. No other state had more than four. Through it Prussia controlled the policy and the constitution of North Germany.

The Parliament of the Confederation was 'elected by universal and direct election with secret votes.' Yet the appearance of democracy was belied in the working of the constitution. It will be more convenient to trace the story when this constitution became that of the German Empire in 1871.

When the constitution began to work it was soon seen that Bismarck had gained another important victory. The Battle of Sadowa had overthrown not only the Austrians but the opposition to

Bismarck's policy in Prussia and the German states of the north. In place of liberty he gave them military glory and the admiration of Europe. Whatever was illegal in his action was covered by an indemnity. More and more, Bismarck became the national hero of Germany, and the opposition to him was soon reduced to trivial proportions.

Another victory awaited him. The states of the south had fought against Prussia in alliance with the Austrians, and it was the hope of French statesmen that their hostility would be intensified by defeat, and that they might be counted on as a permanently hostile force on the flank of Prussia. But the opposite happened. They were drawn towards Prussia by their common German nationality, by their association in the Zollverein, by Bismarck's championship of their interests against France, which we have already noted, and by admiration for the military glory which Prussia had given to the German name. The south would not be strong if it stood alone. Bismarck knew how to make the change of face easy to them. He found assistance from some of their statesmen, especially from Varnbüler of Württemberg. Offensive and defensive treaties were signed between Prussia and the individual states of the south.[1] This meant that in the next war Germany would present a united military front.

The chief interest of these years is to see the forces gathering which produced the great collision between France and Germany in 1870. But first we must turn to Austria and see the enormous change that was passing over the character and organisation of that state.

The changes of 1860–61, already discussed, made some advance towards stability, but the process was incomplete. Two powerful nationalities – the German and the Magyar (Hungarian) – faced one another, and behind them or under them were ranged nearly a dozen others. Before the war with Prussia in 1866 the Emperor was already negotiating for reconciliation with the Magyars and for the settlement of the state on a new basis. The crushing blow of Sadowa quickened the process. If the war had been prolonged the Prussians would have had assistance from the discontented elements of the state and especially from the Magyars. The 'House of Austria' could have no future unless it succeeded in establishing an equal understanding with Hungary, and it is to the credit of the Emperor Francis Joseph that he recognised this. His new aims were admirably served by two capable men. He summoned to his councils Count Beust, who had hitherto been in the service of the King of Saxony, and was a stranger to the passions or resentments that made any solution of the Austrian problem so difficult. The claims of Hungary were presented firmly but temperately and without any trace of revolutionary passion by Fran-

[1] See above, p. 267, note 1. The treaty with Hesse Darmstadt was signed on April 11, 1867.

cis Deák. Both these men had to struggle against violent counsels among their own followers.[1] The settlement was made easier by the fact that the Hungarians ruled over a number of subject nationalities—Rumanians, Serbs, Croats, Slovaks—and were anxious not to give them any opportunity for protest and revolution. So in 1867 a settlement was reached—the *Ausgleich*—by which a complete equality or dualism was established between the two component states, dominated respectively by the Germans and the Hungarians so far as internal affairs were concerned.

Francis Joseph was now, for the first time, formally crowned King of Hungary. His dominions were separated into two parts, divided by the little river Leitha, an unimportant affluent of the Danube; and each part had a Government and administration of its own—the one sitting at Pesth, the other at Vienna—charged with all domestic concerns (which were widely intepreted). In Austria Francis Joseph was Emperor and in Hungary he was King. It was made a legal and punishable offence to speak in public in Hungary of Francis Joseph as Emperor. In addition to these two Governments there was a third, dealing with war and foreign affairs and the finances affecting the two, and acting for both the states. The third Government, which was stronger than Austria or Hungary, was known as the Common Monarchy.

The dualistic system was a piece of wise and conciliatory statesmanship, and it gave to Austria-Hungary nearly half a century of comparative quiet and stability. But in essence it established two national tyrannies in place of one. The national aspirations which had been aroused among the Czechs, Slovaks, Poles, Rumanians, Croats, and Serbs were not in the least satisfied by the new arrangement, nor were they conciliated by the apparently liberal and democratic principles of the new constitution. Bohemia claimed equality with Hungary and used the fifth centenary of the birth of Huss to proclaim her rights. There was discontent and disorder among the Czechs and Ruthenians. These movements were directed against the German majority of the Cis-Leithan state (for so it was sometimes called); but the Magyars in Trans-Leitha had their own difficulties. Croats, Serbs, and Rumanians showed themselves galled by the Magyar yoke, and their discontent was a continuous menace to the dual state. It is sometimes argued that before the twentieth century there could have been further federation: a tripartite system to accommodate the

[1] There were two schools of political thought in Hungary: that of Kossuth which ended in revolution and in a demand for the dethronement of the Hapsburg; and that of Széchenyi, who was a constructive Conservative and who had even played with the idea of a 'Combined Monarch'. Deák represented the school of Széchenyi and adopted a moderate constitutionalism, avowedly based on the British model. He told Francis Joseph that he asked for no more after Sadowa than before, a truly constitutional position.

Czechs followed by a quadripartite system to accommodate the Southern Slavs (Yugoslavs). It did not happen before the War of 1914–18 destroyed the Empire-Kingdom.

In 1867 the position in Central Europe was this. The North German Confederation dominated Germany north of the River Main. South Germany was a group of independent states. The Common Monarchy established by the *Ausgleich* brought together Austria and Hungary in greater harmony then ever before, and seemed likely to provide a counterpoise to the strength of the Prussianised north. Italy was independent but not yet completely united, for Rome, the traditional capital, was outside the Italian Kingdom. The position was, however, far from stable. In all sections there were elements of instability which looked forward to future change. The opportunity came with the Franco-Prussian War, and this arose over the problem of Spain.

Spain had been the chief representative of liberalism in the early part of the century, and the Spanish Constitution of 1812 had been the rallying-cry of liberals in many parts of Europe. But constitutional government did not work easily or well in the Spanish peninsula. The change of Ministries and the succession of Parliaments (*Cortes*) seemed to float on the surface of the state. A revolutionary movement in sympathy with the socialism and even the anarchy of French and German thinkers was to be found under the surface. But among the politicians, though there were political parties, personal rivalries and ambitions were the chief moving force. The army and the Church were often more powerful than the Government. Every Government in turn established a military dictatorship; and until the end of the century it proved impossible to establish religious liberty, except in name, in face of the strong resistance of the Catholic Church and the dislike of the people for all religious variations.

Queen Isabella had been declared of age in 1843, but for ten years after this—even after the Queen had married her cousin Francisco—power still lay in the hands of the Queen Mother, Christina. The chief features of the Government were its strong Catholicism and its resistance to all reforms. A revolution—supported by the army, as is nearly always the case with Spanish revolutions— came in 1854. It was supported by practically all the politicians, whose names fill the troubled parliamentary history of the next fifteen years—chief among them Narváez, Espartero, O'Donnell. The Queen Mother, Christina, was driven into exile: a more liberal era seemed to have begun.

The change in the character of the Government was really not great. A large part of the responsibility for the troubles of Spain during the following years must be put down to Queen Isabella herself. She was superstitious rather than religious; her private life was never free from gross scandals; of real patriotism or of political insight she showed no sign. In her Ministries she rang the changes between Narváez, conservative and autocratic, and O'Donnell, leader of the Liberal Union, who found it impossible to govern with the Queen and who therefore inclined to a change of ruler. Another striking figure in the politics of the time was Prim, who had gained some military reputation in the Moroccan war and was decidedly of the opinion that Queen Isabella must go. O'Donnell died in 1867; Narváez in 1868. An attempt by the Government to arrest and exile the generals of the opposition, especially of the Liberal Union, led to an outbreak. Navy and army declared against the Queen. She neither deserved nor found any effective support. She fled from the country (September 30, 1868) and her reign was declared at an end.

There was a republican party in Spain, but it was thought best not to challenge European opinion by declaring for a republic. It was decided that there should be a constitutional monarchy. But where was the monarch to be found? The Spanish throne was an uneasy seat and proved no attraction to the princes of Europe. Seven candidates were considered or approached. Finally in June 1870 it was believed that a solution had been found and that Prince Leopold of Hohenzollern-Sigmaringen had been induced to accept the crown. It was this candidature which provided the occasion for the Franco-German War. Prince Leopold, indeed, withdrew his candidature when he found how great a storm it was causing, but the War opened nevertheless on July 15. The hunt for a king began again, but although in November 1870 Prim induced the Duke of Aosta, son of the King of Italy, to accept the throne, after a disturbed reign of only two years he refused to continue any longer in an impossible position and abdicated. There followed a short experiment in a republican constitution, and then the old line was restored in the person of Alfonso, son of Isabella. Under him Spain came nearer to constitutional stability.

At midsummer of the year 1870 the international situation seemed particularly calm. In France Émile Ollivier was head of the Government, and he was devoted to peace and resolved to pick no quarrel with Germany; and yet war was declared against Germany on July 15. The immediate causes of this sudden change are no longer in dispute.[1] Once both German and French historians sincerely held that it was a war engineered by their enemies, and that they themselves were entirely innocent of evil intentions or of provocative conduct. In German eyes, Napoleon III was the villain of the piece,

---

[1] See *New Cambridge Modern History* (1960), vol. X, pp. 577ff., using material published in G. Bonnin, *Bismarck and the Hohenzollern Candidature* (1957); cp. A. Ramm, *Germany 1789–1918* (1967), pp. 308–13.

conscious of a tottering throne and anxious to re-establish it by victory against the national enemy. The French saw in all the hand of Bismarck, forcing on France a war that she did not want, in order that he might complete the fabric of German national unity. Certain facts were, however, incontestable. The tension between the two countries was undoubtedly great. German ambition and French jealousy and fear were driving forces of unquestioned importance. The international system of Europe afforded no means of settling peacefully the manifold difficulties which arose from the rivalry of two Great Powers. A French statesman had compared France and Germany to two locomotives running in opposite directions on a single line of rails and had maintained that a collision was inevitable.

The question of the Spanish throne brought the rivalry to a head. There is now no doubt that Leopold of Hohenzollern-Sigmaringen's candidature had been suggested with the approval and support of Bismarck. It had been debated at an informal meeting in Berlin held under the presidency of the King of Prussia and in the presence of Bismarck, Moltke, and Roon, but it was then rejected. It was revived subsequently and secretly by Bismarck and Prim, without the knowledge of King William. Prince Leopold was a distant relation of the Prussian King and a Catholic. His brother had recently become Prince of Rumania. His accession to the Spanish throne would be a great gain to Prussia both politically and commercially. It was feared by France for the same reasons. The French saw the re-creation of the Empire of Charles V against which France had fought for two centuries. When, therefore, De Gramont, the French Minister of Foreign Affairs, received a telegram from Berlin announcing the acceptance of the crown by Leopold, he determined to resist with all his power, and from the first he said that if Prussia insisted on the candidature it would mean war. He tried first to protest through the ordinary diplomatic channels in Berlin, but Bismarck was away and there was no one who could give serious attention to the French claims. It was denied that it was anything but a family matter for the Hohenzollerns, and falsely asserted that the Prussian Government knew nothing of it.[1] De Gramont determined to bring the matter before the French Assembly. He feared that Leopold might have been accepted by the Spanish *Cortes* before the French protest was heard, and that then France would seem to be insulting Spain. He read on July 6 a short speech, which had been approved by the council of Ministers. In grave language he made it plain that if the candidature was not withdrawn France would regard it as a cause for war. Ollivier followed with equally weighty words. 'The Government

---

[1] E.g., by Von Thile, Bismarck's under-secretary, who had been present at the meeting alluded to above!

desires peace; it desires peace passionately; but it must be an honourable peace.'

The war cloud was very threatening, but for a time it seemed as if it would pass. Agencies were set to work from at least four sides to induce Prince Leopold to withdraw his candidature, and on July 12 there came the welcome news that he had consented to do so. Prussia seemed to retreat before the threatening attitude of France. Thiers said that Sadowa was avenged. Guizot said it was the greatest diplomatic triumph he ever remembered. The French Government was not content with it. At a council held at Saint Cloud, at which the Prime Minister, Émile Ollivier, was not present it was decided not to leave the matter where it was but to demand guarantees against renewal of the candidature. Benedetti, the French Ambassador at Berlin, was instructed to demand directly from the King of Prussia, first that he should associate himself with the resignation, and secondly that he should promise not to support the candidature of the Hohenzollern prince if it were raised again. Benedetti presented these demands at Ems on July 13. The King received him courteously, but declared the demands to be inadmissible. In the afternoon he received official news of Leopold's resignation and sent to Benedetti to say that he regarded the affair as ended. Peace once more seemed possible.

It was the action of Bismarck which brought war out of an apparent settlement. He believed war to be inevitable sooner or later, and necessary in the interests of Prussia and Germany. But he did not want war unless and until it would appear in public that France was the aggressor. He was discontented with the King's conduct of the French negotiations. He had made up his mind to resign as a protest, and met his two great colleagues, Moltke and Roon, at dinner in Berlin on July 13 and acquainted them with his resolution. While he was at dinner there came a telegram from the King saying that Benedetti had presented demands that were impossible of acceptance; that in the afternoon he had heard officially that Prince Leopold's candidature had been withdrawn; and that in consequence he had sent one of his aides-de-camp to tell Benedetti that the incident was closed and that he could not see him again on that subject. What had happened seemed to Bismarck and to his associates a humiliating surrender to France, and they were plunged in gloom. But Bismarck had been given permission in the message to communicate the event to the press, and he drew up a version and submitted it to the others. The new version certainly misrepresented the original, for it attributed the King's refusal to see Benedetti again not to the receipt of definite news of Leopold's resignation but to the nature of his demands. The new version was, in Moltke's words, not the signal for a parley, but a note of defiance in answer to a challenge. It was communicated to the press, and circulated to the Prussian legations in Germany the same evening and created profound excitement throughout Germany.

Equally disturbing was the effect of Bismarck's message on Parisian and French opinion. The war was brought about not by what happened at Ems but by the false report of what had happened. There was no effort to discover whether the report was false or true. The statesmen of France—even the pacific Ollivier—treated a question which involved the lives of millions in the temper of duellists. France had been insulted: she had received a box on the ear (*un soufflet sur la joue*) and honour demanded immediate war. At a council on July 14 all in the end voted for war. On the 15th the Assembly supported this decision. Hardly a voice was raised on the other side, though Thiers demanded further information as to the exact proceedings at Ems. Ollivier saw his deeply cherished hopes of peace disappear; but he accepted war. he said, 'with a light heart,' because his conscience was clear.

There were, of course, greater and deeper causes of war than Bismarck's 'doctoring' of the Ems telegram; but it was the communication prepared by Bismarck for the press at the Berlin dinner-table which actually set alight the flames of the great war which led up to the vastly greater war of 1914. A little delay to allow nerves to grow steady and passions to cool, the expedient of reference to an external judgment which might have appeased the sense of honour, these things might have prevented the war, at any rate in the shape in which it came.

Chapter 19

THE FRANCO-GERMAN WAR AND ITS EFFECTS

It was generally believed in Europe that France would win in the war which now began. No Great Power had, however, thought it in its interest to rally to her side; not Austria-Hungary, the most likely, not Russia, not Italy, least of all non-interventionist Britain. The South German States fulfilled their obligations under the treaties of 1866–67 and rallied to the side of Prussia. French military prestige stood high; German soldiers were considered to be inferior in scientific training; and their success against Austria was discounted for various reasons. Both armies had recently been reformed.[1] Though the war worked out very closely according to the German programme, the German victories were won by much narrower margins than is always understood. The siege of Paris was unexpectedly prolonged; but Bismarck succeeded in bringing the war to the desired end without a European Congress, which of all things he most feared. Nor is it difficult to detect the main elements of the German success. The German army was scientifically organised and prepared, and all the problems of war had been thoroughly studied. The command was united in the hands of Moltke, who deployed three armies. The German armies were ready long before the French, and they had in the decisive early stages of the war a great superiority in numbers; the Germans are estimated to have had on the frontier in the first encounters 500,000 against 200,000 men because of the chaos of French mobilisation. Moreover, a great enthusiasm swept over Germany and all party spirit was stifled in the ardour of the moment. On the side of France there were divided counsels. The Emperor nominally commanded, but his health was broken and his direction of the war was never more than nominal. The country would doubtless have been swept away by enthusiasm if victory had crowned the French

---

[1] Technical differences in the use of railways, in weapons, in conscripting manpower, in organisation and staff work are discussed in Michael Howard, *The Franco-Prussian War* (1962), chs. 1 and 2.

arms, but, when defeat came, the divisions of the state were quickly seen. Moreover, campaign plans were constantly changed. Mac-Mahon commanded in Alsace; Bazaine in Lorraine. Bazaine was at first the national hero, though before the war ended he came to be regarded either as a fool or a traitor.

On August 6, 1870, the Prussian Crown Prince attacked and defeated MacMahon at Wörth. The battle opened Alsace to the German invasion. MacMahon withdrew the shattered remnants of his forces towards Châlons. On the same day Prince Frederick Charles defeated Bazaine and the army of Lorraine at Spicheren. These were serious and even terrible events. What line should the French commanders pursue? The first idea was to retreat on Paris and fight the next battle in the neighbourhood of the capital, and this plan has generally found the approval of military experts. But throughout the campaign military motives were constantly being overruled by political considerations, and it was so here. The bad news from the frontier had overthrown the Ollivier Ministry, and power was entrusted to Count Palikao, an old soldier, seventy-five years of age, with no political experience. Through him the Empress Eugénie exercised a preponderating influence on the course of the war until the Empire was swept away by disaster. It was believed that a retreat on Paris would be fatal to the new Government; and the Emperor and Bazaine were persuaded to attempt the defence of Metz. But the Germans struck blow on blow. First the French troops were driven in at Borny, to the east of Metz, and then the German armies marched round to the south of Metz with a view to encircling it and shutting up Bazaine and his troops. Bazaine made a half-hearted attempt to escape from the trap; but in a series of encounters, which are usually known as the Battle of Gravelotte, the effort of the French army to break away was defeated, and Bazaine was cooped up with an army of nearly 200,000 men. Napoleon himself had managed to get away and had surrendered the command which he was no longer able to exercise. The superiority of the Germans in the command and in the rank and file, in discipline and initiative, in weapons and in endurance had been demonstrated throughout the operations.

France was now threatened by a terrible catastrophe; but a wise policy might have given her hope and allowed her to prolong the war until other European Powers entered the arena. MacMahon was near Châlons with a force that was large but much demoralised. The Emperor had abdicated the command into his hands. MacMahon resolved to retreat on Paris, to gain what reinforcements he could, and to fight his next battle with the support of the guns of the Paris forts. The wisdom of this decision is admitted; but again it was overruled for political reasons. The Empress felt that a revolution was preparing and that the retreat of the Emperor and the abandonment of the popular hero Bazaine would precipitate it. She shrank from such a blow for her husband's sake, but above all for the sake of her son, the Prince Imperial. A decision was taken in Paris and communicated to MacMahon. Metz and Bazaine were to be relieved at all costs. MacMahon accepted the decision against his own better judgment. The series of operations which followed would probably in any case have been fatal to France. Their only chance of success lay in rapidity and definiteness of plan. But on the French side there were changes of plan almost beyond counting, while Moltke watched the German movements with an alertness which took advantage of every mistake of the enemy. MacMahon marched towards Sedan by the northern route, choosing such roads as seemed most likely to avoid the enemy, and reached Sedan on August 30. All hope of reaching Metz had now disappeared; the Germans were in greatly superior force and had occupied all the bridges. Moreover, Bazaine had done very little to help the army of relief. There was, however, still a hope that the army, or a large part of it, might get back to Paris by Mézières. But MacMahon, though he had determined on this plan, underrated the imminence of the danger. He waited when every minute was of importance. The Germans attacked on the morning of September 1. There was still one line of retreat open, and MacMahon was determined to take that. But he was wounded early in the battle, and the command was taken over, by order of the Paris Government, by Wimpffen, who still cherished the illusion of the possibility of victory. The French forces were driven into the town at every point, and it was attacked by a constant artillery fire. Late in the day the Emperor and the whole army surrendered into the hands of the Prussian King; 104,000 prisoners were taken.

The news of the disaster was at first disbelieved in Paris. But on September 3 Palikao announced the receipt of a telegram from the Emperor: 'The army has been defeated and taken prisoner; I myself am a prisoner.' The Napoleonic dynasty lived on the traditions of military glory attached to the name and collapsed under defeat. A revolution of some sort was certain. The Assembly met, hoping to maintain the control of affairs in its own hands, though some desired to retain the power of the Empress at least in name. But while they deliberated, Paris boiled into insurrection. The National Guards should have defended the hall but joined with the insurgents, who invaded the body of the hall and the galleries. Amidst great confusion a vote, declaring the Napoleonic dynasty at an end, was about to be taken, when Jules Favre declared that the Hôtel de Ville was the proper place for such a revolutionary decision, and induced the crowd to march thither. At the Hôtel de Ville there was a moderate and constitutional republican party as well as a more violent section, which was later identified with the Commune. In order to exclude this latter party from power, a motion was made to form a provisional

Government consisting of all the deputies of the department of the Seine, including those who, first elected for that department, had later adopted another constituency. Paris thus took the helm in her hands; the rest of France was not consulted. Trochu was Minister of War; Jules Favre took the Department of Foreign Affairs; Gambetta was Minister of the Interior. The title of the new Government was 'the Government of National Defence.' The Republic was not mentioned, nor was the Empress Eugénie threatened. But she was frightened by the memories of Paris revolutions, and the fate of Marie Antoinette had always been before her eyes. She left the palace and found a night's shelter with an American dentist in the suburbs, and the next day made her way to a life-long exile in England.

The Germans had won the war. Could the war end now? Bismarck had shown his diplomatic insight by bringing the war with Austria to an end at the earliest possible moment. Would he act in the same way in this greater war? Germany had overthrown the Empire; could it make peace with the Republic of France? There seemed no absolute reason against it. If the end had come at once Bismarck would have given Europe peace and made alliance between France and Germany not impossible. The stream of European history would have flowed down a different channel from that which has conducted Germany and Europe through three-quarters of a century of unrest. But Bismarck was already preparing the public mind for the annexation of Alsace and Lorraine, and that made a peace or reconciliation impossible.

When the German troops appeared before Paris Jules Favre determined to ask for an interview with Bismarck, and he met his great adversary at Ferrières, near Paris, on September 18. Bismarck made it clear that Germany demanded the Rhine lands. 'You would have had no scruple in seizing from us the banks of the Rhine, although the Rhine is not your national frontier. We recapture our own lands, and we believe that we thus assure ourselves of peace for the future.' Jules Favre had declared that France would not cede an inch of territory or a single stone of her fortresses; and thus peace was impossible. The two men met again later, and Favre shed tears before his iron antagonist; but he could win no concession, and the war went on.

The Germans made no notable additions to their military laurels during the rest of the war. They made no attempt to take Paris by assault, but were content to blockade it and to drive back the attempts of the garrison to break out. They believed that failure of food supplies would produce an early surrender, and they were amazed and exasperated by the long resistance, which lasted from September 20 to January 28. Paris had plenty of men: 80,000 troops of the line, including the naval brigade; 115,000 of the *Garde Mobile*, a sort of reserve, who elected their own officers and were soon notorious for their lack of discipline; and perhaps 350,000 of the National Guards, who also elected their own officers and were quite unwilling to submit to discipline of any kind. Trochu was in command. He was frightened of the Parisians, and did not attempt the rigorous measures which the situation demanded. There was plenty of courage, patriotism, and enthusiasm in Paris, but little discipline, and it was Trochu's great fault that he did not insist on it.

Outside Paris, France had two main sources of hope. Gambetta, one of the few young men in a Government which consisted largely of old men, left Paris in a balloon to organise the war in the provinces. He is the one heroic figure of the war on the French side. He could boast with truth that despair had never come near his heart, and he gave France hope as well. His efforts failed, but the memory of what he attempted has allowed France to look back on these tragic months with pride as well as humiliation. He was immensely helped by an engineer, Freycinet; but his own energy, eloquence, and contagious enthusiasm must be mainly credited with the great results achieved. He raised an army of 600,000 men and equipped it with arms and food, mostly purchased from England. He found some really good commanders—d'Aurelle de Paladines, Faidherbe, and above all Chanzy. On November 9 de Paladines attacked the Germans at Coulmiers, to the north of Orleans, and gained a considerable victory—the only real victory won by the French during the war. It vastly raised the morale of the troops, and Frenchmen began to dream of driving out the Germans from France, as the English had been driven out by Joan of Arc when the outlook for France was even worse.[1]

But there was a third factor on which everything depended—Bazaine and Metz. While they held out, a large German army was kept in inaction, and Bazaine's obvious duty was to hold out to the last possible moment. His actual conduct is still the subject of much controversy. He never accepted the new Government quite loyally, and thought less of the actual war than of what was to come after it. He spoke of his army as destined to become 'the palladium of order,' and he may have hoped to restore the imperial dynasty. His conduct of the siege has found no one to defend it. The sorties that he attempted were conducted without energy. His army and even the civilian population of Metz were in favour of continuing the struggle; and provisions were not entirely exhausted when he capitulated with his army of 173,000 men on October 29, 1870.

Perhaps Gambetta's cry, 'Bazaine has betrayed us,' is not justified, but he was unquestionably right when he said that the avalanche of German troops that poured down from Metz was the ruin of all

---

[1] For the 'arming of the nation' and the importance of the *franc-tireurs*, see Michael Howard, *The Franco-Prussian War* (1962). pp. 244–56.

his schemes. After the war Bazaine was tried, and found guilty of not having done 'all that duty and honour prescribed.' He was sentenced to death, but the sentence was commuted to imprisonment for twenty years. He escaped and died in 1888 in Spain.

Henceforth, though the French fought hard, fortune never smiled on them. Chanzy showed high military qualities in his conduct of the war in the west, but his troops got out of hand. He was beaten at Le Mans and his army dissolved. Faidherbe had no better fortune in the north. He too is reckoned a really fine soldier, but his troops were demoralised, and on January 19 he was decisively and finally beaten near Saint Quentin. In the south-east Bourbaki, an old general of the Empire, tried to relieve Belfort, which was being besieged by the Germans and gallantly defended. He was associated with Garibaldi, who had come to the help of the French in their adversity. But the hero of Italian liberty failed entirely to realise the hopes that were attached to his name. Age had told upon him, and he found the trained German troops proof against the methods which had been so successful in Sicily and Italy. Bourbaki's effort in this region had already failed when the armistice came. Through the negligence of Jules Favre his troops were not included in its stipulations. They were driven into Switzerland, where 80,000 frost-bitten and famine-stricken men laid down their arms.

The avowed aim of all these operations in the provinces was to relieve the siege of Paris. Their failure inevitably brought about the surrender of the capital. The besieged troops had tried to break out, but in vain. The greatest effort was made on November 30 under the command of Ducrot, who declared that whatever happened, 'You will not see me retreat.' Some successes were gained, but were soon swept away, and Ducrot retreated in spite of his promise. The Germans decided at last to bombard the city, but with little effect on the temper of the population. The last attempt at a sortie was made on January 19, and it was a complete failure. There was no hope from the provincial armies, and the food supplies were nearly finished. Jules Favre went to meet Bismarck in Versailles and an armistice was signed on January 28. Bismarck could not recognise the Government of National Defence as capable of speaking for France. New elections were therefore to be held at once, and the Assembly that issued from them was to meet at Bordeaux to accept or reject the terms of peace.

Thus the war ended. But it had been accompanied and it was followed by important diplomatic and political movements which added still further to the significance of its history.

The war was fought out as a duel between the two great combatants. It was the constant fear of Germany and the hope of France that Europe would interfere, and that the war would develop into a European struggle which would call the German armies from the heart of France. Germany was well served by the friendship of the

Russian Tsar, which it had been one of the constant objects of Bismarck to secure. Later, Bismarck publicly thanked him for having prevented the war from developing into a general European struggle.

Of all the French statesmen of the day Thiers had far the highest European reputation. His great learning, his eloquence, and his aloofness from the policy of Napoleon III had made of him one of the foremost of European figures. In September 1870 he accepted the proposal of the Government of National Defence that he should make a tour of the Governments of Europe to secure sympathy and help for France. He was an old man, and the task was laborious, but he carried it through with energy, and it was not his fault that it was not successful. He found Austria-Hungary friendly, but weak; Britain determined to maintain her isolation from Europe; Russia pro-Prussian; Italy prodigal in friendly words, but anxious not to provoke the hostility of Prussia. On his return he attempted to negotiate an armistice so that the opinion of France might be consulted. The attempt failed, as the Germans would allow no revictualling of the besieged city.

There was a moment when it seemed that Russia might unintentionally contribute to the relief of France from her embarrassments. After the Crimean War the victorious Powers—and chiefly France and Great Britain—had forced on Russia a clause in the Treaty of Paris by which the Black Sea was declared neutral, and Russia was thus deprived of the right of maintaining there any military or naval establishment. Probably the clause could in no case have been enforced for long, but now that France was humbled in the dust Russia saw her chance. She denounced the clause. France was powerless to enforce it, but some regarded the action of Russia as a direct challenge to Great Britain, which she could not fail to accept. The British Prime Minister, Gladstone, however, had other views, for he was determined to maintain the peace if possible. He sent a messenger to Bismarck at Versailles: it marks the prestige of Prussia that it was necessary to consult the great Prussian on a question in which Prussia was not directly concerned. A way out was found by means of a conference, which was called to London. The face of Britain was saved by a declaration that no one party to a Treaty could denounce it by herself, and by a restatement of the rules governing the closure of the Straits of the Bosphorus and the Dardanelles; but no effort was made to save the neutrality of the Black Sea. A French representative only appeared at the last session, and France is thought to have neglected a great opportunity of presenting her case against Prussia before the conference, or bringing about a 'general European conflagration' from which she might have reaped advantage.

Just before the armistice, when the victory over France was already secure, Bismarck had realised one great aim of his life. The greater part of Germany was united in an Empire in which Prussia held the predominant position. The stupendous triumph of German arms had united north and south and effaced, at least for the moment, their longstanding jealousies. Before the matter could be accomplished there was delicate negotiation, which was of course undertaken by Bismarck. In 1849 the King of Prussia had refused the German Empire, when offered by hands which seemed to him tainted by democracy. That mistake must not be made again, and the King of Bavaria was induced to make the actual offer. But before the end was reached there were some difficult questions to be solved. The King of Prussia was proud of his royal title and did not relish extinguishing it under the more showy name of Emperor; only the insistence of Bavaria induced him to forgo his objection. Then there was the question whether the new ruler should be Emperor of Germany or German Emperor, which roused some politicians to great excitement, and was finally settled in favour of 'German Emperor' as implying no lordship over German soil. Men asked, too, what relation this Empire bore to the old Holy Roman Empire whose last shadow had disappeared in 1806. Was the German Empire to be established or re-established? No decision was given, but the general opinion of statesmen and historians was that there was real continuity between the old and the new. The final scene took place in the Hall of Mirrors at Versailles on January 18, 1871. William was acclaimed German Emperor. The Crown Prince declared 'the interregnum of sixty-five years is over and the Kaiserless terrible time is past.' To the King himself it was no very welcome change. He is described as 'morose' during the whole day, and he informed the Queen that he 'was inclined to abdicate and hand over everything' to the Crown Prince.

No constitutional difficulties were raised by the new title. The constitution of the North German Confederation had been drawn up with a view to the possibility of the accession of the states of Southern Germany. Bavaria, Württemberg, Baden and Hesse Darmstadt took their places along with Prussia and Saxony, and little protest was raised against the change. Blood shed in common in victorious battle is, declared a Prussian historian, a wonderful cement.

Bismarck had not perhaps desired a national and united Germany, but rather a Prussian leadership of German Princes. On that idea at any rate the structure was based, and the new constitution (1871) bore the impress of the particularism and sectionalism once rampant in the Confederation. It was an adaptation to all Germany of the constitution of the North German Confederation created after the Austro-Prussian War. The King of Prussia, as in 1866, and his Chancellor Bismarck, headed the new Federal organisation. It was termed the German Empire. Its head was merely the hereditary President of a Federation. The key to his power lay in the fact that he was King of Prussia, a state as large as, and more important than, all the other members of the new Empire.

In theory the rights of the smaller states were strictly preserved. The *Reichsrat*, or Imperial Council, was a powerful body. It had the character both of a federal executive and of an upper chamber in a federal legislature. There was no other federal executive. It consisted of fifty-eight members. Of these only seventeen were Prussian, though Prussia ultimately secured control of three more votes. Prussia could be voted down by a majority in ordinary legislation but, as constitutional amendments could be vetoed by fourteen votes (Article 78), Prussia had a permanent veto on constitutional change.[1] In practice the solid front of Prussian delegates, whom smaller states generally followed, was sufficient to enable her to get her way in ordinary legislation. In any case the *Reichsrat* was a thoroughly conservative institution.

The Reichstag, or federal Parliament, was Bismarck's masterpiece. It was elected by universal secret manhood suffrage and contained 397 members. But though in appearance democratic, it was, in reality, limited in all ways. It was much weaker than the *Reichsrat* and much less experienced in the conduct of business. The Imperial Chancellor and Imperial Secretaries of State, after central departments such as the Imperial Treasury (1875) were set up, attended in the Reichstag, but the Secretaries were officials, not politicians, and neither they nor the Imperial Chancellor resigned if their legislative proposals were defeated. The quotas to the army were fixed by previous arrangement with each state and embodied in the constitution. They could not therefore be altered except by constitutional amendment. All that the Reichstag could do was to refuse to vote additions to these quotas. The navy and the Colonies hardly existed in 1871 so that, in later years, the Reichstag had power to vote supplies for them, and could have refused to do so at will. Over foreign policy the Reichstag had little control; for treaties, both diplomatic and commercial, were usually concluded for longer periods than the life of a single Reichstag, with the express object of preventing them from being criticised at an election. There was thus little scope for the assertion of parliamentary control over important matters. And this power was still further impaired by the fact that the Reichstag was always split into many parties, which rendered opposition to the Government difficult. Yet the Chancellor needed a coalition of supporters in order to make a majority to pass his legislative proposals and there were some measures, such as the tobacco monopoly, which he never persuaded it to pass.

---

[1] Voting in the *Reichsrat* was by states not by individuals, e.g. Prussia's vote was cast as a whole, for or against a Bill, and was returned as seventeen votes.

Bismarck had thus settled the internal government of Germany by supplying it with an Imperial Council representing states, with a pseudo-democratic Reichstag representing numbers, with a constitution excluding many matters from the competence of both bodies, and which could not be amended without Prussia's permission. The states retained their separate rulers (Kings, Grand Dukes and Dukes), their separate ministries and separate parliaments. Bismarck had built up the whole fabric of Germany on a firm conservative basis. Prussia, through her prestige, her money, her power, and because Prussian Ministries conducted much imperial business, was emphatically the 'predominant partner.'

The armistice had been concluded in order to allow of the election of a representative French Chamber before which the terms of peace might be brought for rejection or ratification. France generally was weary of the war, though there were some voices raised loudly for its continuance. Gambetta believed in continuing the struggle; and his opposition had to be overcome by force. Faidherbe and Chanzy said, and perhaps believed, that it was still possible to fight on. But France was anxious for peace. No other issue was placed before the electors, and a large majority of the members were pledged to bring the war to an end. The 600 members met at Bordeaux, far from the possible influence of the German army. Thiers, who had been elected by twenty-six constituencies, was appointed 'Chief of the Executive Power of the French Republic'; Jules Favre still held the Ministry of Foreign Affairs, but the real conduct of negotiations was in the safer hands of Thiers. As soon as the Assembly was constituted in Bordeaux, Thiers went off to interview Bismarck at Versailles. There was little negotiation to be done unless he was willing to risk the renewal of war. Bismarck had made up his mind on the general features of the Peace. He was determined to annex Alsace and most of Lorraine. Though he personally would have been willing to hand back the city and fortress of Metz to the French, in the end he yielded to the urgency of the soldiers, and insisted on the cession of Metz as well as of Strassburg. France had to pay a great indemnity, though its figure was reduced from two hundred and forty millions to two hundred millions sterling through the efforts of Thiers. There were many stipulations as to the payment of the indemnity, the conditions of which were stiffened after the outbreak of the Commune in Paris, and as to the maintenance of a German garrison of occupation until the terms of the treaty were complied with. On one point Thiers had gained an important concession. It had originally been proposed that Belfort should be annexed to Germany along with Strassburg and Metz; and Belfort was of the utmost importance as controlling an all-important entry into France from the South of Germany. Thiers threatened to withdraw and leave the

Germans to govern France, rather than abandon this place. Thiers had played his last card. Bismarck, after consultation with the King and Moltke, agreed to leave Belfort in French hands if Thiers would allow German troops to make a triumphal entry into Paris. Thiers accepted at once.

With these terms Thiers hurried back to Bordeaux and submitted them to the Assembly. It was impossible not to accept them, but some strong protests were made. M. Keller, on behalf of Alsace and Lorraine, had declared 'their immutable will to remain French.' Now, when the terms were heard, the representatives of the lost provinces declared that what was done was 'in contempt of all justice and an odious abuse of power.' 'We declare once more that a compact which disposes of us without our consent is null and void.' Violent protest, too, came from certain representatives of Paris. They declared that the Assembly had surrendered two provinces and had dismembered France, and that it was no longer the voice of the country. Several of them resigned as a consequence. Victor Hugo, too—a name venerable to all Europe—resigned. His summary of the situation is noteworthy: 'Henceforth there are in Europe two nations which will be formidable—the one because it is victorious, the other because it is vanquished.'

As a result of the war the French troops left Papal territory (August 19, 1870), a large Italian force entered Rome (September 20), and a plebiscite united her to Italy on October 2.

The Peace Treaty was ratified on March 1. In its definitive form it was signed at Frankfurt on May 10. Thirty thousand German troops entered Paris and stayed there a short time, irritating by their presence the passions of the Parisians which were shortly to boil over into a terrible insurrection.

Chapter 20

THE FOUNDATION OF THE THIRD FRENCH REPUBLIC

The Assembly at Bordeaux had been elected nominally for one purpose only—to establish peace with Germany. Many maintained that it had no mandate for anything else and that when once peace was signed it ought to dissolve. But France was faced by many pressing questions, and it seemed dangerous to have another general election after so short an interval. The Assembly persisted in regarding itself as a sovereign assembly, resting on the choice of the people of France and competent to decide whatever questions presented themselves. The most important question was the form of government under which the country was to live for the future. Of the 600 members of the Assembly at least two-thirds were in favour of a return to some form of monarchy, Legitimist, Orleanist, or Imperial. Yet this predominantly royalist Assembly established the Republic. That is the paradox of the next decade of French history.

The rising of the Commune in Paris had an important influence. There had been, from the Revolution of 1789 onwards, a constant contrast between Paris and the provinces of France; Paris had usually been progressive and radical, while the provinces were conservative. The peasants especially were always ready to reject any measure which seemed to interfere with or endanger the security of their land. Both Napoleons had been able to count on the support of the peasantry, of whom they constituted themselves the champions. Paris, in spite of all Napoleon III's efforts, had remained obstinately republican. The city had suffered severely during the siege, and believed itself to have been badly treated at the Peace. The entry of the German troops had exasperated public feeling, which was also alarmed by political fears for the future. For it was generally believed that the Assembly would establish a monarchy, and against this Paris solemnly protested. Of all the causes that produced the rising of the Commune the fear of the re-establishment of monarchy was, in the opinion of Thiers himself, the most operative. During the first months of the war and after the armistice a vast number of the more prosperous citizens had left the city, and thus the conservative element in the population was weakened. At the same time there was an influx of troops in process of being demobilised. Moreover, the National Guards had not been disarmed. They took the leading part in the outbreak, especially in its early incidents.

Paris had not ceased since 1848 to ferment with eager speculation on all manner of social questions. Saint-Simon, Fourier and Proudhon had each their supporters; there were Blanquists and socialists of 1848; there were members of the International Workingmen's Association, founded in 1864; there were Marxists of a sort. The Communist Manifesto belonged to 1848 and there were many clubs and groups in Paris to spread versions of Marx's system though *Das Kapital* (1867) may not itself have exercised any great influence. Marx, indeed, acclaimed the Commune, quite wrongly, as 'the glorious working men's Revolution', as 'the first revolution in which the working class was openly acknowledged as the only class capable of social initiative'[1]. This was the legend it bequeathed to European communism. It should not be underrated. Legends have their own dynamism. The truth was different. Twenty-five members of the Commune (or municipal council), elected on March 26, were manual workers, the remaining sixty-five were members of the bourgeoisie. The inclusion from time to time of a number of foreigners gave it a certain international flavour. Its programme was a protest against the centralised State. The vision it had of France was a federation of independent Communes or municipalities, which meant a federation of the great cities, organised on a basis of collectivism. The manifesto of the Commune published on April 20, 1871, makes this clear.

> What does [Paris] wish? The recognition and consolidation of the Republic, the only form of Government compatible with popular rights. . . . Absolute autonomy of the Commune extended to all parts of France. . . . The autonomy of the Commune will have as its only limit the right of autonomy equally valid for all other Communes. . . . They are deceived or deceive the country who accuse Paris of aiming at the destruction of the French unity accomplished by the Revolution. . . . . Political unity as Paris desires it, is the voluntary association of all local initiatives.

Its actions in power were to separate Church from State, to pass a number of anti-clerical measures and to enact a few limited laws clearly wished for by the working man: it abolished the variety of fines by which employers arbitrarily reduced wages, it abolished night work for bakers' journeymen, it tried to stop the activities of pawnbrokers, it empowered associations of workingmen to take over

---

[1] Karl Marx, *Civil War in France*, originally an address to the International Workingmen's Association, May 30, 1871.

closed workshops and factories. It did nothing revolutionary.

The movement may be dated from March 18. The Assembly had, partly in anticipation of the coming outbreak, been moved from Bordeaux to Versailles. The number of troops then at the disposal of Thiers was small—not more than 20,000. He ordered them to remove a number of guns from Montmartre. These guns had been made during the siege by the people of Paris and they refused to surrender them. The troops were surrounded by a huge crowd and prevented from taking the guns. Thiers believed that the number of soldiers in Paris was quite insufficient to maintain order, and that they might themselves be overwhelmed. He ordered them to evacuate the city and Paris was to be reconquered from outside. The struggle lasted until May 28—just over two months. Thiers as head of the executive Government had to bear the burden of the responsibility for the suppression of the rising and the reconquest of Paris. He was seventy-four years of age, but he had always taken a keen interest in the organisation and conduct of military operations, and nothing seemed to diminish his confidence or his energy. He had served, as we have seen, the Orleanist dynasty and in theory preferred a constitutional monarchy to a republic; but he had solemnly promised that he would not influence the decision of the Assembly in any unfair way. The confidence which all parties felt in him was a valuable asset for France at this crisis. He induced Marshal MacMahon, recovered from the wound that he had received at Sedan, to accept the supreme command. Thiers refused without hesitation the offer of German help, but he brought home by sea from Hamburg 60,000 French prisioners of war. He had never more than 150,000 men with which to subdue the great city. If the Commune had ever any chance of success it was ruined by the unceasing quarrels and jealousies of the authorities. Nominally, power was in the hands of the Commune which had been elected on March 26. It delegated its powers very largely to a committee of five persons called the Committee of Public Safety, in which Delescluze became later the one dominating personality. But the National Guards were in effect an independent force, and elected a central committee which refused obedience to the Commune.

The Communards were at first confident of victory. The miracles of the first French Revolution would be repeated. The other great cities of France would come to their help. The soldiers fighting for liberty and social regeneration would be inspired by their cause to superhuman efforts. But nothing of the sort happened; and from the first contacts with the troops of Versailles it was clear that the Parisians could not hope to defeat the trained soldiers of France, even though their morale had been shaken by defeat in the German War. MacMahon made careful preparation of artillery. His bombardment of the twice besieged city began at the end of April. Two important forts were taken, and the general assault was arranged for May 23. But in Paris there was no possibility of resistance. The great mass of the Parisians took no part either for or against the Communards. On May 21 a signal was made from the fortifications to the soldiers that the walls had been abandoned, and Thiers superintended the entry of the troops into the suburbs of Paris without encountering any resistance.

Even then the worst was yet to come. The central streets of the city were closed by barricades and obstinately defended, and were only captured after fighting of great cruelty on both sides. Some noble buildings in Paris were set alight with petrol, and some of the most famous—the Hôtel de Ville and the Tuileries among them—were burnt down. On May 24 the Archbishop and some others who had been held as hostages by the insurgents and whom Thiers had refused to exchange for Blanqui, were killed. It was not until May 28 that the last barricade was taken. Then followed a horrible revenge, sometimes under legal forms, sometimes without them. Many were put to death; multitudes were exiled to the penal colonies. The slaughter of the army had already been unparalleled, far worse than in the June days of 1848. After the surrender, between 20,000 and 25,000 people were summarily executed or killed. In addition 38,578 were arrested. Of these 10,137 were convicted during the next two years and nearly half of these were then deported to the penal colonies. 'Paris after the Commune was a different city.'[1] Its suppression was perhaps more important than its life; for that left a legacy of terrible bitterness. The gulf it made between class and class, party and party, lasted into the twentieth century. On the other hand, it is probable that the events in Paris did much to secure the Republic. The Commune had shown the fierce determination of the capital of France not to see the re-establishment of the monarchy.

The defeat of the Commune brought the Assembly face to face with its great tasks. The first of these was the settlement of relations with the Germans. The Treaty had to be signed, and in order to secure the evacuation of French territory by German troops the indemnity would have to be paid. The personality and reputation of Thiers were of immense value to France in dealing with Bismarck, who was inclined to adopt a truculent and suspicious tone towards France. The definitive Peace was signed, as we have seen, at Frankfurt on May 10, 1871; but German troops were still in possession of twenty departments and would remain there until France could raise the required money. Thiers had great financial knowledge and much credit with the financial world. The money required was raised with astonishing ease, and Germany regarded the unexpectedly rapid recovery of France with suspicion and dislike, for the evacuation took

[1] T. Zeldin, *France 1848–1945* (1973), Vol. I, p. 744.

place two years earlier than was anticipated. But she carried out loyally the stipulations of the Treaty. The German troops left, and the Assembly declared that Thiers 'had deserved well of the country.'

It was a great triumph for the aged President, or rather the Head of the Executive, to give him his proper title. But on the future constitution of France the attitude of the President satisfied only a small section of the members of the Assembly. He had promised that he would not exercise any unfair influence on the decision of the Assembly; but he did not think that that promise prevented him from giving advice. He availed himself constantly of the right, which his position as President gave him, to address the House on any topic. He spoke indeed so often and, perhaps we should add, so well that the right was later limited by definite enactment. Thiers's own views were quite clear. He preferred a constitutional monarchy to a republic; but he believed that the actual situation made a monarchy impossible. 'All governments,' he said, 'whatever their names, are now essentially republican in character'; he insisted that events had in fact given France a republic, and that to establish any sort of monarchy would be, under actual circumstances, a real revolution.

The Assembly, however, was predominantly monarchist; and would not accept a republican solution willingly. The restoration of the Empire had few open supporters. If Napoleon III had lived there would perhaps have been some attempt in that direction, but he died in England. There were now two systems and two men who divided the allegiance of the monarchists. The Comte de Paris represented the constitutional traditions of the House of Orleans. He had seen much of the world and was believed to hold liberal opinions. The hope of the Legitimists, of those who clung to indefeasible hereditary right and the close union of the throne and the altar, was Henri, Comte de Chambord. He lived in the neighbourhood of Vienna and was without political ambition. The relations between these two royalist parties raised insuperable difficulties later, but for the moment the first thing was to get rid of Thiers. A motion, which was practically a vote of no confidence, was moved 'regretting that the policy of the Government was not resolutely conservative.' Thiers answered by defending his acceptance of the Republic. 'My reason is,' he said, 'that to-day for you and for me, in fact, the monarchy is absolutely impossible. There is only one throne, and three people cannot sit on it at the same time.' The House voted against him by a small majority and he resigned (May 24, 1873).

He was succeeded in the Presidency by Marshal MacMahon, who immediately nominated a new Ministry. He had hardly mixed in politics at all; but his royalist sentiments and his devotion to the Church were well known. He had no brilliance of thought or speech; but all acknowledged his uprightness, honesty, and seriousness of purpose. The Assembly had suffered under Thiers's continual brilliance, and welcomed the change. His mission was clear. He was to preside over the process by which the monarchy would be established. That was his own wish and the wish of his followers. Yet in fact the Republic was founded during his presidency!

Even if the royalists had been united the monarchy would not have been founded without a sharp struggle. But all attempts to unite them proved unavailing. The Comte de Paris went to see the Comte de Chambord. As Chambord was childless it seemed a natural solution that he should reign first, and that he should be succeeded by the House of Orleans. But if Chambord became king, on what principles would he reign? Would he insist on repudiating all that the French Revolution meant, or would he accept some of its principles? The question was summed up in the symbol of the flag. Would the Comte de Chambord insist on using the traditional white flag of the Bourbon House—the flag of Henry of Navarre and of Louis XIV—or would he accept the tricolour, with all its associations of revolution and of military glory? The Comte de Chambord refused to adopt the tricolour and never yielded. Fusion of Legitimists and Orleanists proved impossible. The cause of monarchy was lost. But the Assembly only slowly and unwillingly came to take the unwelcome decision. First it gave Marshal MacMahon 'the executive power' for seven years and appointed a commission to examine constitutional projects. Various resolutions were brought forward and rejected; but the by-elections ran against the monarchists and had a considerable influence on the Assembly. The decisive vote was taken on an amendment proposed by a deputy named Wallon, determining the method of election of the 'President of the Republic', not of MacMahon personally. On January 30, 1875, it was adopted by a majority of a single vote, and by this narrowest of majorities France was committed to a republic.

A series of measures established piecemeal the form of this Third French Republic. The new constitution was not one of those clearly arranged logical constitutions that France has often loved. It was the result of constant compromises, unwillingly adopted, by an Assembly which hoped that they would not last long. '*Le hasard fût notre maitre*,' said one who took a prominent part in its debates. It came to an end at last on December 31, 1875.

France was to be a republic, and the head of the Republic was to be a President elected by the two Chambers (the Chamber of Deputies and the Senate) in common session. There were strong arguments against this method; but the one argument in its favour was sufficient. The only alternative, that of a plebiscitary election, had brought Napoleon III to power in 1851, and might very likely produce similar results again. So a method was adopted which handed France over to a series of Presidents of small political power and importance. This was not clear until 1877 when MacMahon tested the power of the President and was defeated. There was universal manhood suffrage of all over twenty years of age. Elections to the Chamber of Deputies occurred automatically every four years and to the Senate every three years, though individual Senators were elected for nine years. At first the Senate had contained seventy-five members nominated for life, but this provision was soon omitted. So that in the end all the Senators were elected by the same curious method; chiefly by delegates appointed for that purpose by the municipal councils of France. Gambetta called the Senate 'The Great Council of the Communes of France.' The provinces had a large measure of self-government, but the new Republic maintained the Prefects, the characteristic institution of the First Empire and the descendants of the *intendants* of the old monarchy. They were nominated by the central Government, which gave to France centralised administration and one to some extent protected from popular pressure.

The strength of the new system lay, first, in this administration and in the civil service which staffed the Government Offices and, secondly, in the Chamber of Deputies. The Ministries were unstable. Between 1873 and 1888 there were nineteen Ministries in France, which gives a duration of less than a year to each. Not only did French Ministries have a short life, they also had little control either over their supporters or over the whole Chamber. The explanation of this is not to be found in the French temperament. The instability of French Ministries may at least in part be explained by the following considerations: (1) There were certain Deputies who were recognised as both willing and sufficiently talented to become Ministers and power passed from one to the other according to the coalition of support he was able to negotiate from the spectrum of political opinion represented by the loosely organised parties in the Chamber. There were never two sides, one supporting the Ministry in office and one in opposition offering an alternative Ministry. There was not much sense of party loyalty. Members voted against their own party quite readily; and this tendency was both the cause and the consequence of a multiplicity of parties. (2) The fall of a Ministry was not followed by a general election. In theory the President might, with the consent of the Senate, order a dissolution, but in fact he did not do so. The consequences therefore of throwing out a Ministry were not serious to the individual member: he had not to face at once another election contest with its doubtful issue and its certain expense. (3) This fact enabled the whole Chamber of Deputies to rule effectively. In France Bills were usually introduced by Ministers, but their subsequent development and failure or success depended much more on the whole Chamber, working through its committees or bureaux, which were not chosen on party lines, and decisive changes in a measure were often accepted. The Chamber, conscious of its powers, saw with comparative equanimity the fall of a party

Ministry to which it had for the moment entrusted the executive power.

The Republic was thus founded, and it survived until its destruction by the cataclysm of 1940. But it had come almost by accident and it had many secret enemies. The monarchical parties still existed, though after the death of the Prince Imperial the Imperialists could not agree on any candidate; and the death of the Comte de Chambord did not succeed in uniting the Legitimists and the Orleanists. The President, MacMahon, was by no means prepared to accept the equal and democratic régime which the Republic implied to most of its supporters. He hoped, in close alliance with the Church and by the help of all the agents of government, to maintain the control of the executive and to govern independently of the Chamber of Deputies. The ecclesiastical or Catholic party was very strong and did not accept the Republic. MacMahon was more closely identified with its ideals than with those of royalism itself, and he hoped to maintain the ascendancy of the Church under the Republic. Thus Church and State came into frequent rivalry and conflict, more indeed over educational questions than over politics. The task which the Republic had before it was to control the executive power, to assert its supremacy over the Catholic Church, and to defeat the efforts, secret or open, of the monarchists of every kind.

The year 1877 marked a turning-point in the political development of the Third Republic. In that year MacMahon put the presidential powers to the test. The new Chamber of Deputies, elected in January 1876, had sat for less than a year when he conciliated its majority by putting a new Ministry in office under Jules Simon, an anti-clerical Republican, an ally of Gambetta. The President with his ideas of military honour and discipline and the Republican with his idea of the primacy of the popular will, pulled in opposite directions. On May 16, 1877, MacMahon dismissed the Ministry and dissolved the Chamber. He seemed to have revived personal autocracy. But the President proved unable to maintain the conservative, clerical Ministry he had put in office and the general election, despite his imitation of Napoleon's methods of controlling candidates, produced a Chamber with an even stronger Republican majority. MacMahon refused at first either 'to submit or resign,' but in 1879 in fact resigned, a year before he was constitutionally bound to do so. More important, no President after him dissolved the Chamber before its legal term had expired.[1] France was consigned to a weak presidency for the rest of the nineteenth century.

The Republic triumphed in the choice of his successor, which fell on Jules Grévy, a man of the middle class, in close sympathy with

[1] M. Doumergue, who attempted to assimilate the French Constitution to the British in the power to dissolve, failed and resigned in November 1934.

the peasantry, without any leaning towards monarchism or Catholic ascendancy. The country at this time was making great progress industrially and commercially; she embarked again on colonial and imperial schemes. The possibility of the acquisition of Tunis had been discussed at Berlin during the Congress, and Bismarck thought that foreign adventure would turn the mind of France from brooding perpetually over the past or future of Alsace and Lorraine. Tunis was occupied in 1881. Madagascar was brought under French control in 1884. The movement which brought Tonking into the hands of France began in 1882. The mass of the people of France saw these adventures with alarm, and compared them with the Mexican expedition which had done so much to ruin the power of Napoleon III. At home the chief interest lay in the conflicts with the Church over the organisation of a national scheme of education. This scheme was chiefly the work of Ferry, whose Ministry (from February 1883 to March 1885) was the longest that France had for many years. The work done was of the utmost importance. Following largely the example set by Germany, a complete system of state and lay education—primary, secondary, and university—was organised, the effect of which on the later development of France was very great. It existed for some time alongside a private system parallel with it and largely controlled by the Church. We must note, too, that in 1880 the Chamber came from Versailles and took up its permanent seat in Paris. A year later an amnesty was issued to those who had taken part in the rising of the Commune. Thus something was done to bridge over the gulf that the rising of the Paris Commune in 1871 had made between parties and classes. The State, too, took gradually a more frankly democratic character. In 1884 the life tenure of seventy-five seats in the Senate, on which MacMahon had set such store, was abolished. All the seats in the Senate were henceforward to become elective, and the method of election was made more equal. The freedom of the press was extended and assured. Liberty of association was conceded, and led to the formation of trade unions after 1884. Municipal government became more open to local opinion, when, everywhere but in Paris, the municipal councils were given the right to choose their own mayors.

Most of those changes had been advocated strenuously by Gambetta, who represented more than any other man the ideals of the radical republic. There had always been a conservative element in the ideas of the man whom Thiers had once called 'a raving maniac,' and his language had grown more moderate as time passed. In November 1881 he was made Prime Minister, but his Ministry lasted only for three months and left no permanent mark on the life of France. In the general election of 1885 there was no longer a straight fight between monarchists and republicans. The republicans were divided and the conservatives gained a considerable number of seats, but the Republic itself was not seriously threatened.

Grévy had been elected to a second presidential term, but in 1887, on the discovery of a financial scandal, which touched the honour of his son-in-law, he judged it wisest to resign. The last months of his presidency had seen the beginning of the Boulangist movement. This developed into greater importance under Grévy's successor, President Carnot, but had best be briefly noticed here. It flared up suddenly. On the surface it was an effort to procure a revision of the constitution. What should take its place was by no means clear; but all the supporters of Boulanger were agreed in desiring a strengthening of the executive and a reduction in the interference of the Chamber in the work of administration. This might have led merely to a stronger presidency; or it might have given an opportunity to another adventurer of the type of Napoleon III to make himself ruler; or it might have led to the restoration of one of the old monarchical families. General Boulanger himself would certainly not have controlled the movement for long. He was not the imbecile that he was represented by his opponents. He had distinguished himself as a soldier, and had been a respectable Minister of War. But his chief recommendation was his capacity for appealing to the popular imagination, his handsome personal appearance, his fine horse, his highly coloured and vague rhetoric. He first became a popular figure in connection with a frontier incident. A French officer (Schnaebele) had been illegally arrested by the Germans, and Grévy was thought to have accepted the incident too tamely. Boulanger made himself the spokesman of French nationalism and was supported by the League of Patriots. But he also demanded a change in the whole constitution, and his programme was summed up as 'Dissolution, and revision through a specially elected constituent assembly.' The danger to the republican constitution seemed for a time really great. The claims of Boulanger were pressed on the electors by methods unusual in France and borrowed from America. He became a candidate for every constituency where there was a vacancy, and was elected in many with large majorities. He was elected even in Paris, but made little impression on the resolute republicanism of the south and east. In the end the movement failed through the weakness of General Boulanger himself, and through the strong and even violent measures which were taken against him by the Government. The electoral law was altered and Boulanger was accused of 'plotting against the safety of the state.' He fled from France, and soon afterwards committed suicide in Brussels. Boulangism, more broadly understood, was a movement often among the young in search of a cause, an ideal to serve, but also among industrial workers hoping Boulanger would mean a new Government ready to relieve their distress. It was a kind of nationalist counterpart to imperialism; it was both anti-German patriotism and admiration of German discipline, industry and success. It was also a movement for social reform, the nursery of the followers of Jaurès, the later Socialist leader. It is summed up as an attempt to get out of the rut into which France had fallen.

Chapter 21

RUSSIA AND THE EASTERN QUESTION, 1856–86

The situation created by Germany's victory in 1870 did not immediately produce the changes which German hegemony in Europe seemed to suggest. In eight years Bismarck had humbled Britain, crushed Austria and France, and made the second German Reich. But he was wise enough to see that Germany could do no more at present. He wanted peace and time to consolidate his gains and, during that necessary breathing-space, he was quite ready to let other nations take the lead, and snatch at opportunity in areas where German interests were in no way endangered.

At this distance it is easy to see what the lines of expansion for European Powers were. In Asia and in Africa there were still wide opportunities and still unappropriated lands, to which Bismarck could encourage the expansion of Britain and France and thereby divert their attention from Europe. In Europe itself the only field for expansion was offered by the unrest in the Balkans and the increasing decay of Turkey. Here Russia was alike the most interested and ambitious of Powers, and it was difficult for Germany to oppose her. For it was due to Russia's goodwill and support that Bismarck had triumphed over all his enemies. This chapter will show that the years between 1870 and 1878 were the opportunity of Russia in Europe. The next chapter shows that the years between 1870 and 1883 were the opportunity for France and for Britain in Africa. At the end of that period (as we shall see in chapter 23) Bismarck had fixed his alliances and felt sufficiently strong to intervene both in Europe and overseas. During 1884–85 he picked up colonies in two continents, and between 1885 and 1886 he settled the Bulgarian imbroglio in the teeth of Russia. But the result of this forceful intervention everywhere was to cause a regrouping of the Powers, and ultimately to produce the Dual Alliance between France and Russia.

In 1870 Russia had a great opportunity. She had just got rid of the obnoxious clauses of the Treaty of Paris forbidding her to fortify

Sebastopol or to keep a fleet on the Black Sea. She had subdued the Caucasian and most of the Turkoman tribes, and was therefore ready for intervention in Europe. But the effectiveness of such intervention and the probability of success depended on the moral and material condition of Russia. Had she been armed and ready, an athlete among the nations like Prussia, her success would perhaps have been assured.

During the first quarter of the nineteenth century, under the rule of the brilliant but unstable Alexander I, Russia had suffered from alternative doses of enlightenment and reaction. Nicholas I, who succeeded him, had applied to his vast dominions a rule of stern repression and carried out his system with gigantic energy. It was a system summed up in the three words orthodoxy, autocracy and nationality. During 1848–49 his methods seemed justified, for his peoples remained quiet and his army could leave his own dominions to repress revolution in Hungary. But they had alienated important classes. People educated in the Universities were acquainted with the philosophy (e.g. of Schelling, Hegel, Schleiermacher) and literature, the histories and natural science, the economics and technological progress of the west. They were able to study abroad and came back open-minded and critical. Nor were attempts of the bureaucracy to control the Universities, their entrants, curricula and appointments, successful. Such attempts were stimulants to criticism rather than effective restraints. Young men finishing at the Universities, unless they had estates to manage and were prepared to manage them, or could and would gain admission to the upper ranks of the civil service, or would go into the army, could make contact neither with the state machine nor with the peasants. Russian socialism was born among the gentry in Nicholas I's reign. It attracted, however, educated men from many groups: doctors, lawyers, writers, journalists and University teachers. An alienated intelligentsia had already formed in the thirties and forties before Herzen grew out of his twenties. Alexander Herzen (1812–70) and his circle were of the first generation. He was perhaps to the left of V. Belinski and to the right of Michael Bakunin, to mention only two other names. Herzen was arrested and exiled in 1834. In 1847 he emigrated to the west and like Bakunin became a major revolutionary figure. The radical intelligentsia were revolutionaries with dreams of realising human individuality by social revolution and less concerned with civil rights in practical terms. But there were other educated Russians alienated from the régime. The westernisers were inspired by the French Revolution with ideas of personal freedom, civil liberty and representative institutions for Russia. The slavophils wanted in Russia freedom, civil liberty and universal education, but had no wish to imitate the west. Russia should rely on her own traditions and cultivate her own strong sense of community. This last they believed was the most distinctive feature of Russian life. They wanted, not western parliaments, but a revival of the popular consultative assemblies which had once existed in Russia. The Crimean War revealed the true weakness of Russia. Nicholas's loyalty to those who served him gave him in the end mediocre generals and inefficient administrators. The discredit of the Russian Government earned in the Crimean War drove Nicholas to his death (1855) and his system to an abrupt end.

The problem before his son, Alexander II, was to make peace, which he did at Paris in 1856, and then to renew the strength of his ill-equipped and defeated army and navy. He saw that Russian military and state power could not be repaired without social and economic modernisation. The shock of defeat would make the shock of modernisation less of a risk than if attempted in normal times. Modernisation would make of Russia a more solidly integrated nation and perhaps enable her to realise her great potentiality for wealth and prosperity. Alexander also recognised, as he said to a deputation of Moscow nobility in March 1856, that it was better for change 'to come from above than to come from below.' He was still young and had been trained for his task of ruler; he had some knowledge, some sagacity, though slow, obstinate and indecisive. He did not bring to his task vision or imagination and Russia would continue to be an autocracy, governing through a bureaucracy and dependent on the army and Orthodox Church. Ten years later, when the military and internal problems brought to a head by the war had been solved, Alexander reverted to the reactionary routine more natural to him. During the seventies a new revolutionery movement arose. The Populists or Narodniks did not balk at acts of individual terrorism and Alexander II was murdered by one such act in 1881.

Nevertheless the 'great reforms' of the sixties deserve their title. The emancipation of the serfs (February 19, 1861) affected some fifty million (landowners as well as serfs) of Russia's population of sixty million and involved a new structure for Russian society. The education reform (1863) opened secondary education to the sons of peasants; the institution of the *zemstva* (1864) put local government in the countryside into the hands of the gentry and others who sat in these elected bodies; municipal self-government followed in 1870; the relaxation of the press censorship (1865) gave Russia a political press for the first time; military conscription introduced in 1874 was the last but the army had already been fully reformed. The emancipation of the serfs was the foundation of all the rest, but the institution of elected provincial and district council (*zemstva*) and municipal councils was scarcely less important. The abolition of serfdom did not turn Russia into a land of peasant family farms; but nor did it make agriculture into a food-producing industry with capitalist employers and a wage-earning labour force. By 1881 84.7 per cent of former serfs had become owners of their land though they were still paying for it. Servile status was abolished and the owned serf became a free man equal in status with every other Russian. State serfs, serfs belonging to the imperial family and some other special categories, were dealt with separately from the ten million or more serfs belonging to the gentry, on somewhat more favourable terms. The basic principle was the assertion of the landowner's property in all land. This meant that peasant houses and allotments, both round the house and in the common fields, had to be paid for by rent. The second principle was that such allotments of land, intended to be worked out by local agreements, were for the peasant's permanent use, to become eventually his property. This meant that rents were replaced sooner or later—generally quickly—by so-called redemption payments, paid to the state, which then compensated the landowner for his loss of rent by interest-bearing bonds. The state exercised some control over local agreements by laying down certain maxima for the size of allotments, both to protect the former serf-owner and to safeguard the peasant against insufficiency of land. The third principle was the retention of the *obshchina* and the *mir*. The *obshchina* meant that fields were cultivated in strips worked in common and redistributed periodically among individual households. Strips were also rearranged periodically in different blocks. Because the larger the household the larger the allocation, it was customary to hoard the relatively plentiful commodity, labour, in order to obtain the relatively scarce commodity, land; so that the land was overpopulated. The *mir* was the name given to the community of peasants responsible henceforward to the state as a unit for the payment of taxes. Legal obstacles were put in the way of the peasant leaving the *mir*; so that the emancipation did not increase peasant mobility much or much affect the flow of labour into new economic activities. We shall return later to this subject.

As if to justify the reaction of the sixties, Poland broke out in rebellion in 1863. The revolt was hardly justifiable, except on the principle, dear to Polish hearts, that Russian rule could never be tolerated. During 1862 and 1863 the real concessions, offered by the Russian Government, served only to provoke a Polish revolt, which was as ill-timed as it was heroic and hopeless. The Tsar really had an excuse for reaction now. His offers had been scornfully rejected, and Britain and France had foolishly endeavoured to support the Poles. Brutal repression followed, and the Lithuanians, the Livonians, and the Finns soon suffered for the turbulence of the Poles. From about 1866 a period of gloom and reaction set in, and every non-Russian nationality within the Tsar's Empire was brutally oppressed.

In foreign policy, however, the Russian Government had at last hit upon an illuminating idea. In Asia their expansion was due to penal colonies, to military ambition, or to annexationist greed. In Europe the persistent advance to Constantinople could at last be concealed beneath a cloud of high-flown national and racial aspirations.

It was the adoption of a Panslavist policy which made Russian officials romantic, hid Russia's age-long ambitions beneath a sentimental veil, and enabled her to rally the Slavonic brethren in all lands outside her own dominions. This powerful weapon for propaganda was first discovered and used by the Russian Government in the days of Alexander II.

Panslavism did not arise in Russia, but in Austria-Hungary. In that area were seven Slav races who lamented their subjection to the Teuton and the Magyar. For it is 'the captive peoples who fill their dungeons with legends.' The dreamers dreamed, and the scholars toiled, that the shattered fragments of their race might be fused into one vast spiritual whole. It was in 1824 that Jan Kollár, a Slovak, wrote his famous poem of *Slàvy Dcera* (the daughter of Slava). Two phrases of his show the warmth of his imagination and sum up his ideal: 'Scattered Slavs, let us be one united whole and no longer be mere fragments'; and again, 'All Europe would kneel before this idol, whose head would tower above the clouds and whose feet would shake the earth.' Two years later Šafarik, another Slovak, laid a scientific foundation for this poetic aspiration. His grammar of the Slav languages was the first scholarly investigation of the affinities between the varieties of Slavonic speech. His studies attracted the attention of that learned body of Czechs who were slowly building up the foundations of their nationality anew and seeking to drive out both the German speech and the German rule from Bohemia. This propaganda suited their ideas and their purpose, and it was not an accident that the first ethnic and linguistic conference, uniting all members of the Slav race, was held at Prague in 1848.[1] The same year was memorable because the Catholic Croats and Orthodox Serbs united under the leadership of Jellačić and Austria to attack the Magyars.[2] And when Nicholas sent Russian armies into Hungary, he was regarded by Slavs as assisting the Panslavist ideal. Much sympathy was also aroused among all Slav nations, except Poland, when Russia became involved and was defeated in the Crimean War.

Up to this time the Russian Government had unaccountably ignored the Panslavist movement. Alexander I had been a cosmopolitan, Nicholas a Russian whose eye rested on Constantinople but who sought to win his way there by Russian arms alone. The slavophils, as we have seen, began as an opposition group. Under Alexander II they came increasingly into favour with the Government. Crippled in material force by France and Britain in 1856, Alexander II could only make Russia's influence felt for a time by propagandist

---

[1] It is a curious irony that the different Slav races could not use any common tongue, and finally used German as the language of the Congress.

[2] In 1849 Archbishop Strossmayer took up his episcopal residence at Djakovo in Croatia and began his long struggle for the cultural unity of Yugoslavia. He was also, within limits, an ardent advocate of Panslav ideals.

policies and by a general support of the Slav peoples outside his own Empire. In this way he might turn the Slav peoples of the Balkans into the satellites of the Russian planet.

In 1858 Montenegro, which had already shown strong sympathy for Russia, had beaten the Turks at Grahovo. But, during the next few years, her very existence was threatened by Turkey, and Russia came energetically to her support. Rumania, though not a Slav state, was assisted by Russia to complete her unity in 1861. In 1867 Russia interfered to remove the Turkish garrisons from Belgrade and other Serbian fortresses, and thus renewed her intimate connection with Serbia. Russia failed, of course, to win Poland, as we have seen. But in 1867 she held a great ethnic exhibition in Moscow, where delegates of all other Slav races (except the Poles) appeared, and where the Tsar himself addressed the representatives of the other Slav races as 'brother Slavs.'[1] In 1870, as already related, Russia abrogated the Black Sea clauses of the Treaty of 1856. She announced not only that she intended to restore Sebastopol, the great fortress of Southern Russia, but that the Russian navy should again be rebuilt on the shores of the Euxine. As a demonstration of Russian power this was very impressive to brother Slavs, and no doubt greatly encouraged them to rise against the Turks. In reality the demonstration was an empty one enough for Russia did not succeed in building a large fleet in time to affect the situation. Russia's advance against Adrianople was as much facilitated by her command of the Black Sea in 1829 as it was retarded by her lack of it in 1878.

The year 1870 was marked by an even more important and decisive step on the part of Russia. Up till this year the various Christian Slavs of the Balkans, as Bulgars and Serbs, were under the spiritual jurisdiction of the Greek Patriarch of Constantinople. Religion has always been the handmaid of politics in the East, and Russian statesmen thought that they would aggrandise the Slav element in the Turkish Empire if they could create a Slav Patriarch who would emancipate Slavs from Greek influences and from a Greek Patriarch. In seeking thus to create a new religious authority to rule over Slavs as a distinct nationality, Russia bethought herself of the Bulgars. Macedonia was inhabited by Greeks, Serbs, and Bulgars, but the latter were the most numerous. Hence Russia demanded the creation of a Slav Church and religious leader. The Sultan complied in a firman (edict) of March 10, 1870. He recognised the Slavs as a separate religious nation with a separate religious head, independent of the Greek Patriarch of Constantinople; this religious head was to be a Bulgar and was termed the Exarch.[2]

---

[1] A curious incident occurred. The Poles sent no representatives, but the Czechs expressed a hope that Russia and Poland might be reconciled.
[2] He did not actually function till 1872.

Russia thought she had gained much by this concession. In reality the Turk showed a Machiavellian greatness in conceding it. *Divide et impera* had always been the motto of the Turk, and division between Greeks and Slavs in Macedonia was what he desired. No sooner was the purpose announced than the Greek Patriarch excommunicated the Bulgarian Exarch, and their followers took up the quarrel. Fights soon arose between the Greeks or Patriarchists and Bulgars or Exarchists, and rival brigand-bands soon appeared who 'proved their doctrine orthodox, by apostolic blows and knocks.' The Turk rubbed his hands to see Christians at variance, and did everything to encourage their disputes. Moreover, though this policy certainly created a strong Slav bulwark to Greek influence in Macedonia, it also divided the Slavs themselves. There were Serb, as well as Bulgar, elements in Macedonia, and the Serbs hated a Bulgarian Exarch almost as much as they hated a Greek Patriarch. Hence the Bulgarian Exarchate divided not only Greek from Bulgars but Bulgars from Serbs. And in the strife thus created between Bulgars and Serbs Russia was to find one of the gravest difficulties of her foreign policy in the Balkans. For the moment, however, these difficulties were not perceived, as the Serbs were much weaker in Macedonia than the Bulgars. And the creation of a Slav Exarchate certainly promoted a wave of Slav feeling and propaganda throughout the Balkans.

The first signs of revolt began in Bosnia and Herzegovina. The inhabitants there were nearly all Serbs in blood[1] and notoriously undisciplined and warlike. They adjoined Montenegro, whose inhabitants passed their whole existence in fighting the Turks, and the Montenegrin clan-chiefs planned raids to assist the risings in Herzegovina. The Turkish rule was relaxing, because Turkey was approaching bankruptcy. She could not maintain or arm her garrisons and yet at the same time demanded increased taxation from her already oppressed subjects. The Turkish cup of iniquity was full. A bad harvest in 1874 led to risings in both Bosnia and Herzegovina, which became formidable in 1875.[2] The Great Powers were anxious to localise the rising and to remove the causes of complaint, and a note, with a programme of reforms, proposed by Count Andrássy, the Foreign Minister of Austria-Hungary, and circulated on December 30, 1875, was accepted by other Powers and by the Turkish Government early in the year 1876. A second note of May, from which Britain held aloof — the Berlin Memorandum — carried a threat if the Turkish Government did not carry out the reforms.

---

[1] About a third were Catholic, a third Orthodox, and a third Muslim or 'Turks.'
[2] Peter Karageogević (King of Serbia in 1903) went out as a volunteer and took part in this rising.

The latter had no intention of carrying them out. The Bulgars, who had been excited and encouraged by the grant of the Exarchate, now attempted an insurrection. The rebellion was easily put down, but was followed by a set of revolting atrocities, in which some twelve thousand persons (including women and children) were massacred. These incidents occurred in April, and it was long before the true facts or their import were realised in England.

Disraeli, the Prime Minister of Great Britain, was now confronted with a diplomatic crisis of the gravest importance. He was strongly drawn towards the East and had already shown insight in buying the Khedive's shares in the Suez Canal, and in his policy towards India. But his view of the Turk was a mistaken one, based perhaps on his early travels in the Levant. He certainly admired the Arabs and perhaps confused them with the Turks. Certainly the Turk was gallant and a ruler of men, and Disraeli supposed him capable of progress and useful in resisting Russia. He did not understand that even the pettiest Balkan state could pay its way and could avoid massacring its subjects, and that therefore an increase in their territories tended to tranquillise areas previously seething with revolt against the Turk. He did not see that an Asiatic Power which massacred its Christian subjects, which never intended to sanction reform or progress, and defaulted on its debts, was an increasing danger to Europe.

Disraeli began by minimising the scale of the massacres and by suggesting that the anti-Turk agitation had been got up for political purposes, to cover the aggressions and advance of Russia. In this view he was apparently supported by his Ambassador at Constantinople.[1] But the facts had already been revealed by journalists, and a member of the British Embassy from Constantinople reported that the Bulgarian massacres were 'perhaps the most heinous crime . . . of the present century.' Disraeli's cynicism brought Gladstone from a temporary retirement and induced him to publish a pamphlet called *Bulgarian Horrors*. This lashed the British public to frenzy with its passionate descriptions of the atrocities. It concluded with the oft-quoted words 'Let the Turks now carry away their abuses in the only possible manner, namely, by carrying off themselves. Their Zaptiehs and their Mudirs, their Bimbashis and their Yuzbachis, their Kaimakams and their Pashas, one and all, bag and baggage, shall, I hope, clear out from the province they have desolated and profaned.'[2]

The excitement in Russia was naturally great, and the Panslav

[1] By August 7 Disraeli was complaining of Elliot's 'deficiency of information' (Buckle's *Beaconsfield* [1902], vol. VI, p. 46). Kemal, the only reputable Turkish authority, admitted some 6000 dead.

[2] *Bulgarian Horrors and the Question of the East*, [1876], pp. 61–2. It will be seen that the 'bag and baggage' policy, here expressed, is not expulsion of the Turk from Europe, but from Bulgaria, and (p. 54) from Bosnia and Herzegovina.

appeal was irresistible. Montenegro, whose subjects were always bellicose, and Serbia, though ill prepared for war, could resist the popular pressure no longer. On June 30, 1876, Serbia and on July 1 Montenegro, plunged into war with Turkey. The Montenegrins won many successes, but the Serbs were badly beaten at the end of October, and only an ultimatum from Russia prevented the Turks from advancing on Belgrade. It was now a problem as to whether Russia would not be compelled by popular sympathy to join her brother Slavs. At the end of October the Tsar was informed by Great Britain that, whatever might be the feeling as to Turkish atrocities, she must protect her interests in the Suez Canal and Constantinople. Alexander II, on November 2, gave a solemn assurance that he had no design of annexing Constantinople or Bulgaria. Disraeli, now Lord Beaconsfield, remained unconvinced and violently anti-Russian. On November 9 he spoke publicly at the Mansion House in this sense, and obviously expressed disbelief in the Tsar's pledges and Russia's disinterestedness. The Tsar announced publicly, on the next day after Beaconsfield's speech, that he would act *independently* of the other Powers of Europe, if he failed to secure adequate guarantees from the Turk for the future protection of her Christian subjects.

Meanwhile cooler heads than those of Russian Tsar or British Premier had arranged for a Conference of the Powers at Constantinople. Britain sent to it the man who was to understand the problem best and was now to win his first diplomatic laurels—Lord Salisbury. His first experience was a study in disillusion. Abdul Hamid had become Sultan at the end of August, and, though young, was about to astonish the world with one of those transformation-scenes, of which he was to prove so consummate a master. The day before the Conference of the Powers met at Constantinople to demand reforms, Abdul Hamid endowed Turkey with a constitution. The Sultan, as a liberal and constitutionalist, blandly informed the Conference that Turkey was now a reformed state, and that he ought not to be asked to surrender his sovereign rights over his own subjects, when he had invited them to share in his Government. The Conference, thus nonplussed and baffled, broke up without accomplishing anything. Abdul Hamid, thus at liberty, ended the constitution in May 1877, disgraced Midhat Pasha, its champion, at once, and murdered him a few years later.[1]

It seems quite clear that the action of Abdul Hamid was governed by the belief that Britain would support him against Russia, as she had done in the Crimean War, for a British naval squadron was already in Besika Bay.[2] He was woefully mistaken. When Russia and

[1] Not till 1882, as Britain made efforts to protect him.
[2] It had been ordered there in May 1876.

Britain presented joint demands in April he rejected them, and Alexander replied to this rejection by declaring war. Rumania joined Russia in an alliance, and Montenegro again renewed the war. It was some two months before the Russian and Rumanian armies got into Bulgaria. There they were held up by the military genius of Osman Pasha at Plevna. Behind earthworks this dogged and heroic Turk repelled all assaults and immobilised the European forces of Russia for nearly five months. Finally Todleben, the forgotten hero of Sebastopol, an engineer as able as Osman, drew lines around him that proved too strong to be broken when the gallant Turk made his last sortie. Osman surrendered in December 1877, and before the end of January 1878 Skobelev, the most brilliant of the Russian generals, had opened the way to Adrianople, which fell on the 28th. The Turk was everywhere in retreat. The Serbs had re-entered the war and captured the important strategic centre of Nish, Prince Nicholas of Montenegro had seized Spizza and Dulcigno, and had burst into original poetry on his first sight of the sea. In Asia the Russians had been everywhere victorious and the great fortresses of Kars, Ardahan, and Erzerum, in fact all Armenia, were in their hands. Abdul Hamid sued for peace, and an armistice was agreed on January 31, 1878.

Peace was fairly well assured between Russia and Turkey. Was it assured between Britain and Russia? It was not certain. On January 23 the British fleet was ordered to leave Besika Bay and proceed to Constantinople,[1] and Parliament voted Beaconsfield six millions. The Russian army moved within sight of Constantinople, only to see the ominous black hulls of the British fleet in the waters off Prinkipo island. The danger seemed great to the more timid of the British Cabinet and to the public, but Russia was really helpless. Her army was worn out and exhausted, her supplies were wretched, her finances were in disorder. It was quite impossible for the Tsar to risk a conflict with a new enemy or enemies, for, in all probability, he would have had to fight Austria-Hungary on land as well as Britain on the sea. The dramatic touch, by which Beaconsfield ordered Indian troops to Malta in April, was not needed to prevent Russia from proceeding to extremities.

Russia took the wisest course under the circumstances, and signed a separate peace with the Turks on March 3 at San Stefano. By this she hoped to preserve most of her gains without offending Britain, for she did not enter Constantinople, and proposed to evacuate Adrianople. In Asia she proposed to annex Kars and Ardahan, but, in view of her conquest and evacuation of Erzerum, this was not an excessive demand and did not in fact give her control over most of

---

[1] This was countermanded, but the fleet was ordered to move up to Constantinople on February 9.

Armenia. In Europe direct Russian gains were limited to the recovery of that part of Bessarabia which had been ceded to Rumania in 1856 and to a Russian advance to the mouth of the Danube. Russia proposed to compensate Rumania for depriving her of a fertile province by giving her two-thirds of the barren Dobrudja. This was not generous treatment to a gallant ally in the war, but Rumania was a Latin state and it was the aim of Russia to exalt the Slav.

In this aim she met with considerable difficulties, for the reason that Alexander had already promised Francis Joseph that Austria-Hungary might occupy Bosnia and Herzegovina.[1] Bosnia was the Serb country which Serbia dreamed of annexing. In denying this province to Serbia Russia practically abandoned the Serbs. She insisted indeed at San Stefano on the enlargement of the boundaries of Serbia and on her acquiring Nish. But Alexander could do no more for her, and even recommended her to go to Austria-Hungary for diplomatic help. He seems to have thought that Serbia must fall under Austro-Hungarian influence. For Montenegro he did more. He saw to it that she received accessions of territory—though not a seaport, nor contiguous boundaries with Serbia—and made it clear that he would support her independence against Austria-Hungary.

Russia's trump card was to be the new state of Bulgaria, and the 'Big Bulgaria' she designed at San Stefano stretched the ethnic claims of Bulgaria to an extreme limit. Bulgaria not only included what is now Bulgaria, but added the modern Greek coast-line stretching west from the port of Kavalla to just short of Salonika, and nearly all of what is now Yugoslav Macedonia. Thus a new and great Balkan state of sturdy Bulgar peasants would have been erected. Liberated and (as was hoped) in future dominated by Russia, it would cover all the approches both to Salonika and to Constantinople. In future Russia, having revived her sea power, could operate against Constantinople with the aid of a powerful land-ally on the Turkish flank.[2] The plan was obviously drawn in the Russian interest and based on the idea that Bulgaria, for whose freedom so many thousands of Russians had died, would be the obedient tool and pawn of the Russian Tsar in future. In fact, as events proved, this would not have been the case, and both Beaconsfield and Alexander II were mistaken if they made any such calculation. The San Stefano agreement sinned indeed by giving Bulgaria somewhat too much, but it did not go far enough in justice to the Serbs, to the Greeks, to the Albanians, and to the Rumans. If (as was later done) Albania had been made independent,

[1] In the Agreement of Reichstadt (now Zakupy), July 8, 1876, and in the Convention of Budapest, January 15, 1877.

[2] North-west Macedonia, Epirus and Albania, and Thessaly remained Turkish, but of course were severed by the Big Bulgaria from all connection with Constantinople. Greece, which had not fought, was not to have its boundaries increased. A programme of reform was drawn up for Thessaly and Crete.

if Epirus and Thessaly had gone to Greece, and if Southern Bessarabia had remained to Rumania, the settlement would have been better. Serbia might at this time have been induced to accept Northwest Macedonia and been consoled by it for the loss of Bosnia.[1]

The British view was not determined by any consideration but that of resistance to Russia. Beaconsfield had got rid of the more timid of his Cabinet and made Lord Salisbury Foreign Secretary at the end of March. Though not entirely in agreement with his chief, Salisbury was prepared at any rate to oppose the creation of a 'Big Bulgaria,' which in the British view would have been a Russian stepping-stone to Constantinople. As soon as he became Foreign Minister, on the resignation of Derby, he issued a circular (April 1) to this effect; and began to negotiate with Russia. Great Britain and Austria-Hungary had both already demanded a European Congress for revising the terms of San Stefano. Salisbury finally agreed to accept its main clauses on condition of Russia's abandoning at the coming Congress the plan of a 'Big Bulgaria.' The new Bulgaria was to comprise about one-third of that designed under San Stefano, and to extend merely from the Danube to the Balkans. Macedonia and its southern coast were to be restored to Turkey, and a third section immediately south of the Balkans was to be called Eastern Rumelia and to form an autonomous province directly under Turkish control. The real point of this arrangement was a purely military one. By holding Eastern Rumelia up to the Balkans the Turks would obtain a fortified mountain line which would defend Adrianople and Constantinople against any further Russian advance from the Danube. As this concession was made privately and beforehand by Russia, Great Britain consented to enter the Congress.[2]

Salisbury seems to have thought that he had secured the Turks in Europe by these direct pre-congress negotiations with Russia, of which he did not tell Turkey. He secured Turkey in Asia and the British route to India by direct pre-congress negotiations with Turkey, of which he did not tell Russia. 'Austria will bring about a settlement of the Bulgarian situation,' said he at the Cabinet of March 27. 'It is the Armenian danger which is to be guarded against.' The proposed Russian acquisition of Batum, Ardahan, and Kars was to be met by occupying 'some island or station on the coast of Asia Minor which will neutralise the presence of Russia in Armenia.' Cyprus was the 'key of Western Asia' and could be made a place of arms and a harbour, and was handy for landing at Alexandretta. So a short convention was secretly signed between Britain and the Sultan. If

---

[1] The only flaw in this argument is that Serbia and Bulgaria might have quarrelled over their respective shares of Macedonia.

[2] The agreement with Russia was completed on May 31, 1878, see B. H. Sumner, *Russia and the Balkans* (1937), Appendix viii, pp. 637–51.

Russia annexed Kars, Batum and Ardahan, Britain was to occupy Cyprus, and to guarantee to defend by force of arms the Sultan's remaining Asiatic dominions against Russia. In return the Sultan promised to introduce 'necessary reforms' for the protection of 'the Christian and other subjects of the Porte in these [the Asiatic] territories.' On May 26 it was known that the Sultan would accept this, and the formal Convention was signed on June 4. On the 2nd Beaconsfield and Salisbury had been appointed British representatives and had agreed to attend the Congress. Finally a secret agreement (June 6) had been made with Austria-Hungary to the effect that she should occupy Bosnia and Herzegovina.[1] Britain was thus secretly in agreement with Russia, with Austria-Hungary, and with Turkey before the Congress opened, though neither Austria nor Russia knew of the Cyprus convention, nor Turkey of the Bosnian agreement. As Beaconsfield saw Bismarck before the Congress opened (June 13) and obtained a promise that the subject of Bulgaria should be taken first, there was not much fear as to the result, for the main concession there had already been made. Like most successful Congresses this one was successful because the principal items were agreed to beforehand.

Bismarck had offered Berlin as the seat of the Congress, and himself as 'an honest broker.' In reality his 'brokerage' was open to some suspicion, because he did everything to assist Austria-Hungary in the negotiations, and at times put pressure on her old foe, Russia. Andrássy, the representative of Austria-Hungary, gained most. He had actually declined to join Beaconsfield in a defensive alliance.[2] But his expenditure of ink and paper was more effective in gaining territory than Russian blood and treasure. Bosnia and Herzegovina were handed to Andrássy for political occupation, and the funnel or Sanjak of Novibazar was occupied by Austria-Hungary militarily. This occupation severed Serbia from Montenegro, and the latter, being pro-Russian, was greatly reduced from the boundaries granted it by San Stefano. Serbia was practically brought within the sphere of Austro-Hungarian influence. Serbia, Montenegro, and Rumania were all declared independent states. Russia, which had consented to the reduction of San Stefano Bulgaria to a third of its former size, now sought to deprive this concession of all value. She attempted to prevent the Turks from garrisoning Eastern Rumelia along the Balkan line, to which Beaconsfield naturally refused to agree. But it is probable that her attempt was an intrigue and not a threat to break the peace. At any rate Russia gave way quite early in the Congress, and the Big Bulgaria was trisected on the lines already agreed. Russia

---

[1] It was already known that Russia would not oppose this. See p. 309. n. 1.

[2] Buckle's *Beaconsfield*, vol. VI, p. 227, beacause, though Beaconsfield did not know it, he already had an understanding with Russia.

recovered Bessarabia from Rumania, and compensated her ally by giving her two-thirds of the Dobrudja, which should more properly have gone to Bulgaria.

In Asia Minor the arrangements of San Stefano were startlingly altered by Beaconsfield's *coup* with regard to Cyprus. When Russia intimated her intention to retain Kars, Ardahan, and Batum, he revealed the Convention (July 7) and ordered the British fleet to Cyprus. Russia showed irritation and, despite his assertion to the contrary, seems to have got the better of him in the question of the Russo-Turkish boundary in Asia Minor. He was really much exercised about the route to India, and, in private, made inquiries as to the possible defence of Mesopotamia against Russia. But his scheme of defence was rather unsuccessful in practice.

The Congress was thus over and the Great Powers pacified. Queen Victoria offered Beaconsfield, already an Earl, a dukedom, and gave Garters both to him and to Salisbury, amid the enthusiasm which careful stage management had evoked and which the phrase 'Peace with Honour' embodied. It would be wrong to deny that Beaconsfield had shown great courage at the crisis, but courage in diplomacy should be accompanied by knowledge, and in this Beaconsfied was poorly provided, and he did not try to obtain it from the more instructed Salisbury.[1] He seems to have had no belief in the strength of nascent nationality in the Balkan peninsula and no idea of resisting Russia except by military force. His belief in the virtues of Abdul Hamid and the Turkish desire to protect and ameliorate the condition of their Christian subjects whether in Europe or Asia was woefully mistaken. His policy in Asia speedily came to nought. The despatch of British military consuls to Armenia to arrange for its defence against Russia proved useless. In 1880 Gladstone came into power and substituted political for military consuls, and Salisbury, on resuming office in 1886, like a wise man accepted the change in silence. But political consuls were no more effective in stopping massacres than military ones had been in organising defence. To crown all, in July 1886, Russia announced her intention of disregarding her expressed declaration (Article 69 of Treaty of Berlin) of considering Batum as a port 'essentiellement commercial' and proceeded to fortify it.[2] So neither Russia nor Turkey approved of, or regarded, or upheld Beaconsfield's Asiatic policy. Cyprus was never made a place of arms nor a naval base, and was anything but the 'Gibraltar of the Eastern Mediterranean.' The Sultan never attempted to keep his promises of reform in Asia, and after a time deliberately set to work

[1] Buckle's *Beaconsfield*, vol. VI, p. 337; Lady G. Cecil's *Salisbury* (1921), vol. II, pp. 291–3.
[2] For a somewhat different account see A. Ramm, *Sir Robert Morier* (1973), pp. 223–5.

to massacre his Armenian subjects, without paying any regard to British remonstrances. In 1896 British Blue Books set out the horrible story of these atrocities. In 1898 another Blue Book in recounting the guarantees or engagements of Great Britain, included her obligation to defend Asiatic Turkey and the Sultan's 'promise' to 'introduce the necessary reforms . . . for the protection of Christian . . . subjects.' In other words the Sultan still claimed, and could apparently enforce, the guarantee of Great Britain's protection of Asia Minor, though British Blue Books proved that he had in the most inhuman manner massacred those Christian subjects. He had promised to protect them in the same instrument which guaranteed his own dominions against attack.

In Europe Beaconsfield's policy, though not successful, was not irremediable.[1] Macedonia was indeed delivered over to terrible internecine warfare and suffering, but the blunder by which Bulgaria was separated from Rumelia was ultimately set right. At times Gladstone, by sympathetic insight, hit upon truths withheld from more professional diplomats. He had done so twenty years before the Congress of Berlin. 'Surely the best resistance to be offered to Russia is by the strength and freedom of those countries that will have to resist her. You want to place a living barrier between her and Turkey. There is no barrier, then, like the breast of freemen.'[2] Certainly the union of Moldavia and Wallachia in Rumania proved a more effective resistance to Russia than their separation. The enlargement of Bulgaria produced, in the same way, her liberation from Tsarist Russia.

Russia displayed colossal tactlessness in dealing with the new Bulgaria. In April 1879 Alexander of Battenberg became her Prince. He was a nephew of Alexander II, inexperienced in dealing with his subjects and subservient to Russia. A Russian general became Prime Minister and another one Minister for War. They attempted to dragoon the country and soon aroused the bitter resentment of Bulgars. In 1885 a conspiracy burst out in Eastern Rumelia, and the rebel Bulgars there expelled their Turkish governor and proclaimed the union of 'the two Bulgarias,' inviting Prince Alexander to be their ruler. Russia was hostile to this movement, but Stambulov, the strong man of Bulgaria, informed Prince Alexander that he would be expelled if he did not accept the Union. Prince Alexander capitulated and accepted. Russia was furious and withdrew all her officers from the Bulgarian army. Bulgarians were glad enough to see them go. Russia appealed to the other Powers to prevent the union of Eastern Rumelia with Bulgaria. Austria-Hungary, however, made no objection, because she realised that a strong Bulgaria would be anti-

---

[1] Thus the Greek frontier was extended to include Thessaly in 1880, and Montenegro acquired a port at Dulcigno, as a result of Gladstone's aid.
[2] House of Commons, May 4, 1858.

Russian. What would Britain do, Britain which had created Eastern Rumelia and risked war in 1878 rather than consent to its fusion with Bulgaria? Lord Salisbury was now Britain's Prime Minister and would surely support Russia. But, to the great surprise of everyone, he did not do so. Lord Salisbury had learnt the lesson if others had not, and he quietly acquiesced in a union which he knew would make for permanent peace. And the 'living barrier' formed by the 'breast of freemen' was thus drawn across Russia's path to Constantinople.[1]

Bulgaria, though united, was not to escape entirely either the anger of Russia or the jealousy of her Slav neighbour. For Serbia now sought to intervene. One of the gravest defects of the Congress of Berlin was the disregard of the just claims of Serbia. She is said to have been told by Russia to apply to Austria-Hungary for support, and in 1881 she signed a secret Convention with Austria-Hungary which made her commercially dependent on her. It was followed by a political agreement which made her an Austrian satellite. Now she suddenly declared war on the new Bulgaria (November 14, 1885). In a three days' battle at Slivnitsa the Bulgars were victorious. They began to advance into Serbia, when Prince Alexander received an ultimatum from Austria-Hungary which warned him to turn back.[2] He obeyed and went back to rule 'the two Bulgarias.' He soon found that he was not to rule in peace. In August 1886 the hapless Prince was kidnapped by the supporters of Russia and taken to Russian territory. There was a speedy reaction in his favour in Bulgaria, but he humiliated himself in a telegram to the Tsar and was compelled by Stambulov and the Bulgarian patriots to abdicate. Thereafter, in 1887, Prince Ferdinand of Saxe-Coburg became the ruler of Bulgaria and pursued a strong anti-Russian policy.

In this fashion some of the worst consequences of the Congress of Berlin were liquidated in the decade following it. But certain ineradicable evils remained. There was suffering and atrocity in Armenia, but danger as well as misery in Macedonia. For, while the Great Powers ultimately allowed the Sultan to massacre at will in Armenia, they were not prepared to allow him the same freedom in Macedonia. For in Macedonia there were men of Greek, Bulgarian, and Serb blood, and in Macedonia there were endless opportunities for Russian and Austro-Hungarian intrigue. It was quite certain that these evils could not go on for ever, but the year 1886 marks roughly the period at which a temporary lull ensued, and when men could consider other great European problems.

Bismarck's support at Berlin for Austria-Hungary alienated Rus-

---

[1] Lord Salisbury owed a good deal to the influence of Sir William White, for a time acting Ambassador at Constantinople and truly great diplomat.

[2] Austria-Hungary, of course, could not allow a dependent Serbia to be laid in the dust by Bulgaria. During 1886–87 Bismarck's aid supported her against Russia.

sia and made an estrangement that was only temporarily repaired in 1881. Alexander II was so seriously annoyed at Bismarck's attitude at the Congress that he wrote a letter to the German Emperor William I in April 1879, expressing doubts as to whether peace could be preserved between Russia and Germany. That irritation became much greater during 1885–86 when Russia found Bismarck would not support her in the Bulgarian crisis. So that in 1878 we have the remote origin of the estrangement between Russia and Germany, which divided Europe into two camps, the Franco-Russian and the Austro-Italo-German Alliances. But, before we survey the construction of these great Alliances, which ultimately came into conflict, we must turn to other fields. This chapter has shown how Bismarck allowed Russia an opportunity in the Balkans, how she failed to make full use of it, and how in the end was compelled to restrain her activities. The next chapter will show how Bismarck permitted France and Great Britain to have their opportunities in the area of colonial enterprise, until he himself entered that field and limited their ambitions. The fact that even Bismarck thus in the end found himself limiting the activities alike of Britain, France, and Russia, may explain why his feebler successors ultimately succeeded in alienating all three Powers.

Chapter 22

THE GROWTH OF COLONISATION, OF TRADE, AND OF OVERSEAS EMPIRE, 1815–98

That great transmarine colonisation and activity took place in the seventeenth and eighteenth centuries is universally admitted. The nineteenth century saw a revival of colonising activity and the participants now included Italy, Germany and Russia as well as Britain and France, the traditional colonising countries. The great colonising career of France in Africa began in 1830, and colonisation, in the wider sense, was a policy actively pursued by all the European Powers, though it was not always pursued overseas. Colonisation for Russia meant the plantation of Siberia and penetration into Central Asia, and it was peculiarly active in the nineteenth century. For the German States, all active colonisers in the eighteenth and nineteenth centuries, it meant the plantation of waste areas in their own borders or in Europe herself[1] beyond which they did not look till the last quarter of the nineteenth century. Then united Germany, like united Italy, took colonies overseas and Russia extended her colonial interests to Tibet and the Pacific coast of China. At the beginning of the twentieth century there appeared the first of the many theories of imperialism with which that century was to abound. These were important in bringing the word as well as the fact into bad repute.

Colonising proper seems to mean the settlement of alien districts with white inhabitants. But there are other activities, which can hardly be classed under one head, and include everything from barter and huckstering to military and economic imperialism. The arrival of traders, or travellers or of missionaries is usually the first step. After that the situation leads gradually on to a sphere of influence, a chartered company, a protectorate, or to full economic or political control. There are cases where the greed of a company, the enter-

---

[1] During the eighteenth century the sand wastes of Brandenburg and Polish Prussia, and the areas re-won from the Turk in Hungary, were planted and peopled by settlers from all parts of Germany. The process was curiously analogous to French and British settlement on the North American Continent.

prise of an individual, or the decision of a naval or military officer in hoisting a flag, have determined the fate of provinces or of nations. There are yet others where the desire of a State to possess a strategic post like Kiao-Chau or Aden has led to direct governmental interference. But there is a real distinction between all these processes and that of colonisation. That has normally taken place only in deference to the overpowering need of a surplus population for fresh land, and we find generally that such a flow has moved only to the British Empire, to the United States, and to Siberia.[1] But nearly all European Powers have pursued a policy of trading with, exploiting, 'protecting,' or subjecting native races.

As our emphasis is rather on Europe than on Britain, the growth of the British Empire can only be outlined. In 1815, Britain could have taken all the colonies she wanted from either France or Holland. She concentrated on strategical protection of sea routes and commerce, and handed back the rich isles of Guadeloupe and Martinique to France and the immense wealth of Java to Holland. But she took care to retain the strategical outwork of St. Lucia in the West Indies, and secured the route to India by acquiring Cape Colony from the Dutch and Mauritius from France. Sir Stamford Raffles protected the route to China by acquiring Singapore in 1819, and the acquisition of Aden in 1839 still further assured the route to India.

Meanwhile, as the routes were protected, colonial settlement proceeded apace and imperialist expansion in India was steadily pursued. The process was completed by the annexation of the Punjab just before the outbreak of the Indian Mutiny in 1857. From about this time we may date the vigorous life of Britain's white colonies. Canada had led the way in self-government (1840), but before 1860 the colonies in Australia and New Zealand were developed enough to receive the grant of full responsible government. In 1867 Canada went further and united her different provinces in a federal system which provided full protection for the French settlers of Quebec.

The story of South Africa was less happy, and Cape Colony did not receive responsible government till late in the seventies. Her prospects had been injured by the abolition of colonial slavery (1834). Differences over native policy with the Boers led to their secession in 'the Great Trek' and to the foundation of Boer Republics (1848), repudiating the sovereignty of Great Britain. This situation, and the anomalous status of the Transvaal, caused three wars (1848, 1881, 1899–1902), but was ultimately solved by the combination of Dutch and British in the Union of South Africa (1909–10).

Britain had succeeded during the nineteenth century in peopling waste or sparsely inhabited areas with white populations. The sources of population were various. It had begun with the penal settlements

---

[1] The case of the French in Algeria was exceptional and is treated below.

and transport of political and other criminals to Australia. Then there had been a State-aided settlement in South Africa, mostly of ex-soldiers. Finally, and most important, the industrial revolution produced a surplus population in Britain, and want and distress, during the period of the 'hungry forties,' led to an immense emigration both to the United States and to Canada. Britain was so far ahead of other countries in her industrial revolution that she had already peopled parts of three continents before the rest of Europe began to send its stream of emigrants overseas. In 1881 Canada had a population of four millions and a half, Australia of two millions, New Zealand of half a million. Thus before the scramble for overseas possessions became general in the eighties, the main areas of white colonisation were already well settled by colonists of British blood or feelings, and formed, in fact, areas occupied by nascent white nations.

After 1815 France retained Guiana as well as most of her West Indian isles, but the Monroe Doctrine and the attitude of Canning soon caused her to abandon any attempt at expansion in America. As expansion in Europe was impossible it was sought in Africa, while Syria and China were also considered as objects for the possible extension of French influence. Africa was selected as the point of attack, and the plan was formed by the Ministers of Charles X, the last Legitimist Bourbon King of France. As so often in French history, the foreign policy of the Legitimist Bourbons was inherited and continued by those who overthrew them. When France again became one of the great colonising Powers she opened the era of nineteenth-century imperialism, some say by taking Algeria in 1830, some say by taking Tunis in 1881. Imperialism was a factor both in causing the war of 1914–18 and the decolonisation to which the war of 1939–45 was the prelude. Decolonisation was a stormy process in Algeria and one profoundly affecting the domestic history of France.

The Algerian pirates, or 'Barbary Corsairs' as they were called, had a government of their own, but were technically subject to the Turks. They had for many centuries infested the Mediterranean as pirates, and robbed and enslaved Christian peoples. In 1814 a United States squadron released 500 Christian slaves, and in 1816 a British squadron bombarded Algiers and liberated 3000 more. The French had plenty of justification for interference on general grounds, but they seem to have intended from the first to use their opportunity to control and finally to annex Algeria. In the middle of 1830 a French expedition appeared and occupied the city of Algiers. France gradually extended her sway westwards and eastwards along the coast, and then began to press into the interior. The usual campaigns followed, in which Western science and persistence gradually overcame Oriental valour and indiscipline. Fugitive Algerine chiefs found refuge in Morocco and brought reinforcements from over the Moorish border. It was not until the French ships had bombarded Tangier and Mogador, and a French army had defeated the Moorish forces on land, that the Sultan of Morocco gave way and abandoned the Algerian cause. As a result the end came quickly and all Algeria was subdued by 1847. Thus the future was curiously foreshadowed, and the fate of Morocco seen to be involved in that of Algeria.

The French system of colonisation was a new and exceedingly interesting one. It was half-way between the British idea of white settlement by fortuitous individuals, and the ordinary idea of imperialism, i.e. economical control of the backward races and of their resources by Western companies or Governments. It was, from the first, a system of colonising Algeria with a white population, which was to rule the Arab and other native races. The programme of the Molé Ministry in 1838, 'France is going to revive Roman Africa,' was literally and exactly correct. In complete contrast to the haphazard and individualistic methods of Britain, State support and State direction controlled the plan. First, roads were made and canals cut, legal security was given to foreign merchants and the native Jews were made French citizens. Then about 1841 colonisation, or a State-aided plan of importing true French citizens into the country, began. These Frenchmen were settled on the State lands confiscated from the Bey and from other leading Algerians, or in strategic centres, precisely as Roman colonists were planted by Rome in Spain or in Gaul. In the same way French soldiers in Algeria were encouraged to visit France towards the end of their period of service, to procure a wife and to bring her back to Algeria and settle there. Free land was given by the Government,[1] and intermarriage with the natives discouraged. The latter were treated with a judicious mixture of firmness and conciliation. The French manners, the *Code Napoléon*, the glittering splendours of their military displays, both attracted and impressed the natives. The population of France herself did not increase very rapidly or emigrate very willingly, and the lack of white settlers caused a partial failure of the original plan. What the French really aimed at doing is shown by the population of Algiers itself, where there were in 1936, 149,549 Frenchmen, 25,526 other whites, and 77,246 Arabs and natives. This represents an ideal which France would have been glad to have realised throughout Algeria, and perhaps elsewhere also.

The political conception underlying this colonisation scheme is clear. Algeria became nearly as much France as the department of Les Alpes Maritimes or of the Seine. At times efforts were made to establish customs barriers between Algeria and France or to limit the franchise of white settlers. All such attempts failed, and Algeria became a sort of overseas department or 'extension of France,'

---

[1] I.e. from 1841–83, with a brief interval between the years 1860–71.

returning members to the Chamber, reading the French newspapers, and taking a modest part in French internal politics.[1] Agreeably to the same conception the shipping between Algeria and France was reserved as a coastal trade. The whole principle was fundamentally different from the Anglo-Saxon one. The idea that British colonies were municipal corporations, inseparably connected with the montherland, was thrown overboard with the tea into Boston Harbour when the American Revolution began. A white colony, if planted by Britain, expected always and ultimately to develop a will and consciousness of its own. The French idea was to plant a colony which was an express image and counterpart of the motherland, and organically connected with it.

The international implications of the conquest of Algeria were perhaps even more important than the system of colonisation pursued there. For a long time France did not try to advance her boundaries, but the very fact of her occupation tended ultimately to make such advance inevitable. Advance into the Sahara with the ultimate design of joining up with the French settlements in West Africa was a necessary result of establishment at Algiers. Friction with neighbours on both sides, that is with the Sultan of Morocco and the Bey of Tunis, was hardly avoidable. But these incidents had no serious consequences until Italy began to cast longing eyes on Tunis, and Spain (and ultimately Germany) began to think of securing 'a place in the sun' in Morocco. It was then seen that international questions of the first order had been raised by the French priority of settlement in Algeria. French expansion to the equatorial Sudan led to conflict with Britain and confrontation on the Niger and at Fashoda. And the French desire to possess Morocco had a dominant influence in bringing about the Anglo-French Entente in 1904.

During the thirties and forties some important French interests favoured a policy of active commercial enterprise in various quarters of the world. The French support of the rebellious Egyptian Pasha, Mehemet Ali, was obviously influenced by a desire to exploit, and perhaps to control, Syria. Palmerston defeated this attempt in 1840 and drove Mehemet Ali back upon Egypt. But the French interest in the Levant remained, and her commercial schemes and religious missions might at any time have been used to support active political projects. The strange genius of Michel Chevalier and other followers of Saint-Simon suggested the 'Mediterranean system' of communications which led on to an actual project of cutting a canal through the Suez peninsula. The French consul at Tunis, Ferdinand de Lesseps, caught up the idea, reduced it to practice, and persuaded the

---

[1] If Algeria had not had a Governor-General she would have been exactly like a French department. All French colonies (whether regarded as departments like Algiers or not) sent deputies to Parliament.

Khedive of Egypt to grant him a concession (1854). He was bitterly opposed by Britain in the shape of Palmerston, who considered that the canal would open India to attack by a new route. But this opposition was in vain, and de Lesseps completed his great work between 1859 and 1869. Britain had done almost nothing but oppose it, but in 1875 Disraeli suddenly intervened and bought the Khedive's holdings for the British Government. Disraeli's action was an important gesture, but did not much, if at all, increase British influence over the Canal Company, since each shareholder was limited to ten votes however large its holdings. Nevertheless by 1880 it was clear that Britain was deeply interested in Egypt, France in Morocco, and Italy in Tunis

French imperialistic schemes were active in America as well as in the Levant, and the Suez was not the only canal which French enterprise thought of cutting. One of the motives of Napoleon III in his disastrous imperialistic venture in Mexico was to control Panama and perhaps to cut a canal through it.[1] As told elsewhere the Mexican enterprise failed in shameful humiliation, and from this time forward France abandoned any annexationist ambitions in Latin America.

In China and the Far East, French ambitions were conspicuous, whether France was Bourbon, Orleanist, Napoleomic, or Republican. The British were the first to break down Chinese seclusion. In 1830 a working relationship had long existed between the Chinese authorities and the East India Company. It enabled foreign trade to be carried on through the Chinese port of Canton. It broke down, first, because foreigners brought in more and more opium, in defiance of China's ban on it and, next, because the East India Company lost its trading monopoly. The British Government exercised naval and military force to make a new arrangement. This was important because the Treaty of Nanking, August 29, 1842, was the first treaty which China concluded with any Western maritime country. It provided for the cession of Hong Kong to Britain and the opening of four more ports, the chief of which was Shanghai, to foreign trade. The United States and France were not to be left behind and concluded treaties with China in 1844 in their turn. The French treaty contained provision for China's lifting her ban on Catholic Christianity. Toleration was soon extended to Protestantism. European missionaries now came to China but led a precarious existence when they penetrated into the interior. Shanghai grew spectacularly as a commercial port and a so-called International Settlement developed outside its walls which became famous as a kind of independent city-republic with its own laws and administration. Fresh disputes, caused fundamentally by the weakness of the Chinese Government but superficially by the Chinese habit of registering their shipping under a foreign flag as far as Britain was concerned and, as far as France

[1] Napoleon III had written a pamphlet on this subject. For Mexico, see pp. 245–47.

was concerned, by the torture and execution of a Catholic mission-
ary, led to fresh Anglo-French naval and military action against
China. The Tientsin Treaties were signed by Britain and France with
China in 1858. They provided for the opening of eleven more treaty
ports, conceded the right of travel into the interior and the right of
diplomatic representation in Peking and confirmed toleration for the
Christian religion. But since they had been imposed China evaded
their fulfilment. War was resumed and ended with the execution of
the treaties and further small concessions in 1860. About the same
time Russia, which had already occupied the Amur Province of China
and bordered on Korea, reached the Pacific and built a harbour at
Vladivostok. As a result of all these measures China was more definitely thrown open to foreign commerce and the European diplomatic representatives were finally established at Peking. Up to 1880,
therefore, no special attempt had been made, or success achieved,
by any European Power in establishing special advantages for herself
in China, though the French had gained rights which might give them
great advantages in the future. But circumstances prevented their
making use of them, and diverted their attention to an area south of
China proper. As a result of the murder of some French missionaries,
Napoleon III sent an expedition which conquered and annexed the
three Eastern provinces of Cochin-China (1862). This led also to the
annexation of Cambodia (1863) and the rest of Cochin-China (1867).
Difficulties about the opening of Tongking, the chief port of Annam,
led to a further expedition which turned the whole of Annam into
a French protectorate. The Chinese Government at Peking sent
troops to reassert its shadowy authority over these areas, but these
were easily defeated by the French, and China was forced to acquiesce
in the French annexation of Tongking and Annam by the Treaty of
April 4, 1885. It was, therefore, hardly possible for any single Great
Power to make further moves against the integrity of China without
awaking the jealousy of other Great Powers. The Balance of Power
had already extended its evil influence over the Far East. In 1897–98
three Powers acted simultaneously: Germany leased the port of Kiao-
Chau, Russia Port Arthur, Britain Wei-hai-Wei.

Nicholas I is once said to have asked Wellington to advise him as
to Russian policy in Central Asia. The Duke, who knew Asiatics
well, replied that short punitive expeditions by military commanders
might be undertaken without difficulty, but that, if civil officials once
replaced military ones in districts even temporarily occupied, Russian
prestige would forbid withdrawal and involve serious commitments.
In other words, if an advance in Central Asia was once begun, there
could be no thought of subsequent withdrawal. 'You could never
go back.' And, if you could never go back, you were likely to go
forward.

The motives of Russian advance into Asia were various. In Siberia there was colonisation by immigrant peasants, by convicts, and by political criminals. In the Caucasus and in Turkestan frontier disputes led to punitive expeditions and to Russian conquest. In China the advance was due mainly to conscious governmental policy and to the search for an ice-free port on the Pacific. But, everywhere and always, the truth of Wellington's dictum was proved. The advance, once undertaken, continued and seemed to gain speed from each fresh annexation. A factor of great importance in its history was the existence of Tartar and Muslim tribes in the Caucasus. Russia had no difficulty in occupying the coast of the Black Sea, south of the Caucasus. But strategic reasons prevented her from attacking the Turks in Asia Minor from the rear, so long as the mountain tribes of the Caucasus were still unsubdued. The campaigns against them began in 1830, and seem to have been inefficiently conducted, for they were not subdued till 1859. Had this resistance been less stubborn, Russia might have scored important advantages in Asia Minor during the Crimean War. As it was, now that her communications were secure, she easily obtained the Province of Kars from Turkey in 1878. Beaconsfield's firm attitude in that year was unquestionably influenced by the fact that he realised the danger of Russian penetration into Armenia.

The colonisation of Eastern Siberia was persistent and led naturally to occupation of Chinese provinces, such as the Amur, in the way that has already been described. Russia advanced steadily and was only stopped by the sea when she built a port at Vladivostok (1860). As, however, it was not an ice-free one in winter, she began to think of acquiring a warm-water harbour. This could only be done by her advancing directly southwards into Korea or threatening Peking. But in 1880 she was diverted to Asia Minor and Turkestan.

In Central Asia the chief peoples to be subdued were the tribes of Eastern and Western Turkestan, the former a nominal province of China.[1] The raids of robber horsemen gave every Russian governor of a border province a perpetual excuse not only for punitive expeditions, but for policing (or annexing) territory contiguous to his district. But up till 1860 the steppe land between the Russian post of Orenburg and the Khanates of Khiva and Bokhara prevented any effective advance. Science and more geographical knowledge finally overcame these difficulties, and the first important step was the fall to Tashkent (1864). It was followed by the Russian capture of Samarkand, the famous city from which Genghis Khan and Tamerlane had ruled their immense empires. Russia enormously enhanced her prestige in Central Asia by this triumph, and all Eastern Turkestan soon fell into her hands. Western Turkestan held out longer,

---

[1] Turkestan may be roughly described as the area south of European Russia and Siberia, and north and west of Persia and Afghanistan.

but the Khan of Khiva was finally compelled to cede his territories to Russia in 1873. One further tribe of Turkomans remained to be subdued. This was accomplished by Skobelev, the hero of Plevna, in 1880, and Russia and Britain, whose influence was then dominant in Afghanistan, seemed face to face.

Had not the time, prophesied by Palmerston in 1840, at last arrived? 'It seems pretty clear that, sooner or later, the Cossack and the Sepoy, the man from the Baltic and he from the British Islands will meet in the centre of Asia. It should be our business to take care that the meeting should take place as far off from our Indian possessions as may be convenient and advantageous to us. But the meeting will not be avoided by our staying at home to receive the visit.'[1] In 1880 the British, Russian, and Chinese Empires practically met at one point, for the British had not stayed at home. They had pushed westwards almost as rapidly as the Russians had pushed eastwards. The deserts of Persia and the mountains of Afghanistan were now the only barriers between Russian and British territory. All this Skobelev saw with the clear eye of a soldier and prepared a plan for the invasion of British India. Five years after the Russian diplomats had seen the plan, the moment seemed to have arrived for putting it into action.

Afghanistan was a buffer state dependent on Great Britain, and in 1885 Russian local forces got into dispute with the Afghans and occupied part of their frontier. Gladstone himself took a serious view of the situation. He asked Parliament to vote him eleven million pounds and accused the Russians of unprovoked aggression against a small and weak neighbour. Russia and Britain certainly came to the verge of war, though at the last moment the Penjdeh incident was smoothed over. The gravity of the crisis proved in the end to have been a fortunate thing, for it deeply impressed the Tsar. During the crisis he had carried his head high in order to conciliate Russian public opinion. But he sought anxiously to avoid any similar incident in future. Lord Salisbury advised people who feared the Russian danger to buy large maps to judge distances and to estimate the strength of mountain barriers. The Russians, and the Tsar among them, took that advice, and they found the line of least resistance to lie not towards India but towards China. For an advance depended on railway possibilities, and the deserts of Persia and the mountains of North-west India presented the most formidable barriers known to man, behind which lurked the troops of a well-armed Great Power. In comparison the physical difficulties offered to the railway penetration of China were small, while the power of the Celestial Empire was crumbling. So in 1892 the Tsar turned his face away from India and towards China, and began to build a Trans-Siberian railway with

[1] C. K. Webster, *The Foreign Policy of Palmerston* (1951), Vol. II, pp. 738–9.

French money. Russia thus took a step which she hoped would lead to a speedy conquest over an effete Asiatic Empire, but which, in fact, led to humiliating defeat at the hands of a virile one—that is, of Japan. But, whichever way it led, it led away from conflict with the British Empire in India. Hence the year 1892, when the Russian cloud shifted from the Himalayas and began to settle over Manchuria, is a year of supreme importance in Russo-British relations. It is also supremely important because Russia drew away from Germany and towards France.

Before the Russian advance had been diverted from Central Asia to Manchuria, a general scramble for territorial spoils had begun in Africa. France and Great Britain began the game, and they were followed at a short interval by Germany, and more distantly by Italy (though she had first planted her foot on the Eritrean Coast in 1869), by Belgium, and by Spain. The first definite acquisition in point of time, though not of importance, was the French annexation of Tunis. At the Congress of Berlin France had been reconciled to the British occupation of Cyprus by the suggestion that she should occupy Tunis. Lord Salisbury continued to favour this suggestion, and was supported by Bismarck, who wished to make France forget Alsace-Lorraine in Tunis. France therefore proceeded to negotiate with the Bey of Tunis. Like her near neighbour, Egypt, Tunis was nominally under Turkish rule and actually in chains to her bondholders. A triple financial control by Italy, France, and Great Britain had been set up in 1869, but had not produced much result. Having concealed their aims from Italy, which also cast envious eyes on Tunis, the French Government massed a force on the borders of Algeria and attacked Tunis in April 1881—Britain was surprised, Italy was indignant, but Germany approved. Turkey tried to protest, but thirty thousand French troops were soon in the country, and by the Treaty of Bardo (May 12, 1881) Tunis became a French protectorate. Resistance by scattered tribes in the interior was soon ended and France congratulated herself on a new acquisition and a great stroke of policy. It is doubtful if it was the latter, and it is curious that Clemenceau was the only parliamentary deputy who voted against the new accession. He did so on the ground that 'it profoundly modified the European system and chilled precious friendships cemented on the field of battle.' The reference was to Italy, and Clemenceau saw further than anyone else in France. Italy's just resentment at her treatment over Tunis drove her into the Triple Alliance with Austria-Hungary and with Germany, and Italian hostility remained a danger to France for many years.

France had scored an acquisition by smartly anticipating a rival in one quarter. But in Egypt she thought herself outwitted by another competitor, with the same result of establishing twenty years of bad feeling and hostility between victor and vanquished. Britain and

France were both interested in Egypt, for it lay on the road to India. The genius of de Lesseps and his successful completion of the Suez Canal gave France the preliminary advantage. But the purchase of the Khedive's shares in the company already mentioned, balanced that advantage. A series of financial crises brought Egypt down. The first time the Khedive suspended payment of the interest on the foreign debt, or went bankrupt, was in April 1876. A fund into which revenues were paid, managed by the interested Powers (Britain, France, Germany, Italy, Austria-Hungary), the *Caisse de la Dette* was the result. The third suspension was in February 1879. The consequence of this, in November 1879, was the Anglo–French Dual Control which became control not of finance only but of the whole administration. This lasted till 1883. It did something to relieve the peasant, introduce western efficiency and even institutions. All might have gone well if hatred of foreign interference had not produced a kind of national movement. Khedive Ismail had already been deposed by the Sultan of Turkey at the suggestion of Britain and France (June 1879) and the new Khedive Tewfik's subservience to foreign Powers precipitated an ebullition of national feeling led by Arabi Pasha, and Egyptian general. On September 9, 1881, he led 5000 soldiers to the Khedive's palace, and demanded a change of ministers, an increased army, and a National Assembly. The Khedive yielded, and Arabi was thus supreme, though his dictatorship was decorously veiled for a time.

A collision between Arabi and foreign Governments, interested in preserving their property and protecting their subjects, was probably inevitable. At any rate a Franco-British Note, presented to the Khedive on January 8, 1882, rendered it so. It was one of those unfortunate attempts at intervention from outside, weakening the position of the Khedive whom it meant to support, and strengthening the resistance of the Nationalists whom it meant to intimidate. Arabi, from being a military dictator, now became a national hero. An Anglo-French naval squadron made a demonstration off Alexandria, which only served to irritate the Egyptians and to strengthen Arabi. On June 11 riots began in Alexandria, the mob killed fifty Europeans, and drove both Turkish and European residents from their great cities.

Britain for once acted vigorously and decided not to negotiate but to overthrow the military party in Egypt first. France refused to cooperate, so, on July 11, the British squadron alone opened fire on the forts of Alexandria and promptly destroyed them. Military action speedily followed upon naval. A British force under Sir Garnet Wolseley caught Arabi Pasha napping at dawn, stormed his trenches and utterly overthrew him at Tel-el-Kebir (September 13). Arabi was made prisoner and the Khedive, thus restored by British military action, again mounted his throne.

At the time only Bismarck and Germany supported Great Britain. Italy stood aloof, Russia agreed with Turkey in condemning British action, and France was the most indignant of all. She 'resumed full liberty of action,' a phrase well understood in diplomacy, and covering anything from sullen obstruction to almost open hostility. The consequences could easily have been foreseen. France had been invited to join with Britain in intervening and had declined. Britain had to act alone, and the Dual Control was dismantled. Gladstone promised to clear out of Egypt as soon as affairs were settled. But they never were settled, and Britain, without perhaps meaning to do so, occupied Egypt 'in a fit of absence of mind.' She acquired with it the extreme enmity of France, and it was not till 1904 that she succeeded in conciliating her,[1] and not until 1922 that she cleared out.

The colonial appetites of France and Great Britain had been thus, to some extent, sated, when Germany very suddenly appeared as a Colonial Empire-seeker. Bismarck himself had long opposed a policy of German colonial enterprise. But German oversea commercial interests increased and gradually converted him to their views. Once having decided on the policy he acted with characteristic resolution. In April 1884 he proclaimed a protectorate over the whole of Southwest Africa (except Walfisch Bay) from south of Portuguese Angola to the northern boundary of Cape Colony. In the same month he deliberately deceived the British Government as to his aims in the Cameroons, and in July (while the British Consul was on holiday) formally annexed its coastline as well as Togoland. In May of the same year a German New Guinea Company was formed, and this led, after further disputes with Britain, to a division of New Guinea into a northern or German sphere and a southern or British one.[2] During the years 1884 and 1885 similar methods resulted in the German annexation of Tanganyika (Tanzania) or German East Africa. In about two years Germany became possessed of some millions of square miles of territory, 'without a fleet and without moving a soldier.'

Another equally pacific conquest over even a vaster extent of territory was due to the ability and pressure not of a nation or a government but of a single man. King Leopold II of Belgium, who was as far-sighted as he was unscrupulous, had already seen the importance of Africa and had financed the famous explorer Stanley in expeditions which founded stations and persuaded chiefs to sign treaties to form a new state on the Congo (1878–84). This Congo Associ-

---

[1] The revolt of the Mahdi in the Soudan in 1881 led. ultimately, to the reconquest of the Sudan by Lord Kitchener in 1898 in the names of the Khedive and of the Queen-Empress of Great Britain. The Fashoda crisis arose owing to the attempt of France to annex the equatorial or Behr-el-Ghazal area of the Soudan. This was defeated by the firm stand of Lord Salisbury.

[2] The Dutch already occupied the north-west part.

ation was technically international and commercial in character. Its development caused active apprehensions to France and to Portugal and produced a Conference of the Great Powers at Berlin (October 1884 to February 1885).[1] In result the Berlin Act, signed by the various Powers, handed over the vast basin of the Congo to this new organisation, which was termed the Congo Free State (or the Independent State of the Congo). King Leopold in fact personally ruled a state a million miles square. The provisions made for international control and international free trade were systematically violated by the unscrupulous monarch. He instituted a system of monopolies which prevented international competition and substituted Belgian for international control.[2] The system of government was corrupt and tyrannical, but it served the purpose of its author. By using those international sanctions (which he had no scruple in violating when it suited his own pocket or interests) he was able to prevent any single Power, great or small, from encroaching on the boundaries of the enormous territory he had acquired and ultimately bequeathed to his country.

The history of colonial development in Africa does not seem an edifying one. Britain accused the Boers, and the Boers Britain, of chicanery and deceit. And Britain, though promising that her occupation of Egypt was temporary, finally made it permanent. France deliberately deceived Italy over Tunis, and Germany Britain over South West Africa and the Cameroons. Finally King Leopold, by a masterpiece of guile, tricked all Europe into giving him the richest of colonial plums. The exploitation of the Congolese to procure rubber made the worst scandal of this colonial era.

The partition of Africa was completed between 1885 and 1898. France expanded inland from points on the coast: from Gabon to make the French Congo; from other points to make Dahomey and Senegal further north. If she linked the last two she would cut off from further expansion the British Gold Coast Colony (Ghana) also racing for the interior. Britain, whose special position on the middle Niger had been recognised by the Berlin West Africa Conference, mentioned already, also met pressure from France coming south from the French Sahara. On the Red Sea Coast Italy took Eritrea, but when she attempted to push into Ethiopia was defeated at the Battle of Adowa (1896). In East Africa Britain and Germany were the main rivals and British Kenya and Uganda as well as German Tanganyika (Tanzania) were the outcome of expansion followed by frontier delimitation. In South Central Africa British Nyasaland

---

[1] See S. E. Crowe, *The Berlin West African Conference, 1884–1885* (1942).

[2] In 1889 his will, leaving his Congo estate to Belgium, was published. After much criticism during the next twenty years, Leopold finally made over the Congo State to Belgium during his lifetime. The accession of King Albert was marked by a striking improvement in the Congo administration.

(Malawi), Northern and Southern Rhodesia (Zambia and Zimbabwe) emerged by the same process. Here the African ruler (the Transvaal), Portugal and Britain in the form of Rhodes's South Africa Company, were the main contestants. In this last stage the criteria which the Berlin Conference had evolved (the right of a coastal colony to adequate hinterland, prior treaty rights, and effective occupation) in order to regulate European penetration all proved ineffective. The Balance of European Power, difficult to work out in Europe itself after the small states of Italy and Germany had been amalgamated, was being worked out in Africa by a series of bargains, diplomatic crises and frontier delimitation. Africa, of which hardly one tenth had belonged to European states in 1870, had let her interior land fall into European hands so that Africans retained hardly one tenth in 1900. The Empire of Morocco was the one independent kingdom of North Africa, and it was natural that both Germany and France should cast longing eyes upon it. Ultimately France gave up her claims on Egypt to secure British support in Morocco. And the origins of the Anglo-French Entente and its subsequent evolution were thus profoundly affected by colonial developments in North Africa.

No less striking was the situation produced by colonial or imperialistic expansion in Asia. Russia, after long treading the road to India, turned aside towards China in 1892. She thus postponed, though she did not avert, a conflict with Britain in Asia. Britain finding Germany reluctant to assist her in stopping the Russian advance against China, accepted the Alliance of Japan (1902) for that purpose. And Japan declared war on Russia two years later. Expansion in Asia thus led directly to an alliance and to war. Expansion in Africa led to an Entente in 1904 and perhaps to war in 1914.

Chapter 23

BISMARCK AND THE FORMATION OF THE TRIPLE AND DUAL ALLIANCES, 1879–94

The two preceding chapters have shown how the Eastern question revealed a gulf between Russia and Germany, and how this fact had not prevented Bismarck from securing colonial advantages at the expense of both Britain and France during the years 1884–85. The explanation lies in the system, originated by Bismarck in the early seventies, which continued developing until 1914, the system of the great European alliances. This remarkable arrangement of inter-national checks and balances for a long time preserved peace among the peoples, but by the very fact of its existence ultimately engen-dered strife. For the system was one of competing alliances, not of a universal league. It was a Balance, not a Concert, of Power. As one combination strengthened or developed, its growth alarmed other states outside its orbit and mechanically produced a counter-combination. Competing alliances produced competing armaments, and the rivalry of hatred and of fear ended in the two opposed groups carrying their competition to the battlefield. In 1914, when it seemed clear that war was inevitable, the German Foreign Under-Secretary 'expressed regret that Germany, France "and perhaps England" had been drawn in—none of whom wanted war in the least and said that it came from "this d—d system of alliances, which were the curse of modern times." '[1] He forgot that Bismarck had been the chief archi-tect of the alliance system.[2]

Before 1870 the Great Powers in Europe were singularly divided. There was a close entente between Bismarck and Russia, but France was separated from Britain. Austria-Hungary and Italy hovered uneasily in the void. After the war of 1870, the three Great Powers

---

[1] G. P. Gooch and H. Temperley, *British Documents on the Origins of the War* (1927–38), vol. XI, p. 284.

[2]. Cp. A. J. P. Taylor, *The Struggle for Mastery in Europe* (1954), chs xii–xv. For texts of engagements, see A. F. Pribram. *The Secret Treaties of Austria-Hungary* (1920–21), 2 vols.

of Eastern Europe drew together, and a meeting at Berlin of the Emperors of Russia, Germany, and Austria resulted in the entente known as the Three Emperors' League. But the ideas of Austria-Hungary differed essentially from those of Russia. Austria-Hungary wished to absorb Serbia, to annex Salonika, but to preserve the Turkish Empire if she could. Russia wished to dominate Bulgaria, to annex Constantinople, and to break up the Turkish Empire if she could. Between these two views there could be no real reconciliation. Warning was given of that even in 1876, when the Tsar had asked Bismarck this embarrassing question: Would Germany remain neutral in case of a war between Austria-Hungary and Russia? Bismarck was compelled to answer that Germany would have to see to it that neither belligerent lost her influence or independence as a Great Power. He meant, to put it in plain words, that Germany would never allow Russia to crush Austria-Hungary. The Tsar did not forget the warning, and on January 15, 1877, he secretly promised to connive at the Austro-Hungarian occupation of Bosnia-Herzegovina, in return for Austria-Hungary's neutrality in the coming war. At the Congress of Berlin, when war had ceased, the Tsar, already warned and suspicious, thought he perceived that Germany had weighted the scales against Russia. And his letter to the Emperor William in April 1879 even suggested to Germany that war might be the result of thus estranging an old friend.

The attitude of Russia brought Bismarck face to face with a very grave decision. The exposed position of Germany in Central Europe rendered a close alliance necessary with someone. Italy and Britain were hardly suitable, for he hated parliamentary states and did not think that any alliance with them could be permanent or stable. Austria-Hungary alone supplied him with what he wanted, so he was forced to approach her. Andrássy, the very able Austro-Hungarian Foreign Minister, was tottering to his fall. But he remained in office just long enough to conclude an arrangement. He played the gigantic fish with a master-hand. He knew that Bismarck feared a Franco-Russian combination and saw in this an opportunity to sell the Austro-Hungarian Alliance at a high price. He refused to engage to assist Germany against France, and treated the menaces of Bismarck with indifference. After a visit to Vienna in October, Bismarck came to an unexpected decision. 'If you will not accept my terms,' he said to Andrássy, 'I am forced to accept yours.' And thus, for once in his lifetime, the Iron Chancellor capitulated. But he found it a difficult matter to convince William I, that 'old gentleman of eighty-two . . . with whom habit exercises enormous influence.' The aged Emperor was deeply attached both by sentiment and conviction to the old bond with Russia, but Bismarck prevailed with him at last, as he always did. The Treaty, held up by various preliminaries, was finally signed on October 7, 1879. It was, in form, simply a defensive alliance. By Article I each agreed to assist the other, if attacked by Russia. By Article II each agreed to observe 'benevolent neutrality,' if the other was attacked by 'another Power,' i.e. France. If Russia joined France, 'either by active co-operation or military measures,' however, Austria and Germany agreed to act together. The Alliance was to continue valid for five years, with a possible extension. It was renewed in 1883 and at subsequent intervals and, after 1902, was automatically renewed at the end of every three years until 1914. Andrássy succeeded in his great object by not committing Austria to war with France alone, but he failed to prevent the existence of the Treaty being made known to Russia before the end of the year. For the moment the effect was satisfactory, and Russia stopped 'breathing fire and flame.' But, taking long views, it ensured the estrangement of Russia from Germany, though the separation might be, and was, delayed. Even Bismarck's legerdemain could not prevent a result which lay in the logic of events.

Thus, secure in a firm alliance with Austria-Hungary, Bismarck felt strong enough to approach Russia once more.[1] On June 18, 1881, the *Dreikaiserbund* was defined by a secret treaty signed at Berlin. By Article I Austria-Hungary, Germany and Russia agreed to 'observe benevolent neutrality and to localise the war' if hostilities occurred between one of them and a fourth Great Power. This applied not only, of course, to France, or perhaps Britain, but also to Turkey. In the latter case it was, however, stipulated that the three Powers must reach a previous agreement as to the results of the war before Turkey was attacked. By Article II Russia recognised the Austro-Hungarian position in the Balkans as created by the Treaty of Berlin. By a separate protocol Austria-Hungary was to be allowed to annex Bosnia-Herzegovina whenever she chose, and to continue to occupy the Sanjak of Novibazar. Russia's compensation for this was that the other Powers undertook not to oppose but amicably arrange for the addition of Eastern Rumelia to Bulgaria, if and when produced by the force of circumstances. By Article III the three Powers agreed to compel Turkey to maintain the principle of closing the Straits of Constantinople to warlike operations.

The *Dreikaiserbund* Treaty was renewed in 1884, but expired in 1887, three years before Bismarck's fall. It unquestionably served a useful purpose, for it enabled Bismarck to intervene with effect whenever friction occurred, as it frequently did, between Austria-

[1] At one time he tried to sweep Britain into the net of his combination, and actually suggested an Austro-German-British alliance against Russia. Beaconsfield declined the overture. He let it be known that Britain would not take any step hostile to France, but would, in all probability, support Germany and Austria against Russia. Bismarck troubled no more about Britain, and during 1880 the project of an Austro-Russo-German *rapprochement* was taken up again. Cp. A. J. P. Taylor, *The Struggle for Mastery in Europe*, (1954), p. 265.

Hungary and Russia. But this arrangement could not be permanent, and in fact it broke down in the Bulgarian crisis of 1885–87. Article I of this *Dreikaiserbund* Treaty provided for the contingency of a Great Power (or Turkey) attacking one of the three Powers. But it stipulated for nothing more than 'benevolent neutrality,' and was therefore far less strong than the Austro-German Treaty of 1879, which bound Germany to defend Austria against Russia by arms. For the 1879 Treaty was a real Alliance of two Powers: that of 1881 a vaguer Entente between three. And against the iron of the Alliance the earthenware of the Entente was bound to be shattered in the end.

By 1881 Bismarck was secure in Europe. He encouraged Britain and France in annexationist designs oversea, so that Britain occupied Egypt and France occupied Tunis. Italy had long had her eye on Tunis, but Bismarck had thoughtfully omitted to inform her of France's intentions. Italy, in some indignation, felt herself isolated and turned to her old enemy Austria-Hungary for help. But Bismarck turned to advantage even the irritation of Italy. He induced Austria-Hungary to put pressure on Italy, and obtained an invitation to Germany to form part of a new combination, and thus secured a further defence against France.

On May 20, 1882, Italy, Germany and Austria signed a Triple Alliance Treaty at Vienna, which may be described as one of neutrality and guarantee. In the case of a French attack on Italy, Germany and Austria-Hungary would aid her. Italy agreed to help Germany against a French attack. In case one or two of the signatory Powers were attacked by two other Powers (i.e. Russia and France), all the signatory Powers would unitedly make war.[1] The arrangement was to hold for five years and to be kept secret. This treaty benefited Germany, for she obtained from Italy that promise of support against France which Austria-Hungary had refused. Italy gained even more, for she was not bound to aid either Austria-Hungary or Germany against an attack by Russia *alone*. And she *was* protected against Austria-Hungary by the very fact of the Alliance. Thus at one and the same time Bismarck had given Germany treaties of alliance or defence against Russia and France, and yet included Russia in one of his treaties, and extended his general system of control to Italy and Rumania.[2]

The efficacy of all these arrangements was tested in 1885. In that year Eastern Rumelia revolted from Turkey and threw in her lot with

---

[1] Italy specially stipulated that the treaty was in no case to be directed against Britain.

[2] In 1883 Austria-Hungary also made a secret treaty with Rumania, by which the two Powers agreed to support one another against Russia if attacked by her. Bismarck acceded to this treaty at once, and Italy in 1888.

Bulgaria. The complications of this Bulgarian imbroglio have already been described elsewhere. It is enough to say here that Russia regarded Bismarck as having pursued a double-faced policy in the Balkans, and blamed him for a result which he had not desired and could not avert. The Tsar Alexander III was deeply moved, and articles, openly advocating a Franco-Russian Alliance, began to appear in Russian papers in the autumn of 1886. To all intents and purposes, the *Dreikaiserbund* Treaty was already dissolved, though Bismarck was still secure by his Alliances with Austria-Hungary, with Italy and Rumania. But Russia was alienated and might soon become hostile.

The Reichstag received evidence of the gravity of the situation when a vote for the increase of the army for seven years was demanded in January 1887. Moltke openly said that Germany must be ready for war, and Bismarck declared that, while he did 'not expect an attack or hostility from Russia,' he had to be prepared. 'The difficulty is not to keep Germany and Russia but Austria and Russia at peace, and to ingeminate peace in both Cabinets.' The peace-maker, in Bismarck's view, would only be effective if he obtained new weapons of war. Turning then to France, he declared that he wished to be at peace with her; that he would not attack her on the theory of 'preventive war,' i.e. because war was inevitable; but that, if war did occur, the war of 1870 would be child's play compared with that of 1890. In such case France 'would bleed us white, and, if we won, after being attacked, we would do the same.'[1]

The attitude of Russia had become almost menacing for Bismarck in 1887. The press attacks on Germany had continued, and Bismarck knew that the Tsar had refused to repress them. But the *Dreikaiserbund* of 1881 expired in 1887 and thus provided Bismarck with an opportunity. For the triple bond he substituted a dual arrangement between Russia and Germany, which history knows as the Re-insurance Treaty. It was signed on June 18, 1887, together with 'an additional and very secret protocol.' The chief provisions were: (1) If one Power was at war with a third Great Power, the other would maintain benevolent neutrality and try to localise the conflict. (2) Germany recognised the preponderant influence of Russia in Bulgaria, and agreed to prevent the restoration of Prince Alexander. (3) Maintenance of the principle of closing the Straits of Constantinople, on the lines of the *Dreikaiserbund* Treaty of 1881.

Bismarck, by this Treaty, in effect, counterworked Austria-Hungary. He maintained that he was really benefiting her because he kept a certain restraining hand over Russia by the Re-insurance Treaty.

---

[1] General Boulanger, as War Minister, had recently been agitating France, but Bismarck's coolness and prudence in refusing to take offence prevented serious consequences.

But Austria-Hungary and Russia were now on the brink of war, and the former suspected Bismarck, and with some reason, of duplicity. The inconsistencies of Bismarck's position become clearer if the Re-insurance Treaty is compared with the Mediterranean Agreement signed in December 1887 by Britain, Austria-Hungary and Italy with Bismarck's encouragement, for this was founded on the principle of maintaining the 'independence of Turkey' from 'all foreign preponderating influence,'and referred specifically in this connection to the position of Bulgaria.[1]

Such were the complications of the international situation when Bulgaria selected Ferdinand of Coburg as her prince, and when that prince, having failed to obtain the consent of the Powers, proceeded to Bulgaria and took the oath as her ruler (August 14, 1887). Russia at once proposed to eject him; but this suggestion brought Britain and Italy closer to Austria, and made it clear that they might support her in her opposition to Russia's design to make Bulgaria a vassal-state of her Empire. The tension in Austria-Hungary and Russia became so great that Bismarck finally intervened. In February 1888 he published the Austro-German Treaty of 1879, thus announcing to the world that Germany would not permit Austria, if attacked by Russia, to lose her independence or her position as a Great Power. In the Reichstag he referred openly to the danger from France and to her connection with Russia. He said Germany was strong enough to defend herself, and to protect her 'safe friend' Austria-Hungary. 'Bulgaria is not an object of sufficient magnitude to set Europe aflame in a war whose issue none can foretell. I do not expect an early breach of the peace. But I advise other countries to discontinue their menaces. We fear God and nothing else in the world.' This proud speech evoked hearty cheers from the German Jingoes and was plainly intended to bring pressure to bear upon Russia.

For a few weeks Russia still pressed for the exclusion of Ferdinand from Bulgaria. Bismarck, bound by the Re-insurance Treaty hedged; but Austria, Italy and Britain showed no sign of yielding. Finally, therefore, Russia collapsed and accepted, though with an ill grace, the inevitable. Ferdinand remained as Prince of Bulgaria, and Bulgaria became in fact independent both of Russia and of Turkey. Austria-Hungary's position in the Balkans was stronger, for Serbia and Bulgaria both leaned on her for support. Britain and Italy were in the background. Germany still occupied the centre of the stage with her pledge of protection to Austria-Hungary, but she was no longer able to reconcile it with her Re-insurance Treaty with Russia.

[1] The Triple Alliance Treaty was renewed in 1887. Italy made agreements on two points with Germany and Austria separately: (1) Germany promised Italy to support by arms her claims to Tripoli and to check those of France in Morocco, in return for a renewed Italian offer to aid Germany against France in Europe; (2) Austria recognised Italy's interests in the Balkans, thereby making a great concession.

The old Emperor William told Bismarck that he was like a rider on a horse, who tossed five balls in the air and caught and threw them up again as they fell. The incomparable wizard had reached a time when he could no longer keep up all five. So long as no one except Russia knew of it, the Re-insurance Treaty was useful enough. Though .it had not prevented Russia from being defeated it had averted war over the Bulgarian affair. But Bismarck had only averted war by publishing the 1879 Treaty, which proved that, in the last resort, Germany would stand by Austria-Hungary. In that case Russia must find another ally who was not bound to Austria-Hungary and that ally could only be France. Bismarck's wizardry was not indeed exhausted and the Franco-Russian Alliance not yet concluded. In 1890 he renewed negotiations for a further Russo-German understanding, as the Re-insurance Treaty was just expiring. They failed just after Bismarck's fall (1890). But it may be doubted whether even his jugglery could have kept the five balls still in the air. The 1879 Treaty and the Triple Alliance Treaty ultimately conflicted with the Re-insurance Treaty. The time was now coming when the choice had to be definitely made. Was there to be a German alliance with Austria-Hungary and with Italy, or with Russia? There could not be one with both, and Bismarck had to stand by the Triple Alliance of Germany, Austria, and Italy. Bismarck's own policy therefore tended, in the long run, to throw Russia into the arms of France.

A general survey of the Bismarckian policy between 1870 and 1890 shows that it was primarily inspired by the idea of keeping France in order and enabling Germany to develop her new possessions and her enormous resources undisturbed. He encouraged Italy and Britain to rival France in colonial development so as to divert her attention from Alsace-Lorraine. He secured Germany against France by alliance with Italy, and against Russia by alliance with Austria. The problem Bismarck could not solve was how to remain on good terms, or in alliance, both with Austria and with Russia at once. The impossibility was made manifest in 1888, when he published to the world the German-Austrian Treaty of 1879 which pledged him to protect Austria against Russia. Russia knew, though the world did not, that the Re-insurance Treaty pledged Germany to be neutral if Russia was at war with another Power (i.e. Austria). Genius can make black look like white for a time, but not for ever, and Russia at last knew in 1888 that the great diplomatic artist had tricked her. That he could have continued to trick her in the future seems highly improbable. Bismarck was bound more tightly to Austria-Hungary than to Russia, and the truth was out at last. It is true that Russia had not finally severed her connection with Germany when Bismarck fell in 1890. And it is probably true that his puny successors drove Russia into opposition more quickly than he would have done. But that the ways of Russia and Germany lay apart after 1888 seems morally certain. Indeed there is reason to believe that Bismarck himself recognised the fact and was looking for compensation elsewhere. Bismarck's policy of walking along the knife-edge that separated two dangerous alternatives had in the end failed. However that may be, the great Chancellor fell in 1890, and the brilliant, impulsive and reckless William II became German Emperor in fact as well as in name. The real cause of the failure of the Bismarckian system was not the contradictions implied in it—they were many and had been in it from the beginning—but that these ceased to be latent. They ceased to be latent as soon as the alliance obligations were activated. As long as it was a system of possibilities only and Germany made no actual claim on an ally the system worked to give Germany friends and a free hand in Europe. As soon as Germany ceased to be a satisfied Power, as soon, that is to say, as she adopted a colonial policy she was likely to claim the support of one of her allies and the system would cease to be one of possibilities and become one of actualities. That is why Bismarck's decision, mentioned in the previous chapter, to adopt a colonial policy was so important. Germany had now become a driving Power and to drive forward in any direction, in China, Morocco or the Ottoman Empire, and she drove in all these directions under William II, caused her to claim the support of Austria-Hungary and to lose that of Russia.

Even in 1888 Russian policy had been tending in the direction of France, but Tsar Alexander III was slow to move and hard to convince. His Ministers and relatives moved more quickly, and, as a result of the visit of a Grand Duke to Paris in November 1888, agreements were made for the supply of French armaments and munitions to Russia. The Grand Duke Nicholas assured the French Premier in 1889 that the two armies, 'will be one in time of war.' French diplomats and generals planned and executed a careful campaign of cajolery and flattery. And in 1891 Russia was revealed to all the world as absolutely isolated in Europe. For in that year the Triple Alliance was again renewed for six years, and Britain, still hostile to Russia, showed a friendly interest in this renewal. The French Government saw their opportunity, redoubled their attentions and floated Russian loans in Paris. In August 1891 the outlines of agreement were sketched out. (1) the two Powers agreed to an *Entente Cordiale* and to confer on every question of a nature to threaten peace. (2) If peace was in danger, and especially if one of the two were menaced by aggression, they agreed to concert measures. But the stubborn Tsar was still reluctant to commit himself, and it was not until December 27, 1893, that a Military Convention, supplementing this agreement, was accepted. Russia agreed to assist France if attacked by Germany or by Italy supported by Germany. France agreed to assist Russia if attacked by Germany, or by Austria-Hungary supported by Germany. The French promised to employ 1,300,000 and the Russians 700,000 to 800,000 men against Germany. The Dual Alliance was thus practically complete.[1]

The Alliance was suspected at the time, but was not definitely revealed till 1895. It was an event of the greatest importance. The Dual Alliance was now opposed to the Triple Alliance and Germany thus had a formidable enemy on either flank. Europe was thus divided into two camps and each was necessarily an armed one. The balance was, for a time, fairly even, though in fact the Franco-Russian combination was probably the weaker. Italy was an uncertain and suspected ally to Austria-Hungary and to Germany. But, so long as Britain did not take one or other side, there was still a chance that European peace would be preserved. And a decade was to elapse before Britain's old hostility to France was overcome. During that period Britain approached both Russia and Germany with proposals for an alliance, and each time in vain.

Bismarck may well have given pride of place to the conduct of foreign policy, but without constantly safeguarding his position with the Emperor, with the Reichstag and with public opinion he might well have lost the Chancellorship and the very position which enabled him to make foreign policy. His partnership with the Emperor was one of the most successful partnerships between ruler and minister that history affords. With the Reichstag an appearance of success concealed his manoeuvres and surrenders which made the relationship workable. As for public opinion, though his reputation declined after 1888, he never quite lost that public favour which caused most towns to have their Bismarck memorial, street or square. The defeat of the Second Reich in the War of 1914–18, the collapse of the Third Reich in 1945 and the subsequent division of Germany have caused a reassessment of Bismarck's statesmanship. It is now noticed that he left a legacy of internal tension to William II by his skill in handling domestic problems without solving them and, above all, by his manoeuvring among the parties—reducing them in the process to mere interest groups—to gain support for his preconceived policy instead of making his policies with a party of his own under his own leadership.

Certainly one part of his policy after 1870 was a failure and he recognised it as that and reversed it. This was the *Kulturkampf* or the battle between the Prussian State and the Catholic Church. It is not wholly fair to ascribe the battle to Bismarck alone. There was a *Kulturkampf* in Baden too and indeed, in so far as the Catholic Church and Liberalism were opposed, there was a universal *Kulturkampf*

---

[1] All these documents are in A. F. Pribram, *The Secret Treaties of Austria-Hungary* (1920–21), vol. II, pp. 204 *ff*.

after 1870. Pius IX had published the Encyclical Quanta Cura and the Syllabus of Errors in 1864 in condemnation of much that Liberals accepted and, as we saw in chapter 16, proclaimed Papal Infallibility. But Bismarck brought matters to a head in Prussia in a way which created agitation and real distress. There were Catholics in East Prussia, in Prussian Poland, in Silesia and in the Prussian Rhineland. Prussia was no longer the Protestant state she had been in the eighteenth century. The Prussian constitution as revised in 1850 appropriately provided for the religious neutrality of the Prussian State. It also safeguarded the property and rights of all religious communities equally. The stipends of clergy and the upkeep of Churches and their services were financed by the State. Taxation levied for this purpose assumed that everyone belonged to one Church or another. It was this doctrine that Bismarck's policy would have set aside in favour of a third position where the state was neither identified with one Church, nor neutral between Churches, but neutral as between churches and those who belonged to no church. This position meant secular schools and civil marriage. In 1871 the Prussian *Landtag* enacted a law which protected those who left a Church from any action on its part to recover them. In 1874 it made civil marriage legal. But the *Kulturkampf* waged by Bismarck and the Prussian Minister for religious affairs and education, Adalbert Falk, was specifically against the Catholic Church. Bismarck seems to have believed that the Catholic Church endangered the coherence of the newly unified German State and through its strength in France, Belgium, Italy, Austria, Poland and its universal claims endangered his foreign policy. All Catholics were possible enemies of the Reich. Political Catholicism, in the shape of the Centre Party, strong in both the Reichstag and the Prussian *Landtag*, was independent, and often in opposition, with its own social and political ideas. First the Catholic section of the Prussian Ministry for religious affairs and education was abolished and then the *Landtag* enacted the legislation known as the May Laws (1873). These limited the Catholic Church's control (and at the same time extended the Government control) over the appointment of its clergy, the education of children, the training of priests and the religious direction of its own members. In 1873 the Reichstag by its anti-Jesuit law banned the Order in Germany. The Reichstag had fired a shot at the very heart of Liberalism for the law discriminated against one group of Germany's citizens. Meanwhile in Prussia the conflict took the form of episcopal and clerical protest answered by the suspension of stipends. Sees and parishes were declared vacant when their incumbents refused to submit and in due course state appointees appeared in them. In 1875 the articles protecting the Churches were dropped from the Prussian constitution and all religious orders in Prussia dissolved. When in 1878, Pius IX was succeeded by Leo XIII Bismarck began the process of repairing damaged diplomatic relations with the Papacy, of dismantling the May Laws and allowing gradually the state appointees in the parishes to be replaced by clergy acceptable to both Church and State. The last of the laws bringing religious peace to Prussia was passed in 1883 and the conflict was over by 1886. Civil marriage and secular education for children whose parents wished for it and powers for the State to object to clerical appointments, which it dared not use, were the meagre outcome of much disturbance.

In 1878–79 there occurred in Germany something of a change of course. Bismarck moved away from the policy which, with the support of the National and Left Liberals in the Reichstag, he had so far pursued in other areas as well as the ecclesiastical. Another piece of discriminatory legislation was passed by the Reichstag: the anti-socialist law of October 12, 1878. Bismarck thus fired another shot at the heart of Liberalism and it reached its target. It was also a bid for independence from the Liberal Parties upon which he had so far relied. He had great difficulty in putting the law through. An attempt to assassinate the Emperor was the pretext for it, but the attempt could not convincingly be blamed on the socialists; nor could a second attempt in this same year, 1878. So Bismarck persuaded the Emperor to dissolve the Reichstag and trusted to the general *malaise* produced by the assassination attempts to bring him a favourable majority in the General Election which followed. This is what happened and with a smaller liberal representation the Reichstag passed the law which lasted until September 1890 when William II caused it to lapse. It did not destroy the Socialist Party or socialist representation, which increased, in the Reichstag. It allowed police action against those who threatened the harmony of social classes or public peace. It could, therefore, mean much or little as the State chose. Its political importance was greater in so far as it was part of a manoeuvre by Bismarck against the Liberal Parties.

It will be recalled that from the time of the Zollverein onwards Germany had favoured a trade policy of low tariffs. In 1873 there came, by the standards of those days, a drastic economic slump. This caused a general stock-taking on the tariff question. There was public pressure for a change of policy. Certainly Bismarck wished to do what was in the economic interest of German farmers and industrialists. He also had political reasons for proposing the protective tariff enacted by the Reichstag on July 15, 1879. It put moderate duties on imported foodstuffs and manufactured goods, and was part of the general European move away from free trade at this period. Politically and in its German context it was part of a coherent and systematic revision of attitudes which would both give Bismarck a new coalition of supporters in the Reichstag and strengthen the financial position of the Reich. For its revenue the Reich depended upon contributions from the individual states or upon loans. Revenue from import duties would increase the Reich's resources and do so without increasing its dependence upon the Reichstag, because such duties enacted by law for a period of years would not be subject to annual budgetary control. Bismarck was always to fail in attempts to increase Reich revenue and he was only partially successful this time. The Centre Party, always an opponent of centralisation and a supporter of State rights, carried an amendment which set a limit to the amount to be received by the Reich from the new duties. Anything above the limit was to be returned to the States who were responsible for collecting them at the ports. The policy was for the time economically advantageous. Finally, the balance of power between the parties in the Reichstag was completely changed by the passage of the tariff law. It changed in favour of the Conservative Parties and the Centre Party. The National Liberals disintegrated to the advantage of the Left liberals and the Socialists.

With the support of a new coalition of parties in the Reichstag Bismarck now put through social legislation designed to win back the working classes antagonised by the anti-socialist law; designed also to establish a measure of social security far ahead of that which any other State yet had. The Reichstag enacted sickness insurance for workingmen in 1883, accident insurance in 1884 and pension insurance in 1889, all financed by contributions from the State, the employer and the employee. But the political balance of power had once again changed and imposed a new set of manoeuvres upon Bismarck. A new moderate Liberal Party had organised itself and showed its strength in the elections of 1887. The Centre Party, the Left Liberals and Social Democrats had begun a campaign against the high expenditure on the army. The campaign coincided with a Court intrigue against the Minister of War. The intriguers used the campaign to cut down his control over the army. The result of their efforts was to increase the isolation of the army from the nation, to associate it more closely with the Emperor and to give grounds in William II's reign for talk of the rising militarism of Germany. Meanwhile the immediate consequence of the attack was that Bismarck feared that the increased military budget for 1887 might have difficulty in passing the Reichstag. Once again Bismarck manoeuvred to provide the Government with a new set of supporters. So the Cartel, as it was called, came into being: a coalition of the new Liberal Party and the Conservative Parties directed against the Centre Party and the Left Liberals. Bismarck was perhaps more successful in domestic than in foreign politics in walking the knife-edge between extremes and in keeping his options open. But if this was so, it was at the expense of the quality of party politics, and social peace.

Chapter 24

THE NATIONS OF EUROPE AT THE END OF THE NINETEENTH CENTURY, 1890–1905

The last decade of the nineteenth century was the last period when the scale on which Europe's affairs were conducted was still small. The twentieth century, when the scale was the scale of massed populations, mass production in industry and global distances, seems in retrospect further away from the nineties than the nineties seem from the age of the French Revolution. But the scale was already changing. There will, therefore, be much to say in this chapter of population growth, of industrialisation, of railways. There will also be much to say of a new theme which connects the nineteenth century with the world wars of the twentieth century: political instability. This is why Russia comes first in this chapter. She was the first state to experience revolution—in 1905—in the twentieth century. So that the instability of the autocracy was really important though not particularly striking to contemporary observers. France comes next, by way of contrast. She was taken by observers as the very type of a politically instable country, because of her constant change of Ministers. The reality was different from the appearance, because below the surface important stabilising factors operated. Germany and Austria-Hungary come next, because they too form a pair of contrasting states. Germany was powerful, dynamic and assertive, but directed on an uncertain course. Austria-Hungary was internally paralysed because the *Ausgleich* was coming under pressure from new forces which did not fit into the structure of the Monarchy made by it, but the direction of her external policy was steady. Britain will not figure in this chapter and Italy will take up little space, because the changes being dealt with have worked themselves out earlier in Britain and will happen later in Italy. This grouping of the states also corresponds with the two armed camps into which Europe by 1907 was divided, but the chapter will stop before the division has been completed. It has been shown how Russia and France came together and will be shown in the next chapter how Britain and France reached an understanding but not Russia and Britain. On the other side, Austria and

Germany and Italy stand together as they had stood since the Treaties of 1879 and 1882. But Italy's independence of the Triple Alliance is already marked.

In the later years of Alexander II's reign the slowness and indecision of the Tsar caused everything to stick in bureaucratic routine. There were those at Court and at the head of the administration who continued to be interested in relaxing the autocracy and bringing about a wider sharing of political power. One of these was Loris-Melikov, just appointed Minister of the Interior. A constitutional plan which he had brought forward was widely thought to be on the point of signature when the Tsar was assassinated (March 1881). Under Alexander III, who now succeeded his father, the constitutional movement evaporated. A baffling passivity lay upon Russia. The new Tsar had much intelligent good sense, courage, loyalty and moderation. But authority he did not have. He had an imperfect control of the conflicting impulses playing upon Court and Government. Moreover a shadow of plots, Jewish pogroms and revolutionary agitation hung over the régime and disabled it. But, as we have seen, he and his advisers in foreign policy had sufficient decision to make the alliance with France. Nicholas II, the last of the Tsars, succeeded Alexander III in 1894. He was indecisive, inconsistent and even more at the mercy of the last man with whom he had spoken than Alexander. But he and his advisers were also to make decisions in foreign policy.

Though there was passivity in the autocracy, there was great activity among its subjects. This was the period when industrialisation began and Russia experienced something like economic growth. In the nineties growth reached an average annual rate of more than 8 per cent. Characteristically in Russia the stimulus came from the centre: though some of the consequences of the emancipation of the serfs made the situation favourable to industrialisation and no stimulant could have been successful without a good deal of independent entrepreneurial activity. This stimulus was possible despite the general passivity, because it came from the Ministry of Finance whose area of policy was one which the Tsars traditionally regarded as less their concern than 'high policy', that is foreign relations, army and navy and broad political issues. Under the last two Tsars, first, I. A. Vishnegradksi from 1887 and then Count Witte from 1892, had in succession virtually a free hand in financial and economic matters. They were men of great energy, knowledge and force, Witte rather more so than Vishnegradski. They were helped to a free hand by the only change in government which was made in Alexander's reign. This was the establishment of a Council of Ministers which worked something like a western cabinet and allowed Ministers to support each other in a common policy apart from the Tsar.

First, let us study the way in which the emancipation of the serfs may have favoured industrialisation. It is obvious that free men can move out of farming, can go to the towns, can provide the labour necessary for mines, factories and textile mills. It is also obvious that free men may cultivate their land better than serfs, that landowners may capitalise farms that they had not bothered to improve when they could call upon unlimited supplies of unpaid labour; that farming may, therefore, produce more, may, indeed, produce enough to supply the new industrial areas. These things could have happened in Russia and, probably, in a general way and in the long term did happen. But there are certain awkward facts difficult to fit into this scheme. First, there was no great movement from countryside to town until the twentieth century. Second, industrialisation happened in Russia without a proportionately large increase in the labour force of industry. This was because Russia was able to import skill, technology and all available labour-saving devices from countries which had already been industrialised. There were advantages in being late in the field. Third, many industries, mining especially, had been worked in Russia by serfs: freed serfs hastened to leave hated mines and factories. If we think now of the food supply, we find no great increase in production. We find more farm produce coming on to the market. This was because it was the Finance Minister's policy, Witte's policy especially, to tax the peasants more and more heavily. The peasant had to sell more to have the money to pay tax. This policy might render the peasant destitute and increase peasant unrest, but it was a quick way of feeding the cities and industrial areas, without depending on a slow and doubtful improvement of farming. But since it was also the Finance Minister's policy, again Witte's especially, to stimulate the export of grain in order to give Russia a favourable balance of payments, more production for the market did not much improve the food supply for the cities. We must also remember that Russia's population grew from 97.7 millions in 1880 to 113 millions in 1887, to 118 millions in 1890, to 133 millions in 1900 and this affected both the supply side and the comsumer side of the economy.[1]

We may sum up the ways in which it is known that the emancipation helped industrialisation. It enlarged the reservoir from which entrepreneurial talent could be drawn and was drawn. The redistribution of land as between landowner and peasant in the more fertile parts of Russia brought fresh land into cultivation and more crops on to the world market. The redemption payments increased the part played by money in the peasant's way of life, encouraged him to think in terms of contracts, markets and long-term transactions, encour-

---

[1] These figures include the population of Russian Poland and except for the last are estimates, since no census was taken before 1897. They are taken from the *Cambridge Economic History of Europe* (1966), pp. 811 and 826. Cp. below p. 385.

aged him in short to come into the economy as a consumer of industrial goods. The end of the privilege of owning other men, a privilege belonging exclusively to one class, reduced the status and exclusiveness of that class and it was precisely the class with a vested interest in resisting industrialisation. There was a psychological effect among the peasants too, which made for mobility, open-mindedness to change and for the development among them of a rich class, the kulaks.

Let us now set out a few facts and figures to show what industrialisation amounted to before depression set in soon after 1900. In 1887 with a population of 113 millions there was an industrial workforce of just over one million; in 1900 in a population of 133 millions the work-force was about three millions. This is not perhaps a very large increase, but since industry was concentrated in relatively few areas the expansion was large where it happened. Both the number of industrial enterprises increased and the size of enterprises. Some of these such as the Putilov iron works outside St. Petersburg were very large by any standard. The main industrial areas of Russia were the St. Petersburg (Leningrad) area, and the nine provinces of the centre, including Moscow, the Donetz basin for coal, Russian Poland and the Urals. In other words, industry developed where it had always existed. There were, however, three new industrial areas. The exploitation of oil in the Caucasus, associated with one man above all others, Louis Nobel, began; heavy industry appeared in Poland and the metal industries of the Ukraine came to the fore. The main industrial products of Russia were textiles—that is, cotton cloth with the raw material coming overland from the east, and woollen cloth—coal, metals (chiefly pig-iron, but also steel), metal goods, oil and sugar. Russia also made great strides in mechanical engineering and started electrical engineering.

The whole was preluded by railway building and accompanied and followed by an expansion of banking and stock-exchange business. There was an expansion of the business classes to match the expansion of the industrial work-force. But the whole development took place in the context of artisan or craft industries. In the textile industry artisan activity quietly declined. But some artisan manufacturing benefited from the general development of business and the rise in living standards which appeared with industrialisation. The real decline of artisan industry did not occur until the twentieth century and then happened because the artisan found it difficult to fit himself into the increasingly large scale on which business activity, especially marketing, was taking place rather than because mechanised industry displaced him.

The stimulus to all development came from the centre in more than one way. The great Russian railway network, the finest part of which was the Trans-Siberian railway, decided upon for a political

345

purpose in 1891, was built by the State. Railways were always important in industrialisation, because of the scale of capital and materials they needed and the stimulus which the iron rails and the steam locomotives gave to the iron and coal industries, both in their building and subsequent running. Many mining and metallurgical enterprises were owned now as always by the State. Much of the capital which financed industrialisation came from abroad. It was the Ministry of Finance which borrowed abroad and brought in foreign capital for both state and private enterprise. Then, too, there was the Finance Minister's protectionist tariff policy. Above all Russia's financial policy in this period created confidence among prospective investors, domestic and foreign.

Something more, then, must be said of Vishnegradski and Witte. Vishnegradski had begun life as a schoolmaster, and made a fortune in trade and gained appointment to the civil service, was rapidly promoted until he became Finance Minister in 1887. He raised a series of great loans on the European money market. Russia was already borrowing less from Germany and more from France. He used the proceeds for railway building and other projects for which private capital was not available. He brought order into the national budget and was responsible for a number of debt conversions which reduced the cost to the State of the national debt. It was this policy which Witte continued. Witte's forebears came from the Baltic, but he himself was born and educated in Tiflis. His career had begun in the railway administration, in the very generating station, that is, of the new economic power. Witte is reputed to have made the peasants pay for the industrialisation of Russia. They were heavily taxed, it is said, to raise the capital necessary for new railways and new state factories and mines. They were certainly heavily taxed. Witte increased indirect taxation. Because this takes a disproportionate amount from a small cash income, it was harder on the peasant than anyone else. He made the sale of vodka and spirits a state monopoly and the Government spirit and wine shops charged high prices. He levied a heavy duty on sugar and used the proceeds to subsidise exports of sugar. Nor were these the only indirect taxes. Of the direct taxes the poll tax, which brought in little revenue, had been abolished before this period and the land tax was paid by both landowner and peasant. But like the indirect taxes and for the same reason, it was a heavier tax on the peasant than on the landowner even when they paid the same amount. Moreover the landowner assessed himself and could keep his assessment down, whereas the peasant was assessed by Government officials. Local taxation was twice as high on the peasant as on the landowners and for some local taxes the peasant alone was liable.

Witte is known as the Finance Minister who raised vast loans and committed Russia finally to borrowing from France. He made profitable deals on the international money market. He reorganised the State Bank to encourage it to lend money to prospective or established industrial enterprises; he stimulated saving and savings banks to provide industry with domestic capital. In Witte's period Russia came to be part of the international finance and banking network, a country tied to the international money market. This was partly because in 1897 he put Russia on the gold standard, now used by all the European countries (Austria, the last to do so, had adopted it in 1892). The tariff of 1891 put heavy duties on imported manufactured goods and on exported raw materials. Despite this protectionist tariff Russian trade expanded and expanded at an increasing rate. A favourable balance of payments brought Witte a large gold reserve. It was this that enabled him to put Russia on the gold standard. His motive for this measure was that it would increase, as it did, foreign confidence in Russia. It brought not only loans to the Government which carried the heavy expenditure of the Ministries for War, for the Navy and for Communications, but attracted foreign capital for investment in private industrial companies and attracted foreign companies to establish themselves in Russia.

It was not Witte's fault if Russia's prosperity encouraged her to embark on imperialist expansion in Manchuria and Korea which brought her to war with Japan, to fresh defeat and, in 1905, revolution. Nor was it his fault if industrialisation brought with it an industrial proletariat, ill-paid, ill-housed and badly exploited. It may have been partly his fault that the land settlement of 1861, now much in need of revision, was not revised. Though in 1896 Witte reduced the land tax by half for the next ten years, this did not abate the generally disproportionately high level of peasant taxation. Witte, as we have seen, provided some justification for the view that the peasant, as always, was the most oppressed part of the population. There were already in 1902 peasant riots in the provinces of Kharkov and Poltava. Nor, of course, was it Witte's fault that the radical intelligentsia was now throwing out truly revolutionary offshoots for discontented workers and peasants to use to some purpose.

In the seventies the Narodniks or Populists had arisen. They believed that Russia's future lay with 'the people', whom they distinguished from the landowners and the educated intelligentsia. They were perhaps right to distinguish between themselves, as the intelligentsia, and 'the people', for they were not understood. They were less understood than were the landowners, however valiant their own efforts to understand. The truth was that 'the people' for them was an idealised abstraction. They were not averse to individual terrorist acts. One of their number, Vera Zasulich, had assassinated Alexander II. She with others became Marxists, who will be considered presently. In the seventies and eighties their leading writers were N. K. Mihailovsky, N. Danielson and V. P. Vorontsov. They were political and moral theorists, preaching respect for the individual and the importance of elective institutions at local and national level and seeking universal education. They detested, above all, that any man should have absolute power over other men. They were sharply repressed in the late eighties. But opposition nevertheless grew.

By the nineties the other face of Russia,the face of the opposition, was seen in some five groups. There was already a Marxist group to which the modern Communist party traces its ancestry. It was organised in the League of Struggle for the Liberation of theWorking Class, founded in Russia in 1883. To this Vladimir Ulyanov (Lenin) belonged. He had been expelled from the University of Kazan for his revolutionary activities. He sought a meeting with the League's leader, Plekhanov, who had been a Narodnik, and he became a member. In 1898 the Russian Social Democrat Workers' Party was founded and held its first tiny congress. There were Social Democratic Circles, or discussion groups, all over Russia, and the handful of men at the congress came from these circles. The members of the Party at the congress were arrested soon afterwards. Lenin was already in punitive exile in Siberia. So it was that Plekhanov, Martov, Axelrod, Zasulich and Potresov organised Russian Marxism from outside Russia. Their newspapers—*Iskra* (the Spark) and *Zarya* (Dawn)—were published abroad and were laying the basis for the Social Democracy of the twentieth century. In 1903 Lenin's dynamic personality split the Party into two: so arose the Menshevik and Bolshevik Parties.

Inside Russia was a second group, called the legal Marxists, because they lived legally and were neither *émigrés* nor prisoners. They kept within the limits allowed by the censor in the articles they published in their journals. This they could do by writing on economics and avoiding social questions. One of their journals rose to a circulation of 5000, largely because of Maxim Gorki's contributions. They did much to make Marxism a matter of general interest and its terms and ideas familiar, though not perhaps understood. Peter Struve, Tugan-Baranovsky, Berdaev, Bulgakov, Frank were the principal writers. They were all university men. Peter Struve belonged to a family of German origin and scientific interests. He published in 1894 *Critical Notes on the Question of the Economic Development of Russia*.

Third, were the Socialist Revolutionaries. They carried forward into the twentieth century what the Populists in the seventies had stood for, in other words, they were prepared to execute individual acts of terrorism and had a combat brigade from 1902–07 for the purpose; and they looked forward to the inevitable social revolution. Their distinguishing characteristic was their belief in the *obshchina* and they looked to the peasants, not to the proletariat, to make the revolution. They believed that the customary, communal life of the *obshchina* would enable Russia to step straight into the Socialist Revolution without a bourgeois interlude. There was even continuity of membership with the Populists; for by the nineties some of the Populist groups had begun to meet again. They were not Marxists. Their new name was intended to distinguish them alike from the Social Democrats and their own Populist past. By 1901 the most important groups came together in the Socialist Revolutionary Party and published abroad a journal called *Revolutionary Russia*. They were to play a part in the first Duma; Russia's first parliament, set up in 1905.

Fourth, were the so-called Economists, whose intellectual leader was Kuskova. The 'Imperial Free Economic Society' was a chartered society, originated by Catherine II for conducting research into various aspects of agricultural science. Its so-called literary committee was set up after the famine of 1891, to publish cheap good books for working-class and peasant readers. When it became a centre of progressive thought of all kinds the Government closed it (1895). The members, however, continued the work as individuals. They included a group who concentrated on agitation for reform. They had a programme of democratic reform to be achieved in alliance with the liberals and they wished to postpone the Socialist Revolution. 'For the Russian Marxist there was only one way: to support the economic struggle of the proletariat and to participate in liberal opposition activity.' Characteristic of their position was the belief that the worker was only interested in economic questions; that this was the natural result of Russian history and the long exclusion of the people from politics. The Economists were in touch with working men and knew more of the realities of their lives than other groups did. The group acquired impetus from a great success. It was responsible for the great law of June 2, 1897. This was important as the first piece of factory legislation in Russia, not on account of its liberalism for it established a normal working day of eleven and a half hours. It did not prevent strikes. The strike among the St. Petersburg weavers of 1895 began the year of strikes of 1896–97 which continued after the law, in 1898, and were accompanied in 1899 by student unrest.

Lastly there were the Liberals. Many young radical idealists found an outlet for their idealism in the day-to-day work of the Zemstva and City Council secretariats. There was enough to do in the provision and maintenance of schools, hospitals and public works and the defence of their activities against the encroachment of the administration. Their hope was for civil liberties and greater freedom of expression and some channel whereby the views of a much wider group of classes among the Russian people could penetrate to the Court and Government, but they were rebuffed by Nicholas II on his accession. During his reign, before 1905, they concentrated on gaining some sort of national union of Zemstva and bringing forward

Zemstva opinions. They were important also in the 'Imperial Free Economic Society' and took part in enquiries into trade unionism or the economic conditions of Russia. By 1900 Peter Struve had led the legal Marxists out of social democracy into the Liberal movement. From then onwards he published the *Liberator* as the Liberal organ, abroad, in Stuttgart. The Liberals were to provide the backbone of the Cadet Party in the first Duma.

The condition of France throughout this period was at once fluctuating and perplexing. The Republic which we last saw in the grip of Boulangism now had a Government of compromise and the second-best. Ministries continued to be short-lived, 'lute-string administrations', fading with the summer or changing with the wind. Gusts of popular passion, such as the one which caused Grévy to resign the Presidency in 1887, continued to force sharp, unexpected changes. The year 1889 saw the end of Boulangism, but its underlying causes were only smothered and would come to life again. The year 1892 had witnessed, on one hand, the solid achievement of the Franco-Russian *entente* (to become an alliance in 1893–94) and, on the other, an appalling exposure of the way Deputies sold their votes and accepted money for favours to be given to dubious speculators. That particular instance related to the Panama Canal. The years 1894–99 saw the Dreyfus Affair when a miscarriage of justice at the expense of a Jewish Army colonel, wrongfully convicted of spying for the Germans, raised great questions, ranging from anti-semitism to Army and Church justice versus Republican virtue. But these crises were symptoms of the way the French political system worked and did not in fact mean that France was either on the edge of collapse or a new *coup d'état*.[1] There was more unity in France in the nineties than there had been in the seventies or eighties. The Royalties were no longer of any real importance; Bonapartism had been laughed out of existence by the parody of it which the colourful side of Boulangism had been; the clericals were assimilated after the Pope's Encyclical of 1892 had enjoined them to accept the Republic; the Socialists were divided.

In view of their future importance a little more may be said of the Socialists. Some followed the dour, authoritarian Jules Guesde, a Marxist, into the *Parti Ouvrier Francqis* with 16,000 members in 1898 and 13 seats in the Chamber, but never master of the trade unions. (These were active after the law of 1884 permitted their existence.) Some followed Paul Brousse, who led a group to break away from Guesde and revolutionary Socialism. Some followed a much greater man than either of these, Jean Jaurès. It was he who eventually created a unified Socialist Party on a broad human basis, less doctri-

---

[1] See T. Zeldin, *France 1848–1945* (1978). vol. i, pp. 581 and 640.

naire, less authoritarian. Jaurès accepted some Marxist doctrines, but mixed them with liberal beliefs. He was both a practical politician and a great orator. In 1905 he created a united Socialist Party known as the French Section of the Workers' International. He was greatly respected in the French Chamber, where he sat as Deputy for the Tarn in the years 1885–89, 1893–98 and 1902–14.

The first decade of the twentieth century brought to France somewhat accelerated economic growth and some decline of artisan industry in favour of factories. But she remained a thinly populated country—40.7 millions against Britain's 38.2 millions in 1900—though she no longer had a rate of decline instead of a rate of growth in population. The Méline tariff of 1891 had perpetuated tariff protection of the home market for both agriculture and industry and may have discouraged any great increase in production in both. The urban and industrial problems of unemployment, trade union action and strikes were increasingly important. They were much in the mind of successive Governments, especially when the Syndicalists, who aimed at using the general strike to destroy parliamentary institutions, came to the fore. But social problems did not constitute the stuff of parliamentary battles. Nor could they in the period cause any massive expansion of Socialism. It was, however, increasingly important. A sign of its growing importance was Waldeck-Rousseau's appointment of a Socialist, Millerand, as his Minister of the Interior. He, like later Radicals, depended on the alliance with the Socialists for his parliamentary majority. The Radicals, organised as a Party with an annual conference from 1901 onwards, continued to be dominant in the Chamber. Indeed, they increased their representation at each of the General Elections of 1902, 1906 and 1910. But in the period covered by this chapter they could not form a Government with a majority over all other Parties without the votes of the Socialists and others on their left.

France was really governed by her Chamber of Deputies. Its membership continued remarkably stable in contrast to the instability of Ministries. It effectively checked any Government's supremacy over it by frequent motions of censure, by constant interpellations which held up Government business, by the right which each Deputy had of introducing a Bill, which, if he could get the support of the appropriate Ministry, became as important as a Government measure, and, above all, by the system of permanent parliamentary commissions. Each commission had to report on every Bill in its field of competence and the Chamber acted on its report as much as on the Government's initial proposal. In so far as France was not governed by her Chamber of Deputies she was governed by her civil service and her Prefects. The Deputies, the same men over long periods, the civil servants and the Prefects, sub-Prefects and Mayors were all important elements of stability in France. Moreover, her slow industrialisation gave France a basic stability which was rare in Europe at the end of the nineteenth century.

The Church, the Army, state finance and taxation were the matters on which parliamentary politics turned. Under Combes, Rouvier and Sarrien in succession the Radicals between 1903 and 1905 treated the Church with such an outburst of their traditional anti-clericalism as to provoke something of a reaction. By the law of 1905 the system under which the Church had lived since Napoleon's Concordat was brought to an end. Church buildings continued to be public property, maintained by the Communes, but Church and State were separated. The Catholic Church and other religious communities were henceforward independent bodies, paying their own clergy and maintaining themselves from their own funds and those of their congregations. Anticlericalism was now exhausted as the main characteristic of Radicalism, but it had little else to put in its place. The prolonged period of the Radicals' ascendancy thrust Conservatives and Catholics into a kind of alienation from the State. Bergson, the philosopher, Charles Maurras with the group of *L'Action française*, Barrès, Peguy, Agathon were powerful writers who attracted followers. They were without an outlet in the Chamber and Government. They criticised the State and the whole political system: they never had to work it. Their prolonged period of ascendancy had also deprived the Radicals of the dynamism which had once entitled them to be thought of as the party of movement and reform. In 1900 France was still in the rut of the eighties and arguments about the length of service in the Army (reduced by Boulanger's reform and then again, in 1905, when liability to serve was freed from exemptions) were no substitute for much needed measures of social and economic change.

This period witnessed in Wilhelmine Germany a decline in the authority of the Emperor. He made too many bombastic speeches, invented too many all-too-memorable phrases and intervened in policy too often, in too many contradictory directions. The period witnessed, too, a decline in the power of the Chancellor. No successor of Bismarck, neither Caprivi (1890–94) nor Hohenlohe (at seventy-five in 1894 older than Bismarck when he resigned) nor Bülow (1900–09) knew how to exercise the legacy of power which Bismarck had bequeathed. There were able Ministers in Prussia, such as Johannes von Miquel, a notable Finance Minister, and G. von Gosslar, who tried to settle the schools question. Though the Prussian Ministry might serve the Reich it was never able to focus the power of the Reich. Nor could the *Reichsrat*, hampered by the dual allegiance of its members, all of them Ministers in their own states as well as members of the *Reichsrat*, do so. Had Germany had a central Ministry whose members were members of the Reichstag and responsible to it, the Reichstag might have done this. Though at the beginning of the twentieth century there were many who thought such a Ministry should be constituted and worked for it, they were too few and too weak. The Emperor's response to such agitation, or to attempts of the Reichstag to change policy, was to contemplate a *coup d'état*. He first spoke of this in 1894. The *Staatsstreich* has been much written about by historians, but it was a fantasy. The Emperor never bent his efforts to any one aim in any one direction long enough to have carried it through. Another feature of this period was, after the economic recession of the late eighties and nineties, another leap forward in economic expansion based on the continuous growth of population and production. This was accompanied by the building of a monolithic economic structure. Industry in Germany was highly concentrated with single organisations—cartels—controlling the exploitation of the raw material and the manufacture and distribution of its product, or with all the businesses engaged in the manufacture or distribution of a product, grouped horizontally in great price rings. The banks were similarly concentrated so that by the end of this period banking throughout the country was controlled by the four great, so-called D. banks[1] whose policy in turn was controlled by the Reichsbank, which took directions from the Government. Since industry in Germany was largely capitalised by the banks, who had seats on the boards of most companies, one could simplify the structure and represent it as a great pyramid culminating in the Reichsbank. Alternatively, one could think in terms of powerful anonymous organisations all intermeshed. Yet not entirely anonymous, for the greatest captains of industry and finance were known by name (Krupp, Thyssen) and the great firms were known, if not all their ramifications: but anonymous enough for Germany to seem in the period the prey of great dynamic forces, imperfectly directed. Germans had the sense of much being owed to them on account of their vitality; they had also the sense that it was not accorded them. They believed they were without the position in the world that all this vitality justified. This frustration might have been avoided by a consistent policy pursued steadily by a Government as powerful—or apparently powerful—as it had been in the seventies. But Bülow attempted to move in too many directions simultaneously. Another consequence of the absence of a real focal point in the Government was the fragmentation of German society. This was exacerbated by the way in which the political parties continued to represent, not different opinions, but different social and economic interests, thus emphasising these divisions rather than harmonising them.

This may be illustrated from the time of Caprivi's new tariff policy.

---

[1] The Deutsche Bank, Disconto-Geselschaft, Dresdener Bank, and Darmstädter Bank.

Caprivi in 1893 attempted to modify Bismarck's tariff policy by sub-stituting a more flexible system of tariff treaties for his rigid system of fixed duties, and by tipping the tariff policy to favour industry and the city consumers instead of agriculture and the food producers. The response of the parties in the Reichstag made plain their several economic interests. The Right Conservatives were aligned with the agricultural interests of the large landowners and large peasant farm-ers; the Left Conservatives with officials and professional men; the Right Liberals with industry; the Left Liberals with the petty bourgeoisie. Only the Social Democrats (SPD) and the Centre Party escaped this kind of classification, but they were aligned with other possible soures of social conflict, the one with social, the other with religious opposition. The Government, by allying with any one party, as it had to do for the sake of Reichstag support for its measures, made it impossible for itself to harmonise the various economic interests in the State. Caprivi's very sound labour legislation of 1890, setting up arbitraton machinery for industrial disputes, and of 1891, establishing a code of practice as to hours and conditions of work in factories and workshops, was the last occasion when the State suc-cessfully transcended the developing social conflict.

Behind the political parties stood the pressure groups, strength-ening their divisive influence. These were of three kinds. Some like the Chambers of Commerce or Artisans' Chambers were corpora-tions, sometimes chartered, simply to organise people with the same trading or professional interests. In the second group, came organi-sations formed not only to protect an interest, but to exercise delib-erate pressure on the Government to further it or to change policy in its favour. The best known of these was the Central League of German Industrialists, formed in 1876. In a third group were organ-isations set up to galvanise the public in their interest as much as to put pressure on the Government. In 1893 the League of Landlords was formed for propaganda to the public on behalf of the agricultural interest and against Caprivi's trade treaties. This type of organisation became more and more common and more and more demagogic in its methods. The Pan German League and the Navy League are good examples.

The Pan German League was strong among the National Liberals and in the Reichstag. At the end of our period, thirty-four members of the Reichstag were members of the League and nearly half of those who at one time or another since the League's foundation in 1890 had been both members of the Reichstag and of the League were National Liberals. The remainder belonged to various parties of the Right. Its aims were to arouse patriotism, to keep alive among Germans, living outside Germany, their sense of nationality and to promote the assertion of German power in Europe and overseas. The Navy League and the Hansa League were both organised to gain public support for the policy of building a navy and winning sea power.

The parties split up in the general political frustration. By the time of Bülow there were three, instead of two, Conservative Parties and while the National Liberals survived united, the Left Liberals had split into three groups, led respectively by Barth, Richter and Payer. Under Naumann there was a group of Liberals associated with the idea of *Mitteleuropa*, i.e. Central Europe, including Austria-Hungary, organised economically under German dominance. Only the Social Democrats and the Centre Party retained cohesion. All parties, but especially the SPD, had become highly organised. Indeed, there was an element of organisation for organisation's sake. Parties had their newspapers, their funds, their lists of members, their programmes, their salaried bureaucracies. What they were without was the chance of making a Ministry from a Reichstag majority. It has already been indicated that there was no Reich Ministry, only one Reich Minister, the Chancellor. The Secretaries of State were civil servants.

The Chancellor was, indeed, finding it increasingly difficult to get his measures through the Reichstag. In 1895 Hohenlohe had difficulty: his measure to curb the expression of social discontent failed. Between 1901 and 1902 Bülow had difficulty in changing tariff policy to make it, once again, favourable to the landowners. In order to save his tariff policy, Bülow dissolved the Reichstag and ran the elections of 1903 so as to gain the support of the Centre Party. He hoped to use the Centre Party to counteract the conflict his tariff policy had roused between urban and rural interests.

The Navy Laws and the increases in the Army were the principal laws enacted in this period. The appointment of von Tirpitz as Secretary of the *Reichsmarineamt* was the appointment of a quite exceptional man in this period of lesser men. He was a man with a clear aim, a consistent policy and the nerve to sustain it. Tirpitz was to build the great Battle Fleet, not to outdo the British Fleet but so to match it that it would never risk battle with the German Fleet. His theory is known as the risk theory. By such sea power Germany would win her due place in the world. The appointment of Tirpitz in 1897 marks the beginning not only of naval building but also of *Weltpolitik* (world policy). Tirpitz dominated naval policy from 1897 to 1917. The basic plan was laid in October 1897 and enacted by the Navy Law, which Hohenlohe put through the Reichstag in March 1898. It added 12 ships of the line to an existing 7; 10 large crusiers to the existing 2; 23 small cruisers to the existing 7. It provided also for 8 armoured coastal defence vessels. In January 1900 new proposals were put before the Reichstag and were passed, after some cuts imposed by the Centre Party, as the second Navy Law of 1900. It committed Germany far ahead by a plan of naval building, with appropriate alterations in dockyards and naval installations.

The general absence of direction that was felt internally was not redressed by the consistency with which Germany developed her naval and world policy, because Bülow, as we shall see, attempted to follow too many initiatives all together; both in the Far East and in Morocco; both in Samoa and in Black Africa. Behind a multi-sided diplomacy the actual colonial situation was in fact bad. At the end of 1904 the Hereros and Hottentots rebelled against German rule in German South West Africa. A force of 17,000 men was sent out and appeared to have crushed the rebellion, but guerrilla fighting continued for another two years. Germany's whole colonial administration was under attack. Bülow dissolved the Reichstag and ran the elections this time on a colonialist and nationalist platform against the Centre Party and the SPD. But this was in 1907 and outside the period of this volume.

Austria-Hungary was a power in Europe compelled by her situation, rather than her strength, to form part of the great diplomatic combinations. Francis Joseph understood that European peace was essential for Austria-Hungary's survival and his policy was on the whole, after the period of Andrássy, one of restraint until, on Aehrenthal's advice, he again attempted limited self-assertion. In domestic policy Francis Joseph observed the *Ausgleich* between Austria and Hungary, but he was stronger in the first than the second. The *Ausgleich* brought stability to the Monarchy for over two decades. By the nineties instability characterised the Monarchy as it characterised Russia, though in a very different way. Instability arose because the two partners pulled in opposite directions in their policy: over constitutional development; over trade and economic development; and over the nationalities. In all three areas Austria seemed the more liberal and Hungary the more rigid partner.

Austria had parliamentary institutions. Parliaments in her separate provinces were called Landtage and her central parliament was called the Reichsrat and had 352 members. The real rulers of Austria were, however, the Emperor and his advisers and the slow, efficient, incorruptible bureaucracy. Yet the Emperor's Ministers, though they might be officials and not politicians, sought and obtained the Reichsrat's sanction for their measures. Moreover, the Reichsrat was made increasingly representative. The lower House of the Reichsrat was elected (like the Landtage) by four so-called curiae. The landowners, grouped into one curia, sent more of the 352 members to the Reichsrat than the rural or urban communes, which formed the fourth and third curiae. But in 1873 the numbers elected by the landowners were reduced and those elected by the urban communes increased. (The second curia was composed of Chambers of Commerce, that is of merchants and professional men.) In all four curiae, direct replaced indirect election. Then in 1882 the franchise was widened for the urban and rural communes of the third and fourth curiae. Thus the electorate was much increased, to include shopkeepers and artisans in the urban communes and a large peasant vote in the rural communes. In 1896 a fifth curia was added to the system, returning seventy-two members to the Reichsrat. To vote in this curia one had only to be male, literate, over twenty-four, and to have resided six months in the constituency where one lived. There were two great Ministers during this period who organised their support in the Reichsrat to get measures through or modified their measures there to make them acceptable: Count Taaffe, 1879–93, and Ernst von Koerber, January 1900 to December 1904. These two long periods of calm had their sterile years as well as fruitful and constructive ones, but were less disturbing than the short Ministries between 1893 and 1900, and much less disturbing than what was going on in Hungary, where only the years of Kálmán Tisza, 1875–88, were calm.

The constitutional structure of Hungary was quite distinctive and, *within* its gentry and magnate aristocracy, but not otherwise, more democratic than the Austrian. It was distinctive in its counties and county boroughs with their elective assemblies dominated by the gentry. These were real communities, something more than administrative units. The system was reorganised in 1876 to take in parts of Hungary, hitherto outside it and to get rid of dwarf counties and rotten boroughs, leaving 73 counties and 24 boroughs of county status in addition to Budapest and Fiume. The central parliament (Diet) in Hungary had two houses like the Austrian. The Upper House continued to be composed of hereditary magnates, archbishops and other church dignitaries and some nominated members. The Lower House was more representative than the Austrian in that it was directly elected without a curial system, but the franchise was extremely narrow. The Hungarian Diet governed Hungary no more than the Reichsrat governed Austria; for the Ministry was often made up of officials. Yet the Minister President for thirty years was a member of the Liberal Party, substantially represented in the Diet, and did pass his measures through the Diet with a coalition of supporters of which it was an important part. But the franchise was only once changed and that to make it more rather than less restrictive. The constitutional turning-point in Hungary was 1903. It had for some time been necessary to increase the intake into the Austro-Hungarian army—a single institution for the two halves of the Monarchy. The size of the annual intake of conscripts was not only out of proportion to the size of the population, which had much grown since it was last fixed, but out of step with that of Germany, Russia and France. The increase was put through the Austrian Reichsrat with some difficulty; it failed altogether in the Hungarian Diet. In 1903 the Hungarian Diet used the Emperor's need as its opportunity. It bargained for concessions in return, which would make the army, so far as this was possible, more Hungarian. This was conceded on one side and that on the other, but neither side really got nearer its objective. This dragging but impossible situation may have been a motive for the important event of 1905.

In November 1905 Francis Jospeh decided to introduce universal manhood suffrage for both the Reichsrat and the Hungarian Diet. In Austria the decision was carried out. The curial system was abolished and an arrangement of constituencies, to make them roughly uni-national, was effected. The first parliament elected by the new franchise met in 1907. In Hungary the decision was never carried out. The army question was settled by conceding the postponement of franchise change. Thus by the end of this period Austria looked constitutionally modern, Hungary old-fashioned. The important reality was that each was out of step with the other: or better expressed the *Ausgleich* of 1867 was now producing Delegations—the common parliamentary institution composed of delegates from the two separate parliaments—quite different, the one from the other.

Economically the dualism of 1867 was even less satisfactory. The two halves still made a free trade area in the seventies in which, schematically, Austria supplied manufactured goods for both halves and Hungary wheat, livestock and wine for both. But trade routes took Hungary's exports north, south and south-east, not west into Austria. And Austria, after American grain invaded Europe, could get grain from Western Europe. Moreover, *both* halves were slowly industrialising. Finally Hungary remained the much poorer half. This poverty, as well as parallel, instead of complementary, economic development, proved a source of instability for dualism. Population expanded in both countries as the following figures, in millions, show:

	Austria	*Hungary*
1869	20.5	15
1880	22+	no figure is fair because of cholera
1890	24	17.5
1900	26+	19.25

In both halves there was further differentiation of the population through urbanisation and the development of business classes, professional classes, shopkeepers and clerks.

Both Austria and Hungary were still, of course, mainly rural and agricultural. In 1890 in Austria agriculture employed 62.4 per cent of the working population; industry and mining 21.2 per cent of those gainfully employed. The number employed in textile and metal industries, organised on a factory basis, was not unimpressive and a total industrial work-force of 2,880,000 meant much more industrialisation than the comparable figure out of a very much greater population in Russia. Hungary lagged behind Austria, but in 1900 was in a comparable position to Austria in 1890. By 1900, 14.2 per cent of her population derived its livelihood from industry and 1 per cent from mining. Textiles, chemical manufacture and sugar refining were all beginning.

Then, at the turn of the century, Austria experienced another spurt forward. (There had been a recession at the end of the nineties though not one comparable to the crash of 1873.) In 1900, 25.9 per cent of those gainfully employed were earning their living from industry or mining and 52.1 per cent from agriculture, fisheries and forestry. The move into the towns was continuing and Vienna, Prague, Trieste, Lemberg, Graz were considerable cities. Austria had forty-four towns apart from these with over 20,000 inhabitants. Hungary was hampered by the absence of the kind of peasantry from which industrial entrepreneurs might have been recruited. She was hampered by the extreme poverty of those who were poor. Emancipation of the serfs had brought prosperity to many and they had become well-to-do farmers and were content to remain so. But there were many who had not stood up to the bracing, but harsh, wind of freedom. They became tenant farmers, share-croppers, landless labourers—and many went down the whole scale. The condition of the landless labourers was intolerable. They attempted combined action and a strike and gained some improvement, but emigration was really their only hope.

Finally the nationalities question exposed the *Ausgleich* to an extreme strain. It was the one under which it was eventually to succumb, though not until the war of 1914–18. The Nationalities problem for Austria was this: how could the supra-national Monarchy and its Ministers cope with the Czechs of Bohemia and Moravia and the Slovenes, scattered in Styria, Carniola and Carinthia. It was only in the twentieth century that the supra-national position of the Monarchy became difficult to maintain. The difficulty with the Czechs had, however, already begun in 1874 when the Party of the Young Czechs constituted itself in the Reichsrat. They had no scruples about recourse to obstruction to make it impossible to get business done in the Reichsrat. The Austrian Government was liberal in response to Czech pressure. The language law of 1882, for example, bound officials in Bohemia and Moravia to use either Czech or German according to the language of the person or persons with whom they were dealing. There were endless difficulties of interpretation. Conflict was exacerbated and, with conflict, difficulty of interpretation, when national divisions began to coincide with new economic ones: employers were often Germans and wage-earners Czech. Badeni, then Prime Minister in Austria, made new language laws which bear his name in 1897. The Badeni decrees came so near to putting the two languages on an equal footing that they produced German protest. The decrees were repealed (1899) and the Czechs renewed their obstruction in the Reichsrat. A new attitude now came to the fore. Under the leadership of Dr. Kramař the Czechs widened their horizons and began dangerously to work in the general Slav interest. But Kramař was only leader of the Young Czechs in the Reichsrat. T. G. Masaryk, who stood outside the Young Czechs, was a greater figure with a wider vision. He had been teaching at the Czech University of Prague since it was founded in 1882. By 1900, he had begun to build up that enormous moral ascendancy which was to lead him eventually to be the first President of the Czechoslovak Republic. As long as the Czechs were aiming only at concessions for their language, they could be controlled by the Monarchy's policy of accepting discontent as inevitable, and yet trying to harmonise national interests or, in Taaffe's phrase, keeping them 'in well-modulated discontent.' The Monarchy might even have solved the Czech problem by becoming a trialist instead of a dualist monarchy. Neither of these things was possible as soon as a nationality problem was shared with Hungary. And the Czech problem was shared as soon as it became a Slav problem. This was so because it was then a problem where Czechs and Slovaks acted together and the Slovaks lived in Hungary. Hungary's attitude to the nationalities was quite different from Austria's for two reasons. First, Hungarians had never thought of their state as multi-national or non-national. The Hungarian state had always been inconceivable to Hungarians except as a Magyar state. The policy of Hungary was to Magyarise and to use the schools, which were largely confessional, for this purpose. The second reason for a different attitude was that those of other than Magyar nationality lived on the perimeter of a solid Magyar block in the central plain, protected by mountain barriers. Thus the policy of Magyarisation was successful when applied to those who came into the Magyar area or when it was a matter of pushing outwards from the Magyar centre. In the eighties, successful Magyarisation was carried on against the Slovaks. The Government dissolved three Slovak gymnasia and reduced the number of primary schools where instruction was in Slovak by a third. By 1900 Magyarisation was no longer a successful policy. The Slovaks had found leadership from Prague and especially from Masaryk: 1896 saw the foundation of the *Czechoslovak Society* to free the Slovaks, who lived in Upper Hungary, from Magyar domination. There was also a popular Slovak movement. To intensify Magyarisation was no answer. As the Czech and the Slovak problem became one, so the different policies, of Austria to appease and Hungary to oppose, became a further reason for the *Ausgleich* to fail.

The pattern was repeated in relation to the Serbo-Croats, but there were important exacerbating factors here. We have seen two reasons why Hungary's attitude to other nationalities was different from Austria's. The Croats show a third reason at work; for the Croats were a sufficiently consolidated national group on the Hungarian southern perimeter to stand in much the same relationship to Hungary as Hungary stood to Austria. The *Magodba* of 1868 complemented the *Ausgleich* of 1867, except that the Croatian Parliament was strictly subordinated to the Hungarian Diet and not on an equal footing with it. The occupation of Bosnia and Herzegovina in 1878 brought into the Monarchy two provinces with no industry, no modern communications, no schools, no medical services and much brigandage. These things could be and were remedied. Brigandage disappeared, industry increased, health improved, communications were built, the three religious groups were equally protected and conscription in the Austro-Hungarian army applied. What could not be remedied was the wish of the Croats, who formed part of the population, to join with a wider Croatia. This might be centred on Zagreb, the capital of the Croatia which formed part of Hungary. It might, more doubtfully, be centred on Sarajevo, the capital of Bosnia. It might, and here lay the danger, be centred on Belgrade, the capital of the Kingdom of Serbia. The first possibility had seeds of fresh conflict between Austria and Hungary, the second was too unlikely to need much thought. The third contained one of the seeds of the War of 1914–18. There were three important events in 1903. One— the army reform—we have already discussed; the second was the murder of Milan Obrenović and the accession of the Karageorge ruler in Serbia. This was supremely important because Serbia now became hostile to the Monarchy and the southern Slav question or Yugoslav question began to take shape. As the nineteenth century closed it was a question, as a Yugoslav question, for the future, but as one causing the Croat question to be one common to both halves of the monarchy—therefore to be one on which Austria and Hungary thought differently, therefore to be one which made the *Ausgleich* a source of instability—it was a question for the present. The third event of 1903 was unfavourable to Hungary, for the year saw a hardening of attitude on Francis Joseph's part and, unrelated, the emergence of Francis Ferdinand his nephew and, since 1896, the heir apparent, who blamed Hungary for the Monarchy's difficulties.

Italy during the reign of King Humbert (1878–1900) and King Victor Emmanuel III (1900–46) was harvesting the uncertain fruits of unification. Though a unitary and not a federal state, united Italy proved not to be a concentration of power such as the federal state of Germany was. Such was her political history in the eighties and nineties that some historians have doubted whether united Italy was fitted for parliamentary government. The truth is that with a high degree of illiteracy and a large peasant population, labouring for too long hours for too little return to have time or inclination for politics, a narrow franchise made sense. In some constituencies only a hundred or so men qualified. In 1882 the tax-paying qualification for the vote was lowered to give an electorate of some two million. The political nation was, however, further reduced by the Papal *non expedit* (1874), an instruction to Catholics not to take part in elections. It was not widely ignored until the Elections of 1904. No Minister after 1876 was a devout Catholic and few diplomats were. In her short-lived Ministries Italy seemed more like France than Britain. But the practices, outlined above, which gave much power to the Chamber of Deputies in France, did not exist in Italy. The system was nearer eighteenth-century English practice than any other. There was no change from one side to the other in government, but a circulation of ministerial office among a small group of men ready to be Ministers. Ministries were brought down by the coalescence of parliamentary groups, which did not then stay united to provide an alternative Government. Ministries were transformed rather than replaced. The system was called *trasformismo*. The era of Depretis (d. 1887), the first Minister from the Left to come to power (1876) and an excellent administrator, was followed by the era of Crispi, also from the Left, and the era of Crispi followed by that of Giolitti, still from the Left. These were simply the most important political figures in their periods and they were not continuously in office. Depretis was in office for short periods with others such as Cairoli in between; Crispi was Prime Minister from late 1887 to 1891 and again from 1893 to 1896. Giolitti was Prime Minister in 1892 to 1893, but the era of his ascendancy was from 1901 to 1914. Elections were managed and there were no political parties organised with German efficiency. There was little political discussion, in the absence of elective local institutions, on any level other than the parliamentary and, in the eighties and nineties, not much there. The system of making a majority to pass a measure through the Chamber was a system of clientèles. Those who had ambition for ministerial office had each his clientèle of supporters, whose support he would offer to the Government in return for some contract for public works of personal or local advantage. Deputies took money for favours and Italy, like France, had her scandals. The most notorious were the bank scandals of 1893–94 in which Giolitti was involved. She had a brief interlude at the end of the nineties when parliamentary politics became quite unworkable. General Pelloux, from the Right, ruled for a brief period without parliament.

Italy was also plagued by social unrest. Railways and improved communications and military service brought the peasants into contact with the towns and higher standards of living. The eighties were a period of agricultural depression. So that peasant unrest, such as occurred in Sicily in 1893–94, was blind protest against poverty and high taxation. It was not inspired by Socialism, though the Socialists sympathised with the peasants. In January 1894 the marble workers of Massa and Carrara in the north rioted. The revolt was suppressed by a régime of martial law, but the roots of the evil were economic, and not pulled up. In 1898 there were bread riots in Milan. Italy could not have, while the Catholic withdrawal from politics lasted, a Catholic Centre Party such as Germany had. But she did have a Socialist Party under Turati with, from 1882, a small representation (3 seats in 1882, but 32 in 1900) in the Chamber of Deputies.

Economic development was not for Italy, as it was for Germany, a source of strength. Indeed, it is doubtful whether Italy constituted a single economy. By the end of the nineteenth century the industrial north and the agricultural south are best thought of as constituting two separate economic systems. A protective tariff had been introduced in 1887. It put heavy duties on imported grain, but it did not prevent the north with its more developed economy from being dependent, not on food grown in the south, but on imported food. The peasant could not produce enough grain and cereals for the industrial centres and cities of the north. The rate of per capita production from the land rose steadily after 1860, but not fast enough to meet the demand. Railways were built and banking developed. Behind them was private capital and some state aid. Nevertheless the seventies and eighties were not years of intense economic activity even in the north. Italy only began to experience economic growth after about 1896 and then only in the north. Like Russia, she was a late entrant into industrialisation, but for a different reason. Italy, unlike Russia, lacked raw materials. She was to specialise in the twentieth century in industries which needed dexterity and ingenuity (the manufacture of motor cars, bicycles, tyres, sewing machines) rather than in heavy industry which demanded raw materials she did not possess. Her population, however, grew, from 29.6 millions in 1880 to 31.7 millions in 1890 to 33.9 millions in 1900. Her surplus population remained on the land and was not absorbed into an industrial work-force. It emigrated certainly, but above all it provided Italian politicians with justification for colonial expansion. She had begun in 1869 with Assab Bay (on the west coast of the Red Sea) to which she added Massawa in 1885, eventually to make Eritrea. She was to claim Ethiopia, but to be defeated by the Ethiopians at the Battle of Adowa in 1896.

Meanwhile her Foreign Ministers pursued an extremely clever foreign policy. She had signed the Triple Alliance with Germany and Austria-Hungary in 1882 and developed it to her advantage at each renewal. It was renewed every five years. In 1887 she had gained an Austrian promise of compensation in Albania for any Austrian gains in the Balkan Peninsula and a German promise of support for pos-

Chapter 25

INTERNATIONAL RELATIONS
1895–1905

In 1895 a new factor had been introduced into world diplomacy by
the modernisation of Japan and the irruption of the European Powers
into her relations with her Chinese neighbour. Japan had ended her
two-hundred-year seclusion in 1845. From 1854 she had diplomatic
relations with the European Great Powers. From 1868, the date of
the accession of the Emperor Meiji, industries of a western kind
began to appear. By 1889 she had a parliament of two Houses and
western-type Ministries. But the Emperor and his group of personal
advisers, the *genro*, or elder statesmen, comprising much of the military, financial and diplomatic talent of the nation, played a significant part in the Government of the country in addition to the
Ministries. The Prime Minister came from among the *genro* and was
virtually chosen by them. Between 1871 and 1873 a Japanese mission
toured the western capitals and paid special attention to the industrial
organisation of Great Britain from whom the mission raised a series
of loans for railway building. While first French and then German
officers helped in the modernisation of the Japanese army, a mission
from the Royal Navy between 1873 and 1882 reorganised the navy.
Between 1870 and 1900 most Japanese battleships were built in British dockyards. On July 16, 1894, Britain and Japan had signed a commercial treaty, which ended the unequal relationship established
between the two countries by the Treaty of Edo of 1858 and provided
the pattern for Japan's commercial relations with all other countries
including the United States. The common interest of 'the two Island
Empires' in restraining Russia in Korea had already been established.
Indeed, Britain's occupation of Port Hamilton in April 1885 was as
much related to her Korean objective as to her fear of war arising
with Russia out of the Penjdeh incident (above, p. 324). She left Port
Hamilton in 1887 when Russia had given China assurances about
Korea.[1]

[1] I. H. Nish, *The Anglo-Japanese Alliance* (1966), p. 18.

It is not, therefore, surprising that Britain did not take part in the European irruption into Japan's China policy in 1895. Japan had made war upon China and, to the astonishment of the West, the little athlete had utterly defeated his gigantic opponent. *Punch* produced a cartoon entitled 'Jap the Giant-Killer', representing a tiny dwarf bestriding a huge Colossus and administering the *coup de grâce* with a sword. As a result of the Treaty of Shimonoseki (April 17, 1895), Japan obtained from China the independence of Korea, while she annexed for herself the island of Formosa and the peninsula of Liaotung, including the harbour of Port Arthur. The latter was a warm-water harbour, was near to Peking, and was regarded with greedy eyes by Russia. She organised a collective demand to Japan to evacuate the Liaotung peninsula and Port Arthur (April 23). Japan quietly obeyed, but she did not forget. She felt no anger against France, which had only acted with her ally, but she bitterly resented the action of Germany. The German Government, having already got Russia to promise to support her future claim to a port in China, had addressed Japan in terms of extraordinary rudeness, expressing her intention of 'removing all menaces to peace in the Far East.' Twenty years later Japan demanded the evacuation of the port which Germany had obtained in terms which repeated the exact words of the German ultimatum to herself. Over Russia, as we shall see, Japan's revenge came sooner. One Great Power in the west had abstained from taking part in the Franco-Russo-German demand. That Power was Britain. Japan, humiliated, decided to lie low while she built up her armed strength. When she returned to international diplomacy she would have to choose between taking the opportunity of agreement with Britain or making a local bargain with Russia.

In the New Year of 1896 the first signs of a rift between Germany and Britain began. At the end of 1895 Jameson led his famous 'Raid' against the Transvaal Republic. And on January 3, 1896, William II sent his even more famous telegram to President Kruger, congratulating him on the defeat of armed bands invading his territory. This was interpreted in Britain as a German attempt to interfere with her in the Transvaal and provoked much indignation, especially among the British public. The German Government promptly retreated from their position, but left a lingering trail of suspicion behind them.

As we have seen, 1897 brought Tirpitz to power in Germany and Germany became Britain's naval rival. On November 14 Germany seized Kiao-Chau, thus obtaining a fine naval base in the Far East. It marked the beginning of Germany's *Weltpolitik*.

Russia, which had reluctantly acquiesced in Germany's seizure of spoil, now looked about for compensation, knowing well that neither France nor Germany would oppose her. Britain approached Russia in January 1898 with proposals for an understanding with special reference to China and Turkey; but Russia, after some consideration, declined the overture.[1] She went ahead alone and seized Port Arthur. By way of compensation Britain seized the harbour of Wei-Hai-Wei and France that of Kwangchuan. Neither of these places were much of a compensation. These ports were not annexed, but leased from China, but Russia had at last obtained a warm-water anchorage in the Pacific. Britain wished to preserve the Yangtse-kiang valley as an economic sphere for herself. She felt it absolutely necessary to stop the pressure of Russia upon China. Germany's foundation of a first-class navy and initiation of a world policy made the years 1898–1901 a turning-point in relations between Germany and Britain. Both Powers recognised what they had in common. These years were to show that this was insufficient for a political alliance. Their common interest in holding Russia back from China was the substance of overtures from March to April 1898, initiated unofficially by the British Colonial Secretary, Joseph Chamberlain, in talks with Count von Hatzfeldt, the German Ambassador in London. The possibility of a defensive alliance or of a treaty with the Triple Alliance was also discussed. Bülow, appointed Foreign Secretary in October 1897, rebuffed this overture. He believed time was on Germany's side and doubted Britain's reliability. Soon after these abortive discussions of a general agreement, a limited agreement on a specific subject was successfully concluded. On August 30, 1898, Germany and Britain signed an agreement about the Portuguese colonies. They agreed on securities for a joint loan—Portugal was not eventually to require it—to Portugal: the customs revenue of Portugal's west-coast African colonies for Germany and of her east-coast colonies for Britain. In somewhat hazy terms it was secretly agreed that if Portugal abandoned her colonies each might take possession of her share. The discussion with Germany made a play in three acts. Each act was to have the same pattern: the failure of a general agreement and the achievement of a limited one.

Before the next act the possibility of hostilities between Britain and France suddenly loomed up. In 1898 Britain had at last begun the reconquest of the Soudan, lost by Egypt in 1885, when the British was the only army in Egypt. On September 2, Kitchener broke the Soudanese army at Omdurman, and entered Khartum immediately afterwards. He then heard that a small French expedition under Captain Marchand had reached Fashoda and there hoisted the French tricolour. On September 19 Kitchener with a small force proceeded in person to Fashoda, but could not induce Marchand to lower his flag or to abandon his pretensions. The struggle was transferred from Khartum and Fashoda to London and Paris, and a crisis was soon at hand. The Marchand expedition had been proposed by Marchand to

[1] G. P. Gooch and H. Temperley, *British Documents on the Origins of the War*, (1927), vol. I, pp. 5–18.

Hanotaux in 1895, but authorised in November 1895 by Berthelot, his successor. When Marchand began to leave for Africa in April 1896 Bourgeois was in charge of foreign affairs, but Hanotaux was back that same month and he was to take responsibility for the expedition and to generalise its character. It had begun with the object of laying claim to the equatorial hinterland of the Soudan, principally in the Behr-el-Gazal area, and of obtaining, by a presence on the Upper Nile, a lever with which to reopen the Egyptian question and to induce Britain to evacuate Egypt. Without altering the instructions which Marchand had from the Colonial Office, Hanotaux minimised its political character and certainly made no diplomatic preparations for a clash with Britain, though he did bring dragging negotiations with her about the Niger to a rapid conclusion in the summer of 1898. Marchand raised the tricolour at Fashoda in July 1898, but it was for Delcassé, yet another French Foreign Minister, to deal with the consequences of his refusal to yield to Kitchener. The threat of force, rather than force itself, decided the issue. Delcassé was under pressure from President Faure, who was facing a ministerial crisis as well as the Dreyfus affair.[1] Both Kitchener and Salisbury sought contrivances to save peace. Kitchener hoisted only the Egyptian and not the British flag at Fashoda. The British Foreign Secretary, Lord Salisbury, did not 'drive' Delcassé 'into a corner' and talked vaguely of the possibility of negotiated frontier rectification in the Behr-el-Gazal region. Nevertheless, the Mediterranean Fleet was alerted and the Channel Fleet sent to Gibraltar. On the morning of its arrival, November 3, Delcassé told the British Ambassador in Paris that Marchand would be withdrawn. Victory in a war, an actual military confrontation, over Fashoda would have been pointless.

Thus it came about that Anglo-French differences led to an *entente*. Delcassé, despite his humiliation, had the courage to speak of the need of *une bonne entente* with Britain. France, with relentless logic, recognised that there must be no intrusion into the Upper Nile, and that her differences with Britain had better be made up. Delcassé made clear his desire by deeds as well as by words, for he promoted two pro-British and anti-German diplomats, Carmille Barrère, whom he sent to Rome, and Paul Cambon, whom he sent to London. And Cambon was in six years to be the French architect of the Entente.

In the middle of 1898 the Tsar had issued an appeal for peace, which resulted in the First Hague Peace Conference (May to July 1899). The personal sincerity of the Tsar has usually been admitted, though cynics have suggested that the backward state of the Russian artillery rendered a delay in armaments advisable. There was, at any

---

[1] G. N. Sanderson, *England, Europe and the Upper Nile 1882–1899*, (1965) has a complete and up-to-date account of all the events connected with Fashoda and corrects much misinformation.

rate, no serious attempt made to limit armaments. When it was proposed, Germany made a vigorous opposition which negatived all possibility of success. But Britain made a vigorous and successful effort to establish an Arbitration Tribunal. It was opposed to the last moment by Germany, and the Emperor, when he finally gave way, remarked that he should depend not on arbitration but on his own sharp sword for safety.

The Hague Conference had hardly risen when war began between Britain and the Boer Republics of the Transvaal and Orange Free State (October). The war was one between combatants immeasurably unequal in resources. But the heavy losses of Britain in December 1899 made it seem for a moment as if success was doubtful. Much popular hatred was shown towards her on the Continent, particularly in Dutch, Belgian, French and German newspapers. But the policies of Governments were unaffected. France and Russia were more interested in remodelling the Dual Alliance than in intervention in South Africa. In August 1899 Delcassé and Muraviev widened its scope to include the preservation of the European balance of power and made its duration independent of that of the Triple Alliance. Delcassé was guarding France against German expansion into Austria-Hungary, Asia Minor and the Mediterranean. Germany was more interested in replacing her joint rule of the Samoan Islands with Britain and the United States by her sole rule over the most important of them than she was in intervening in South Africa. Over a month of serious negotiation on this subject was brought to a conclusion on November 14, just before the Emperor paid a personal visit to Queen Victoria. That visit was the occasion for the second act of the drama of Anglo-German relations to be played, for Joseph Chamberlain spoke to him of his desire for a general alliance in which the United States might be a third partner. But the Emperor shared what was also Salisbury's view, that the time for such an alliance had passed. Once again the general proposal failed and the limited one succeeded. By the Samoan Treaty of 1899, Germany acquired the islands she coveted and Britain took the Tonga group to which she attached importance. Britain accepted partition, not because she feared European intervention in South Africa, but because she attached no naval strategic importance to the islands remaining after the United States had taken Pago-Pago, the only good harbour, for a coaling station. No improvement in Anglo-German relations followed. Nor did William II's propensity to give advice on the conduct of the Boer War help in the matter. Peace was made with the Boers in May 1902, and all danger of intervention was thus ended.

Events in China in 1900 introduced the third act in the drama of Anglo-German relations. In June the German Consul was murdered in China, and this was the prelude to a siege of the Foreign Legations in Peking, and to a pronounced anti-foreign movement (secretly encouraged by the Chinese Government) known as the 'Boxer' revolt. After much trouble an international force advanced and relieved the Legations at Peking. A German, Count Waldersee, was appointed Generalissimo of this force, and various indemnities and humiliations were exacted from the Chinese. The Emperor, who had openly exhorted the German contingent to act towards the Chinese like Huns, was foremost in the work of vengeance. Britain sought to turn the situation to her advantage by making an agreement with Germany. This agreement (signed October 16, 1900) arranged for joint action of the two Powers to maintain the 'territorial condition' of China, and the 'open door' in commerce wherever they could exercise influence. The terms were not clear, but Britain thought that she had at last got Germany to support her against Russia's aggression in North China. But she was soon undeceived, for on March 15, 1901, Bülow, Chancellor since October 1900, publicly stated that the Anglo-German Agreement applied only to the Yangtse-kiang valley and not to Manchuria.

Negotiations were once more simultaneously taking place for a general alliance. They were handled by Lansdowne (who had succeeded Salisbury as Foreign Minister) and by the indefatigable Joseph Chamberlain. Germany seems to have wished to include Britain in her existing Triple Alliance (Germany, Austria-Hungary and Italy). Lansdowne, on the other hand, favoured a separate alliance or, preferably, a much looser agreement. By this time Britain was getting dissatisfied and made it pretty clear to Germany that, if these negotiations failed, she would turn to France and Russia. This warning was regarded as 'bluff' and once again the general proposal failed, but this time the specific one, on China, had only half succeeded. By December 1901 all real chance of success in improving Anglo-German relations had faded away. The reasons for this failure may be summarised. First, it must be said that different traditions of diplomacy prevailed in the two countries. In Germany the Bismarckian tradition of tightly defined obligations for the event of war was still respected. The implications of such a treaty outside the specific obligations might be negligible, but, if it was taken seriously, might extend to a mutual control of each other's policy. Britain preferred agreements on precise disputes without any obligations about the future, but conceived with the deliberate purpose of leading to habits of co-operation where common interests existed. There were, unfortunately, no disputes arising from past conflicts of interest to be cleared away between Britain and Germany. A deeper cause of failure was that Germany at this time was an ambitious Power interested in colonial expansion. Britain, on the other hand, preferred to retain the existing territorial balance, which exactly suited her. The deepest cause of all was that Germany was a continental Power in the first place and a world Power only in the second place. This situation was for Britain reversed. The British Empire made her interests world-wide and reduced her continental interests to a subordinate place. Germany, committed as she was to Austria-Hungary and her preservation, and always placed between France and Russia, could never sacrifice continental considerations for naval ones, however important these now were to her. Yet there was still a long way to go before the bitter antagonism of the twentieth century developed.

Meanwhile, it was not to France and Russia that Britain had turned, but to another sea Power: Japan. Japan had shown herself ready. But she did not approach Britain alone; she also tested the possibilities of agreement with Russia. Nor did she approach Britain before she was sure that Britain would accept her as a counterpoise to Russia's influence in North China. She had by 1898 doubled the size of her army and enormously extended her naval building programme. The first soundings were made in that year, tentatively on both sides. There were two options for Japan, as we have seen, and it was not until the balance of advantage was proved to lie with an agreement with Britain, who had shown by the arrangement with Germany over China of October 16, 1900, already mentioned, how much she valued her naval interests in the Far East, that Japan was ready to bring the negotiations to a conclusion. Lansdowne signed with Hayashi on January 30, 1902. The Anglo-Japanese Alliance was of epoch-making importance, but not because it was a departure by Lansdowne from his predecessor's policy. In February 1901 Salisbury had professed himself 'not opposed in principle to an engagement with Japan to join in defending the coasts' which should be preserved from Russia's grasp. Nor was it a departure from isolation, if isolation meant being without friends. If isolation was the name given to avoiding military commitments for contingencies of which the consequences could not be foreseen, as Castlereagh had urged Britain should in his State Paper of May 5, 1820, and Canning had re-urged, Britain had perhaps made an unprecedented move. But the importance of the alliance did not in fact lie in such commitments, though they existed. Each promised the other to remain neutral in the event of its being engaged in war with a third Power and to come to the other's assistance if a fourth Power joined the third. Indeed, the Treaty might be said to be aimed against Russia and France. The importance of the Treaty lay rather in the affirmation by each signatory of its interest in maintaining the independence of China and Korea. The Treaty, though negotiated in secret, was at once published by the two signatories. Its importance lay, then, in the clear warning which it publicly administered to Russia that an expansion of her influence in the Far East would not be tolerated by either signatory. This kind of warning was in entire conformity with British nineteenth-century practice. The naval part of the alliance was contained in secret notes exchanged at the same time. They contained no commitment, but a statement of intention. Each intended to keep in the Far East 'as far as may be possible, available for concentration' a naval force superior to that of any other Power. On what really mattered Britain had taken no open-ended commitment. The second Treaty of Alliance, concluded on August 12, 1905, did go beyond what was normal British practice, but by then long-term commitments were less dangerous, for the Russo-Japanese war had been fought and Russia defeated. This alliance by periodic renewals remained in force until 1925.

The effect of the alliance in 1902 was that it tended to draw Britain still further away from Germany. There had at one time been a question of including her in it. Japan had favoured this and Lansdowne was, at least, anxious to communicate the Treaty to Germany in anticipation of its publication.

If Germany was not included, it became all the more important for France and Britain to compose their differences. Delcassé was able to organise French foreign policy during a long period in office (1898–1905) and with a unique degree of independence. In 1900 as a measure of insurance in advance, he further developed the scope of the Dual Alliance so that it might even be used against Britain, if necessary. In 1900 and 1902, as we said, from the Italian side, he developed a relationship with Italy which virtually nullified the anti-French direction of the Triple Alliance. He was then prepared to develop friendship with Britain. Relations between Britain and Germany had once again suffered from their very co-operation, this time in Venezuela. Germany induced Britain to unite with her in a combined naval demonstration against Venezuela, undertaken in order to collect debts for British and German bondholders. As this incident came just after a visit of the German Emperor to Sandringham, public opinion was greatly excited in Britain. The neglect of popular feeling in Britain by her statesmen was quite as maladroit as the disregard for the views of the Government of the United States. In 1895 America had indicated clearly to Britain that she interpreted the Monroe Doctrine as meaning that the United States was 'the predominant partner', who had to be consulted by European Powers before they interfered in South America. Now, two European Powers proposed to intervene without consulting her first. The British public viewed the affair as a German 'dodge' to embroil us with the American Government. Both considerations combined to make British statesmen retreat hastily from their positions.[1]

The year 1903 was memorable for the continental journey of Edward VII, who visited Lisbon, Rome, Paris and Vienna. All these

---

[1] Before this time Britain had refused, largely owing to popular clamour, to join in the Baghdad railway scheme with Germany and France. The question came up formally in April 1903 and the British Government declined co-operation.

visits were connected by German journalists at the time, and by German historians afterwards, with the *Einkreisungspolitik* or 'encirclement policy' of this alleged Machiavelli among kings. In reality they seem to have been visits of ceremony or of pleasure. But the State visit made to London by the French President and by Delcassé (July 6–9, 1903) was the occasion for the beginning of serious talks on matters in dispute between Britain and France. During the year the relations of Japan and Russia became steadily worse. The details need not concern us, for there was one cause of them, and one only: Russia had occupied Manchuria and was threatening Korea. Japan was resolved to fight if Russia occupied Korea, and unless she could get definite assurances against Russian aggression in Manchuria. When Russia would not give these pledges, Japan broke off the negotiations and declared war (February 1904).

During the autumn of 1903 Lansdowne and Delcassé worked hard at a Franco-British Entente. The main aim of the British statesman was undoubted; it was finally to settle half a dozen old difficulties in Africa, America and Asia, on which France and Britain were at variance. These questions were due to old-time treaties or aggravated by recent hostilities, and on any one of them war might arise through a careless Governor or an impetuous soldier. These questions Lansdowne meant to liquidate altogether, or, at any rate, to remove from the danger zone. The aim of France was not only a settlement but an ally. Delcassé thought that, if France gave the one, he could gain the other. He needed an ally for the forward policy he was evolving in Morocco. On April 8, 1904, the Franco-British Declaration regarding Egypt and Morocco was signed, the most important among a group of similar agreements dealing with special areas. From that date the Franco-British Entente was virtually operative.

There were concessions by one side or another in the minor questions, Newfoundland, Siam (Thailand), West Africa. But the two main questions concerned Egypt and Morocco. Britain wanted a free hand in the one, France in the other, and, somewhat to Britain's surprise, France made little difficulty about Egypt. She secured some advantages in respect of the Suez Canal, but agreed not to obstruct Britain's action by 'asking that a limit of time be fixed for the British occupation or in any other way.' In return for this, France stated that she had no desire to alter the political status of Morocco, and Great Britain promised not to obstruct her action there. This was what was published. But secret articles were also signed on April 8, 1904, which were not revealed until 1911. One of these provided that, in case of modification of the *status quo* in Egypt or in Morocco, there was to be as before freedom of trade, unobstructed passage of the Suez Canal, and prohibition of fortifications opposite the Straits of Gibraltar. The Capitulations were to be abolished in Egypt, if desired by France or Britain. Finally another secret article stipulated that, whenever the Sultan of Morocco ceased to exercise authority over it, a specified part of Morocco should be transferred to Spain. In plain language, these secret articles provided for the annexation of part of Morocco by Spain. That meant, of course, that the rest of Morocco would, or might, be annexed by France, whenever she chose, and that Britain would have to give diplomatic support to this arrangement.

The secrecy of these arrangements is in itself suspicious. For, while France secured Italy's good will in 1900 and 1902 by promising her Tripoli, and Spain's good will shortly afterwards by promising her a part of Morocco, nothing was done by Britain or France to enlighten Germany as to the secret deal over Morocco. But Germany understood the meaning of the public Declaration well enough. In October 1904 it was summed up by one of her diplomats: 'England wished to obtain a sanction *de jure* for her *de facto* position in Egypt, whilst France wished to make a reality of her so far theoretic aspirations in Morocco.' The German Foreign Office began to prepare a campaign for countervailing advantages for Germany.

The German Government held back from overt action because the Russo-Japanese war necessarily increased the danger of misunderstanding. In this war German sympathies were with Russia, and this was of great importance because of the alliance between Britain and Japan. On Trafalgar Day (October 21, 1904) the Russian fleet off the Dogger Bank shot at an English fishing-vessel, believing it to be a Japanese torpedo-boat. A tense situation ensued, which was eventually ended by Russia's promise of full apologies and compensation. But in December of this year Germany took care to assure Russia of her support, in case of conflict with Britain. And, on the British side, the fleet in the North Sea was permanently strengthened. So that both Germany and Britain had become more irritated with each other than before.

Bülow opened the Moroccan question in 1905 with no limited aim in view. Basing his case on the international Treaty of 1880, giving its signatories the right to be consulted before any change in the *status quo* in Morocco, he kept his options open. At the least, Germany would prevent her exclusion from developing commercial possibilities in Morocco; at the most, she would challenge the Entente or, indeed, even gain a port on the Atlantic coast. Early in February 1905 a French envoy made new demands on the Sultan of Morocco. This was Bülow's opportunity and he approved the project of sending William II himself as a kind of counter-envoy to Morocco, suggested by Holstein, that singular wire-puller, now back in the Foreign Office after a long absence. On March 29 Bülow spoke in the Reichstag, demanding 'the open door' for German trade and the political *status quo* in Morocco. On March 31 William II landed from his yacht at Tangier and made a speech. He declared that he recognised the sovereignty and independence of the Sultan, whom he considered as 'absolutely free.' 'I hope that under his sovereignty a free Morocco will remain open to the peaceful competition of all nations, without monopoly or annexation, on a policy of absolute equality.' This speech meant two things. It meant, first, that Germany considered herself in no way bound either by the Entente or by the Franco-Spanish Treaties; next, that she would endeavour to safeguard the integrity and independence of Morocco. And these points were speedily emphasised. For on April 11, Bülow issued a circular demanding the summoning of an international Conference on Morocco. He was promptly backed up by the Sultan of Morocco, who now repudiated all his previous concessions to France, and invited a conference at Tangier of those Powers who had signed the Treaty of 1880 which had settled the status of Morocco. It is significant that the Schlieffen plan, the piece of German General Staff planning, designed to save Germany from a war on two fronts by the 'knock-out blow against France', was given its final formulation at this time.

Bülow's policy was a failure. He embarked on negotiations with France for an agreement to share the opportunities of affording adminstrative and financial assistance to the Sultan. It is clear that he could have had this, if he had been prepared to give up the Conference. He preferred to insist on the Conference, from which Germany was to emerge with a loss of prestige and no gains. France turned the negotiations into a successful limitation of the agenda of the Conference. Moreover, his policy, far from weakening the Entente, caused Britain and France to draw closer together. Britain gave France a precise assurance of support in resisting any demand by Germany for a Moroccan port and offered 'consultations' before sensitive questions reached dangerous crises. Bülow's one gain was the fall in France of the anglophil Delcassé, on June 11, 1905. Delcassé's colleagues had feared he was going too far in antagonising Germany and Delcassé, who already had resigned a month before but returned to office, now gave up the struggle against them. But even this was not an unqualified gain, for his fall roused the French public against Germany's alleged intervention in French affairs. Rouvier, the French Prime Minister, who now also took on Foreign Affairs, tried to reach agreement with Germany. Bülow failed to respond and continued to insist on the Conference. In December 1905, Germany was using the language about France that she had used in the War Scares of 1875 and 1887. But as with earlier War Scares there was alarm, but no change. The Conference met after an American intervention. Germany and France both appealed to President Theodore Roosevelt, who persuaded all parties to agree to a Conference at Algeciras.

One more event of this year of turning-points is well worth a mention though it had no influence on the way international relations were developing. In July 1905 the brilliant and impulsive William II achieved what he considered a master-stroke. He paid a surprise visit in his yacht to the Tsar's yacht at Björkö (July 24). There next day he persuaded the impressionable Tsar, who had no political advisers with him, to sign a treaty 'before God, who heard our vows' as William II afterwards said. The Tsar wrote that he felt a moisture all over him and saw the hand of God in this achievement. 'July 24', said he, 'is a cornerstone in European history and a great easing of my dear country's situation.' This astounding treaty contained four provisions. First, each state promised to join the other 'with all its forces' if attacked by any European state. Second, neither would conclude a separate peace. Third, the treaty came into force on conclusion of peace with Japan and a year's notice was necessary for cancellation. Fourth, Russia was to make its terms known to France and invite her to sign it as an ally.

This treaty, described by the Emperor as 'a Continental combine ... to block the way to the whole world becoming John Bull's private property', would indeed have been a triumph. It would have compelled France either to obey Germany or to abandon Russia, and have isolated Britain completely. But Russian statesmen were not quite mad, and soon made it clear to the Tsar that Russia's ally, France, could not be treated thus. Even Witte, who was at first inclined to favour it, said that the pact was absurd. He became Prime Minister on October 20, 1905, and at once assumed a correct official attitude. The Tsar wrote formally to the Emperor through the ordinary official channels, and the Russian Ambassador at Berlin took the attitude, under instruction, that the treaty was inoperative as it contravened the Dual Alliance, and that France must agree to any revision of the latter. It took the Emperor some time to realise that his plan, though as brilliant as a soap bubble, was also as frail, and destined to the fate of all bubbles.

Before the Conference of Algeciras met, Balfour had resigned (December 4, 1905) and in Britain a Liberal Government was in office, with Grey as Foreign Secretary. He was to hold that office for a longer period than any other man in the nineteenth or twentieth centuries.[1] His first action gave a new aspect to the Anglo-French Entente. During the summer British and French soldiers had been discussing their separate plans for the event of war. In January 1906 Grey and Paul Cambon agreed that unofficial communications between the Admiralty and War Office and the French Naval and Military Attachés should take place about suitable action if the two

---

[1] Grey held office from December 1905 to December 1916; Castlereagh, the next candidate, from March 1812 to August 1822. The reference is to a continuous period of office. The most recent work on Grey is a set of essays, F. H. Hinsley (ed.), *British Foreign Policy under Sir Edward Grey* (1977).

countries found themselves in alliance in war against Germany. They might be 'unofficial', but if they were authorised, as they now were, they had a most serious meaning. It was Churchill's view that they constituted 'an exceedingly potent tie.'[1] Mere conversations between experts about contingency plans might be rash, vague, technical, hypothetical. When they were once authorised they could not be so described, for they were governed by an assumption: namely, that the contingency planned for was a war between the Germans on one side and the French and British on the other.

Let us now sum up so far as we can the position reached by the beginning of 1906. Lansdowne might claim that the Anglo-Japanese Alliance had prevented France (and perhaps Germany) from being involved in the Russo-Japanese war. The Treaty of Portsmouth, making peace between Russia and Japan, was actually signed on September 5, 1905. This surrendered Port Arthur, Manchuria, Korea, and half the isle of Sakhalin to Japan, while Russia refused to pay any war indemnity. Just before this on August 12, 1905, Britain and Japan signed the second Treaty of Alliance. Britain pledged herself in future to give help to Japan if attacked by only one Power (instead of two). In return Japan agreed to defend India against attack. This new obligation would tend to preserve peace in the future in this local area of the Far East, and Russia's defeat deprived it of dangerous implications.

As regards the Entente with France: it meant something more in January 1906 than in April 1904. The scope of the understanding had been widened by conversations of April and May 1905 over Morocco, and an arrangement which seemed at first likely to be limited in effect to Morocco had become the basis of a general practice of co-operation between the two countries. Moreover, by the military and naval conversations of 1906 the Entente was made little different from an alliance.

The main difficulty between Britain and Germany consisted in the rise of a dangerous popular prejudice on both sides. Popular opinion had embarrassed their relations in the South African War, had wrecked the Baghdad Agreement, had rendered difficult the Venezuela question, and had just inflamed the Tangier crisis. Repeated negotiations with Germany in 1898, in 1899, in 1901, had failed to create a working agreement or to promote an alliance between the two countries. Britain had, indeed, been more eager than Germany for an understanding. She had failed thrice, and popular opinion made it dangerous to renew the attempt at once. It was not possible to negotiate an Entente, for there were no outstanding diplomatic difficulties. There was only a dangerous popular tension on both sides, while opinion against Germany's driving ambition so hardened

---

[1] Winston Churchill, *World Crisis* (abridged and revised ed, 1931), p. 35.

Conclusion

INTERNATIONALISM IN EUROPE

The period covered by this volume is full of wars, which were progressively more destructive of life and property, for the development of science put into the hands of combatants means of destruction greater with each generation. It is also a period with long spells of peace between the Great Powers: 1815 to 1854 and 1871 to 1914 (or 1905 to keep within the bounds of the volume) are long. Efforts to avoid war and to link together the nations of Europe and the world were more serious and more conscious of the goal than anything that the world had previously seen. They also penetrated deeper down the social scale. The peace movement began outside the Governments soon after 1815 when peace societies were established in several countries. The first World Peace Congress met in London in 1843. The separate peace societies were federated in 1848 and a programme with clear and realistic aims adopted. The International Peace Bureau in Berne had decided to summon the twenty-first World Peace Congress in Vienna for September 1914, but was foiled by the outbreak of war in August.

Among the Governments the project of a world union of Christian States was put forward at the close of the Napoleonic Wars by Tsar Alexander I, though it soon became overlaid by other motives—fear of revolution and ambition for power. It had not the slightest influence on the public policy of Europe, and is usually treated as unworthy of serious consideration. It can clearly be riddled with practical criticisms. Its motives were too narrow and indefinite; it took no account of the non-Christian world; it lacked entirely organisation and machinery. Before this time another and a more practical project had been inaugurated. When the Allies were pressing upon Napoleon after the Battle of Leipzig and had followed him on to the soil of France, a treaty of permanent alliance was signed at Chaumont on March 9, 1814. The moving spirit of the time was Castlereagh, the British Foreign Minister, so bitterly hated in his own time as a reactionary and supporter of tyrants. He proposed that the four Great

379

Powers who were fighting against Napoleon should not separate when hostilities came to an end but renew their meetings periodically: what we should call Summit meetings. His ideas were expressed later in the terms of the Quadruple Alliance of 1815. The words of the all-important clause which owes its origin to Castlereagh have been quoted in the footnote to page 141 above.

Here at least was the recognition that the peace of Europe required and deserved regular attention. There was no effort to secure the co-operation of the states of Europe in matters of common interest; there was no appeal to arbitration or to international law. It was just such an alliance of Great Powers as Europe had frequently seen. None but the Great Powers had part or lot in it. But the meetings at regular intervals, and the hope of securing permanent peace in Europe by dealing with difficulties before they become too serious for conciliation were new and fertile ideas. There was no effort to win for it the support of public opinion though some support would have been available. The Monarchs and their Ministers went their own way without any attempt to justify themselves in the eyes of the outside world, and very soon this attempt, which was genuinely intended to secure the 'peace and prosperity of Europe,' came to be regarded with the most vehement hostility by all that was progressive and humanitarian in European thought.

It is important to note that in 1818 at the Congress of Aix-la-Chapelle the Tsar made an attempt to carry the idea of European unity further and to create something which would have borne fairly close resemblance to an embryonic League of Nations. He proposed a general alliance of all the signatories of the Treaty of Vienna, to guarantee to every legitimate sovereign his throne and his territory. Such an alliance, the Tsar contended, would be favourable to both order and liberty, for the security of governments would be assured if international law were placed under a guarantee similar to that which protected the rights of the individual. In such an event the governments would be relieved of the fear of revolution, and would then be able of their own free will to offer constitutions to their subjects. It was a grandiose but not impossible scheme, containing perhaps elements that might be dangerous to popular causes, but capable of development and reform, had the times been favourable to its growth. The tendency of the age that was beginning was, on the contrary, towards national movements, often revolutionary in character.

While Europe thus turned back on the ideals of the Holy Alliance and went forward to the wars between 1854 and 1871 which sprang from the very principle of nationality, the problem was becoming more urgent. For the era of invention had come, and the contacts between nations and states were being multiplied with amazing rapidity. It is hardly possible to exaggerate the gap which separates the twentieth century from the early nineteenth in the material and mechanical sides of life. Invention soon turned its attention to weapons of war and gave soldiers powers of destruction beyond anything that even Napoleon had dreamed of. The world, moreover, was linked together as never before. England knew more of Austria, Italy, or America than Kent had known of Yorkshire a hundred years previously. Since the beginning of the nineteenth century the movement has gone on with constantly increasing acceleration. It is many-sided and has had many different results, but its chief effects have been to produce rapidity of transit and of communication beyond all that was dreamed of in an ealier age; and with these results has gone a proportionate increase in the destructive powers of man. The need for some method of avoiding war was immensely greater than in any earlier age.

In the eighteen-thirties and forties international co-operation manifested itself only in the meetings of the Foreign Ministers of the Great Powers, or their representatives, to solve problems arising from disputes between small nations (Belgium and Holland, Greece and Turkey, Egypt and Turkey, Schleswig-Holstein and the German Confederation) and to prevent their leading to war between Great Powers. The Great Powers acting in this way formed the Concert of Europe. The general problem of preserving peace was not again raised until after the Crimean War. The Congress of Paris provided no adequate solution, although on the initiative of Clarendon, the British Foreign Secretary, a protocol was issued declaring: 'the Plenipotentiaries do not hesitate to express, in the name of their Governments, the wish that States between which any serious misunderstanding may arise, should, before appealing to Arms, have recourse, as far as circumstances might allow, to the Good Offices of a friendly Power.' The pious wish of the Paris plenipotentiaries remained quite without effect, and in the next fifteen years four European wars were fought. The period of comparative calm which followed in western Europe saw the revival of international feeling and organisations, and in commercial, labour, cultural and scientific fields there was in Europe, in the period 1871–1905 and beyond, a real unity. Moreover the Concert of Europe was even more active than before and played a part in preserving peace between the Great Powers to the end of the period covered by this volume.

The most constructive proposal of the second half of the nineteenth century was for the development of the practice of arbitration. The idea of international arbitration was indeed as old as Periclean Athens, or older; but it is during the past century only that it has been seriously and almost continuously urged. Between the Battle of Waterloo and the end of the period covered by this volume arbitration in some form was applied to nearly 300 international disputes. The universal acceptance of the idea was prevented by the refusal of the great states of the world to admit any procedure which even seemed to encroach on their complete independence. No European Government was willing to adopt arbitration or to appeal to any authority except force 'upon issues in which the national honour or integrity was involved.' So, though arbitration smoothed many diplomatic difficulties and provided useful machinery for the settlement of many secondary disputes, it did nothing to remove the tension between the Great Powers out of which the War of 1914 came, or to reduce the burden and expense of armaments.

A great effort—emanating from and really supported by the Tsar of Russia—was made to regularise and extend the application of international arbitration in the two Peace Conferences held at The Hague in 1899 and 1907. There was in the Tsar's mind, and in the minds of many who supported him, a genuine humanitarian desire to lighten the burden of armaments which weighed on all Europe, and to find if possible some means of removing from Europe the menace of war. The attempt to secure disarmament failed completely, as all attempts up to the present time have failed. The large number of Powers assembled at The Hague in 1899 would only declare that 'the restriction of military charges, which are at present a heavy burden on the world, is extremely desirable for the increase of the material and moral welfare of mankind,' and this was something far weaker than the words which the Tsar had used in sending out his invitations to the Conference. The armies of Europe increased rather than diminished during the following years. But though the movement for disarmament failed there was a unanimous belief that something might be done to maintain peace among the nations by the development of the practice of arbitration and the definition of its methods. And here something of real importance was done. The arbitration movement was given definite shape. A permanent arbitral system was set up, which could be called into action whenever two Powers wished to use it for the settlement of any disputes. Various methods were suggested to meet various circumstances. In some instances mediation might be used; in others a mixed commission of inquiry might examine and report on matters of fact; disputes which lent themselves to such treatment might be submitted to a court of arbitration, which was set up in a permanent form and was to be governed by fixed rules of procedure. The Conference also met in 1907, and again upon the initiative of the Tsar; but the second Conference was something of a disappointment. It was seen once again that nothing could be done to disarm Europe, and many saw that without disarmament there could be no permanent peace. The wisdom of arbitration was reaffirmed, and the methods were reconsidered and improved.

The Conference at The Hague gave an impetus to the signing of arbitration treaties among the states of the world, and these were of real use in promoting a peaceful atmosphere among the smaller Powers of Europe. Not only had the number of arbitration treaties increased but a most important advance was also made in their form. It was hopeless, however, to expect that arbitration would maintain the peace of the world while the most important questions were formally excluded from its scope. Most of the great wars in history have been fought, not for the interpretation of clauses in a treaty, but for what were considered to be 'affairs of honour and vital interests'. The movement to include these matters within the scope of arbitration began in America. It encountered much opposition even there, but by September 1914 arbitration treaties between the United States and both France and Great Britain were drawn up, accepted and duly signed. By these treaties all disputes of whatever kind which could not be settled by the ordinary procedure of diplomacy were to be submitted to a joint International Commision, whose constitution and procedure were carefully defined and regulated. The Commission was to report within a year, and during this time the signatory Powers were to take no step of any kind towards any other solution of their difficulties. Europe was already at war.

Another theme which has been followed in this volume with some consistency is the rise and decline of European liberalism. The volume opens at a point in European history when the monarchies have lost their efficiency and authority. The idea that sovereignty rightly rests only in the general will of the people has been put into words by Rousseau and, by the French constitution of 1791, supposedly put into practice. During the French Revolution much was done in the name of that doctrine which was illiberal, and as régime succeeded régime during the Revolutionary and Napoleonic period the participation of the people in the political life of the state now widened and now contracted. But all Governments in France after 1791 acknowledged that they were in some sort responsible to the nation and controlled by it. Even under Napoleon I and Napoleon III, the most autocratic of later régimes, this was acknowledged by the use of plebiscites. Nor did France ever again lose the parliament she acquired in 1791, though its form changed some eight times after that year. Freedom of the press, freedom of association, freedom from arbitrary arrest, freedom of religious opinion, freedom to bear arms in some form of national militia were liberal claims and the expression of liberal individualism from the time of the French Revolution onwards. Other countries followed France, either during the Revolutionary Wars or after them, in gaining parliaments and some part of the individual rights just enumerated. The south German states all had parliament before 1820, Belgium and Holland had separate parliaments after 1830, Greece, Spain, Portugal, Piedmont-Savoy, Prussia, Austria and Hungary all had elective parliaments by the mid century. The Balkan States followed in the second half of the century as they obtained their freedom from Turkey. United Germany in

1871 obtained a parliament elected by universal manhood suffrage, but retained a strong, not to say autocratic, Government. By this date liberal gains, where they existed, were taken for granted; the parliamentary constitution had lost its savour. It had not proved the cure of all evils which liberals had once expected it to prove. When Metternich and other rulers feared the Revolution, they were afraid of conspirators, threats to public order and demands for the safeguards of liberal individualism listed above. But after the middle of the century when men feared revolution, they feared social revolution.

This idea of social revolution can also be followed forward from the French Revolution. But to understand this it is necessary first to follow three lines of thought. During the years after 1793, under pressure of the need to organise, in order to win the war, and under pressure to provide bread, work and security for the crowds in Paris and other cities, the French Government learnt its own strength. The Jacobins improvised a form of economic control. It did not survive the war but economic control as a concept survived. In the first part of the nineteenth century the economic action of Governments was most conspicuous in the field of tariff regulation and in its negative rather than positive aspect. The European free trade movement gathered momentum. The abandonment of tariff walls within the German Zollverein, the lowering of tariffs by trade treaties, such as the Anglo-French of 1860 or the last such treaty, the Franco-Italian of 1865, and the levelling of tariffs by the use of the most-favoured-nation clause were the marks of economic liberalism. They were accompanied by the relaxation within the several countries of a number of domestic economic controls. Then the movement stopped and after 1870 was reversed. The French, who favoured indirect taxation as the source of national revenue, had a war indemnity to pay to Germany and denounced the free trade treaty of 1860 and raised their tariffs to increase revenue. Italy adopted a moderate protectionist tariff. Germany followed in 1879. Faith in *laissez-faire* and economic freedom declined at the same time as constitutionalism was taken for granted and lost its attraction for progressive thinkers. These men began to think of the economic and social responsibilities of Governments and claims began to be made on them in the last quarter of the nineteenth century for economic and social legislation. At the time when such claims were made, Governments were, indeed, becoming increasingly powerful. The number of states in Europe had fallen from 54 in 1815 to 14 in 1871. Before the end of the period covered by this volume there was to be a small addition when Bulgaria, Serbia and Montenegro were freed from Turkey. But the difference made by the unification of Germany and Italy to the configuration of Europe and above all, to the strength of the Governments of the six Great Powers—and they set the pattern for the rest—was a permanent change.

The second line of thought to be followed relates to the scale on which men lived. The population of the largest European countries may be set out at four dates as an indication of the change of scale, which happened during the period covered by this volume:

	Population (*in millions*)			
	1800	1850	1880	1900
Austria (Austria-Hungary)	see figures on p. 358			
France	26.9	36.5	39.2	40.7
Germany	24.5	31.7	40.2	50.6
Great Britain	—	22.3	31.1	38.2
Italy	18.1	23.9	29.6	33.9
Russia	41.0 (?)	58.6 (?)	—	94.3[1]
(no census before 1897)				(for 1897)

By the end of the century Europe was living on the scale of massed populations, dwelling in cities, industrial centres, urban areas and large towns. Britain was already experiencing industrialisation when the period covered by this volume opens. Belgium and Germany came next, but German industrialisation did not gather pace until the fifties. France evolved somewhat differently and more gradually, with the emergence of the great banking, trading and textile houses in the forties and expansion of coal, iron and steel industries gradually under the Second Empire and Third Republic. She was a rural country with industrial problems rather than a fully industrialised country as Germany was by 1905. Italy and Russia developed in a more lop-sided manner as has been seen, but similarly had their urban and industrial problems. The wealth of the several European countries by the end of the period covered by this volume can be best expressed in figures for the production of coal, iron and steel, that is, in the production of large-scale industry. It is the measure of the change of scale that has happened and it is commensurate with the enlargement of the power of Governments.

The third line of thought relates to social change. Two phenomena concern us here: the decline of the old ruling aristocracies, so far as it had happened, and the release into the general society of the nation and into its economy of men—serfs—who, so far as Governments were concerned, had before had no individual existence. These two changes can similarly be followed forward from the time of the French Revolution. Britain, the land of tenant farmers and gentry, kept her old ruling classes unimpaired until after the second reform

---

[1] See *Cambridge Economic History of Europe* (1966), pp. 62–3, for difficulties of estimating Russian population, and above, p. 344. The figures given above do not include Russian Poland.

Industrial development 1850 to 1900 (in million metric tonnes)

	Germany	France	Britain	Russia
Annual coal production				
1850	5.1	4.5	57.0	—
1871	29.4	13.3	118.0	—
1890	109.3	26.1	184.5	5.0
1900	149.0	32.7	225.1	16.5
Annual pig-iron production				
1850	0.2	0.4	2.2	—
1871	1.5	1.4	6.5	—
1890	4.7	2.0	8.0	0.08
1900	7.5	2.7	8.9	2.0
Annual steel production				
1850	—	—	—	—
1871	0.2	0.1	0.3	—
1890	2.2	0.6	3.6	0.06
1900	6.7	1.5	4.9	2.8

Austria, Hungary and Italy have negligible quantities.

bill (1867) and had no serfs to lose. For her, social change was more noticeable in the period both before this volume opens and after it closes. In France the *émigrés* of the Revolutionary period returned and some recovered land, but they did not press forward into the ranks of the Prefects or parliamentary Deputies. Some old families withdrew from public responsibilities, some were absorbed lower down the social scale, Serfdom had disappeared before 1789. There has been much argument whether the Revolution stimulated or retarded capitalist development and the arguments cannot be weighed up here. Suffice it to say that the medium-sized property owner and the small peasant proprietor or the poorer share-cropper (*métayer*) were preponderant elements in the French population throughout the period covered by this volume. In Germany, especially in the north, where the large estate was characteristic, the landowner continued to dominate the countryside. Throughout the period covered by this volume some of the landowners of East Prussia were able to exclude Government officials from their estates. In the small-town-dwelling population characteristic of south-west Germany and in the industrial Rhineland the large landowner was less evident. But the old ruling aristocracy tended in Germany to absorb the new industrial entrepreneur and to remain rather than either to withdraw or to be absorbed lower down. Towards the end of the nineteenth century many middle-sized landowners were badly struck. They had over-mortgaged their estates and much of their land came on to the market. It was they who lost their social level rather than the most wealthy. Great social change only came to Germany after the War of 1914–18. The emancipation of the serfs was enacted during the Napoleonic Wars, as we have seen, and the German peasant farmer, like the French, continued to form a stable social foundation. But the class contracted in Germany and especially in west Germany, more rapidly than in France. Italy was characterised, as we have seen, by the withdrawal of the old families from political life after 1874—the date of the Papal instruction against political activity—and 1876—the date of the first Government from the Left. Land-hunger, extreme provery and illiteracy continued to mark peasant life in southern and, to some extent, central Italy. These social changes left Austria and Russia untouched until the emancipation of serfs in Austria and Hungary in 1848 and in Russia in 1861. In these countries social change was inextricably involved with sharp political problems relating in the first two to the nationalities and in the third to the movement against autocracy. So there is great diversity in European social change. It cannot be averaged out into a broad generalisation that the old aristorcracy declined and the peasant classes acquired a new political status from the beginning of the century. Nevertheless, broadly speaking the enlargement of the scale on which life was generally lived, and the increase in the power of Governments, was accompanied by a trend all over Europe towards greater social equality.

If we now attempt to draw the conclusions from these three lines of thought, we can say that change in these three respects reinforced the decline of liberal individualism and tended to put in its place a preoccupation with society and social theory as distinguished from the liberal preoccupation with the state, whose powers liberals wished to see reduced to the minimum, and with political theory. Notice has been taken in this volume of the early socialists in France and Italy, of Fourier and Proudhon, and should perhaps have been taken of Lassalle in Germany. All European countries had Social Democratic Parties by the date at which this volume closes. The Party in France under Guesde dated from 1879; the Italian Parliamentary Party under Turati from 1882; the German Party under Bebel and W. Liebknecht from 1869; in Russia there were at least three socialist opposition groups by the end of the century. Of all these the German expressed their aims most clearly, for the formal Party programme was a characteristic of German politics. It may be quoted as an illustration of what Socialism might mean in the broad European context. The quotation is taken from the Eisenach programme of 1869.

Every member of the Social Democratic Workers' Party undertakes to stand for the following principles with all his strength:

1. The political and social conditions of today are in the highest degree unjust and therefore to be fought against with the greatest energy.
2. The struggle to free the working classes is not a struggle for class privileges and advantages, but for equal rights and equal duties and to do away with the predominance of any one class over others.
3. The economic dependence of the worker on the capitalist, forms the foundation of slavery in every form and the Social Democratic Party, therefore, strives, by abolishing the present methods of production (the wage system), to obtain for each worker through co-operative work the full earning for his labour.

There was no talk here of the public ownership of the means of production, distribution and exchange, still less of the dictatorship of the proletariat. There was no notion of the state's withering away. Indeed, the programme opened with the sentence, which precedes the quotation above: 'The Social Democratic Workers' Party strives for the establishment of the free people's state.' It was not a Marxist programme. The full adoption of Marxist objectives by Communist Parties belongs to the twentieth century. It is appropriate, therefore, that a discussion of the ideas of Karl Marx and Friedrich Engels should be postponed to the second volume.

The Eisenach programme has a further point of interest. It goes on to affirm that 'political freedom is the indispensable prerequisite of the economic freedom of the working classes. The social question cannot be separated from the political. Its solution requires and is only possible in the democratic state.' It went on, therefore, to demand universal, equal, direct and secret suffrage, a people's militia, the separation of Church and State, compulsory and free primary education, the independence of the courts and the introduction of the jury system and an end to all restrictions on the press, on the right of association and other demands made earlier on by liberal movements. Germany, like Russia, was an exception to the generalisation that on the whole liberal demands had been realised. Liberal ideals were not realised in Germany until the Weimar Constitution of 1919, nor in Russia until the first Duma and then imperfectly. Neither was a success and both were to swept aside by more extreme movements, as will be related in Volume 2.

MAPS

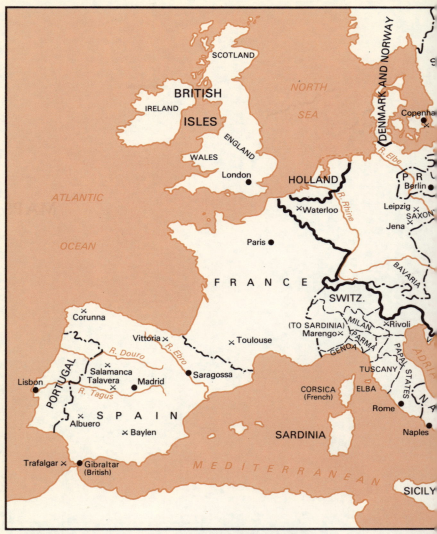

1. European resistance to the French Revolution and Napoleon

St. Petersburg

Moscow
× Borodino

R U S S I A

E D E N

BALTIC SEA

Tilsit
× Friedland

POLAND

SILESIA

R. Vistula

GALICIA

A
× Austerlitz
× Wagram
Vienna

USTRIA

HUNGARY

R. Danube

C E   T U R K E Y

SEA

Constantinople

IONIAN IS.
(Venetian)

SEA

Boundary of the Empire

The boundaries are those of 1792

The length of each line indicates
the resistance made by each
country, expressed in war-years

Gt. Britain........	20
Austria	8¾
Spain.............	8
Portugal	7
Russia	7
Prussia	6
Holland	4
Sweden	4
Naples...........	3
Turkey...........	3
Denmark.........	2
Italy	2
Tuscany	2

0   300 mls
0   300 km

2. Europe at the height of Napoleon's power

France at the end of 1802
Acquisitions 1803–05
Acquisitions 1805–10
Kingdom of Italy, directly ruled by Napoleon
Dependent states
Boundary of France, 1792
Boundary of Confederation of the Rhine

0   300 mls
0   300 km

SWEDEN

Copenhagen
BORNHOLM

BALTIC SEA

Danzig (Rep.)
Tilsit
× Friedland

PRUSSIA

Berlin

GRAND DUCHY OF WARSAW

Posen

Warsaw

R. Oder

SILESIA

SAXONY

esden

Cracow

Dresden

R. Elbe

GALICIA

Prague

BOHEMIA

Austerlitz

AUSTRIA

Wagram ×

R. Danube

Pressburg

Vienna

Pesth

AUSTRIAN

EMPIRE

HUNGARY

TRANSYL-VANIA

R. Dnieper

R. Dniester

MOLDAVIA

R. Pruth

R U S S I A

BLACK SEA

Venice

WALLACHIA

BOSNIA

SERBIA

R. Danube

Bosphorus

ADRIATIC SEA

NAPLES

ples

Maida

lermo

SICILY

MONTE-NEGRO

TURKISH

ALBANIA

Janina

IONIAN ISLANDS (French)

MOREA

Constantinople

Dardanelles

EMPIRE

ASIA MINOR

Smyrna

MALTA (British)

CRETE

3. Europe in 1815

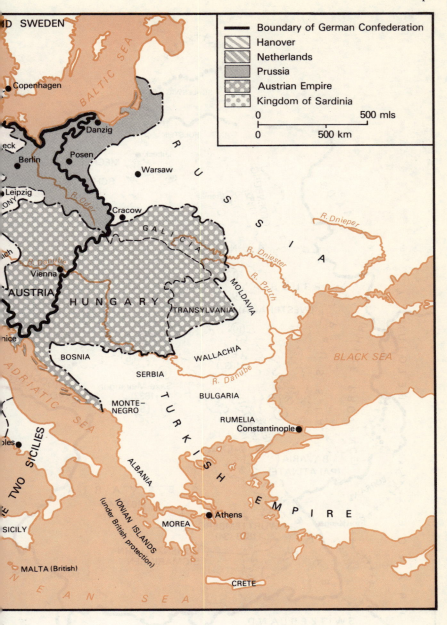

Boundary of German Confederation
Hanover
Netherlands
Prussia
Austrian Empire
Kingdom of Sardinia

0   500 mls
0   500 km

SWEDEN

BALTIC SEA

Copenhagen

Danzig

Berlin · Posen

Warsaw

Leipzig

Cracow

R. Oder

R U S S I A

R. Dnieper

GALICIA

R. Dniester

Vienna

R. Danube

AUSTRIA

HUNGARY

MOLDAVIA

R. Pruth

TRANSYLVANIA

BOSNIA

WALLACHIA

SERBIA

R. Danube

BLACK SEA

MONTE-NEGRO

BULGARIA

RUMELIA

Constantinople

T U R K I S H

ALBANIA

E M P I R E

ADRIATIC SEA

THE TWO SICILIES

IONIAN ISLANDS (under British protection)

MOREA

Athens

SICILY

MALTA (British)

CRETE

E A N   S E A

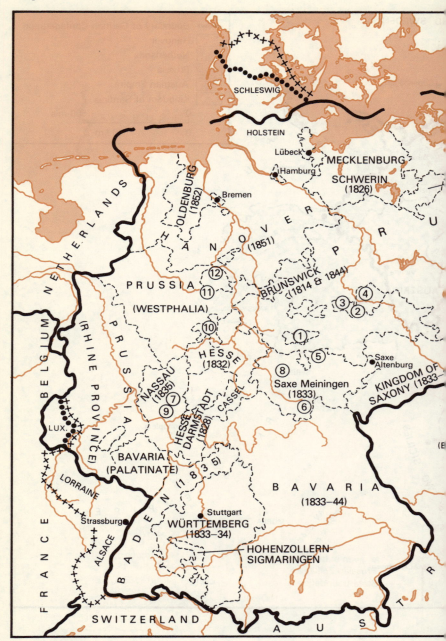

4. Germany in 1815

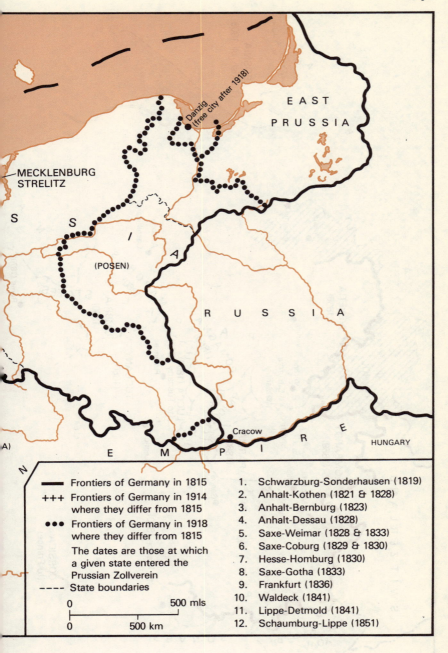

EAST PRUSSIA

MECKLENBURG
STRELITZ

Danzig
(free city after 1918)

S

S

I

A

(POSEN)

R U S S I A

Cracow

R   E

HUNGARY

A)   E   M   P   I

N

───	Frontiers of Germany in 1815
+++	Frontiers of Germany in 1914 where they differ from 1815
●●●	Frontiers of Germany in 1918 where they differ from 1815

The dates are those at which
a given state entered the
Prussian Zollverein

---- State boundaries

0   500 mls

0   500 km

1. Schwarzburg-Sonderhausen (1819)
2. Anhalt-Kothen (1821 & 1828)
3. Anhalt-Bernburg (1823)
4. Anhalt-Dessau (1828)
5. Saxe-Weimar (1828 & 1833)
6. Saxe-Coburg (1829 & 1830)
7. Hesse-Homburg (1830)
8. Saxe-Gotha (1833)
9. Frankfurt (1836)
10. Waldeck (1841)
11. Lippe-Detmold (1841)
12. Schaumburg-Lippe (1851)

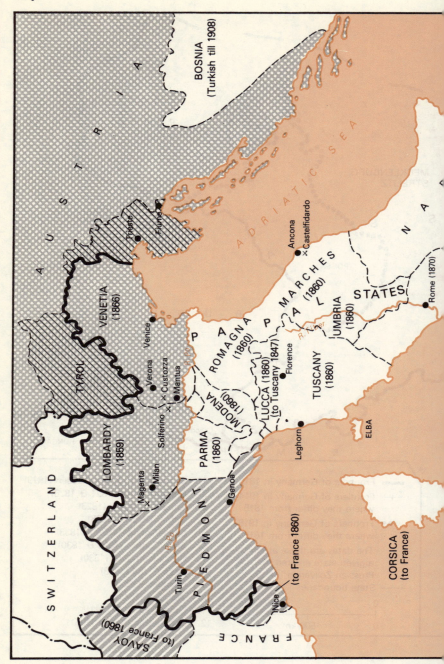

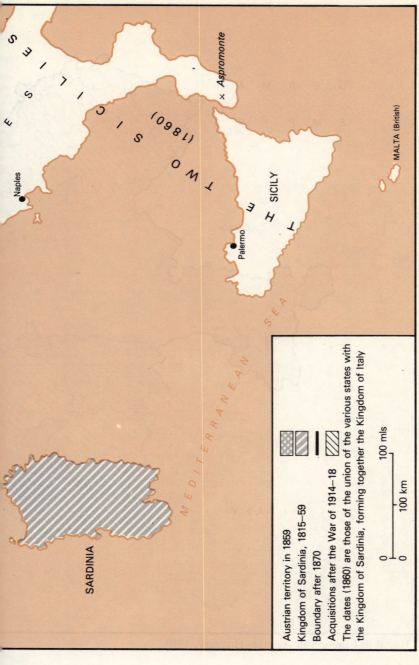

5. Italian unification

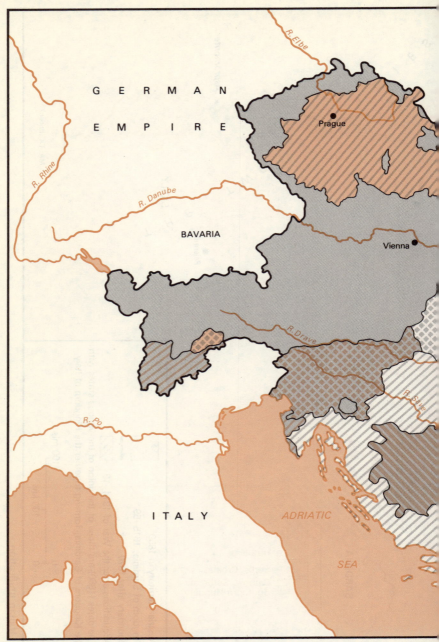

6. Racial distribution in Austria–Hungary, 1910

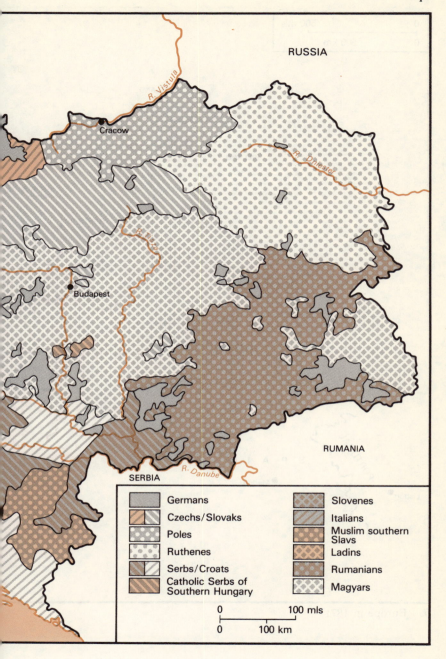

RUSSIA

Cracow

R. Vistula

R. Dniester

R. Tisza

Budapest

SERBIA

R. Danube

RUMANIA

Germans		Slovenes	
Czechs/Slovaks		Italians	
Poles		Muslim southern Slavs	
Ruthenes		Ladins	
Serbs/Croats		Rumanians	
Catholic Serbs of Southern Hungary		Magyars	

0   100 mls

0   100 km

7. Europe in 1871

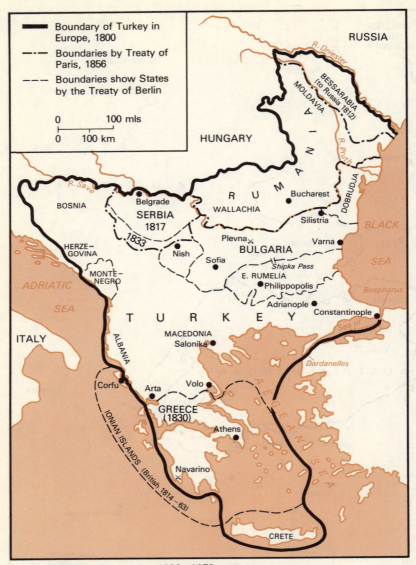

Boundary of Turkey in
Europe, 1800

Boundaries by Treaty of
Paris, 1856

Boundaries show States
by the Treaty of Berlin

0   100 mls

0   100 km

RUSSIA

R. Dniester

BESSARABIA
(to Russia 1812)

MOLDAVIA

R. Pruth

HUNGARY

R. Save

RUMANIA

Bucharest

DOBRUDJA

BOSNIA

Belgrade

SERBIA
1817

1833

WALLACHIA

Silistria

BLACK

HERZE-
GOVINA

Nish

Sofia

Plevna ×

BULGARIA

Shipka Pass

Varna

SEA

MONTE-
NEGRO

E. RUMELIA

Philippopolis

Bosphorus

ADRIATIC

SEA

Adrianople

Constantinople

ITALY

T U R K E Y

Sea of

ALBANIA

MACEDONIA

Salonika

Dardanelles

Corfu

Arta

Volo

IONIAN ISLANDS

GREECE
(1830)

A E G E A N   S E A

Athens

(British 1814 – 63)

Navarino
×

CRETE

8.   The Balkan Peninsula, 1800–1878

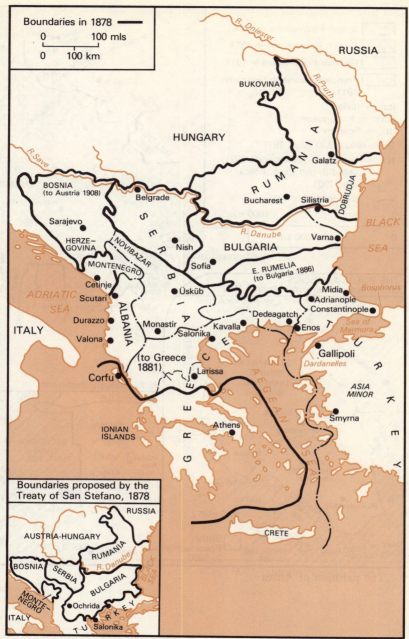

Boundaries in 1878 ⎯⎯⎯

0   100 mls
0   100 km

RUSSIA

BUKOVINA

HUNGARY

R. Dniester

R. Pruth

R. Save

RUMANIA

Galatz

BOSNIA
(to Austria 1908)

Belgrade

Bucharest

Silistria

DOBRUDJA

BLACK
SEA

Sarajevo

HERZE-
GOVINA

NOVIBAZAR

S E R B I A

Nish

R. Danube

BULGARIA

Varna

MONTENEGRO

Sofia

E. RUMELIA
(to Bulgaria 1886)

ADRIATIC
SEA

Cetinje

Scutari

Üsküb

Midia

Bosphorus

A L B A N I A

Adrianople
Constantinople

ITALY

Durazzo

Monastir

Dedeagatch

Valona

Salonika

Kavalla

Enos

Sea of
Marmora

T U R K E Y

(to Greece
1881)

G R E E C E

Larissa

Gallipoli
Dardanelles

ASIA
MINOR

Corfu

A E G E A N   S E A

IONIAN
ISLANDS

Athens

Smyrna

CRETE

Boundaries proposed by the
Treaty of San Stefano, 1878

RUSSIA

AUSTRIA-HUNGARY

RUMANIA

R. Danube

BOSNIA

SERBIA

BULGARIA

BLACK
SEA

MONTE-
NEGRO

Ochrida

T U R K E Y

ITALY

Salonika

8.   The Balkan Peninsula, 1800–1878

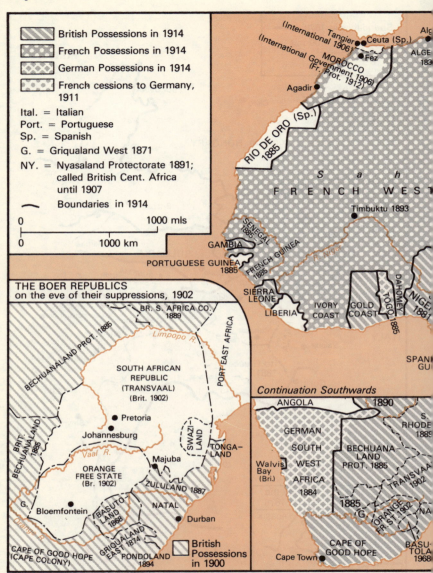

9. The partition of Africa

Tunis

MALTA (Br.)

MEDITERRANEAN SEA

Tripoli

TRIPOLI
(Ital.) 1911
(Turkish till
then)

EGYPT
(British occupation
1882)

Cairo

Suez Canal 1869

R. Nile

RED SEA

A R A B I A

a

RICA

Chad
1898

1911
Germany
to France

ANGLO-EGYPTIAN
SOUDAN 1898–99

Omdurman

Khartum

ERITREA
(Ital.) 1885

FRENCH
SOMALILAND 1888

SOCOTRA
(Br.)

Aden 1839

ERIA
5

Fashoda
1898

BRITISH
SOMALI-
LAND
1887

CAMEROON
1884

BAHR-EL-
GHAZAL
1894

ABYSSINIA

FRENCH
1880

CONGO

R. Congo

BELGIAN CONGO
(CONGO FREE STATE
1885–1907)

Leopoldville

UGANDA
PROT. 1894

L. Victoria

BRITISH
EAST AFRICA
1888

Protectorate
1894

ITALIAN SOMALILAND
1892

INDIAN

OCEAN

GERMAN
EAST
AFRICA
1884–5

ZANZIBAR
1890 (Br.)

L. Tanganyika

ANGOLA
(Port.)

NORTHERN RHODESIA
1890

GERMAN
SOUTH WEST
AFRICA 1884

BECHU-
ANALAND
PROT.

SOUTHERN
RHODESIA
1889

NY.

L. Nyasa

PORTUGUESE EAST
AFRICA
1884–5

MADAGASCAR

INDEX

408